Ex Libris

CABALA

THE BROTHERHOOD

The Brotherhood - Compiled with graphics and edits by Darrell Jordan, Copyright © First Edition 2024. All rights reserved.
No part of this book may be reproduced in whole or in part without the written permission from the publisher, nor stored in any retrieval system or transmitted by any means, electronic, mechanical, photocopying, recording, or other, without the written consent of the publisher.
For bulk purchases, please contact the publisher.
Enquiry@Athenaia.Co

Library of Congress Cataloging-in Publication Data
Names: Westcott, Wynn | Atkinson, William W | Jordan, Darrell
Title: The Brotherhood, Darrell Jordan
Description: First U.S. edition. | Coeur D'Alene, Idaho: Athenaia [2024]
Identifiers: LCCN (pending) |
ISBN 979-8-88556-057-3 (First Edition hardcover)
Subjects: OCC040000 BODY, MIND & SPIRIT / Hermetism & Rosicrucianism | REL071000 / RELIGION / Leadership | PHI036000 / PHILOSOPHY / Hermeneutics
LC record available at https://lccn. loc.gov

On the internet: Parallel47North.com/collections/esoteric-books
Managing Editor: Darrell Jordan
Original Authors and Essays: Wynn Westcott, William W Atkinson, and The Rosicrucian Brotherhood
Executive Producer: Yuka Jordan
Book Cover Design by Yuka Jordan
Book Cover Art and Illustrations: Jessica Naomi [JessicaNaomiDesigns.com]
Image Credits: Darrell Jordan's personal collection
Printed and bound in the United States

Publisher: Athenaia, LLC
2370 N Merritt Crk Lp, Ste 1, Coeur D'Alene, ID 83814 The United States

This book is a collection of select articles from The Rosicrucian Brotherhood and various published books, magazines and interviews. The original authors' work is now in the public domain, but their intellectual insights still apply today, and we wanted to preserve their precious wisdom, and to help you further study Rosicrucianism, mysticism, hermetism and other occultism work.

The Brotherhood

Darrell Jourdan

Hand-drawn by artist Jessica Naomi

Table of Contents

INTRODUCTION   11

By F. LEIGH GARDNER. 1857–1930

INTRODUCTION   15

By Wm. WYNN WESTCOTT, M. R. 1848-1925

IX. S. M. of the Soc. Ros. in Anglia, P.M., P.Z., P.G.D., 30°.

ROSICRUCIAN AND MASONIC ORIGINS   19

By MANLY P. HALL - 1901 - 1990

THE ROSY CROSS   39

By THE ROSICRUCAE - 1898

THE ROSE AND THE CROSS   48

By MAURICE MAGRE - 1877-1941

CONSIDERATION OF THE MORE SECRET PHILOSOPHY   63

By PHILIP À GABELLA

THE SHADOW OF THE UNKNOWN MASTER   85

By MAGUS INCOGNITO – 1862 - 1932

THE IMMORTALIZED JESUS   95

By PAUL TYNER – 1860 - 1926

THINGS WORTH THINKING ABOUT   99

By DR. T. J. BETIERO - 1864 - 1917

THE ARCANE TEACHING — 103
By WILLIAM W. ATKINSON – 1862 - 1932

A MANUAL ON THE PATH OF KNOWLEDGE — 126
By JNANA MARGA – 1928 - 1997

SECRETS OF THE ROSICRUCIAN'S — 153
by a Frater of the Rosy Cross

A ROSICRUCIAN PROBLEM — 159
By MANLY HALL – 1901 - 1990

HOW IS KNOWLEDGE OF THE HIGHER WORLDS ATTAINED? — 165
By RUDOLF STEINER – 1861-1925

FROM THE MASTER TEACHER TO HIS NEOPHYTE — 212
By R. S. CLYMER -1878 - 1966

JOHN — 239
By CHARLES FILLMORE – 1854 - 1948

VOYAGE TO THE LAND OF THE ROSICRUCIAN'S — 248
A. E. WAITE Collection – 1857 - 1942

THE HEAVENLY FIRE — 277
By MANLY HALL 1901 - 1990

ANCIENT AND MODERN INITIATION — 291
By MAX HEINDEL – 1865-1919

ARCANA COELESTIA — **360**

By EMANUEL SWEDENBORG – 1688 - 1772

THE ROSICRUCIAN'S OR KNIGHTS OF THE ROSY CROSS — **387**

(From "The Dreamer," London, 1754.)

THE PHILOSOPHER'S STONE — **391**

By FRANZ HARTMANN 1838 - 1912

A ROSICRUCIAN ALLEGORY — **394**

By JOHN HEYDON - 1629 – 1667

THE PHILOSOPHER'S STONE — **397**

By Gen. N. B. BUFORD - 1807 – 1883

THE ROSICRUCIAN'S — **415**

By ALEX. WILDER, M. D. - 1823 - 1909

CHRISTIAN ROSENKREUZ AND THE ROSICRUCIAN'S — **428**

By W. WYNN WESTCOTT, M. D. - 1848 – 1925

THE HERMETIC PHILOSOPHERS — **444**

By HARGRAVE JENNINGS - 1817 – 1890

EARLY ROSICRUCIAN'S — **453**

By Frater WILLIAM CARPENTER - 1797 – 1874

THE RED BOOK OF APPIN — **458**

BY Gen. E. A. HITCHCOCK - 1798 – 1870

THE ROSICRUCIAN'S IN THE UNITED STATES	**464**
BY S. C. GOULD, VIII° - 1840 -1909	
HERMETIC BROTHERHOOD TEMPLE TALKS	**472**
By SOLARIUS	
THE ROSIE CRUCIAN PRAYER TO GOD	**479**
JESUS Mim OMNIA.	
ORIGINAL AUTHORS' PORTRAITS	**483**
REFERENCES	**489**
OTHER BOOKS BY THE MANAGING EDITOR	**490**
ABOUT MANAGING EDITOR	**491**

EMBLEMA 5
AVRI POTABILIS CHIMICE
PRÆPARATI

Introduction

By F. LEIGH GARDNER. 1857-1930

The name of "Rosicrucian" does not appear to have been known until the commencement of the Seventeenth Century, when Europe was beginning to emerge from the depths of the intellectual darkness of the Middle Ages. The Reformers, notably Calvin and Luther, had to a great extent broken up the ground preparatory to a new era.

This welcome change did not, however, prevent religious fanatics of many sorts from trading on the credulity of the masses, as is witnessed by the number of quacks who extorted money, under the pretense of being able to tell fortunes, and to perform transmutation, even by means of a compact with the evil one. It seemed as though a horde of sharpers was let loose, and they gulled people in a wholesale manner. Things were in this state when in the year 1614 two anonymous pamphlets appeared, the one called The Universal and General Reformation of the whole wide World, and the other The Fama Fraternitatis, or Brotherhood of the Praiseworthy order of the Rosicrucian's, a message to the Governments, Nobles, and Scientists of Europe.

These works caused an immense excitement, and were translated into several languages; a large number of pamphlets were circulated in reply, and the whole of Christendom was stirred to its utmost depths. This state of things went on for some considerable time, and finally seemed to exhaust itself; but curiously enough fresh evidences of interest in Rosicrucianism crop out at intervals. In the *Encyclopaedia Metropolitana* it is stated definitely that in 1630 there was a London College of Rosicrucian's.

Another remarkable instance occurs in the work No. 132, by a Count Eckhoffen, who wrote under the Pseudonyms of Pianco VIII and Phaebron; in this work a very important Folding Table appears; this was translated into English and published by Kenneth Mackenzie in his now scarce work The Royal Masonic Cyclopcedia (p. 617), it contains the full details of an order based upon Rosicrucian design.

The Places of Assembly, Consulates, Countries, Symbols, etc., are given, and the contents of the work reveal to my mind sufficient evidence that about 1750 such an Order undoubtedly existed, and was worked on Kabalistic lines. In further confirmation of this actual existence of the Order I must refer my readers to an article that appeared in a German publication called The Sphinx, published at Brunswick, and a translation of which appeared in the Theosopht, for April, 1886; it is written by a certain Karl Kisewetttr, who states that he found amongst his great grandfather's papers documents shewing that he was the then Imperator of a Rosicrucian Lodge (1769); he goes on to say that in 1792 it was decided to release the Brethren from their oath of secrecy, and to destroy the Library and the Archives.

Whether this was done or not, there is no evidence forthcoming, but he dwells at length on the "innumerable secret arts with which the Rosicrucian's were acquainted." In the present day we have an organization of Masonic Students, who are joined together under the title of "*Societas Rosicruciana in Anglia*" and whose ramifications extend' to Germany, and abroad to India and the United States of America, and in whose service I have the honor to be Secretary to the Supreme Council, and of which my worthy colleague, Dr. W. Wynn Westcott, is M.W. Supreme Magus. We have a number of earnest and thoughtful students and Literati in our ranks. Considering all of the collected evidence it is certainly a fact that the Rosicrucian's did exist. They did work Lodges, and were in possession of knowledge that was not accessible to the man in the street; neither did they adopt the modern scientific method of making every discovery public property, the propriety of which many even now question.

They evidently adopted high ideals, as they worked unselfishly for the good of the world and accepted no remuneration for so doing; they made no display from motives of vanity, and worked unknown and unostentatiously, leading quiet and secluded lives, secure in their own knowledge which was not to be obtained by any but worthy people. This- knowledge was also not to be purchased for money, but descended from lovers of the Hermetic art to others who trod in the same footsteps. "We wrap ourselves in mystery," says one, "in order to avoid the censure and violent importunity of those who regard us as no philosophers but wanting in common prudence, except we employ our knowledge to some worthy use and profit."

Whether as some writers suggest, this knowledge has descended from the Ancient Philosophers of Egypt, the Chaldeans, the Persian Magi, or the Gymnosophists of India, it, hardly falls within my province to discuss, but I may mention *en passant* that the Rose and Cross are Symbols of Great Antiquity—the former was dedicated to Venus as the Symbol of Secrecy and Immortality and is sacred both in Life and Religion; the latter according to the Christians is well known to typify Salvation ; but it is of much greater antiquity than Christianity, and amongst the ancient Egyptians it symbolized "Life."

According to Masonic Tradition it was foreshadowed in King Solomon's Temple; again, the Rose and Cross combined were the badge of a Knight Templar. Robert Fludd or his friends who wrote the "Summum Bonum" state its meaning to be "the Cross sprinkled by the rosy blood of The Christ" which is a purely religious illustration. Again, there is the Rose of Sharon, and amongst the Indians, the Mystical Rose is continually met with in legends; so that we may have to look to the East for its origin. Lord Beaconsfield declared that the Secret Societies and the Papacy were the only two Institutions endowed with permanency; and this is possibly the reason why the latter has always been so persistent in its intense hatred of the former.

In fact, any Order that is possessed of real Occult knowledge is hated by the Church of Rome, which brooks no rivals; its history is one of unrelentless cruelty and spiritual despotism; its pathway is strewn with the human wrecks, whom it has used as its tools in the service of its restless ambition; power was its one goal, and achievement was desired irrespective of cost; the end alone justifying the means. As in the present day I have no desire to perpetuate the follies of the middle ages, nor to suggest to anyone the necessity of yielding up his freedom of thought and will to any Imperator, Magister, or to the Chief of any secret society, however high sounding and high faluting a title may be assumed, rightly or wrongly; so I think it advisable at this point to caution any would-be aspirant in mysticism against dangers which I know to be current at the present day. Certain quasi-Secret Orders, which pretend to impart occult knowledge, and which possibly do possess some slight qualifications sufficient to justify their existence, are used simply as a means of obtaining money.

I am informed on credible authority that the daughter of an English nobleman recently applied for admission to such a society as I have described, and after the ceremony had taken place, the chief had the audacity to demand a sum of money approaching five and twenty pounds; fortunately, both the mother and daughter were not such pigeons as they were supposed to be, and I do not suppose they troubled the gentleman again. I merely mention this case to impress upon my readers the fact that true Rosicrucian's have always taught "That Divine wisdom is not to be bought nor sold for private gain."

Introduction

By Wm. WYNN WESTCOTT, M. R. 1848-1925

IX. S. M. of the Soc. Ros. in Anglia, P.M., P.Z., P.G.D., 30°.

THE history of the Rosicrucian Fraternity, the date and manner of its origin, and the peculiar doctrines and pursuits of its members have always been subjects of the greatest interest to such literary men as find a charm in tracing the developments of genius along what are now considered somewhat erratic lines. The proceedings of those societies which are credited with the pursuit of a knowledge of the Occult world, of magic and of alchemy, in secret assemblies and with solemn ceremonials, have always attracted certain students who fail to find full satisfaction in the pursuits of common life, and the subjects of general literature.

The Rosicrucian Fraternity was brought to public notice in Germany by means of two tractates, the "Fama Fraternitatis," and the "Confessio Fraternitatis," which were printed at Cassel in 1614 and 1615. The former work, the "Fama," narrates the history (or as some critics say—the myth) of the founding of the Fraternity by one Christian Rosenkreuz, who appears to have been born circa 1378, and who was educated in a monastery. He is said to have started upon a tour in the Holy Land as companion to a learned monk, his master and teacher.

This brother died in Cyprus, but Christian Rosenkreuz continued his travels, visiting many countries, of which the Holy Land and Damascus, Egypt and Fez are mentioned, and sought out in every place "such as were learned." In this manner he gained great wisdom, and studied the ancient Chaldean religion, the theology and magic of Egypt, the philosophies of Alexandria, and the Kabalah of the Hebrew rabbis. From Africa he returned by way of Spain to his native land — Germany, and there settled down to form a society of learned men, to which he might impart the results of his long and laborious researches in foreign lands.

The narrative goes on to say that he first chose three fraters, in the year 1408, and with their aid a dwelling and temple for the home of the new Society was erected and named "Domus Sancti Spiritus." These fraters, under the tuition of C. R., wrote a

Dictionary of his occult lore, and composed a ritual of instruction called the Book M. In 1410 tour more fraters were admitted to the private studies and practical researches of the Society.

Peace and prosperity appear to have blessed the new venture, and after a time of probation some fraters went away on travels of benevolence, using healing arts and comforting the afflicted. In view of his approaching death, and when of great age, C. R. designed a Vault for the reception of his remains. He collected in it all manner of symbols representing the hidden truths of nature, and the occult relations of the planets and stars to man; and many marvelous devices.

Above all, it is noted that "into this Vault the sun shineth not, yet was it illuminated by another light placed in the flat heptagonal ceiling." In the year 1459 was written by C. R. the extraordinary volume, entitled the Chymische Hochzeit, or "The Hermetic Romance of the Chymical Wedding." In 1484, the Founder, Christian Rosenkreuz died, full of years and honor, and was buried by the survivors of the early adepts in a private manner in the Vault so long prepared for his body.

C. R. appears to have wished that this Vault should remain closed for one hundred and twenty years, after the expiry of which time, if the Society survived, the Vault was to be opened, the existence of the Society declared, and a fuller admission of students to membership should be invited. This long period passed away; the universality of Catholicism had been wrecked, and the Reformed religion had become notable; the Vault was opened, and the embalmed body with its curious surroundings was displayed to view.

The survivors, or their nominee, who is now generally thought to be Valentine Andrea, a German theologian and mystic, published the "Fama," to the world; and next year republished the "Fama" with the "Confessio." This latter tract explains the aims of the Society, many of its doctrines and its attitude to the outside world, and gives the primary rules. The "Fama" views Christianity as contrasted with Paganism and Mohammedanism, while the "Confessio" adopts the views of the Reformed Lutheran religion.

The publication of these two works caused a storm among the learned; intense interest was excited, and the land was flooded with pamphlets, some written against the possibility of the existence of the Fraternity and others loudly welcoming the foundation of such a home of learning and benevolence. Do these works refer to a myth, or do they narrate a history? Each alternative has been supported by men of great eminence, but no final decision has been arrived at; no Domus Sancti Spiritus has even been seen by the uninitiated; that much is certain; but how many persons were received into the Society no one can say.

All that can be stated is that from 1616 onward there have been always some persons who claimed to be Adepts of the Rosicrucian Fraternity. Some few of them have Issued printed works relating to Rosicrucian subjects; others have signed themselves with the official motto, R. C., and others appear to have written in defense of the Society anonymously, or under the guise of a Latin Motto. The Soc. Ros., in Anglia is composed of Freemasons alone, and derives its title from some descendants of the older Rosicrucian's of Germany; it does not profess Magic, nor claim the possession of the Philosopher's Stone; but "The aim of the Society is to afford mutual aid and encouragement in working out the great problems of Life, and in searching out the Secrets of Nature; to facilitate the study of the system of Philosophy founded upon the Kabalah and the doctrines of Hermes Trismegistus, which was inculcated by the original Fraters Rosae Crucis, of Germany, a.d. 1450; and to investigate the meaning and symbolism of all that now remains of the wisdom, art and literature of the ancient world." It numbers about five hundred members, who carry out, so far as may be, the objects of the Society.

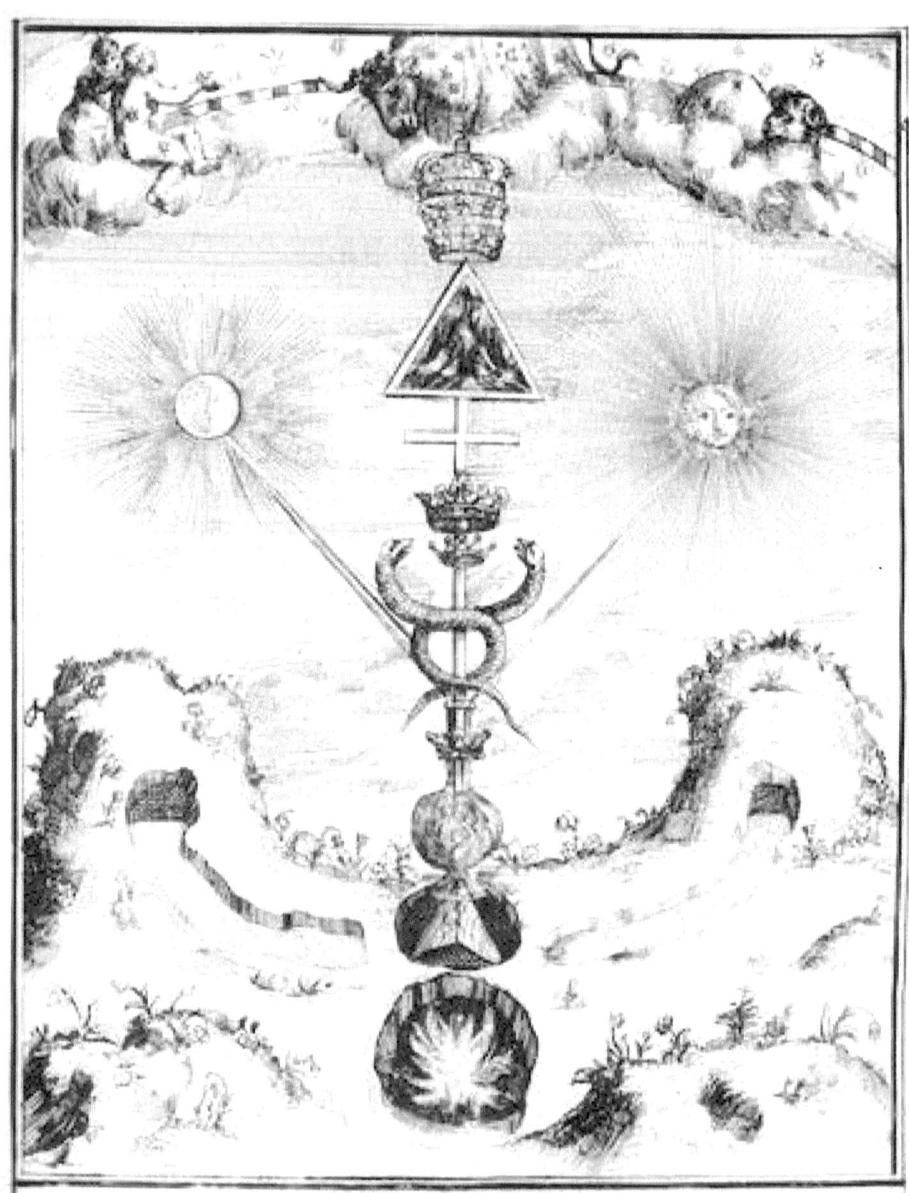

ROSICRUCIAN AND MASONIC ORIGINS

By MANLY P. HALL - 1901 - 1990

FREEMASONRY is a fraternity within a fraternity—an outer organization concealing an inner brotherhood of the elect. Before it is possible to intelligently discuss the origin of the Craft, it is necessary, therefore, to establish the existence of these two separate yet interdependent orders, the one visible and the other invisible. The visible society is a splendid camaraderie of "free and accepted" men enjoined to devote themselves to ethical, educational, fraternal, patriotic, and humanitarian concerns. The invisible society is a secret and most august fraternity whose members are dedicated to the service of a mysterious arcanum arcanorum. Those Brethren who have essayed to write the history of their Craft have not included in their disquisitions the story of that truly secret inner society which is to the body Freemasonic what the heart is to the body human. In each generation only a few are accepted into the inner sanctuary of the Work, but these are veritable Princes of the Truth and their sainted names shall be remembered in future ages together with the seers and prophets of the elder world. Though the great initiate-philosophers of Freemasonry can be counted upon one's fingers, yet their power is not to be measured by the achievements of ordinary men. They are dwellers upon the Threshold of the Innermost, Masters of that secret doctrine which forms the invisible foundation of every great theological and rational institution.

The outer history of the Masonic order is one of noble endeavor, altruism, and splendid enterprise; the inner history, one of silent conquest, persecution, and heroic martyrdom. The body of Masonry rose from the guilds of workmen who wandered the face of medieval Europe, but the spirit of Masonry walked with God before the universe was spread out or the scroll of the heavens unrolled. The enthusiasm of the young Mason is the effervescence of a pardonable pride. Let him extol the merits of his Craft, reciting its steady growth, its fraternal spirit, and its worthy undertakings. Let him boast of splendid buildings and an ever-increasing sphere of influence. These are the tangible evidence of power and should rightly set a-flutter the heart of the Apprentice who does not fully comprehend as yet that great strength which abides in silence or that unutterable dignity to be sensed only by those who. have been "raised" into the contemplation of the Inner Mystery.

An obstacle well-nigh insurmountable is to convince the Mason himself that the secrets of his Craft are worthy of his profound consideration. As St. Paul, so we are told, kicked against the "pricks" of conversion, so the rank and file of present-day Masons strenuously oppose any effort put forth to interpret Masonic symbols in the light of philosophy. They are seemingly obsessed by the fear that from their ritualism may be extracted a meaning more profound than is actually contained therein. For years it has been a mooted question whether Freemasonry is actually a religious organization. "Masonry," writes Pike, however, in the Legenda for the Nineteenth Degree, "has and always had a religious creed. It teaches what it deems to be the truth in respect to the nature and attributes of God." The more studiously-minded Mason regards the Craft as an aggregation of thinkers concerned with the deeper mysteries of life. The all-too-prominent younger members of the Fraternity, however, if not openly skeptical, are at least indifferent to these weightier issues. The champions of philosophic Masonry, alas, are a weak, small voice which grows weaker and smaller as time goes by. In fact, there are actual blocs among the Brethren who would divorce Masonry from both philosophy and religion at any and all cost. If, however, we search the writings of eminent Masons, we find a unanimity of viewpoint: namely, that Masonry is a religious and philosophic body. Every effort initiated to elevate Masonic thought to its true position has thus invariably emphasized the metaphysical and ethical aspects of the Craft.

But a superficial perusal of available documents will demonstrate that the modern Masonic order is not united respecting the true purpose for its own existence. Nor will this factor of doubt be dispelled until the origin of the Craft is established beyond all quibbling. The elements of Masonic history are strangely elusive; there are gaps which apparently cannot be bridged. "Who the early Freemasons really were," states Gould in A Concise History of Freemasonry, "and whence they came, may afford a tempting theme for inquiry to the speculative antiquary. But it is enveloped in obscurity, and lies far outside the domain of authentic history." Between modern Freemasonry with its vast body of ancient symbolism and those original Mysteries which first employed these symbols there is a dark interval of centuries. To the conservative Masonic historian, the deductions of such writers as Higgins, Churchward, Vail, and Waite—though ingenious and fascinating-actually prove nothing. That Masonry is a body of ancient lore is self-evident, but the tangible "link" necessary to convince the recalcitrant Brethren that their order is the direct successor of the pagan Mysteries has unfortunately not been adduced to date. Of such problems as these is composed the "angel" with which the Masonic Jacob must wrestle throughout the night.

It is possible to trace Masonry back a few centuries with comparative ease, but then the thread suddenly vanishes from sight in a maze of secret societies and political enterprises. Dimly silhouetted in the mists that becloud these tangled issues are such figures as Cagliostro, Comte de St.-Germain, and St. Martin, but even the connection between these individuals and the Craft has never been clearly defined. The writings of early Masonic history is involved in such obvious hazard as to provoke the widespread conclusion that further search is futile. The average Masonic student is content, therefore, to trace his Craft back to the workmen's guilds who chipped and chiseled the cathedrals and public buildings of medieval Europe. While such men as Albert Pike have realized this attitude to be ridiculous, it is one thing to declare it insufficient and quite another to prove the fallacy to an adamantine mind. So much has been lot and forgotten, so much ruled in and out by those unfitted for such legislative revision that the modern rituals do not in every case represent the original rites of the Craft. In his Symbolism, Pike (who spent a lifetime in the quest for Masonic secrets) declares that few of the original meanings of the symbols are known to the modern order, nearly all the so-called interpretations now given being superficial. Pike confessed that the original meanings of the very symbols he himself was attempting to interpret were irretrievably—lost; that even such familiar emblems as the apron and the pillars were locked mysteries, whose "keys" had been thrown away by the uninformed. "The initiated," also writes John Fellows, "as well as those without the pale of the order, are equally ignorant of their derivation and import.

Preston, Gould, Mackey, Oliver, and Pike—in fact, nearly every great historian of Freemasonry-have all admitted the possibility of the modern society being connected, indirectly at least, with the ancient Mysteries, and their descriptions of the modern society are prefaced by excerpts from ancient writings descriptive of primitive ceremonials. These eminent Masonic scholars have all recognized in the legend of Hiram Abiff an adaptation of the Osiris myth; nor do they deny that the major part of the symbolism of the craft is derived from the pagan institutions of antiquity when the gods were venerated in secret places with strange figures and appropriate rituals. Though cognizant of the exalted origin of their order, these historians-either through fear or uncertainty-have failed, however, to drive home the one point necessary to establish the true purpose of Freemasonry: They did not realize that the Mysteries whose rituals Freemasonry perpetuates were the custodians of a secret philosophy of life of such transcendent nature that it can only be entrusted to an individual tested and proved beyond all peradventure of human frailty. The secret schools of Greece and Egypt were neither fraternal nor political fundamentally, nor were their ideals similar to those of the modern Craft. They were essentially philosophic and religious institutions, and all admitted into them were consecrated to the service of the sovereign good. Modern Freemasons, however, regard their Craft primarily as neither philosophic nor religious, but rather as ethical. Strange as it may seem, the majority openly ridicule the very supernatural powers and agencies for which their symbols stand.

The secret doctrine that flows through Freemasonic symbols (and to whose perpetuation the invisible Masonic body is consecrated) has its source in three ancient and exalted orders. The first is the Dionysiac artificers, the second the Roman collegia, and the third the Arabian Rosicrucian's. The Dionysians were the master builders of the ancient world. Originally founded to design and erect the theaters of Dionysos wherein were enacted the tragic dramas of the rituals, this order was repeatedly elevated by popular acclaim to greater dignity until at last it was entrusted with the planning and construction of all public edifices concerned with the commonwealth or the worship of the gods and heroes. Hiram, King of Tyre, was the patron of the Dionysians, who flourished in Tyre and Sidon, and Hiram Abiff (if we may believe the sacred account) was himself a Grand Master of this most noble order of pagan builders. King Solomon in his wisdom accepted the services of this famous craftsman, and thus at the instigation of Hiram, King of Tyre, Hiram Abiff, though himself a member of a different faith, journeyed from his own country to design and supervise the erection of the Everlasting House to the true God on Mount Moriah. The tools of the builders' craft were first employed by the Dionysians as symbols under which to conceal the mysteries of the soul and the secrets of human regeneration. The Dionysians also first likened man to a rough ashlar which, trued into a finished block through the instrument of reason, could be fitted into the structure of that living and eternal Temple built without the sound of hammer, the voice of workmen or any tool of contention.

The Roman collegia was a branch of the Dionysiacs and to it belonged those initiated artisans who fashioned the impressive monuments whose mins still lend their immortal glory to the Eternal City. In his Ten Books on Architecture, Vitruvius, the initiate of the collegia, has revealed that which was permissible concerning the secrets of his holy order. Of the inner mysteries, however, he could not write, for these were reserved for such as had donned the leather apron of the craft. In his consideration of the books now available concerning the Mysteries, the thoughtful reader should note the following words appearing in a twelfth-century volume entitled Artephil Liber Secretus: "Is not this an art full of secrets? And believest thou, O fool! that we plainly teach this Secret of Secrets, taking our words according to their literal interpretation?" (See Sephar H' Debarim.) Into the stones they trued, the adepts of the collegia deeply carved their Gnostic symbols. From earliest times, the initiated stonecutters marked their perfected works with the secret emblems of their crafts and degrees that unborn generations might realize that the master builders of the first ages also labored for the same ends sought by men today.

The Mysteries of Egypt and Persia that had found a haven in the Arabian desert reached Europe by way of the Knights Templars and the Rosicrucian's. The Temple of the Rose Cross at Damascus had preserved the secret philosophy of Sharon's Rose; the Druses of the Lebanon still retain the mysticism of ancient Syria; and the dervishes, as they lean on their carved and crotched sticks, still meditate upon the secret instruction perpetuated from the days of the four Caliphs. From the far places of Iraq and the hidden retreats of the Sufi mystics, the Ancient Wisdom thus found its way into Europe. Was Jacques de Molay burned by the Holy Inquisition merely because he wore the red cross of the Templar? What were those secrets to which he was true even in death? Did his companion Knights perish with him merely because they had amassed a fortune and exercised an unusual degree of temporal power? To the thoughtless, these may constitute ample grounds, but to those who can pierce the film of the specious and the superficial, they are assuredly insufficient. It was not the physical power of the Templars but the knowledge which they had brought with them from the East that the church feared. The Templars had discovered part of the Great Arcanum; they had become wise in those mysteries which had been celebrated in Mecca thousands of years before the advent of Mohammed; they had read a few pages from the dread book of the Anthropos, and for this knowledge they were doomed to die. What was the black magic of which the Templars were accused? What was Baphomet, the Goat of Mendes, whose mysteries they were declared to have celebrated? All these are questions worthy of the thoughtful consideration of every studious Mason.

Truth is eternal. The so-called revelations of Truth that come in different religions are actually but a re-emphasis of an ever-existing doctrine. Thus, Moses did not originate a new religion for Israel; he simply adapted the Mysteries of Egypt to the needs of Israel. The ark triumphantly borne by the twelve tribes through the wilderness was copied after the Isiac ark which may still be traced in faint has-relief upon the minds of the Temple of Philae. Even the two brooding cherubim over the mercy seat are visible in the Egyptian-carving, furnishing indubitable evidence that the secret doctrine of Egypt was the prototype of Israel's mystery religion. In his reformation of Indian philosophy, Buddha likewise did not reject the esotericism of the Brahmins, but rather adapted this esotericism to the needs of the masses in India. The mystic secrets locked within the holy Vedas were thus disclosed in order that all men, irrespective of castely distinction, might partake of wisdom and share in a common heritage of good. Jesus was a Rabbin of the Jews, a teacher of the Holy Law, who discoursed in the synagogue, interpreting the Torah according to the teachings of His sect. He brought no new message nor were His reformations radical. He merely tore away the veil from the temple in order that not only Pharisee and Sadducee but also publican and sinner might together behold the glory of an ageless faith, substances of his own mind. Neither prophet nor savior preached a doctrine which was his own, but in language suitable to his time and race retold that Ancient Wisdom preserved within the Mysteries since the dawning of human consciousness. So, with the Masonic Mysteries of today. Each Mason has at hand those lofty principles of universal order upon whose certainties the faiths of mankind, have ever been established. Each Mason has at hand those lofty principles of universal order upon pregnant with life and hope to those millions who wander in the darkness of unenlightenment. Father C. R. C., the Master of the Rose Cross, was initiated into the Great Work at Damcar. Later at Fez, further information was given him relating to the sorcery of the Arabians. From these wizards of the desert C. R. C. also secured the sacred book M, which is declared to have contained the accumulated knowledge of the world. This volume was translated into Latin by C. R. C. for the edification of his order, but only the initiates know the present hidden repository of the Rosicrucian manuscripts, charters, and manifestos. From the Arabians C. R. C. also learned of the elemental peoples and how, with their aid, it was possible to gain admission to the ethereal world where dwelt the genii and Nature spirits. C.R.C. thus discovered that the magical creatures of the Arabian Nights Entertainment actually existed, though invisible to the ordinary mortal. From astrologers living in the desert far from the concourse of the market-place he was further instructed concerning the mysteries of the stars, the virtues resident in the astral light, the rituals of magic and invocation, the preparation of therapeutic talismans, and the binding of the genii. C. R. C. became an adept n the gathering of medicinal herbs, the transmutation of metals, and the manufacture of precious gems by artificial means. Even the secret of the Elixir of Life and the Universal Panacea were communicated to him. Enriched thus beyond the dreams of Croesus, the Holy Master returned to Europe and there established a House of Wisdom which he called Domus Sancti Spiritus. This house he enveloped in clouds, it is said, so that men could not discover it. What are these "clouds," however, but the rituals and symbols under which is concealed the Great Arcanum-that unspeakable mystery which every true Mason must seek if he would become in reality a "Prince of the Royal Secret"? Paracelsus, the Swiss Hermes, was initiated into the secrets of alchemy in Constantinople and there beheld the consummation of the magnum opus. He is consequently entitled to be mentioned among those initiated by the Arabians into the Rosicrucian work.

Cagliostro was also initiated by the Arabians and, because of the knowledge he had thus secured, incurred the displeasure of the Holy See. From the unprobed depths of Arabian Rosicrucianism also issued the illustrious Comte de St. Germain, over whose Masonic activities to this day hangs the veil of impenetrable mystery. The exalted body of initiates whom he represented, as well as the mission he came to accomplish, have both been concealed from the members of the Craft at large and are apparent only to those few discerning Masons who sense the supernal philosophic destiny of their Fraternity.

The modern Masonic order can be traced back to a period in European history famous for its intrigue both political and sociological. Between the years 1600 and 1800, mysterious agents moved across the face of the Continent. The forerunner of modern thought was beginning to make its appearance and all Europe was passing through the throes of internal dissension and reconstruction. Democracy was in its infancy, yet its potential power was already being felt. Thrones were beginning to totter. The aristocracy of Europe was like the old man on Sinbad's back: it was becoming more unbearable with every passing day. Although upon the surface national governments were seemingly able to cope with the situation, there was a definite undercurrent of impending change; and out of the masses, long patient under the yoke of oppression, were rising up the champions of religious, philosophic, and political liberty. These led the factions of the dissatisfied: people with legitimate grievances against the intolerance of the church and the oppression of the crown. Out of this struggle for expression materialized certain definite ideals, the same which have now come to be considered peculiarly Masonic.

The divine prerogatives of humanity were being crushed out by the three great powers of ignorance, superstition, and fear—ignorance, the power of the mob; fear, the power of the despot; and superstition, the power of the church. Between the thinker and personal liberty loomed the three "ruffians" or personifications of impediment-the torch, the crown, and the tiara. Brute force, kingly power, and ecclesiastical persuasion became the agents of a great oppression, the motive of a deep unrest, the deterrent to all progress. It was unlawful to think, well-nigh fatal to philosophize, rank heresy to doubt. To question the infallibility of the existing order was to invite the persecution of the church and the state.

These together incited the populace, which thereupon played the role of executioner for these arch-enemies of human liberty. Thus, the ideal of democracy assumed a definite form during these stormy periods of European history. This democracy was not only a vision but a retrospection, not only a looking forward but a gazing backward upon better days and the effort to project those better days into the unborn tomorrow. The ethical, political, and philosophical institutions of antiquity with their constructive effect upon the whole structure of the state were noble examples of possible conditions. It became the dream of the oppressed, consequently, to re-establish a golden age upon the earth, an age where the thinker could think in safety and the dreamer dream in peace; when the wise should lead and the simple follow, yet all dwell together in fraternity and industry.

During this period several books were in circulation which, to a certain degree, registered the pulse of the time. One of these documents—More's Utopia—was the picture of a new age when heavenly conditions should prevail upon the earth. This ideal of establishing good in the world savored of blasphemy, however, for in that day heaven alone it was assumed could be good. Men did not seek to establish heavenly conditions upon earth, but rather earthly conditions in heaven. According to popular concept, the more the individual suffered the torments of the damned upon earth, the more he would enjoy the blessedness of heaven. Life was a period of chastisement and earthly happiness an unattainable mirage. More's Utopia thus came as a definite blow to autocratic pretensions and attitudes, giving impulse to the material emphasis which was to follow in succeeding centuries.

Another prominent figure of this period was Sir Walter Raleigh, who paid with his life for high treason against the crown. Raleigh was tried and, though the charge was never proved, was executed. Before Raleigh went to trial, it was known that he must die and that no defense could save him. His treason against the crown was of a character very different, however, from that which history records. Raleigh was a member of a secret society or body of men who were already moving irresistibly forward under the banner of democracy, and for that affiliation he died a felon's death. The actual reason for Raleigh's death sentence was his refusal to reveal the identity either of that great political organization of which he was a member or his confreres who were fighting the dogma of faith and the divine right of kings. On the title page of the first edition of Raleigh's History of the World, we accordingly find a mass of intricate emblems framed between two great columns. When the executioner sealed his lips forever, Raleigh's silence, while it added to the discomfiture of his persecutors, assured the safety of his colleagues.

One of the truly great minds of that secret fraternity—in fact, the moving spirit of the whole enterprise-was Sir Francis Bacon, whose prophecy of the coming age forms the theme of his New Atlantis and whose vision of the reformation of knowledge finds expression in the Novum Organum Scientiarum, the new organ of science or thought. In the engraving at the beginning of the latter volume may be seen the little ship of progressivism sailing out between the Pillars of Galen and Avicenna, venturing forth beyond the imaginary pillars of church and state upon the unknown sea of human liberty. It is significant that Bacon was appointed by the British Crown to protect its interests in the new American Colonies beyond the sea. We find him writing of this new land, dreaming of the day when a new world and a new government of the philosophic elect should be established there, and scheming to consummate that end when the time should be ripe. Upon the title page of the 1640 edition of Bacon's Advancement of Learning is a Latin motto to the effect that he was the third great mind since Plato. Bacon was a member of the same group to which Sir Walter Raleigh belonged, but Bacon's position as Lord High Chancellor protected him from Raleigh's fate. Every effort was made, however, to humiliate and discredit him. At last, in the sixty-sixth year of his life, having completed the work which held him in England, Bacon feigned death and passed over into Germany, there to guide the destinies of his philosophic and political fraternity for nearly twenty-five years before his actual demise.

Other notable characters of the period are Montaigne, Ben Jonson, Marlowe, and the great Franz Joseph of Transylvania—the latter one of the most important as well as active figures in all this drama, a man who ceased fighting Austria to retire into a monastery in Transylvania from which to direct the activities of his secret society. One political upheaval followed another, the grand climax of this political unrest culminating in the French Revolution, which was directly precipitated by the attacks upon the person of Alessandro Cagliostro. The "divine" Cagliostro, by far the most picturesque character of the time, has the distinction of being more maligned than any other person of history. Tried by the Inquisition for founding a Masonic lodge in the city of Rome, Cagliostro was sentenced to die, a sentence later commuted by the Pope to life imprisonment in the old castle of San Leo. Shortly after his incarceration, Cagliostro disappeared and the story was circulated that he had been strangled in an attempt to escape from prison. In reality, however, he was liberated and returned to his Masters in the East. But Cagliostro—the idol of France, surnamed "the Father of the Poor," who never received anything from anyone and gave everything to everyone—was most adequately revenged. Though the people little understood this inexhaustible pitcher of bounty which poured forth benefits and never required replenishment, they remembered him in the day of their power.

Cagliostro founded the Egyptian Rite of Freemasonry, which received into its mysteries many of the French nobility and was regarded favorably by the most learned minds of Europe. Having established the Egyptian Rite, Cagliostro declared himself to be an agent of the order of the Knights Templars and to have received initiation from them on the Isle of Malta. (See Morals and Dogma, in which Albert Pike quotes Eliphas Levi on Cagliostro's affiliation with the Templars.) Called upon the carpet by the Supreme Council of France, it was demanded of Cagliostro that he prove by what authority he had founded a Masonic lodge in Paris independent of the Grand Orient. Of such surpassing mentality was Cagliostro that the Supreme Council found it difficult to secure an advocate qualified to discuss with Cagliostro philosophic Masonry and the ancient Mysteries he claimed to represent. The Court de Gebelin—the greatest Egyptologist of his day and an authority on ancient philosophies-was chosen as the outstanding scholar. A time was set and the Brethren convened. Attired in an Oriental coat and a pair of violet-colored breeches, Cagliostro was haled before this council of his peers. The Court de Gebelin asked three questions and then sat down, admitting himself disqualified to interrogate a man so much his superior in every branch of learning. Cagliostro then took the floor, revealing to the assembled Masons not only his personal qualifications, but prophesying the future of France. He foretold the fall of the French throne, the Reign of Terror, and the fall of the Bastille. At a later time, he revealed the dates of the death of Marie Antoinette and the King, and also the advent of Napoleon. Having finished his address, Cagliostro made a spectacular exit, leaving the

French Masonic lodge in consternation and utterly incapable of coping with the profundity of his reasoning. Though no longer regarded as a ritual in Freemasonry, the Egyptian Rite is available and all who read it will recognize its author to have been no more a charlatan than was Plato.

Then appears that charming "first American gentleman," Dr. Benjamin Franklin, who together with the Marquis de Lafayette, played an important role in this drama of empires. While in France, Dr. Franklin was privileged to receive definite esoteric instruction. It is noteworthy that Franklin was the first in America to reprint Anderson's Constitutions of the Free-Masons, which is a most prized work on the subject, though its accuracy is disputed. Through all this stormy period, these impressive figures come and go, part of a definite organization of political and religious thought—a functioning body of philosophers represented in Spain by no less an individual than Cervantes, in France by Cagliostro and St.-Germain, in Germany by Gichtel and Andreae, in England by Bacon, More, and Raleigh, and in America by Washington and Franklin. Coincident with the Baconian agitation in England, the Fama Fraternitatis and Confessio Fraternitatis appeared in Germany, both of these works being contributions to the establishment of a philosophic government upon the earth. One of the outstanding links between the Rosicrucian Mysteries of the Middle Ages and modern Masonry is Elias Ashmole, the historian of the Order of the Garter and the first Englishman to compile the alchemical writings of the English chemists.

The foregoing may seem to be a useless recital of inanities, but its purpose is to impress upon the reader's mind the philosophical and political situation in Europe at the time of the inception of the Masonic order. A philosophic clan, as it were, which had moved across the face of Europe under such names as the "Illuminati" and the "Rosicrucian's," had undermined in a subtle manner the entire structure of regal and sacerdotal supremacy. The founders of Freemasonry were all men who were more or less identified with the progressive tendencies of their day. Mystics, philosophers, and alchemists were all bound together with a secret tie and dedicated to the emancipation of humanity from ignorance and oppression. In my researches among ancient books and manuscripts, I have pieced together a little story of probabilities which has a direct bearing upon the subject. Long before the establishment of

Freemasonry as a fraternity, a group of mystics founded in Europe what was called the "Society of Unknown Philosophers." Prominent among the profound thinkers who formed the membership of this society were the alchemists, who were engaged in transmuting the political and religious "base metal" of Europe into ethical and spiritual "gold"; the Qabbalists who, as investigators of the superior orders of Nature, sought to discover a stable foundation for human government; and lastly the astrologers who, from a study of the procession of the heavenly bodies, hoped to find therein the rational archetype for all mundane procedure. Here and there is to be found a character who contacted this society. By some it is believed that both Martin Luther and also that great mystic, Philip Melanchthon, were connected with it. The first edition of the King James Bible, Bible, which was edited by Francis Bacon and prepared under Masonic supervision, bears more Mason's marks than the Cathedral of Strasburg. The same is true respecting the Masonic symbolism found in the first English edition of Josephus' History of the Jews.

For some time, the Society of Unknown Philosophers moved extraneous to the church. Among the fathers of the church, however, were a great number of scholarly and intelligent men who were keenly interested in philosophy and ethics, prominent among them being the Jesuit Father, Athanasius Kircher, who is recognized as one of the great scholars of his day. Both a Rosicrucian and also a member of the Society of Unknown Philosophers, as revealed by the cryptograms in his writings, Kircher was in harmony with this program of philosophic reconstruction. Since learning was largely limited to churchmen, this body of philosophers soon developed an overwhelming preponderance of ecclesiastics in its membership. The original anti-ecclesiastical ideals of the society were thus speedily reduced to an innocuous state and the organization gradually converted into an actual auxiliary of the church. A small portion of the membership, however, ever maintained an aloofness from the literati of the faith, for it represented an unorthodox class—the alchemists, Rosicrucian's, Qabbalists, and magicians. This latter group accordingly retired from the outer body of the society that had thus come to be known as the "Order of the Golden and Rose Cross" and whose adepts were elevated to the dignity of Knights of the Golden Stone. Upon the withdrawal of these initiated adepts, a powerful clerical body remained which possessed considerable of the ancient lore but in many instances lacked the "keys" by which this symbolism could be interpreted. As this body continued to increase in temporal power, its philosophical power grew correspondingly less.   The smaller group of adepts that had withdrawn from the order remained inactive apparently, having retired to what they termed the "House of the Holy Spirit," where they were enveloped by certain "mists" impenetrable to the eyes of the profane. Among these reclusive adepts must be included such well-known Rosicrucian's as Robert Fludd, Eugenius Philalethes, John Heydon, Michael Maier, and Henri Khunrath. These adepts in their retirement constituted a loosely organized society which, though lacking the solidarity of a definite fraternity, occasionally initiated a candidate and met annually at a specified place. It was the Comte de Chazal, an initiate of this order, who "raised" Dr. Sigismund Bacstrom while the latter was on the Isle of Mauritius. In due time, the original members of the order passed on, after first entrusting their secrets to carefully chosen successors. In the meantime, a group of men in England, under the leadership of such mystics as Ashmole and Fludd, had resolved upon re-popularizing the ancient learning and reclassifying philosophy in accordance with Bacon's plan for a world encyclopedia. These men had undertaken to reconstruct ancient Platonic and Gnostic mysticism, but were unable to attain their objective for lack of information. Elias Ashmole may have been a member of the European order of Rosicrucian's and as such evidently knew that in various parts of Europe there were isolated individuals who were in possession of the secret doctrine handed down in unbroken line from the ancient Greeks and Egyptians through Boetius, the early Christian Church, and the Arabians.

The efforts of the English group to contact such individuals were evidently successful. Several initiated Rosicrucian's were brought from the mainland to England, where they remained for a considerable time designing the symbolism of Freemasonry and incorporating into the rituals of the order the same divine principles and philosophy that had formed the inner doctrine of all great secret societies from the time of the Eleusinia in Greece. In fact, the Eleusinian Mysteries themselves continued in Christendom until the sixth century after Christ, after which they passed into the custody of the Arabians, as attested by the presence of Masonic symbols and figures upon early Mohammedan monuments. The adepts brought over from the Continent to sit in council with the English philosophers were initiates of the Arabian rites and thus through them the Mysteries were ultimately returned to Christendom. Upon completion of the by-laws of the new fraternity, the initiates retired again into Central Europe, leaving a group of disciples to develop the outer organization, which was to function as a sort of screen to conceal the activities of the esoteric order.

Such, in brief, is the story to be pieced together from the fragmentary bits of evidence available. The whole structure of Freemasonry is founded upon the activities of this secret society of Central European adepts; whom the studious Mason will find to be the definite "link" between the modern Craft and the Ancient Wisdom. The outer body of Masonic philosophy was merely the veil of this qabbalistic order whose members were the custodians of the true Arcanum. Does this inner and secret brotherhood of initiates still exist independent of the Freemasonic order? Evidence points to the fact that it does, for these august adepts are the actual preservers of those secret operative processes of the Greeks whereby the illumination and completion of the individual is effected. They are the veritable guardians of the "Lost Word"— the Keepers of the inner Mystery-and the Mason who searches for and discovers them is rewarded beyond all mortal estimation.

In the preface to a book entitled Long-Livers, published in 1772, Eugenius Philalethes, the Rosicrucian initiate, thus addresses his Brethren of the Most Ancient and Most Honorable Fraternity of the Free Masons: "Remember that you are the Salt of the Earth, the Light of the World, and the Fire of the Universe. You are living Stones, built up a Spiritual House, who believe and rely on the chief Lapis Angularis which the refractory and disobedient Builders disallowed. You are called from Darkness to Light; you are a chosen Generation, a royal Priesthood. This makes you, my dear Brethren, fit Companions for the greatest Kings; and no wonder, since the King of Kings hath condescended to make you so to himself, compared to whom the mightiest and most haughty Princes of the Earth are but as Worms, and that not so much as we are all Sons of the same One Eternal Father, by whom all Things were made; but inasmuch as we do the Will of his and our Father which is in Heaven. You see now your high Dignity; you see what you are; act accordingly, and show yourselves (what you are) MEN, and walk worthy the high Profession to which you are called. * * * . Remember, then, what the great End we all aim at is: Is it not to be happy here and hereafter? For they both depend on each other. The Seeds of that eternal Peace and Tranquility and everlasting Repose must be sown in this Life; and he that would glorify and enjoy the Sovereign Good then must learn to do it now, and from contemplating the Creature gradually ascend to adore the Creator."

Of all obstacles to surmount in matters of rationality, the most difficult is that of prejudice. Even the casual observer must realize that the true wealth of Freemasonry lies in its mysticism. The average Masonic scholar, however, is fundamentally opposed to a mystical interpretation of his symbols, for he shares the attitude of the modern mind in its general antipathy towards transcendentalism. A most significant fact, however, is that those Masons who have won signal honors for their contributions to the Craft have been transcendentalists almost without exception. It is quite incredible, moreover, that any initiated Brother, when presented with a copy of Morals and Dogma upon the conferment of his fourteenth degree, can read that volume and yet maintain that his order is not identical with the Mystery Schools of the first ages. Much of the writings of Albert Pike are extracted from the books of the French magician, Eliphas Levi, one of the greatest transcendentalists of modern times. Levi was an occultist, a metaphysician, a Platonic philosopher, who by the rituals of magic invoked even the spirit of Apollonius of Tyana, and yet Pike has inserted in his Morals and Dogma whole pages, and even chapters, practically verbatim. To Pike the following remarkable tribute was paid by Stirling Kerr, Jr., 33? Deputy for the Inspector-General for the District of Columbia, upon crowning with laurel the bust of Pike in the House of the Temple: "Pike was an oracle greater than that of Delphi. He was Truth's minister and priest. His victories were those of peace. Long may his memory live in the hearts of the Brethren." Affectionately termed "Albertus Magnus" by his admirers, Pike wrote of Hermeticism and alchemy and hinted at the Mysteries of the Temple. Through his zeal and unflagging energy, American Freemasonry was raised from comparative obscurity to become the most powerful organization in the land. Though Pike, a transcendental thinker, was the recipient of every honor that the Freemasonic bodies of the world could confer, the modern Mason is loath to admit that transcendentalism has any place in Freemasonry. This is an attitude filled with embarrassment and inconsistency, for whichever way the Mason turns he is confronted by these inescapable issues of philosophy and the Mysteries. Yet withal he dismisses the entire subject as being more or less a survival of primitive superstitions.

The Mason who would discover the Lost Word must remember, however, that in the first ages—every neophyte was a man of profound learning and unimpeachable character, who for the sake of wisdom and virtue had faced death unafraid and had triumphed over those limitations of the flesh which bind most mortals to the sphere of mediocrity. In those days the rituals were not put on by degree teams who handled candidates as though they were perishable commodities, but by priests deeply versed in the lore of their cults. Not one Freemason out of a thousand could have survived the initiations of the pagan rites, for the tests were given in those strenuous days when men were men and death the reward of failure. The neophyte of the Druid Mysteries was set adrift in a small boat to battle with the stormy sea, and unless his knowledge of natural law enabled him to quell the storm as did Jesus upon the Sea of Galilee, he returned no more. In the Egyptian rites of Serapis, it was required of the neophyte that he cross an unbridged chasm in the temple floor. In other words, if unable by magic to sustain himself in the air without visible support, he fell headlong into a volcanic crevice, there to die of heat and suffocation. In one part of the Mithraic rites, the candidate seeking admission to the inner sanctuary was required to pass through a closed door by dematerialization. The philosopher who has authenticated the reality of ordeals such as these no longer entertains the popular error that the performance of "miracles" is confined solely to Biblical characters. "Do you still ask," writes Pike, "if it has its secrets and mysteries? It is certain that something in the Ancient Initiations was regarded as of immense value, by such Intellects as Herodotus, Plutarch and Cicero. The Magicians of Egypt were able to imitate several of the miracles wrought by Moses; and the Science of the Hierophants of the mysteries produced effects that to the Initiated seemed Mysterious and supernatural." (See Legenda for the Twenty-eighth Degree.)

It becomes self-evident that he who passed successfully through these arduous tests involving both natural and also supernatural hazards was a man apart in his community. Such an initiate was deemed to be more than human, for he had achieved where countless ordinary mortals, having failed, had returned no more. Let us hear the words of Apuleius when admitted into the Temple of Isis, as recorded in The Metamorphosis, or Golden Ass: "Then also the priest, all the profane being removed, taking hold of me by the hand, brought me to the penetralia of the temple, clothed in a new linen garment. Perhaps, inquisitive reader, you will very anxiously ask me what was then said and done? I would tell you, if it could be lawfully told; you should know it, if it was lawful for you to hear it. But both ears and the tongue are guilty of rash curiosity. Nevertheless, I will not keep you in suspense with religious desire, nor torment you with long-continued anxiety. Hear, therefore, but believe what is true. I approached to the confines of death, and having trod on the threshold of Proserpine, I returned from it, being carried through all the elements. At midnight I saw the sun shining with a splendid light; and I manifestly drew near to the Gods beneath, and the Gods above, and proximately adored them. Behold, I have narrated to you things, of which, though heard, it is nevertheless necessary that you should be ignorant. I will, therefore, only relate that which may be enunciated to the understanding of the profane without a crime."

Kings and princes paid homage to the initiate—the "newborn" man, the favorite of the gods. The initiate had actually entered into the presence of the divine beings. He had "died" and been "raised" again into the radiant sphere of everlasting light. Seekers after wisdom journeyed across great continents to hear his words and his sayings were treasured with the revelations of oracles. It was even esteemed an honor to receive from such a one an inclination of the head, a kindly smile or a gesture of approbation. Disciples gladly paid with their lives for the Master's word of praise and died of a broken heart at his rebuke. On one occasion, Pythagoras became momentarily irritated because of the seeming stupidity of one of his students. The Master's displeasure so preyed upon the mind of the humiliated youth that, drawing a knife from the folds of his garment, he committed suicide. So greatly moved was Pythagoras by the incident that never from that time on was he known to lose patience with any of his followers regardless of the provocation.

With a smile of paternal indulgence the venerable Master, who senses the true dignity of the mystic tie, should gravely incline the minds of the Brethren towards the sublimer issues of the Craft. The officer who would serve his lodge most effectively must realize that he is of an order apart from other men, that he is the keeper of an awful secret, that the chair upon which he sits is the seat of immortals, and that if he would be a worthy successor to those Master Masons of other ages, his thoughts must be measured by the profundity of Pythagoras and the lucidity of Plato. Enthroned in the radiant East, the Worshipful Master is the "Light" of his lodge—the representative of the gods, one of that long line of hierophants who, through the blending of their rational powers with the reason of the Ineffable, have been accepted into the Great School. This high priest after an ancient order must realize that those before him are not merely a gathering of properly tested men, but the custodians of an eternal lore, the guardians of a sacred truth, the perpetuators of an ageless wisdom, the consecrated servants of a living God, the wardens of a Supreme Mystery.

A new day is dawning for Freemasonry. From the insufficiency of theology and the hopelessness of materialism, men are turning to seek the God of philosophy. In this new era wherein the old order of things is breaking down and the individual is rising triumphant above the monotony of the masses, there is much work to be accomplished. The "Temple Builder" is needed as never before. A great reconstruction period is at hand; the debris of a fallen culture must be cleared away; the old footings must be found again that a new Temple significant of a new revelation of Law may be raised thereon. This is the peculiar work of the Builder; this is the high duty for which he was called out of the world; this is the noble enterprise for which he was "raised" and given the tools of his Craft. By thus doing his part in the reorganization of society, the workman may earn his "wages" as all good Masons should. A new light is breaking in the East, a more glorious day is at hand. The rule of the philosophic elect-the dream of the ages-will yet be realized and is not far distant. To her loyal sons, Freemasonry sends this clarion call: "Arise ye, the day of labor is at band; the Great Work awaits completion, and the days of man's life are few." Like the singing guildsman of bygone days, the Craft of the Builders marches victoriously down the broad avenues of Time. Their song is of labor and glorious endeavor; their anthem is of toil and industry; they rejoice in their noble destiny, for they are the Builders of cities, the Hewers of worlds, the Master Craftsmen of the universe!

THE ROSY CROSS

By THE ROSICRUCAE - 1898

THE origin of the Rosy Cross is known only to the oldest initiates of the order. Its symbols are as ancient as the Egyptian Mysteries and its principles underlie all religions, ancient and modern. In modern times the names of Christian Rosenkrutz, Robert Fludd and Francis Bacon have figured prominently in its literature; but historically, there are few exoteric landmarks of the Order. Rosicrucice is spiritual, not material; a Fraternity rather than an Order. Its members are gathered from the East and the West, from among the lofty and the lowly, the learned and the unlearned, wherever there are free souls, and sympathetic and aspiring natures. It embraces all ages, races and climes, and reaches from the visible far into invisible realms of being.

Silence, secrecy and unpretending good works are its characteristics, and one member may pass his life next door to another and neither be aware of the bond between them unless some stress of need draw the curtain aside. The law of Silence is particularly emphasized, obedience to the injunction to "enter into the closet and shut the door" being imperative on all who would have access to the sources of power. Each age calls for restatements of truth, specially adapted to its understanding and use, and the present age is no exception. That which was hidden from the ignorant and vicious under symbols and figures in the past is emerging from its outgrown shell so that he who runs may read.

The veil of Isis has become a misty cloud, destined to disappear in the broader light of the coming century, and while the Rosy Cross has its lodges, passwords and signs, these external forms are regarded with indifference by the genuine Rosicrucian, who is aware that he can become a complete epitome of the Order only through development of its principles within himself. While the Rosy Cross has no creeds or dogmas to which the initiate must subscribe, there are certain principles which all true Rosicrucian's accept. Among them is belief in the impartial Fatherhood of God and the universal Brotherhood of Man, thus recognizing the Unity of Spirit in all manifestations of Life. Reincarnation is generally accepted as a truth, and salvation is the freedom of the soul from successive embodiments in earthy forms, wherein pain and pleasure alternate; where the glow of genius is dimmed by the darkened understanding of age, and the flame of passion is quenched by the chill of disease and death.

Humanity desires happiness, but none ever fully attains it, because it is sought in individual conditions and possessions, while it can be gained only through the uplifting of all souls everywhere. Life is homogeneous, and perfect rest will come to the individual soul only when the soul of the race is at rest. Therefore, whatever makes for the kingdom of heaven among men is the way to happiness for the individual.

Men and women are born free and equal, but each one comes immediately into conditions destructive of freedom and equality, - conditions which man himself has created in the evolutionary processes of thought and life. He binds himself with creeds, forms and codes of action which divide man from man, create the iron bondage of caste, and limit freedom of thought by fear.

The recognition of universal brotherhood and of the truth that all are entitled to equal rights and privileges in the house of the Common Father and Mother is an important step in the path the soul must travel toward the perfected life.

The cult of the Rosy Cross embraces the culture of the whole man, and this is carried on through vibrations set up in the emotional or soul nature by the Will. These vibrations exalt and expand the energies of the soul, and this culture is the work of salvation, which is not freedom from consequences, but deliverance from evil desires and tendencies.

That which is recorded cannot be erased, but a new record may be made which will cast the old into the limbo of forgotten things. The past belongs to God, with all its failures and sins; but the future is man's to mold and fashion as he will, for himself and for the race. Vibrations may be indefinitely transferred by oral or mental suggestion, and the instructed soul consciously arouses, excites and directs the thoughtless and ignorant through vibrations.

Ignorance unguards the soul, furnishing conditions of receptivity to good and evil suggestions, which uplift or degrade. Mind responds to mind, soul to soul, spirit to spirit, through vibrations in the ether. The invisible world of spirit is drawing near to the earth-plane, and the souls of men respond wherever they are sensitive to etheric vibrations.

The Rosy Cross has long sensed this incoming spiritual tide and confidently expects the breaking away of the clouds of ignorance which have long obscured the light of the inner heavens. The pyramids, the buried cities, the tombs and mountain retreats of the old world are giving up their long-hoarded secrets to the push and enterprise of the age; but their wealth of knowledge and wisdom, though grand and wonderful, sinks into insignificance when compared with the treasures of the kingdom concealed in the soul of man ready to be revealed for use.

This is the Kingdom of Heaven which is taken by force, the force of persistent desire and effort. Thoughts are not things, - they are greater than things. Thought is the energy, the inherent force of things, and comes from the Primal Intelligence which is above and beyond all things. The mind is an instrument manipulated by unseen, but not altogether unknown forces.

Its energies do not belong to us; they are lent for use, and the only merit which we can claim because of superior adaptability of the instruments is in the quality of their use. The power to project this force or energy of the soul is inherent in human nature, and our department of the Rosy Cross culture is devoted to instruction and training in its use.

To vibrate the etheric atoms of the body is to set in motion the ether of space; to exercise the Will in breathing is to connect with the space of Will, charging the body with electricity, power and life; but the fervent desire to attain to any condition sets in vibration the finer essences of spirit that connect with the love-soul of the universe, the Infinite Love. Every aspiring soul reaches some plane in spirit that corresponds to itself, and which it can absorb and use. There are Seven Spaces of Spirit corresponding to the Seven Great Powers, - four Mundane and three Spiritual, or psychic. Those corresponding to the Mundane Powers are, Mineral, Vegetable, Animal, Human; the Spiritual Spaces are, Faith, Will and Love.

All the spaces are filled with Societies, Orders, Associations, and Brotherhoods, which correspond to every condition possible to man. Connection with the beings inhabiting these spaces may be attained by systematic training and effort. This is not mediumship, so called, but the entering into and possession of the knowledge and power of the space contacted.

Man, body and soul, is the Temple of the Infinite Spirit, and in him are etheric atoms belonging to all spiritual states and spaces; some active, some latent. Those which are active connect the individual with the space with which he has the closest affinity, and the influx from it is largely unconscious. To illustrate: Beethoven was by nature affiliated with the Musical Societies and, being a fine instrument attuned to the inspirations of that space, he holds the world entranced by superhuman melodies. Socrates contacted the Philosophical space, Napoleon, the Strategic; but the full soul of the Prophet of Galilee came forth from and breathed the inspiration of the most interior space, the space of Love.

To aspire is to become, in time and in eternity; for aspiration connects the soul with the spaces of spirit vibrating with immortal energies. Man makes and unmakes himself; "He fails, sickens and dies through feebleness of will." Physical life is only a series of vibrations whose intensity may be greatly increased by persistent use of spiritual forces.

Degrees of soul-force depend on the rapidity of the vibrations of the flame uniting the three powers which constitute the human ego. This trinity of Intelligence, Will and Love is a manifestation of the Divine Trinity in Unity, making of man a microcosmic God. The soul is a glowing spark in an Infinite Flame. The vibrations of these triune forces develop heat, which is generally diffused throughout the body as a gentle warmth. This heat may be powerfully increased and drawn to a center in the breast, where it burns with a pure and conscious flame.

This is the baptism with fire and the Holy Ghost (Geist, Spirit) and is typified by the fire kept burning on the altars of the ancient temples. It is also the transmuting fire of the Rosicrucian's, which certain of the old alchemists misunderstood and materialized to mean the transmutation of the baser metals into gold. This flame in the breast is evidence of the Christ-union, the seal of immortality, and is possible only to the pure in heart.

To the impure and unholy, the increase of spirit vibrations fills the soul with an unquenchable thirst and an insatiable hunger, which destroy soul and body by a slow combustion of unrest, impure desires, disease and death. This flame is the point of contact with the source of all power and knowledge, and sometimes it finds a voice. With Moses it objectified in the form of a burning bush, and the "still small voice" of spirit became audible to the external ear. Referring to this flame the great Persian sage, Zoroaster, says, "When you see the fire, listen for the voice of the fire."

This inner fire burned with conscious power when the disciples walked with the risen Jesus on the way to Emmaus. "Did not our hearts burn within us, while he spake to us on the way?" It has well-nigh ceased to burn on the altars of human hearts, but the Rosy Cross has preserved a spark of it and now calls to the wise virgins, whose lamps are trimmed and burning, to unveil the light for the illumination of the world. Love is the only antidote for Evil; force will suppress, but will not prevent it.

The peaceful, gentle, forgiving vibrations of love open the invisible spaces from which descends purifying and regenerative power. Through the vibrations of love, war will cease, crime and its vindictive punishment will pass away, and practical help will supersede sermons, prayers and the legal restraints with which society now ignorantly strives to protect itself. Crime should be prevented rather than punished, criminal tendencies detected, undermined and destroyed, and the transmission of criminal instincts rendered impossible.

All this may be done through spiritual vibrations, and this is one of the fields of work which specially engages the attention and efforts of the Rosy Cross. The concentration of effort and the union of many minds in one vibration creates societies, sects, governments, on the plane of its action; in the same way spirit, by projection, creates and destroys. Spirit individualized in a human body is no less spirit than when disrobed. There are conclaves in the spaces of spirit in which the souls of men and women who are still of the mundane world take part, equally with those who have cast off the body.

Convocations are held when the interests of earth-life are represented by those in earth-bodies who, in soul projection, are in the spiritual spaces, and questions touching human interests most nearly are considered. Such a convention, giving exclusive attention to the application of the great principles of sex, has long been in session. It has removed the ban of silence from woman, and caused her equality with man to be recognized in many ways; but the projection of this truth into the external world has been difficult, owing to the prejudices and superstitions of men.

Rosicrucian: invites woman's cooperation and has made her eligible to its councils and helpful influences on the same terms as her brothers; it now boldly proclaims the feminine principle as embodied in woman to be the Savior of the Race. Being the most spiritual, she is the vibratory center between God and man. Through her elevation in the thought, will and love of man, the influx of crime, lust, and disease from the lowest hells will be checked, and the incarnation of lofty and pure souls will be facilitated. This can only be accomplished by the cooperation of the visible world of souls with the invisible.

Sex is of the body, soul and spirit, and is as eternal as is the Creative Power, for by and through its principles all things exist. Its activities are always creative, for generation on one plane creates another plane similar but a little higher. Vibrations of the body are the result of vibrations of spirit, which they involve, and all vibrations are creative in accord with their plane of activity. Sound vibrations reach the ear, thought vibrations the mind; but the powerful and far-reaching vibrations of emotion move the soul, and the motion is infinitely sustained.

Love is the creative center and the vibrations that harmonize the conditions, interior or exterior, of each individual are generated at that center. It is the love of one, not of many; for all sincere and genuine Rosicrucian's are monogamists. Love in the physical has its correspondence in the spiritual nature, it is one, for Love is Spirit, and all its vibrations are creative.

What we name matter is an effect produced by spirit transforming itself through vibratory motion. Nature makes no mistakes; she is the word of God to which nothing can be added or taken away by man except to his own hurt. The separation of the masculine and feminine in thought, emotion, or physical life, is destructive, not constructive. In their perfect blending on all planes, lies the secret of power, and the Lost Word is unity - one.

The natural use of the organs of the body, as of the faculties of the mind and powers of the soul, is an imperative duty to all who would perfect the human nature. The orderly exercise of mind and will is required to preserve the harmonious balance of being, so that life on all planes shall march together in orderly sequence. To be self-poised and perfect in rhythmic motion, like the worlds swinging in space, is the prerogative of every human being; but only those who have found the center, and lighted the flame on that altar, approach that condition. It is not attained by ignoring the selfhood or in disuse of the functions of body or mind.

The Rosy Cross makes no noise; it loves the Infinite Silence, and works through vibrations of Thought, Will and Love. It is ready to point out the path and to clasp hands with any who desire to work for the advent of the new civilization. To this end, the fraternity desires souls rather than money; earnest, active, sincere students and workers. Not all who knock can enter. Before one can become a member of the visible Fraternity, he or she is already enrolled among the Invisibles. "Not everyone who saith Lord, can enter into the kingdom," saith the Christ, and one before Him affirmed "Many are the wand-bearers, but few are the true Bacchanals." Those who can recall the conditions of life fifty years ago will appreciate the gigantic strides man has made along the lines of progress.

The twilight of the stage-coach has broadened into the noonday of steam and electricity; the inspiration of books has largely given place to scientific certainties, to ascertained truths and facts of things, thus widening and deepening the scope of free thought. Dr. Franklin ushered in a new age, the age of electricity, when he called forth a message from the shadow of God which pronounced the death sentence on the limitations of matter, annihilating time and space by putting "a girdle around the earth in forty minutes," as prophesied by Shakespeare's tricky sprite.

As the age of crude force merged into the electrical age, bringing with it everything worth preserving, so the wires and dynamos and circuits, which now witness to the external activities of man's restless intelligence, will give place to the simpler methods of the mental age, when the possibilities of mind will become manifest. The present laborious processes of education will become obsolete, and telepathy will take the place of the old, cumbrous methods of instruction in the imparting of knowledge.

Daguerre pictured the outside of things fifty years ago; modern photography reproduces the inside, and it is only a question of a little more time and a few more experiments when mental states will be photographed and man's nature will be mapped out, as physical geography maps the surface of the planet. The swamps and lagoons in human nature which send up the malaria that generates crime, disease, death, will be located, as will the life-giving seas and breezy, moral mountain tops. Mind will be generated, rather than adipose tissue, and God will be enthroned in the heart of the world, rather than in some far-off anachronistic City of Gold.

Speed characterizes the electrical age; let us move· quickly to help God save the world. He demands only the sacrifice of meanness, of enmity to our brother man; and this is the only bar to infinite progress. No one can borrow the light of the Spirit. Each virginal lamp must shine by its own light, and each man stands or falls alone. "God helps those who help themselves." His tables are laden with flowers and fruits which are not forced on anyone; the command is, "Help yourself" Recognizing the value of organization for certain work which is before us, the Western Cult of the Rose Cross has established a bureau of instruction, where those who desire to learn and work with the Fraternity may apply. By order of HER WHO is NAMELESS.

THE ROSE AND THE CROSS

By MAURICE MAGRE - 1877-1941

Rosicrucians took the union of the rose and the cross for their symbol because this union embodies the meaning of their effort and emphasizes the fact that that effort must be made by all men. For immemorial ages the wisest among us have discovered that the aim of humanity on earth is to attain divine wisdom. Two ways lead to divine wisdom: knowledge and love. The cross is the oldest symbol in the world. Ever since the appearance of the earliest civilizations it has denoted mind or spirit moving towards perfection. The rose symbolizes love because by its perfume, color and delicacy it is Nature's masterpiece of beauty, and beauty excites love, just as love transforms into beauty the elements on which it is bestowed. By the rose blooming in the middle of the cross the meaning of the universe is explained, the only true doctrine is summed up, the truth shines out with splendor.

In order to realize his possibilities and become perfect, man must develop his capacity for love to the point of loving all creatures and all forms perceptible to his senses; he must enlarge his capacity for knowledge and understanding to the point of comprehending the laws that govern the world, and of being able to proceed, through the intelligence, from every effect to every cause. He who breathes the perfume of the rose and savors its beauty, who sees the branches of the cross open towards the four cardinal points of the spirit, may take the wrong road, may go backwards, may be for the time overwhelmed by ignorance. But he holds his anchorage in the storm, he sees the light on the hill-top; sooner or later he will once more find the right way.

All glory to the messenger who found this safety-giving signal and fixed it in wood or stone that it might be transmitted! All glory to the messenger who, through the virtue of the symbol, created the possibility that the truth should be preserved! He has added name and number to the milestone; he has been the comfort of the traveler, the safety of the lost wanderer.

Christian Rosenkreutz made rules for his disciples' life. The first of these rules was unselfishness, which will always be the most difficult virtue to put into practice. The men who have a reputation for unselfishness and live among us with a vague halo of generosity, are only men who are less greedy than others. Nobody is unselfish. There is not a single example in our modern society of a man big enough to break the terrible bond of riches and pass readily and unostentatiously from wealth to poverty or even from poverty to greater poverty. As soon as the mind has reached a certain level it understands that it is in this direction that the first step must be taken. Yet it does not take that step. One of the bravest men of all, and one most deeply convinced of the virtue of poverty, Tolstoy made up his mind only a few hours before his death to become a wandering beggar. But he was too late. Another essential rule was absence of pride.

The Rosicrucian had to pass unnoticed, might not pride himself on his knowledge, had to remain so far as possible anonymous. For the ordinary man modesty is as impossible to practice as poverty. It is even a matter of common observation that great intellectual faculties are almost always accompanied by a form of stupid, boastful vanity. And this very vanity is regarded with favor as the sign of genius. The third rule of the Rosicrucian's was chastity. Wise men have always attached great importance to chastity, though neither Pythagoras nor Socrates nor Plato nor the Alexandrine philosophers practiced it rigorously.

Possibly it is nothing more than a preventive measure against excess and against the violence generated by such desires. Logically, if pleasure in eating is not forbidden there is no reason why the pleasure of sex should be forbidden. And these two orders of physical pleasures are in some degree comparable. In the ordinary man they are both equally indispensable to life. But while eating involves only the physical pleasure arising out of a good digestion, the other, if practiced with a person who is loved, contains marvelous possibilities of pleasure and may even be a path to perfection. Only at present nothing is known of this path.

The laws which teach how a high spiritual level may be attained through community of desire and its mutual satisfaction have not yet been written by any master. I have never heard even of there being any oral teaching on that subject. A prudishness that is as old as the world has cut short with a command of silence the forward impulse which humanity might have received through the flesh. We do not, however, know whether the rose in the Rosicrucian symbol may not contain an implicit indication of the secret of love which remains to be found. He who reaches higher knowledge through an enlarged intelligence will be able to love only those persons and things whose machinery he understands, whose movements he sees, whose passions he comprehends as though they were his own.

He who reaches the state of perfect love through the emotional impetus of the heart will see the barriers of ignorance fall before him and will conquer knowledge by the bestowal of himself on that which he loves. For the two ways meet and at a certain level become one. The symbol is well-founded and eternal, and there will be no need of any other for thousands of human evolutions. Every man can weigh himself up by reference to the rose and cross and can find in it a provisional touchstone of good and evil. It is the interrogation point which is formed in many consciences, though they may not confess it to themselves. What is good and what is evil? Am I right to do something which seems good from my point of view and evil from that of others? Naturally the rose and cross cannot serve as a key to every riddle, for there are too many doors in the darkness of the soul.

The agonizing question which every man asks himself at least once in his lifetime and most men ask themselves a thousand times, the question whether it is more important to develop oneself or to help others, whether it is better to sacrifice oneself or to progress by study, remains unsettled. But the two ever-present symbols give man the framework of an answer, if he is sincere with himself. Whenever a man becomes identified through love with that totality of universes which is called God, or with a landscape, or with some creature, though it be only a dog, he is on the way of the rose, protected by it and enriched by its substance.

Whenever he emerges from his ignorance, learns a fact or a law, allows his mind to go a little farther in knowledge of reality, he is progressing towards that super-terrestrial and super-celestial point at which the cross stretches forth its four spiritual branches. That is the message which Christian Rosenkreutz brought to the West. It is a message which may seem very modest to European sceptics (who are convinced that they possess all knowledge and consider hate more important than love). But it was brought very humbly by a messenger who gloried in concealing his name and who, after journeying for more than a century to transmit his little truth, has left no other trace of his passing than the design of the open flower at the center of the cross.

Southern France there are certain districts covered with pines which are periodically ravaged by fires. Often the pines grow again, and where before there was nothing but calcined dust you may see, some years later, a new forest of resinous trees. But sometimes, as though the violence of the fire had reached the very seeds themselves, the hill that was once covered with pines remains bald and barren. Then on the top of the hill there springs up a single tree, which, strangely full of life, rises solitary as though to attest the lost presence of a dead forest. So, of the great Albigensian forest, which was cut down, burned and reduced to ashes, there survived but one man, who was to perpetuate the doctrine by transforming it.

Like the solitary pine on the hill, he plunged his vigorous thought deep into the human soil of his time and saw it rise high into the blue heaven of the centuries with its foliage of books. From the Albigenses there sprang in the middle of the thirteenth century the wise man who is known under the symbolical name of Christian Rosenkreutz and who was the last descendant of the German family of Germelshausen. There are no precise data here-only a tradition, a story told orally. There is no written text, no historical proof. How could there be? So intense was the desire to suppress the heresy that not only were the bodies of the heretics destroyed, but even the stones of the houses that had sheltered them, and the documents which might have enshrined their thought. Besides, these heretics very soon realized that their only chance of survival lay in wrapping themselves in obscurity, hiding under false names, corresponding in cipher.

History can no longer be traced except under the disguise of legend. But a man who has left so deep a mark after a life so obscure and so lacking in wonders and miracles cannot have been created by legend. Discretion, modesty, unostentatious goodness, knowledge without parade-these are not the attributes of legend. Christian Rosenkreutz is as real a figure as Jesus or Buddha; their attributes may be more glorious, but their historical foundation is scarcely more secure. The Albigensian doctrines had spread fragmentarily to the north of France, the Low Countries and Germany. Families of refugees had found their way there.

Solitary men had escaped, begging their way, from the sunny land in which they were thenceforward outlaws and accursed. Many of them died. But some reached the distant countries where the vine does not grow, where the rivers are more rapid and the sun less hot. And some of them gave an account of what they had heard in their low houses under the shelter of the ramparts of Toulouse or in the shadow of Montsegur; they imparted to others what was still a flaming truth in their hearts. A few of them were understood. Little nuclei of Albigenses formed round a preacher, a spare, brown-faced man, who looked like a Saracen.

The seed carried by the wind was thus to germinate in the country to which chance had brought it. Under the influence of a wandering Albigensian the doctrine crossed the fir-grown mountains and flowered in the Rhon district, on the border of Hesse and Thuringia. In the middle of the Thuringian Forest stood the castle of Germelshausen. The men who inhabited it were a grim, sullen family, half-brigands, whose Christianity was mixed with pagan superstitions. They spent their time fighting their neighbors, and they did not disdain to ambush and rob travelers. They venerated an idol of worn stone, the origin of which was unknown to them. It was probably the fruit of some long-past pillaging expedition.

It might have been a Greek statue of Athene. It stood in the courtyard of the castle beside the chapel door. The period was the middle of the thirteenth century. Germany had just been devastated by the fanatical Dominican, Conrad of Marburg, the envoy of Pope Gregory IX. Another Dominican, Tors, carried on his work. He was accompanied by a one-eyed layman called Jean, who claimed that his single eye had been given the divine faculty of distinguishing at first glance a heretic from a good Christian.

Almost all who came within the field of view of this terrible eye were marked with the mark of heresy. It was no doubt enough for him to catch a glimpse, through the rocks and firs, of the towers of the castle of Germelshausen to discover from the color of its stone that it sheltered a brood of heretics. Perhaps something of the power of the eternal spirit was given off from the ancient statue that stood in the courtyard. Landgrave Conrad of Thuringia, who had razed to the ground the little town of Willnsdorf, decided on the destruction of the castle. He besieged it several times, at intervals of some years.

The castle fell at last, and the whole family of Germelshausen (which now adhered to the mystical doctrine of the Albigenses, practiced its austerities, and believed in reincarnation and in the consolamentum, which delivers from reincarnation) was put to death at the final assault. The youngest son, who was then five years old, was carried from the burning castle by a monk who had taken up his quarters in the chapel and who had been struck by the amazing intelligence shown by the child.

This monk, this ascetic dweller in the chapel of the Germelshausens, was an Albigensian adept from Languedoe, and it was he who had instructed the family. He took refuge in a monastery nearby, into which the breath of heresy had already penetrated. It was in this monastery that the last of the Germelshausens, who was to be known by the name of Christian Rosenkreutz, was brought up and educated. He learned Greek and Latin and, with four other monks of the community, formed a fraternal group determined to devote themselves to the search for truth. They made a plan to seek this truth at the source whence it had always sprung, the East. Two of them started out, Christian Rosenkreutz, who was then fifteen, and one of the four monks whom the Fama Fraternitatis calls Brother P.A.L. The pretext of their journey was a pilgrimage to the Holy Sepulcher.

Their real aim was to reach a center of initiation, and they no doubt had precise knowledge as to where it was to be found. Brother P.A.L. died in Cyprus, where the hazards of travel had led the two companions. Christian continued his journey and, no doubt as a result of directions he had received, made for Damascus. He did so because the tie with the East, which was about to be broken, still existed. Just as Apollonius had learned from the Pythagorean groups among whom he lived the exact whereabouts of the abode of wise men, so Christian Rosenkreutz knew, probably from the adept who had instructed the Germelshausens, that Damascus lay on the path to initiation. It cannot have been easy to leave the Christian kingdom of Cyprus for the country of the infidels. But to him who sincerely seeks truth all religions are alike; and when he left Christian territory Rosenkreutz assumed the dress and appearance of a Mussulman pilgrim. At that time Damascus was under the dominion of the Mamelukes.

All the learned men and poets of Persia had taken refuge there from the invading Mongols under Hulagu. The destruction of

Bagdad and Nichapur and the annihilation of their universities and libraries convinced the intellectuals of the East that thought was dying. There were rumors of the end of the world. There had been great earthquakes in Syria and a rain of scorpions in Mesopotamia. The Mongols occupied Persia and watchers on the ramparts of Damascus searched the horizon anxiously for the appearance of their advance guards. How great must have been Christian's astonishment in the city of the three hundred mosques, among men learned in the literature of the East!

What discoveries for a young man so greedy for knowledge. He read the Guide of the Erring, by Maimonides; the Alchemy of Happiness, by Gazali; the Golden Meadows, by Mazoudi. He heard Omar Khayyam's poetry recited and made every effort to understand his books on algebra and Euclid. He discussed astronomy with the disciples of Nazir Eddin. He meditated on the Masnavi, the sacred book of the Sufis, and was. amazed to find in it the mystical pantheism of his spiritual fathers the Albigenses. How barbarous Germany must have seemed to him amid the intellectual effervescence which surrounded him in the presence of the great Arab civilization now drawing to its close he understood still more clearly the necessity for his mission, which was to preserve the spirit and transmit it to the men of his race. After several years' study at Damascus, when he had acquired the greatest sum of knowledge possible to a man whose sole aim is to learn, he thought to obtain a higher knowledge, for which he was then ripe.

The enigmatic name of the place to which he directed his steps has been preserved by tradition. It was Damcar, in Arabia. At Damcar, which name probably designates a monastery in the sand, there was at that time, and possibly there still is, a center of initiates. Damcar was for him what the abode of wise men was for Apollonius. He remained there some years, then went to Egypt, crossed the Mediterranean, visited Fez. In the reign of Abou Said Othman there was in Fez, the city of the six hundred playing fountains, which was then at the height of its splendor, a school of astrology and magic. It had become secret since the persecutions of Abou Yusuf. It was there that Rosenkreutz learnt divination by the stars and certain laws which govern the hidden forces of Nature. But he was eager now to return to his own country.

He left Fez and took ship for Spain. It was probably at this time that he took the name of Rosenkreutz, which embodied the essence of his beliefs. He entered into relations with the Alumbrados, a secret society in Spain which had come into being under the influence of the Arabs, and which studied the sciences and practiced a mysticism derived from that of the Neo-Platonists. They were engaged also in the search for the philosopher's stone in accordance with the writings of Artephius. This secret society was a little later to be wiped out by the Inquisition. The Fama Fraternitatis recounts an echo of the disappointment experienced by Christian Rosenkreutz. He was anxious to communicate to others the new truths that he was bringing in the domain of science and philosophy. He hoped to set right mistakes, to transmit with love that which he had learned. He was received with scorn and laughter. In all times half-knowledge has enveloped pseudo-scholars in an illusion of certainty which prevents them receiving any new idea. Before a mediocre mind can grasp an unfamiliar truth, habituation is necessary, even though the truth be radiant as the sun. It was then that Christian Rosenkreutz realized that only slowly can wisdom enter the human heart.

He had to remember the persecutions that had struck down too precocious possessors of the truth. And, though he wondered at the time necessary for the spirit to develop, whereas a flower opens in a single day and a tree reaches its full height in a single century, he reconciled himself to leaving the acorns to the pigs and keeping the pearls for the elect, at the risk of occasionally mixing with the acorns an infinitesimally small amount of pearl dust. He considered the fine filters through which thought must trickle to the men of his race in rare, microscopic drops, so that they might not be consumed by it. He counted up how many he would be able to initiate and saw that their number could not be more than eight. He laid the foundations of an occult group which was so secret and the members of which were bound together by an oath that was so terrible, that the group was able subsequently to act as he had ordered, to pursue and attain its aims, for three centuries without its existence being known, except by vague whisperings.

The curiosity of superficial men who find pleasure in anecdotal history may have been disappointed by this secrecy. But who could maintain that it is due to the egoism of a superior minority scorning to enlighten their fellows and share their knowledge with them? How many men are there in Europe at the present day who are sufficiently free from intellectual pride to entertain an absolutely new idea? Is not this pride a barrier which precludes even the approach of a new idea? If Christian Rosenkreutz disembarked today from Fez and tried to explain that the problem of the unity of matter is linked with the development of love in man-would he not appear ridiculous to every academy in the world? If he tried to teach, would he not find, on the part of those who wish to learn, this incapacity to receive? To help him without hope of reward, would he find now, as he found then, even eight faithful monks?

Christian Rosenkreutz passed through France without leaving any trace. It must have been the time when the mystic Marguerite Porete was burned in Paris, and Christian was anxious to get back to Germany. Long years had passed. Germany was affected by all sorts of mystical currents which sprang from the Albigensian heresy. There were the Brothers of the Free Spirit, who affirmed the vanity of external cults and sacraments, denied purgatory and hell, said that man was a fragment of God, which must, after a long series of lives, return at last to the divine essence. There were the Friends of God, who aimed at emancipation from desire, and were addicted to practices analogous to those of the Yoga system, while their philosophy was modelled closely on the Hindu theology. But the Church organized. its persecution more intensely than these sects propagated themselves. Christian Rosenkreutz, seeing the number of imprisonments and burnings, was compelled to weigh the danger into which the spiritual light brought those among whom it spread. He went back to Thuringia to find the three monks who had been the companions of his early studies.

They formed a brotherhood of four members, and the number was increased a little later to eight. It was at this time that the brotherhood of the Rosicrucian's had its greatest efflorescence and contained a greater number of true initiates than was ever again reached. All the members of the brotherhood were Germans, except the brother designated by the Fama Fraternitatis under the initials I.A., who came from another country, probably Languedoc.

Christian Rosenkreutz first of all taught his disciples the secret writing and the symbols by which adepts corresponded with one another. He wrote for their use a book which was the synthesis of his philosophy and contained a summary of his scientific and medical knowledge. The role played by the brotherhood seems to have been to influence the few men in the West who were at that time interested in science, so that science might be turned in the direction of disinterestedness. It is possible that this was the great cross-road of our civilization. If the aim of the Rosicrucian's had been attained, science, instead of being organized for material ends only, might have been the source of a boundless development of the spirit.

We have seen that it has not been so. The men designated by the symbol of the rose and cross travelled all over the world, each one with a mission to fulfil. But with one exception nothing was ever heard of them again. Brother I.A., according to the Fama, returned to Southern France, where it may have been his task to rekindle the old Albigensian flame. But he must by that time have been very old.

Did he succeed in resuscitating the sect with the same secrecy which surrounded the Rosicrucian's? Tradition reports only his death near Narbonne. Historically, nothing is known of the activities of Rosenkreutz during the last part of his life, that is to say, at the beginning of the fourteenth century. It may, however, be supposed, without great fear of error, that he inspired Jean de Mechlin, who preached in High Germany, and that at Brussels he was the source of truth from which the mystic Blomert drew.

This inspired woman performed miraculous cures and published writings in which she taught the liberation of the being through love. Her disciples asserted that on either side of her they saw a seraph, who advised her. It was in all probability Christian Rosenkreutz who was the mysterious visitor (as to whose identity so much has been written) of Johann Tauler. Johann Tauler was the most celebrated doctor of theology of his time. The learned world of Europe came to Strasburg to hear his sermons. One day he was visited by a layman whose name he never divulged and who converted him to a mystical philosophy, the ideal of which was absorption into the divine essence. For two years he kept silence and became a member of the sect of the Friends of God. This sect possessed the same characteristics as the Albigenses.

It rejected as the expression of evil the cruel God of the Old Testament; it condemned marriage and taught poverty as a practical means of divine realization. Of the death of Christian Rosenkreutz nothing is known. As in the case of Apollonius of Tyana, no burial-place can be determined. It was a rule among the adepts to maintain secrecy with regard both to their birth and to their death. Was it merely to avoid the violation of the grave and the profanation of the body to which the Church condemned heretics? Or was it in some cases to permit the transference of their spirit into another human body, and to prevent even the suspicion of a secret so astounding to ordinary men? There has come down to us nothing more than a childish legend regarding the burial-place of Christian Rosenkreutz.

Two and a half centuries after his death, at the time when the story of his life was beginning to become known, his disciples, or rather men who would have wished to be his disciples, asserted that they had found a geometrically-proportioned cave, in which rested, in artificial sunlight, the still intact body of the master.

In all times men have wished that those whom they considered greater than themselves should not die in the flesh. They attach less importance to the permanence of their spirit, although of course that is the only possible form of eternity for them. Thus, when the bodies of Catholic or Mussulman saints are found, they are said to emit a pleasant odor. But the true fragrance given off by the bodies of wise men in the silence of the earth and in corruption is made of no material quintessential atom, no perfumed volatilization.

The subtle radiations of their soul float over the places where they lie and impregnate them long after the bodies have ceased even to be dust. But you must yourself be a wise man to establish connection with this posthumous life; and if your perception allows you to catch a glimpse of the fact that the best cannot escape the law, it will also make you feel more deeply the sadness inherent in all changes.

TRUE AND FALSE ROSICRUCIAN'S AT the beginning of the seventeenth century there broke out a sort of Rosicrucian mania. The Fama Fraternitatis and the Confessio published, in a naive form, what ordinary men knew of the sect of Rosicrucian's-which indeed was extremely little. A great many philosophers and scholars, as well as many impostors, attracted by the sublime philosophy of the Rosicrucian's, claimed to be their followers. Secret societies were formed, which very soon ceased to be secret owing to the vanity of their members, who boasted of their membership. Most of these groups, when they were not Lutheran, bowed to the authority of the Church.

Every alchemist called himself a Rosicrucian. Descartes tried to establish contact with the genuine brotherhood of Rosicrucian's.

He searched for them in the Low Countries and in Germany, but on his return to France said he had not been able to find out anything definite about them. It has been asserted that Paracelsus, Francis Bacon and Spinoza were Rosicrucian's; but there seems to be no proof of this. In the eighteenth century a new grade that of the Rosicrucian's, was introduced into Freemasonry by the Jesuits, who had made their way inside the movement and everywhere formed groups within it. The hardy independence of the heresies of the thirteenth century had disappeared.

The so-called Rosicrucian's recognized the sacraments, studied the Old Testament as the source of all truth, acknowledged the power of the Church and the infallibility of the pope. This is the line of development which all spiritual currents follow. The tree produces a beautiful flower, a perfect fruit, and falls a victim to an obscure force which poisons the sap and kills the tree. But the true Rosicrucian's carried on their work. Their brotherhood had never ceased to remain secret. Through the self-sought obscurity of each member no one ever knew the identity of those who belonged to the brotherhood. From the assertion of certain men that they were Rosicrucian's the one sure inference was that they were not members of the sect founded by Christian Rosenkreutz.

The influence of this free spirit was felt in the seventeenth and eighteenth centuries by all who struggled against the tyranny of Calvinism and Lutheranism, which were as intolerant as the Inquisition, and against the intransigence of the universities, which tried to submit all thought to the intellectual discipline of Aristotle. But the messengers remained faithful to their vow not to make themselves known.

The message reached its destination, but it was not known who had brought it. Certain characteristics in the lives of certain men may, however, give rise to the supposition that they were the true possessors of the Rosicrucian tradition. Paracelsus practiced medicine gratuitously; his philosophy was Neo-Platonic; he wore only very unpretending clothes and exalted poverty; upon his appointment as professor of surgery by the senate of Bale, he burned in the Amphitheatre before the students the old medical books, which were believed in blindly but which, owing to the respect in which they were held, were actually an obstacle to research.

Philalethes, who possessed the secret of the philosopher's stone, travelled all over the world to heal the sick; his continual preoccupation was to escape the fame which his cures brought him. Although the Comte de Saint-Germain had a fondness for precious stones, he may, for other reasons, be numbered among the true Rosicrucian's. But the same conclusion cannot be drawn in the case of Spinoza from the fact that his seal was in the form of a rose and that he did not sign his work. Certain too zealous writers have assigned to the Rosicrucian's every remarkable figure of the last few centuries.

In 1888 Stanislas de Guaita and Papus founded a cabalistic order of the Rosy Cross, with a ceremonial, grades and, possibly, special dress. These facts, together with the stir which they made over this foundation, were sufficient indication that the new order was not inspired by the tradition of its original founder. The same may be said of the Catholic order of the Rosy Cross founded by Josephin Peladan at the same time. These orders had only an ephemeral life. At the present day there can still be found various groups, almost all of them Christian, calling themselves Rosicrucian's; but they do not correspond to any reality based on initiation. The only true Rosicrucian's, the eight heirs-who have followed one another in unbroken succession of the Albigensian Christian von Germelshausen, have carried on their secret work uninterruptedly.

Some have thought that towards the end of the seventeenth century before the growing materialism of Europe, as though they considered the game lost, they abandoned the races which were greedy only for material well-being and retired into the inaccessible solitudes of the Himalayas. But a game in which the stake is divine can never be lost. Possibly they left Europe at one time and have since returned: The legend of them, after providing one of the chief topics of conversation among European intellectuals, died down after the French Revolution. At the present day it interests only a small number of seekers after knowledge. The eight wise men have returned to their task, though this task has become excessive. By what means are they seeking to accomplish it?

Sometimes it needs very little to turn a human soul in a new and better direction. It may happen that the reading of a book is enough, or a chance word that you hear-even the face of a good man that you catch a glimpse of one evening and that reminds you that good exists. Each one of us, when the moment has come or when he asks with sufficient intensity, may meet one of the eight wandering wise men. Let him not be in a bad temper that day, or inattentive, or tired. Wisdom is not capricious, as luck is; but it visits us much less often.

CONSIDERATION OF THE MORE SECRET PHILOSOPHY

By PHILIP À GABELLA

[A pseudonym, possibly for Raphael Eglinus or Johannes Rhenanus]

This work was published together with the first edition of the Confessio Fraternitatis at Cassel in 1615. It is one of the earliest known Rosicrucian works.

['May God give thee the dew of and the fatness of the earth' Genesis 27: 28]

The Consideration of Philip à Gabella upon secret matters, dedicated to the most distinguished nobleman Bruno Carolus Uffel, a knight of the order of Hass.

Those who seek the hidden and secret origins of all natural things must first trace back the perpetual sources and springs of the rivers and fountains to the oceans itself. They wonder at the ability of the waters to flow back and forth as if by a natural impulse. But does it seem appropriate to tell of those philosophical matters that relate to these secret origins praised by another author, to whom these things were passed on, if not to you (Noble Sir) and thence to me? For it seems right that natural reason would wish to trace the origin of all things in the world, to discover their derivation, and how they come to develop.

I would thus appear ungrateful were I to offer these philosophical meditations to any name but yours, and so may this work, which exalts you as being its great originator, be presented to you. Just as the waters that flow from the great ocean always seek to return, similarly these contemplations flow back to you as I gladly offer you, my work. And just as the salty waters of the ocean become clean and sweet during their long wanderings through the land, I hope that this treatise - more commendable for its value than for its great age - may be decorated by the deeds, the enthusiasm and the diligence of the Rosicrucian Brotherhood.

Whether my gift to you be roughhewn or refined, I beg you to accept it kindly. The gods do not care for solemn pride or for prayers that are merely intended to impress. They think little of those who call upon them with a long procession of words and a fine speech. But you, Sir, if you have regard for my feelings and the prayers of a man who serves you well, then I beg to praise this attempt, made by one who has wished for some record of his respect and of his constant service to you in this work of a period of leisure. I wish to dedicate this work to the eternal memory of your name.

Preface to the Reader How does it come about, gentle reader, that of nearly all the men who wish to learn and to gain wisdom, there is only one in every thousand who acquires through such study even a modicum of knowledge and wisdom? Perhaps it is because they fail to set themselves a specific goal in their studies as they are setting out on the path to knowledge, so that they know whether they are on the right path? For nothing results from their diligent attempts, if they do not at the same time hold steadfastly on the course that they have chosen as the right one. For when they have reached their goal they will find that all their pains and hard work will be worthless, if they have not first worked towards a fixed end, and directed all their thoughts and actions towards it. In such a way do sailors, when they have no harbor to make for, wander uncertainly across the vast ocean, unsure of their course, eventually arriving at an unsuitable harbor, or being wrecked on the shore. For those who do not chose a suitable goal are just like those sailors; they willingly run themselves aground or drive their ship onto sharp rocks.

No sane man has ever doubted that this is a most fitting end to those mocked by Aeolus and Neptune, and those who bring sorrow to their friends and joy to their enemies. Therefore, whoever wishes to know the daughter of alchemical wisdom, resplendent in her brilliant white dress, should, before he sets out on this crystal sea, first train his eyes and prepare his strength for the struggles ahead in the pyronomic art. He should, as it were, first color himself with dyes, and then polish and smooth himself as if with pumice, tweezers and scrapers. But is there not always something obscure in these books? I admit that there is, yet there is just as much - if not more - that can drive ignorance from the mind and lay the foundations of wisdom. What rose could be more beautiful, more sweet-smelling and more beneficial to the mind? Such roses still have spines that tear, and thorns that prick, but even small boys can be taught to avoid these when picking the flowers, and to shun the Hyblaean nectar, even though it is not deadly poison. Such a task is part of a teacher's duties, and such a teacher must show what is to be accepted and what discarded, what is worthy of praise and what of censure. But if anyone should accuse me of obscurity, he should also accuse Hermes, Plato, Seneca and many other philosophers, for it is upon their work that the present contemplation is founded

Chapter One

It is truth that I present to you: Truth, whose brightness drives out all uncertainty. It is not Falsehood, which conceals the truth in the depths of obscurity. Both my own conscience and the learning of the ancient philosophers attest to that. May Plato be a friend to me, and Truth an even greater friend. I will neither write nor teach anything that has not been acknowledged by these ambassadors as being true. Time reveals all things, and you will see that what I say is correct, namely that: The entire march of time reveals what is hidden, yet also does it hide what is revealed.

There is nothing that will not be revealed, and nothing secret that will not be brought into the light. Plutarch in his Problemata wisely sought to discover why it was that in antiquity divine matter tended to arise in Saturn. This is considered important because the truth, which is generally hidden and secret is at the same time revealed here.

Saturn is considered as both the Father of Time and a God, since Kronos can mean Saturn as well as Time. Although it is often said that justice exercises truth a great deal, yet truth itself is not exhausted. Therefore, time must always be given: the light reveals truth. I know enough of this philosophy to know that it is happy to have only a few judges. I prefer it to be judged by learned and good men, rather than the multitude. My aim is only to philosophize, not to observe the heavens; I hope to find the causes and the reasons for secret matters, and above all else acquire knowledge of M, which has its origin in the heavens. All things are moderated by a kind of harmony.

All endeavors and all actions are governed by this premise, which has attracted the downcast eyes of some men, as they look uncertainly upon the earth, and has raised them to gaze upon the heavens: He has given man a sublime countenance for, whereas all other creatures lie flat and gaze upon the earth, man can look upon the heavens, He has ordered man, thus upright, to turn his face to the stars.

Yet there are those who would hide themselves away with their philosophy, and take it with them, only to admire it. These would also carry off language into the shadows. How fitting is Paracelsus' description of them as men who would reap pollen, weave ropes from sand and unravel some unknown thread. Such a private study of philosophy can never hope to bear fruit.

Chapter Two

Learn from this chapter, then, and mark it well. Light and motion are the most salient characteristics of the heavenly bodies. The Sun surpasses all the other planets, since it produces its own light. The Moon, on the other hand, exceeds all others with the speed of its motion. These two planets are therefore deservedly considered the most outstanding of all the heavenly bodies. The Moon is especially powerful, since it rules all aqueous bodies. And just as it follows the brilliant light of the Sun, which is also the principal source of heat, the Moon's motion and its control over humidity are similarly joined, as if by some wonderful analogy.

Through another process of analogy, we can discern a pattern in the year, by simply examining a single day. For each day comprises – by the grace of the Sun and the Moon – its own spring, summer, autumn and winter. All basic qualities are produced by the heat of the Sun alone, partly through themselves and partly by chance, yet they occur in a fixed order, for if we establish a beginning, a middle and an end to each unit of twelve, a pattern emerges. It is indeed beautiful to consider how, all over the earth, each year is like a single day.

You may then consider the natural mysteries of the Trinity, and with reason may you then wish for the blackness of the many-hued night to enshroud your work. From this consideration comes about the first and simplest form and manifestation both of things non-existent and of things hidden in the folds of nature: this is produced from the straight line and the circle. It is through these that we are able to effect marvelous changes in the nature of things, if we urge nature on correctly by the artificial means of pyronomy (by nature I mean here everything created by the Grace of God). But we should not only use this process to produce those things visible and familiar in nature, but also to bring forth those which exist, like seeds, in the hidden places of nature. The wise man can learn about these also, but the ignorant man cannot.

Now whatever emerges from this process throws out its beams all around, penetrating every corner of the world, and filling the world in its own way. And so, every part of the world contains the beams of everything brought about by this process. Is it then by accident or by design that these objects project their own forms? Indeed, it is by design, a far more powerful influence than chance. Those substances which comprise both body and spirit (or which are of spirit alone) are far superior to those which are purely corporeal and comprise changing and impure elements.

How much finer are those first substances than those which only produce an imperfect form: for the perfect form will have the same name as the substance that produces it. But just as God has created all things, beyond all reason and the laws of nature (an act which it is not for us to contemplate), similarly it is impossible for anything to pass into nothingness unless it too is beyond the laws of reason and nature; even then it may do so only by His supernatural power.

Chapter Three

From this second consideration of the ancient philosopher's work we turn to the star, represented by [symbol of circle with vertical line]. The circle cannot be produced without the straight line, nor the straight line without the point. Consequently, things first came into existence through the point and the star, and whatever is on the periphery - however great it may be - cannot exist at all without the aid of the central point. Thus, the central point of the hieroglyphic star represents the earth, around which both the Sun, the Moon and the other planets run their courses and make their impression.

So much does she desire to be imbued with the sun's rays that she appears to have been transformed into him, and disappears from the sky until, a few days later, she reappears as I have shown her here [Symbol of lens-like figure]. By joining together this image of the Moon with its solar complement a single day was made from the evening and the morning. This is the first day according to the philosophers, on which light first appeared. For just as there is the law of first motion without which all would remain motionless, so there is the power of first and sensible form (that is, light) without which other forms would be unable to act.

Next, we see the Sun and Moon resting upon a rectilinear cross which [symbol of circle with horizontal radius] - by a most fitting hieroglyphic interpretation - can signify both the ternary and the quaternary. The ternary consists of two straight lines **[>]** and a common point connecting them; the quaternary consists of four straight lines [symbol of number 4 composed of lines], including four right-angles produced by repeating each line. The octonary (which I doubt many will have seen before) also presents itself here, in a most secret fashion, [symbol of double 8 composed of eight lines] and you should note this especially. According to the first fathers of philosophy the magical contemplation of the ternary encompassed body, spirit and soul. From this we obtain the remarkable septenary, consisting of two straight lines [symbol of number 7 composed of two lines] sharing a common point.

Chapter Four

In the third consideration we saw that the whole encompasses everything that we can perceive. Apart from this there are certain parts, a certain substance, that remain apart from the rest. Every natural thing desires this substance, just as art requires the touch of the artisan. Exactly what this substance is I shall now tell you. Parts of us - the hands, the nerves, the eyes - are substances that are strengthened when food is taken. Blood is also part of us, and it too is a substance, for it prepares other parts of the body and is equal in strength to those other parts. I would now ask you to pay close attention to what I say: of this whole machine (the body) a necessary part is air, for it is air that binds the heavens and the earth, that separates the heights from the depths, and yet also joins them. It receives a certain substance from the earth below, and at the same time hermetically transfuses the strength of the stars to the earth.

I consider this just as much a part of the world as I do the plants and animals. All the species of plants and animals are part of the universe since they are all part of the fullness of the universe. Even a single plant or animal may be considered a part of the universe since, although it is perishable, it is still a part of the whole at its death. In a similar way the air coheres with both the heavens and the earth, and is innate in both. For this reason, the philosophers rightly call it the Hermaphrodite.

Yet the natural part of any thing possesses unity, for nothing is born without unity or without the point. I do not think that you will ask out of ignorance how the earth is both part of the universe and a substance itself, but if you do then you will also need to know how it is that the heavens are also a part. This is because the universe cannot exist without either of them, for the universe is made of them; it comprises them and from both equally is nourishment distributed to all animals, all seeds, metals, minerals and all the stars.

Everything is provided with as much strength as it requires, whether it be a single thing or even the world itself. And so, it may be seen how it is that so many stars, however much they travel and however greedy they may be, are sustained day and night in their work and in their nourishment. For it is in the nature of all things to take as much nourishment as they require, The world, however, would desire the full amount of time that is allotted to it and seize it all in a single revolution. The philosopher provides a mundane rural analogy to explain this serious matter: he says that eggs absorb as many humours* as they need to effect the birth of the animal.

Thus, it is agreed that the earth is ruled by nature, and in this example from the microcosm there exist veins and arteries, the former being channels for the blood, the latter for the spirit. There are similarly in the earth channels through which water flows, and others through which the air flows. It can thus be seen that nature has formed the earth in the likeness of the human body, and that both ourselves and our ancestors have named these channels of water 'veins'. But in us there is not only blood but many types of humour: some essential, some corrupt (these being thicker). There is the brain in the head, the marrow in the bones, mucus and saliva, tears and a lubricant in the limbs which makes them flexible. Similarly in the earth there are many different kinds of humours. Some of these are hardened by nature, and these become the earth of the metals. Of these metals gold and silver are the most sought after by the greedy. There are also those that are turned to stone by the action of petrifying liquid.

All of these, since they contain the four elements, also contain their own seed. From each of these comes forth a pair: male and female. Air is considered to be male when it is gusty and female when cloudy and still. Fire is male when it burns with a strong flame and female when it is harmless to the touch. When the earth is especially hard and rocky it is considered male; when it is easy to farm it is female.

Humoral theory, also known as humorism or the theory of the four humours, was a model for the workings of the human body. It was systemized in Ancient Greece, although its origins may go back further still. In this theory, humours existed as liquids within the body and were identified as blood, phlegm, black bile and yellow bile. These were in turn associated with the fundamental elements of air, water, earth and fire. It was further proposed that each of the humours was associated with a particular season of the year, during which too much of the corresponding humour could exist in the body - blood, for example, was associated with spring. A good balance between the four humours was essential to retain a healthy body and mind, as imbalance could result in disease.

Chapter Five

From the fourth chapter it is clear that the dislocated homogeneous parts of the elements can show that the elements, after they have been removed from their natural places, return to them along straight lines. It will not therefore seem absurd that the mystery of the four elements (into which each compound element can ultimately be resolved) is implied by the four [symbol of four lines meeting at a point] straight lines running in opposite directions from a single point. You should take note and diligently observe that geometry teaches us that a line is produced by the flow of a point. This is similar to the way our four elemental lines are produced by the continuous fall of drops becoming a flow (by drops we mean the points of our star). Thus, does it come about in our mechanical magic. Moreover, the cabbalistic expansion of this quaternary according to the usual method of counting (that is, one, two, three, four) produces, when added together, the perfect number ten.

As Pythagoras himself said, one, two, three and four add up to ten. Therefore, it is not by chance that the rectilinear cross (which is the twenty-first letter of the Roman alphabet and considered to be formed from four straight lines) was chosen by the most ancient Roman philosophers to signify the number ten. Furthermore, its division immediately shows the quinary. Its place in the alphabet is determined also: for by multiplying the power of the ternary by the septenary establishes it as the twenty-first.

It will be seen that this accords very well with the sun and moon, since through the magic of these four elements a most exact separation of the sun and moon into their own lines was effected. In addition, by the circumferences of their lines the conjunction [symbol of circle with four lines meeting at a point] was made in the solar complement (for by the laws of geometry a circle may be described for a line of any length). It then becomes clear how much the proportion of our star - signified by the cross [symbol of four lines meeting at a point] - serves the sun and moon. The dagger-like, pointed zodiacal sign of Aries is well-known to everyone (that is, the figure [symbol of Aries]). It is generally considered that from its position in the heavens comes the fiery ternary.

We have added the astronomical sign of Aries, therefore, to signify the use of fire. It is agreed that this mystical sign, consisting of two semicircles joined by a single point, is most aptly assigned to the time of the vernal equinox. For a period of twenty-four hours, when arranged as at the equinox (that is, equally), denotes our most secret proportions (by 'our' I refer here to the earth). For this reason, wise men have handed down to us the hieroglyphic signs representing the elements and Aries.

Therefore, drink of this truly golden milk, but if you would rather hunt the hare with the sophists, then do not catch hold of the pheasant or the ferret. You should be aware that skill is obtained by increments, for who does not know that the origin of all skills was quite crude and that it was only by the passing of time and the growth of experience (the universal teacher) that they grew to perfection? This is certainly proved by the study of medicine, a skill much sought after and continually developing.

Wisdom always increases in the presence of men. So, you must be taught, says Seneca, as long as you remain ignorant (perhaps throughout our whole lives), if we are to believe in this saying. It is true that all things increase through time and that in this way the arts have developed to such an extent that the practitioners of our day far exceed their predecessors. So it is that your own skill in the study of philosophy has itself grown: if we compare the older students of the true and more secret wisdom with you, we find that they appear quite worthless. If Hermes, the father of philosophy, were to be brought back to life today, there is no doubt that he would be laughed at by the alchemists, just as the sculptors say that if Daedalus was living today and was to make such things as those which made him famous, he too would appear ridiculous. Indeed, the wise men of today far excel their predecessors in increasing the number of syllogisms for our ultimate benefit. Every skill increases: if the well is drawn off it fills up all the better. But once you have arrived at a right decision you must continue along that path, otherwise you will be led astray from the truth before you have even started out on your way. Pile up that which is rare and in short supply in the open air and, after it has been completely soaked by the water, the rotting damp and its location make it waste away.

Chapter Six

In the fifth consideration I did not attempt to demonstrate any other principle except that which Nature Herself has demonstrated. I acknowledge the spagyric art as representing the most skillful and sophisticated of all the arts, through which

I am able to give you my opinion on these matters. For, as if by divine ordinance, it teaches us how to distinguish the pure from the impure, just as logic distinguishes truth from falsehood; it teaches us when to separate substances and when to bring them together; it teaches us the method most favorable to Nature, for it distinguishes between the clear and the confused, the subtle and the gross, the light and the heavy, fire and air, air and water, water and earth. In such a way as this did the Creator Himself show us everything in the First Creation.

We are his imitators, and although we do not try to duplicate his work throughout the entire universe, yet we do attempt it in this small and confined world of ours. It is certain that since each of these considerations concerns the Universal Medicine, each one is also concerned with a method of enquiry. Therefore, I affirm that the Universal Medicine for bodies is the philosophic gold, after it has been separated and drawn to the highest state of perfection. Our common gold has absolutely nothing in common with the philosophic gold we use to begin our task. In that respect common gold is dead and clearly useless. For just as a chicken is not born from a cooked egg, the Universal Medicine will not come from cast gold.

Careful consideration must be given to what must be done, for we must not pervert nature but imitate it accurately to the best of our abilities. All the wise men agree that there is only this one substance, the One Medicine (speaking hieroglyphically), to which nothing is added and only the superfluous is removed (and even this process is achieved naturally). It is therefore a most difficult task to locate this medicine amongst the multitude of substances, although it would certainly be ignorant folly to look for it in an unnatural substance. The search is therefore rightly directed towards the sources of the metals and minerals.

The philosophers set two of these above all the rest, that is, the sources of mercury and of sulphur. But just as they do not mean common gold, neither do they mean common sulphur or common mercury. The philosophers' gold is living, subtle and spiritual. Common gold is dense, hard and unchanging. The philosophers' mercury is the prime material of all things: without it the M cannot exist. But in fact, liquid mercury, or quicksilver, is an impure metal which comes from its own special seed. The philosophers' sulphur is pure, permanent, white or red and flammable.

Common sulphur, however, is combustible and impermanent. Hence it is easy to understand the difference between the philosophers' gold and that of those who are mistaken; between the philosophers' sulphur and that of the foolish; between the philosophers' mercury and that of the ignorant. The difference between heaven and earth is as great as the difference between the truly wise and the sophist.

The philosophers' gold is gold that has not yet solidified or hardened naturally, for if it were to do so then our man-made fire would have no effect on it, and the craftsman would be frustrated by his own skill. It is removed from the prime source of all the metals by pruning and separation through spring water, and in a natural way. For just as the Microcosm was first created out of the Macrocosm without a soul, which was later breathed into it by divine power, in a similar way does our man (mercury) appear. Later, he too receives a soul which is brought forth and kindled by the continuously regulated movement of the fire beneath. When our Mercury is joined with either magnesia or lunaria it is more correctly known as 'aqua sicca' (dry water).

This does not wet the hands and when placed near a fire it flees like a runaway slave. It is also known as Proteus, since it transforms itself into various, distinct forms and is itself transformed by this process. At times it appears in the form of dew, at times like heavenly rain, sometimes even like snow, hail, hoar frost or a cloud, as if it were dressed in a cloak. This transformation can be seen everywhere: however, it comes about, whether in metals, animals or vegetable matter, it is essential for the appearance of the mercury so that the work can be brought to a conclusion.

The mercury of Hermes and of all the Philosophers is water, the water that falls from the sky as rain and which the Sun, as its father, extracts from the earth each day in a very fine vapor and takes up into that part of the sky where the downpour is formed. Here it is condensed into rainwater by the innate natural force of the Moon, its mother, using that same power with which she controls affairs below. Thus, it condenses into rainwater, thickens and falls in drops by its own weight. It is moved around willy-nilly by the air or the wind (which is, after all, nothing more than the movement of the air) until it lands upon the center point, that is, the earth, its nursemaid, who must then carry it in her lap. Perhaps this seems like a Gordian knot, yet one even tighter than Alexander's, which can only be cut by the sword of reason.

As I have often told my sons of knowledge and wisdom, the Philosophers' sulphur is first formed when the water has returned to the earth. At times it floats on the top of the water and is multicolored, like the earth covered in foliage, or like some kind of thick broth. All these different hues derive from the greenness of the vitriol. But experience has confirmed that all water which is without spirit may be hardened by heat, and that which has spirit may be hardened by cold.

He who understands how water can be hardened by heat and how the spirit can be joined with it, will certainly discover something a thousand times more precious than gold, more precious than anything. Therefore, the alchemist should separate the spirit from the water and allow it to decay until it resembles a seed. After the waste has been discarded, he should reintroduce the spirit into the water from above, and effect a conjunction between these two. It is this conjunction or arrangement that will produce an offspring utterly different from its parents.

Chapter Seven

The sixth consideration deals with Nature itself and so we must now define Nature. But Nature is a difficult thing to define, even amongst the wise there was disagreement about which came first, God or Nature. For if Nature came first, then God must have been created, which he cannot have been. But if God came first, then Nature must have been created, for only if Nature can have been born can it really come into existence. But some wise men define Nature as the originator of fire, and it is through fire that it enters sensible matter to enable its reproduction. Indeed, it is clear that all things are created principally by fire. But Plato defined Nature as the Will of God, and this is the definition that meets with the most approval amongst the philosophers, for the Will of God is complete Goodness in its entirety and is present in all things.

His will is born from his Divinity, so that things may be as they are, as they have been and as they always will be, and that Nature may be proof against aging. Nature, sensation and the whole world contains this Nature within them, in fact every living thing contains it. For each sex is fulfilled through procreation and this joining of the two or, more accurately, this unity between them which you may well call desire or love (or both) – is quite beyond our understanding, just as much as are desire and love.

However, if both God and Nature are considered to exist and since neither can come from the other (for it must be that which is born of the first comes second), neither God nor Nature can be considered as having been born. Plato was quite correct when he stated that Nature is the Will of God, for God has always willed and it is necessary that he does so, for this is the truest cause of all things. Since, if it is the Will of God, Nature cannot have been born, then neither it nor God can have been born, and thus we must understand that the nature of the Macrocosm beyond the Microcosm is not Nature at all but God.

For this same Nature, by which the world exists, is the Will of God; but the art that pursues Nature (that is, the Will of God) is the true knowledge of the Microcosm, and of what must be done. For it is not Nature that carries the vitriol from the mountain into the furnace, or builds a fire beneath. The true concern of man, his true art, is to prepare and produce the Medicine. Every man who has known that this art is the only true one may then practice it faithfully.

He who has learned may then assume control. But whoever tries his skill should take care that he does not sin against the Will of God or the Laws of Nature. But the greatest skill is the ability to dissemble that skill, for whoever feels it necessary to put something in writing or in speech about this great study, uses his skill in speaking to conceal his true meaning. This is to be contrasted with our more usual way of speaking, so that we may more easily agree with those appearing to speak naturally, rather than with those who have perverted that natural method of artifice.

For as Euripides says, the use of language is simple, but every man abandons that natural simplicity and comes under our suspicion, just as if they are trying to deceive and defraud us. Consider well, then, the following simple and natural example of the Great Work: the rainwater, after it has been completely covered over and left outside in the bright sun, becomes fetid and mud collects in the bottom. It becomes sticky and has a bitter, foul taste. But in time this foulness is exhausted and disappears. The sediment, or solid matter, will separate from the water and precipitate at the bottom and remain there.

Thus, a pure, clean water is produced that is sweet, fragrant and flavorsome. Pour the water off from the sediment into another glass and once more place it outdoors until the sediment forms a scum. Repeat the process until no more sediment can be found.

This water has been produced naturally and as a result it is incorruptible. One could say the same of oil, wine and other liquids except that spring water, as I shall explain, separates all kinds of solid matter of both contrary and similar qualities, from the vitriol of Venus and Mars. It will do all this gradually and by a natural process. If you combine this pure and perfect material with fire you will produce pyraustae. After these have been left out in the sun they ferment properly.

But those fashionable Galenists and academic doctors who criticize distillation and alchemical matters generally, have not considered these matters seriously enough. They have not understood at all about the heat in wine, for example. This heat is first separated by fire from the parts with which it has been mixed, these being the cooler and more sluggish parts of the mixture. After it has been freed from these parts as if from an enemy it then exists in a fine type of distilled water without any more vigorous operation taking place. For this reason, the philosophers rightly call their work (the Medicine) 'Fortitude', for this signifies the Elixir.

Into its trust they rightly pledge all nature. Furthermore, the work and the true end of alchemy may be briefly described as that of 'the Body into the Body', and those of Magia as 'the Spirit in the Body'. The wise men call their results violent since they use amounts of strength that seem greater than those ordained by nature. There is more about this in the carefully-arranged books of Paracelsus, where there is a cure for diseases that aims to ease and cleanse sickness by using symbols, words and spoken formulae. But this resembles more the casting of lots and is therefore contrary to the Will of God; for this reason, we reject it in our modern age.

Chapter Eight

In the seventh and last consideration I would not want to appear to be pursuing a Euclidean strategy, nor any other: you should learn from the fifth chapter of the fifth book, which concerns the secret deeds performed by the Monarch throughout his long life. In the fourth chapter it says that the Necrolii (or Necrolici) are forbidden a long life, that is, they are barred from the Great Work, which Geber calls the Third Order. The elemental substances in their crude state of blackness (according to Raymond Lull they are of a blackness blacker even than black) can produce a solution for the dead. The Scaiolae are the four elements in the vitriol of Venus after they have been purified. In the Necrolii, that is, in the First Order of the Work, are contained ridiculous travesties, sophistical preparations indeed, that do not withstand the test of fire. Yet they do shed light on the Cyphant, in other words, on the formation of the embryo or infant (as Arnold and Lull refer to it), and which Geber refers to when he says that the instruction is not complete until the preparations of the first order have been made (these preparations were adequately shown in the previous chapter).

Those who get to this stage who do not advance to the other orders and therefore do not produce pyraustae are referred to as Alloeani by Paracelsus, since they are superficial imitators of the form and sophistical white-washers of the tinctures of Venus and the Moon. But if we suspect that anything might go wrong with the liquor then we should proceed as follows: the distillation should be repeated more often so that the favorable path to the good may be sufficiently open to you.

That is, we should distinguish between the right way, which leads to the more perfect material and the left, which relates to imperfect bodies. Some philosophers refer to these enigmatically as the eastern and the western parts. Water envies the Scaiolii and conceals the liquor of the lunaria from them. Now he who possesses the ability to extract spring water in a torrent is known as a water diviner; he who softens using fire is called a fire tongs. Such a man laughs at the sophists, since they have little experience and act just like the easily-disturbed Necrolii when they are dormant, for they do not fix the tincture properly, which develops naturally up to a certain stage before flying from the fire.

They are careless, as has often been said, about the poppy seed, which brings sleep just like the fifth essence of the vitriol. This essence brings about the coagulation of Mercury, which is alternately hard and soft. The alchemists refer to this process as fixing. This essence also brings sleep in a similar way to mandrake. But Aequaster, the anatic material of the completed operation, will not destroy the position of the Scaolii, for it delights to be in that spiritual seat of the Scaolii, that is, of the philosophers' Mercury.

But if the Sun or the Moon is to be added to this crude preparation something must first be removed, in other words, the receiving material must be prepared by transmutation: this is the extent of the medicine of the second order. But the greatest Adech exceeds even this with the medicine of the third order, for the Mercury is first prepared philosophically and then accurately and fully gathered together. Thus prepared, the Mercury advances our purpose since, according to Geber, it brings the material we have already mentioned to advance the work. But this is not all, for in this order there is a difference in the method and the subtlety of the preparation. Once the pure Nymphidic spring water has left the Moon, the latter passes through the water of the Scaolii and undergoes another transformation, where it will remain difficult to work with and virtually insoluble.

This has been decreed by the earthly sun, for this process is indeed death by fixing and life by the lightening of the Scaolii. The White Sun also agrees to join with the Moon in the early stages but he undergoes a change towards the end, since the King turns red at the end of the work. But all that is written at the close of the book concerning travesties and the Nymphidic spring water lead to obscurity, since they pervert the traditional order. This is something which the teachers if this wisdom often do, since (as Augurellus has it) they are dedicated to the laws of this intricate art.

So that we may comprehend the Nymphidic and understand the Aniadic Year, in other words, how we may become immortal through hard work and suffering, we should first learn the characters (known as the gift of Venus) which, as Paracelsus says, even though you may understand them in relation to each other, you do not have practical knowledge of them. For the man who summons Palemon and Leucothea does so in vain if he has not first attracted Nereus. Nor will he attract Nereus if he has not first worked on the primary trinity of life.

His work will have no firm grounding at all unless he has first attracted Vestra. For the aqueous nature of the Moon is referred to mystically as Saturn while it makes one revolution around the earth, by the science of the Scaolii. For the same reason it is also given the name of Jupiter. But after it has turned through the elements three times, we represent it more obscurely, in this way: [symbol of lunar crescent with lower cross], which is usually known as Mercury. You can see how lunar this symbol becomes: [symbol of lens-like figure with lower cross]. Some wise men would hold that it is produced by the fourth revolution, but this in no way contradicts our secret purpose. Only the purest magic spirit will carry out the work of whitening in place of the moon.

Through his spiritual virtue, once he is alone with us, he may speak hieroglyphically without words for almost a whole day, introducing and impressing into the purest and plainest earth prepared by us those four geogamic figures, or instead that other figure shown nearby. But is not the mystical sign of Mars produced by the combination of the hieroglyphs for the Sun and Aries? And is not the teaching of the elements included in this? And is not, I ask, the sign of Venus produced from a fuller exposition of the Sun and the elements?

These planets therefore have regard for the solar revolution and the work of rehabilitating metals by fire, where there arises during its progress that other Mercury, which is indeed the uterine brother of the first. He appears once the lunar magic of the Sun and the elements has been completed, just as the hieroglyphic messenger tells us most expressively, if we will only fix our eyes upon him and give him a more attentive hearing. By the Will of God, he is that most famous Mercury, he is the Microcosm, he is Adam.

Yet some experts would put the Sun in his place, something which we in our present age are unable to do unless we put in charge of this golden work a certain spirit that has been separated from its body by the pyronomic art. This is difficult to do and very dangerous because of the fiery and sulphurous fumes that are produced. But this spirit will be wonderful indeed, joining Venus and even Mars to the disc of the Moon (or at least to that of Mercury) with indissoluble bonds. This then produces the Sun of the philosophers in what they call the third position, which completes our septenary number. Care must therefore be taken when such an operation takes place in the Vitriol to ensure that the central heat can change water into air, so that it an spread out over the flat earth and scatter the residue, with the aid of the rain, throughout the channels of the earth. Finally, the opposite will also come about: the air will turn to water of a particularly fine type. This occurs if you bring about the overwhelming of the gold and silver by the Old Man, that is, our aqueous Mercury, so that the water consumes them: eventually he will die and be consumed as well.

The ashes of the gold are then to be sprinkled on the water, and the water boiled until it is ready. You will then have a medicine for curing leprosy. But take care that you do not use cold instead of hot, or hot instead of cold. Mix like natures together, but if you must use a substance that does not occur in nature then separate it until it resembles a natural substance. In the end - by the Will of God - the Great Work is achieved not by hand but by fire.

Final Chapter

In conclusion, can I really put a price on my work, when all I do is provide a brief sketch of the lunarium of the philosophers? I do not even possess all the required knowledge; and even if I knew how to express myself coherently would I even dare? For I consider this matter to be old enough to be common knowledge, while it is always the modern writers who believe that they can make clearer and surpass the unskilled ancients in their writing. But however, it comes out my work will at least, to the best of its ability, help to recover and restore the ancient lost arts of knowledge and science to their descendants.

By lunarium it is generally agreed that the ancient writers refer to Chalcantum, whether it be cupric orhungaric Chalcantum. Its body is metallic, called 'blacking' by the Romans. It exists in two forms: it can be dug out of the ground and can be produced artificially. When it is out of the ground it is sometimes dark, sometimes pale. Occasionally it is white, occasionally transparent like glass, which is why it is commonly known as vitriol.

You may get to know the bowels of the earth well with this metal, and by purifying it you will discover the Hidden Stone, the True Medicine. Its artificial form is produced by the action of rainwater flowing through the metals and forming a pool. After passing through those substances bound to the metals, it is collected in large clay vessels where after a few days it hardens in the air. Under certain conditions this water can turn Mars into Venus. But what happens if the natural form is improved upon by the pyronomic art? As the vitriol bubbles, two vapors are released from the channels in the stone: these create the metals.

The first is therefore to be found in the elements of earth and water, with the Sun acting upon them and producing the vitriol; the second cause is in the chalcanthus; the third and last in the vapor, that is, in the twin spirits of sulphur and mercury that are the source of the metal, after its mother has first been impregnated by wild nature. The philosophers have laid claim to lunaria themselves, due to the aqueous nature of the Moon. Raymond Lull is chief amongst these, for we find the following repeatedly in his writings: 'take up the stone, whatever its form, and pour on the lunaria'. The flower of the air is considered to be Cheiros, that of Mars is rosemary. The magicians take this for their own and call it Martagon, as if it were born of Mars.

Undoubtedly chemistry cannot be understood without practice and experience. For all metals can be reduced to a vitriol resembling their own aqueous source, without any diminution in their composition. This vitriol is the lunaria, otherwise known as the philosophers' tree. According to Borissa this has seven branches representing the seven qualities of the metals. The root of this tree is the metal-bearing earth; its trunk is red, solid and suffused with black. Its leaves resemble those of marjoram: there are thirty of them in all, fifteen corresponding to the length of the Moon's waxing and fifteen to its waning. Its smell is like that of musk; at the full moon its fruit resembles the finest saffron. If Mercury is removed from it at the time of the full moon or at the waning and replaced there at this same time, it turns into the Moon.

If this is then boiled six times it turns into the Sun. In short, from this pure form flows pure water. But this water, although similar to ordinary water, because it comes from a very deep well, must never be assumed to be too much like ordinary water. For the elements have been interchanged, just as it says in the Psalterium of Sonus:

but although their various names have been changed, yet their influence remains throughout. Such a precise description enables you to bring to a conclusion all that has taken place in the operation. For this reason, have you praised your people in all their endeavors, Lord, and you have honored them with glory. You have not disdained them, rather have you stood by them at all times and in all situations. Thus, nothing of value can arise in man's affairs, unless his mind first spurns all thoughts of grandeur, and wonders at and worships the One and Only God.

Prayer Eternal, unchanging and Infinite God, you who are truly born of yourself, and from whom all other things are created; you who are Good without comparison; you who are great without limit; eternal without time; omnipresent but in no single place. You are the only true virtue, the only perfection that alone embraces all other forms of perfection and enters into each one far and wide.

You appear to us greater than the greatest; you have in your power the way to perfection. Only when we have remained in continual contemplation for a long period of time will we be fortunate enough to achieve this goal ourselves; however ignorant we may be, let us not be ignorant of this at least. Therefore, for as long as we seek you in the wilderness, let us not lose ourselves.

Bestow upon us your fatherly and infinite goodness and mercy, so that we may come to find you in some way at least, by loving your glory and majesty, worshipping, admiring and adoring them. May we embrace and possess them through your only son, Our Lord Jesus Christ, who always welcomes us. We seek this from you and ask of you with our most heartfelt prayers that you will bring it to pass through your Holy Spirit, for you are truly the best and greatest God, because of the love that you freely give to us. May there be praise and honor bestowed upon you, the One Godhead and the Three-in-One, the only Living and True God, for all eternity and for all time, Amen.

THE SHADOW OF THE UNKNOWN MASTER

By MAGUS INCOGNITO - 1862 - 1932

AT TEKELS

When He Came

Couldit have been the smell of the pines that brought the Master to Tekels? For, after all, there are pine trees in Thibet and Hungary, and they are holy abiding places. Or could it have been the call from a few earnest students But, there are earnest students in other places besides Tekels.

Whether from the smell of the pines or the persistent voice of the students that the Master called, is not known to any but the students—and the pines.

He came, a wayfarer from beyond the Great Divide, unrecognized by the many, loved by the few. He came, the bearer of a Great Secret. He knew what it was to die, he knew how it was to live again. He brought a message of hope, peace and goodwill to those who would lend listening ear. fie came as a man, a man who could feel intense pain, bitter anguish, unspeakable joy.

As a man he was simple, believing, cultured and soft voiced, with a sadness in the eyes which bespoke knowledge of the ways of men, sympathy and understanding. To the many he appeared to be dangerous, a fool, an imposter. To the few, a simple-minded, ready-to-help-and-advise fellow.

Sometimes his eyes lit up with a strange light. Someone was suffering and he was sending out helping forces: at such times he was a healer. Sometimes he had a "far-away" look in his eyes: he was then a Master communicating with those Great Ones far beyond the white-ranged mountains. At other times he heard the voices of the wayward desecrating the Divine, cursing humanity, then an awe-inspiring glint came into his eyes. At such times he was dangerous. This strange composite man came to Tekels.

Tekels in the county of Surrey above all places—a wild, uncultured place where trees and ferns grew in abundance, where the hand of man had barely touched for the purpose of building a few houses.

There he found a community of people mixed in their aspirations, some worshipping a Crown which shone like gold but was merely polished clay, others worshipping a Crown of lead which had yet to show its polish. Others worshipped neither Crown.

For what purpose came he? To found a religion, a sect, to enliven and instruct the Community Came he to undo a wrong that had been done, to announce that Tekels was to be a holy abiding place? No.

A place of rest and quietness was offered him, and he had accepted. There he listened to the sighing of the wind, the rustle of the trees and the voice of the birds. Through glades of varied trees, on soft mosses he wandered, then he climbed a small hill. On the hill he spoke.

His voice rose to a pitch which resembled a call, and the sound reverberated through space. It was caught up afar and lo! With lightning rapidity came a response—those in the High Place had responded to his appeal, and the hill became sacred, imbued with subtle power. Here, thought he, is indeed place for inspiration where one can sit in silent attuned meditation with the Brethren.

Work had begun at Tekels. How? Those who climb the hill in humbleness of spirit, who are above the pettiness of small things, who are true to themselves as well as to others, will soon learn. The one who would know the Master must climb the steep hill unaided, and with his back to the sun look downwards whence he came. He will count twelve steps which must be long, and forty steps which must be short. But these steps must be traversed both mentally and physically and in humbleness of spirit. After this he will meditate between breaths, and whisper into the silence the sound—Ah I - aam - ee - oom.

Some day he who writes this will again visit Tekels, and that which stands behind him will hear the call of those who may climb the mount. With those who have already done so, the Master rejoices. They shall reclimb the mount without fatigue.

Neath the Tower of Lympne

It is said that the Masters of Wisdom, through their chosen disciples, visit spots on earth whereon they have trodden during some period of Evolution.

A Master of Wisdom is an out-thinker, a Master of Masters. His disciples are Masters or His chosen disciples. It is the latter we follow, for they are ever directed by the Out-thinkers to such spots. Distinguish then between an Out-thinker and a Master—they are One in essence but two in manifestation.

September 10th, 1931, dawned with a cloud o'er the sun, but as the day advanced the cloud moved and the sun shone with brilliance. The Master, with two of his disciples entered a bus which wended its way to Lympne.

The Master and his disciples alighted, and on foot traversed a road on either side of which were firs, and pines. The trees cast a strange shadow on the road and they swayed slightly as though giving a salutation to those who passed.

A turn to the left and the Castle loomed in sight. Here was quietude and it was proper, for the Castle broods in such quietude—over the past—and with its companion the Church of St. Stephen overlooks that which was once the sea.

The Master and his disciples gazed down towards the sea, now four miles away from the Castle, and the Master with uninterrupted gaze looked back into the night of time. Far down, below the battlements of the Castle, was a magnificent sweep of country, the Romney Marshes, Dungeness to the right and Folkestone to the left. Far away rising from the horizon was a patch of white—France was smiling a peeping welcome to him who gazed. The Master saw these things, but other scenes came before his eyes, things which were not observed by the disciples. The waters of the sea were surging in furrows over the land and the river Ljmen was pouring its waters into the sea.

The priests of St. Stephen were taking turns, swinging lanthorns towards the sailing men who were returning from their voyage to the far lands, with pretty presents, and their minds full of strange stories to tell over the log fires when port was reached, and they were safe within their homes. Then the scene changes, all is noise and bustle. The Saxon Sea robbers have passed up the Channel and have sighted the Castle. The sentinel on the watch tower in Stentorian voice calls to the men-at-arms. Suddenly a Beacon flares upwards from the tower, and the people beyond prepare to intercept this invader who dares to desecrate the precincts of a peaceful village.

Still another scene, and the sea is slowly receding to the ocean, leaving marshes dangerous to the wayfarer. Wild ducks wing their flight, and delight in the struggles of the wayfarer to wend his way cautiously o'er dry places. The priests of the Church ring their bells at intervals, and the wayfarer is cheered by the sound. A light comes into the eyes of the Master, for he sees himself moving towards his friend Gheist, who awaits him in the church.

From the busy affairs of state, from his task of almost tireless writing, he passes into the church and there, in close converse with his friend they speak of days long passed when no monarch of regal bearing arranged the affairs of ecclesiasticism but monks were monks, and a tradition was handed down, a tradition which spoke of tremendous mysteries. The disciples stood still, they knew that the Master was gazing into the Cosmic picture gallery, and that their patience would be rewarded ere long. With him, they entered the Castle and learnt many things. They escorted him to a garden where refreshments were administered to the body.

Thus, it was, that the Master visited a place of the past, and thus it is that he records the visit as an appreciation to those disciples who made the visit possible. We leave Lympne, knowing that the shade of the Roman guard will keep its secrets intact and preserve its peace after the noise and bustle of the long dim past.

Seabrook

Shadows, strange illusive things which come between the light and the objects o'er which they pass. Can one call a shadow darkness, without Light there would be no shadow, therefore shadows are dependent upon light. There are many shadows, some distorted, some sinister, some awe-inspiring—and there are shadows of the Master. Three people looked from, the shingled beach of Seabrook towards Lympne, their eyes rested upon two hills some little distance from each other.

High, above the two hills passed a shadow. The sun had passed behind the clouds and on swept the shadow o'er the hills. For a moment the hills were dark and gloomy then refulgent light once again lit up the verdure tops. The shadow had passed on. He who is the shadow of the Master thought much as he gazed upwards, so did his two disciples—one a young man, the other a mother. That shadow o'er the hills was an omen, Seabrook and Lympne had for a moment been in attuned vibration with those who stand behind. From the far away came a voice, a voice which spoke scarcely above a whisper, but loud enough to say—"The Unknown Master is near, watch for him, for like the shadows of the night he approaches, steals on to you when you least expect him. Be watchful."

The two disciples had known shadows, but they were of suffering, trials, fears, doubts. The mother had the faith of a child and was patient. The young man, too, had faith and was trusting. One knew that soon revelation must crime, the other had soon to learn, for coming events cast their shadows before. Let doubters and those who bear false witness beware for their secret moves are known and recorded in a strange book whose pages cannot be torn, whose records cannot be effaced, whose words speak ever the Truth, in which are inscribed the deeds of men and women greater in number than the shingle on the shore of Seabrook. In this little place, peaceful and quiet, two of the handful of disciples who seek for the unknown Master begin to see with slowly opening eyes.

Quietly, very sensibly, are great problems being solved, slowly and surely are great mysteries being unfolded and in Sacred truth comes the Unknown Master, the mystery of six centuries, into the lives of men. He seeks not to be known to the many, yet he has been known by those who could sigh for knowledge, he may even be known in this record though he is as yet but a shadow. All ye who read this, search your own innermost thoughts and ask yourself if you have found the light. Ask those thoughts if you are true to yourself as well as others, ask if you have condemned others when you yourself might be condemned.

My shadow is stealing over you as it did o'er the hill tops beyond Seabrook, when I come yet ye shall not know me, but Light shall know and if thou art cautious it shall abide with thee.

All Hours at All Places

He who seeks for the Master only during the day shall not find Him. He who seeks for the Master only during the night shall not find Him. Always, at all times, in all places may He be found. He is not confined to any particular country or place. He is in all countries and places. He does not belong to any particular race. He is of all races. He does not favor one and not another. He favors all. He does not make Initiates by recommendation. His disciples must realize Initiation ere they can know Him as Master.

By ordeal and test only does He make Initiates, for Initiation means the crossing of the Threshold, the meeting and controlling of the Dweller on the twilight pathway of illusion, and then sight of the Master in fully awakened Spiritual Consciousness.

Initiates are known only to Initiates, Masters to Masters and Initiates. Gaze at the Kosmic Clock, then realize that there are twelve hours of Initiation both of day and night, and every twelfth hour culminates into a thirteenth. During the thirteenth hour one meets the Master. Until that is known, His shadow only crosses the pathway. Take care, if ye would realize the thirteenth hour, that ye bear none ill will, that ye speak and hear no evil, that ye judge not, for ye shall know during that hour if thou hast evil clone. If thou hast spoken ill of another, during that hour ye shall be judged. To Him who sits in the Inner Sanctuary of Masters, there is neither day nor night, twilight nor shadow, but thou who hast not yet seen the Light knowest only the shadow. From the Inner Sanctuary do the Masters pass amongst men, unrecognized by the many, for they are not prepared to see them.

The Kosmic Clock is the Round Table. Would ye be a Knight and sit in thy place during the day or night If so, be prepared to meet the Master irrespective of His garb or name or of the country in which He resides. Ye would know the shadow of the Master at first by speech, by words of wisdom, by works of art, philosophy, science, drama and the Muses, but ye must seek closely, for oft times a mask is used to test the unwary that their desires to approach the highest might be intensified or weakened accordingly as they seek.

The true disciples of the Master are known by the progress they make, by the knowledge conveyed to them in mystic manner, by their ready answers to questions propounded to them regarding the problems of life.

But if ye ask them who the Master is, they are as silent as night. Ye yourself must go out to meet Him and recognize Him. Very often He is the most unlikely person, if He inhabits a mortal body, be careful. As the Master frequents familiar places, in those places He may not be known as Master. Seek Him then in places unfamiliar, and ye may be rewarded for the effort. Time is but an illusion, yet as the finite mind cannot grasp the idea of space duration, time is conceived in the mind by the interval of events, the movement of the mechanism of a clock. In this sense think of the Sanctuary as representing Greenwich time—it is always the twelfth Hour there, and all Masters know the twelfth Hour which encompasses all hours, all time.

It is always High Twelve to the Master, no matter where He may be, for He is in close contact with the Inner Sanctuary, and He ever conceals the thirteenth, whether in the sense of the Round Table, the Zodiac, the Apostles or the watch that ye have on your wrist or in your pocket. Know then, ye who read, ye who are willing to learn from simple words, who do not consign this message to the flames, who are sincere in desiring to attain to the Highest, who do not slander your fellows—that the shadow of the Unknown Master has moved across the pathway, and He soon may play an active part in thy Spiritual welfare. Be watchful, be wise, Most Wise, and ye may soon see the Light.

Unknown Master

In treble numbers secrets I declared, To those who dare not run before they walked; But those who walked some secrets strange have shared, Whilst those who ran were by an Old Fox stalked. The past, present and future are one and Destiny is made yesterday, to-day and to-morrow for the sake of to-day. To the Infinite Eye Time is but an illusion and to that eye the past and future are to-day. Life speeds on in cycles and the finite mind appreciates but a little of this through events. Some there are who know to-morrow and yesterday through to-day and there is not always pleasure in the knowing.

Love, Hatred, Hope, Inspiration, Pleasure, Pain, Persecution and Peace all wait upon life and they follow in its wake but there comes a period when life has sped on so quickly that these expressions of manifested life become lost in the abstract.

Love is the only thing that persists; it expands from the smallest microbe to the greatest star, from man to God. Man will not always love, for he is prone to hate, prone to misunderstand, prone to persecute his fellowmen, till he knows better. As life speeds on and man lives his life, he makes events and these events repeat in cycles. There come periods of love, periods of hate, periods of persecution, and periods of peace. There are some who at this period of life are experiencing love and peace, others who are experiencing pain and persecution. Shylock is a great symbol, there are always people who want their pound of flesh but when it comes to the cutting, under penalty, they are afraid to cut lest they cut under or above their pound of flesh.

Why do some want their pound of flesh to-day? Because they have wanted it in the past and when they cannot obtain it, without penalty, they seek to persecute and disparage that which appears to be the pound of flesh. THOSE WHO WILL NOT CUT BECAUSE OF THE PENALTY ARE COWARDS.

Supposing a man slandered another man by speech amongst his friends and when asked to put into writing refused, such is a coward, he is base and is not worthy of the company of honored men. He wants his pound of flesh but will not take the penalty. There are such people to-day even against whom there is evidence of such. Three hundred years ago a Master of Science and Philosophy and perhaps a Master of Life also, was slandered and persecuted, but in spite of that his work went on, he knew the Shylocks. Perhaps it is that the Unknown Master knows the Shylocks of to-day, he may even have much evidence against them and in spite of the persecution may be biding his time.

There is soon to be Revelation in various Occult Societies and there may be other revelations also, some which may not bear the light of day, who knows save those who transgress. The Unknown Master has many servers in all grades of life from the highest to the lowest, his arm is long and his memory is long. Many think they know the Unknown Master, but they are mistaken. They have read his works but they know him not. Publishers will not tell who he is, writers who work under his guidance will not tell who he is, the poets who sing his verses will not tell, because they do not know. They, like many others, may fancy they do but fancy is not reality.

The Unknown Master is here now for a definite purpose and his purpose shall be accomplished. Misinterpretation, persecution, will not interfere with the purpose, it shall most certainly be accomplished. There is one thing which is very sure, the Unknown Master comes not for, or to do, evil, if evil manifests it manifests from the hearts of those who think evil and speak evil. In the doing of good for the benefit of your fellow men, you may come to know the Unknown Master, but there is no certainty that you shall. In your real good self you may find him.

There are some who try to link him up with all kinds of people and with all kinds of movements, they are mistaken. You may search through a hundred of his works and not find him, yet with patience find him in one of them. He who is well trained in the Mystic Sciences might find him through the Ciphers in this paper. You may find him in most unlikely places, rarely in the most familiar. To find him you must forget your prejudices, you must clear your hearts of hatred and have ceased to bear false witness against your neighbors.

"The Glory of God is to conceal a thing, The glory of man is to find out a thing. You take more than is granted, You grant less than is proved."

THE IMMORTALIZED JESUS

By PAUL TYNER - 1860 - 1926

In asserting the continued existence on earth of the man Jesus, in the body of flesh and blood, it is by no means intended to deny the law demonstrated throughout the universe in all forms of life, simple or complex, of the progress from birth to maturity, and from maturity to decay, so far as outer form is concerned. What this continued existence of Jesus in a body of flesh and blood means is dominion and control over the law by which construction, destruction and reconstruction are constantly going on in all forms; its deliberate and conscious direction at all times.

As a matter of fact, material form is the very essence of mental flexibility; and this is especially true in regard to the human form. The spirit—which is the man himself, formless and immaterial, is continually building and rebuilding a habitation for himself, calling to himself, out of the universal ocean of matter and force, all the elements he needs, and rejecting and expelling that which he has used, when he has taken from it all that he requires, and it no longer serves his purpose. The apple on the tree comes in to existence, grows and expresses its soul, in form, color and flavor in the same way. In man the process may be made a conscious one. In the true sense, there is no such thing as a "disembodied spirit," cognizable by the senses, psychic or physical.

Spirit and matter are counterparts, and each is essential to the other; but matter varies in degrees of density. Spirit must embody itself for manifestation and expression. Yet the body may be visible on one plane of consciousness, and invisible on another. Jesus, on attaining to spiritual self-consciousness, deliberately and consciously chose, and has since constantly chosen, his embodiment, molding it from day to day, into greater and greater responsiveness to his will. This will is the Cosmic Will, the will of the Father. And this is the secret of harmony and power. He is able to pass through closed doors and stone walls in this body, so consciously controlled, because of his power to change its vibrations. That is to say, he passes through stone walls as ethers or gases pass through substances of lower vibration and greater density. The component elements of the human body, while governed to some extent by the "plan and specifications" of normal human anatomical structure and organization, are really in what might be called a state of flux. The old Greeks considered the universe in a state of flux, as indeed it is. What we know as "flesh and blood" may be resolved instantly into ether, and out of ether as instantly called back into the forms called flesh and blood. In fact, we are now unconsciously and automatically passing through this very process of appearing and disappearing every moment will turn brain and brawn into mental or muscular energy in the activity that results in creation or destruction in every field of effort, and in the individualization of character. In rest, we again crystalize, into individual brawn and brain, so to speak, the universal energy of thought, in air, food, water and environment.

"The life is more than the meat," means simply that the individualized intelligence of the ego is creator of flesh and blood—creator and destroyer—its veritable lord and master. The shadow depends on the sun, not the sun on the shadow. Matter is but the shadow of force; a mode of motion; my body is my mind reflecting itself in motion, a shadow of my soul. Being is reflected in existence; as reflection may therefore, be assumed to be necessary to Being, existence is necessary to Being. Man has no life apart from God.

Death is demonstration of the error of thinking he has. Life in an everlasting body is Jesus' tangible demonstration of the truth that life everlasting is found in acceptance and realization of the life of God as the only life. I am fully aware of the difficulties in the way of de scribing a phenomenon, not merely unfamiliar, but considered impossible to most men. Clear comprehension of what is meant by this "immortalization of the flesh" may however be arrived at through an analogy conveying a very close approximate to the actuality. You are asked to imagine an architect who has planned a very beautiful and perfect dwelling; one whose mind holds the plan very distinctly and completely, and who is himself a master builder, with unlimited command of the force and material needed to embody his plan, and with unerring knowledge of an instantaneous method of building.

Imagine further, that this architect, standing in the midst of the dwelling he has planned and built, should find that by some chance, or rather law, it was burned up every night without, however, burning him, or in the least injuring his powers. Remember that the plan remains intact; that the builder's skill and strength not consumed; that his command of material, sufficient to his needs, and instantaneous in supply, remains with him; that it is placed and combined in due order and proportion at his will. What would happen? Would he not reproduce this dwelling as quickly as it was destroyed? Would there, in fact, be any apparent break into the continuity of the dwelling? The only possible changes would be that, with experience and consequent growth? the plan would expand in beauty and strength, the material part of the building would become ever finer and finer, the adjustment of its various parts one to another more and more delicately exact.

This, in a rough way, conveys an idea of what is meant by the immortal man in an immortal embodiment. No difficulty appears to be found in conceiving the immortal principle in man as embodying itself in a succession of bodies, on an ascending or descending scale—any more than we find it difficult to conceive of the universal principle of life embodying itself in a variety of forms in an ascending or descending scale.

Yet, any such process must be considered complex and uncertain, compared to the simple and definite processes of the cosmically conscious man consciously and deliberately rebuilding, from day to day, that embodiment which best expresses his thought, and which best answers to his requirements. In this, as in other things, evolution of forms and of processes is all in the direction of greater simplicity and of increased economy and efficiency in the doing of our work. It is not the personal Jesus that is immortalized, or that has the power of immortalizing the flesh, but the Christ principle clothed in that personality? Animating it and using it simply as one of its modes of motion, so to speak. Yet, the Christ in Jesus came into such fullness and clearness of manifestation that his personality is indeed the lamp from which shines "the light of the world that lighteth every man that cometh into the world."

THINGS WORTH THINKING ABOUT

By DR. T. J. BETIERO - 1864 - 1917

Is the earth and all of the planets pursue their ceaseless journey around the sun, Astrologers tell us that the whole universe is moving around another greater central sun. They have further calculated that this far distant sun which is many times greater than the orb with which we are familiar, is situated in the Pleiades and is called Alcyone. As the earth crosses the Equinox we have regularly periods of great atmospheric disturbances, storms and, perhaps, earthquakes may then appear. Such being a well-known fact, is it not possible that at some certain point of the universal orbit, the magnetic harmony is likewise disturbed, and far greater cataclysms may result? The first statement is a known fact, the latter is simply a working hypothesis, and, if true, it accounts for some conditions which have for centuries puzzled the geologists.

We know that all ancient races of mankind have progressed to a certain stage, from whence they deteriorated, and, in not a few instances, they have been stricken down suddenly in their work or daily avocation. In confirmation of the first we have but to recall the fate of the Chaldeans the Persians, the Athenians, and later, the luxurious Romans. To illustrate the latter, we find in many parts of the old-world unfinished temples and public buildings whose architecture was on a plane far superior to that of our present time. Travelers going from Teheran to Isfahan are shown the ruins of an unfinished temple whose design excels in magnificence any building of the present day. And a short distance from this hastily abandoned structure a great block of stone can be seen lying at the quarry, dressed and ready to assume its place among the huge pillars of the now ruined temple. This block of granite is said to be more than forty feet in length and so wide that two carriages might pass each other on its surface.

We shall not here discuss the means by which these ancient builders may have intended to transport this huge pillar to its intended place, for notwithstanding the many ingenious theories advanced from time to time, we must finally admit that "we know not."

The question I desire to bring before the minds of readers is: What caused these workmen to stop so suddenly at their task? In other parts of the world, we find many unfinished undertakings which may have been contemporaneous with the work just referred to.

As an answer to this query fraught with such grave interest to humanity we find among the Oriental records preserved at Lahore an account showing that between long periods the earth has been immersed in a cloud that brought death to all animal life. At another period we find that the earth was submerged in water. Not only was the greater part of animal life destroyed, but the narrative goes on to say that the sacred books were lost in this water and Vishnu was sent down to recover them. These accounts proceed to say that at the end of each day of Brahm, the night comes on which lasts for a period so long as to almost baffle the imagination; and before the day changes into the night these great disturbances may be expected.

According to these ancient records we are led to infer that in the progress of the universe around the great central sun there must be a crucial point where the earth encounters so condensing nebulae or solid substance that adheres to the earth, at the same time destroying the greater part of the animal and vegetable life. According to geologists the earth has six distinct layers of this nature, which may be taken for proof that the universe has revolved six times around far-off Alcyone since the dawn of creation (that is since the earth's creation.) Taking this plausible deduction for granted, we may go a step further and inquire into the possible cause of this periodical destruction. We find the answer in the one word—Evolution.

The human race must continually evolve, ever going onward and higher. We are the sixth root race, and the time may not be far distant when we will give place to the seventh or perfected race. Seven is the mystic number of Creation. There are seven days in the week, seven colors, seven perfumes, seven notes of music, and we always find the seventh higher and purer than any other degree of vibration. Therefore, the seventh race, will no doubt, possess and cherish those attributes of the spirit, or inner sense, which now lies dormant in the great majority.

Some may say that such wholesale destruction as we have pictured would show cruelty on the part of Deity. To this I reply: Not so! There is no proof forthcoming to show that death is painful. On the other hand, few know of their birth and we may well suppose that few will know of their death. One of the most delightful sensations of my memory is the time when I was almost fatally injured. True when consciousness was restored my pains were such as might be expected under the circumstances. God in his great wisdom has made such provision that all forms of animal life when about to perish pass into that dreamy condition where they do not care to live.

However, as we are taught by the pure doctrine of Karma and Reincarnation we were here from the beginning and if we use wisely our opportunities we shall be here in the millennium. The material bodies may undergo great changes as do all things in the material plane, but our spiritual natures may be made everlasting.

Then let us not be deceived into accepting the unreal for the real. Let us devote more time to the development of our spiritual self, and let us not lay too much store by the physical whose final object is to die.

The ignorance of evil doth not save from evil: it must roll on the same A part of all things.

—Byron.

THE ARCANE TEACHING

By WILLIAM W. ATKINSON - 1862 - 1932

Lesson I.

The Arcane Teaching has come down to the present age through the corridors of time, from the dim ages of past eras, races, and schools of thought. Even those highest in the councils of "The Custodians of The Scroll," are unable to trace the Teaching, in an unbroken direct line, further back than the time of Pythagoras (about 500 b. c.), and a little later in Ancient Greece, although they find many references to, and extracts from, the teachings of ancient Egypt and Chaldea, which serve to show that the Pythagorean and Ancient Grecian Arcane Schools were founded on occult instruction still more remote, received in a direct line of succession of teachers and pupils extending over centuries.

Investigators have found traces of the Arcane Teaching in the records of Persia and Medea, and it is believed that the inspiration for the original philosophical teaching (not the religion or the pessimism, however) of Gautama, the founder of Buddhism, was received from Arcane sources. Traces are also to be found in the Hebrew Esoteric Teachings of the "Kabballah" and the "Zohar." The Grecian Arcane Teaching was undoubtedly obtained directly from Egyptian sources through Pythagoras, the relation between the early Grecian teaching and philosophies, and the older school of old Egypt, being very close and intimate. Pythagoras is known to have received instruction from Egyptian and Persian hierophants.

Besides the traditions of the Arcanes, there is to be found the closest resemblance between the ancient Grecian teachings, and those of the Egyptian Esoteric Fraternities. Some of the Teachers, however, hold that the Grecian and Egyptian schools, respectively, were but two separate off-shoots of an original and older Teaching which had its origin in the lost continent of Atlantis. There are many Arcane traditions connecting the Teaching with Atlantis, and it is possible that both Egypt and Greece received it from this common source, instead of Greece being indebted to Egypt for the line of transmission. But, be this as it may, it is a fact that all of the traces of teaching that the various occult schools gather from the traditions, scraps of doctrine, and legends regarding Atlantis can be reconciled with the Grecian Arcane Teaching. And it is also a fact that the fragments of the Egyptian Esoteric Teachings, many of which are still preserved in an undoubted direct line of succession, are practically identical, in fundamental and basic points with the Grecian Arcane Teaching. And, as we have said, the Persian, Medean, and Chaldean legends and traditions, and scraps of teaching, show a common source of origin with that of ancient Greece.

We are speaking now of the historical view of the subject, alone. The traditions of the Arcanes hold that the Teaching, in some form, is as old as the race itself, and that it has been known to the advanced minds of every great civilization of the past, many of which disappeared thousands upon thousands of years ago, all traces of them having been lost to the present sub-race. The traditions hold that the Teaching was handed down from the Elder Brethren of the race—certain advanced souls who appeared in the earliest days, in order to plant the seeds of Truth, so that they would grow, blossom and bear fruit throughout the ages to follow.

We do not ask you to accept this statement—it is not material—the Teaching bears the evidence of its own truth within itself, without needing the belief in any such authority. It agrees with the highest reason, and intuition of man, and to those who are ready to receive it, it shows itself as true. We mention the ancient traditions only that you may know what is accepted as truth by those high in authority among the Arcanes. The word "Arcane" is derived from the Latin word, "arcanus," meaning "shut up, closed, hidden, away," being derived from "arca," meaning "a treasure chest." The English word means:

"Hidden; concealed; secret; esoteric; mystic;" etc. So, the term "The Arcane Teaching." means "The Secret Doctrine." The Arcanes are a loosely organized body of men, who have lived in all countries, in all times, since the days of the Ancient Greece, and probably for thousands of years before. They keep alive the old Teaching, traditions, legends, and instruction, and give the same to the few whom they meet who are deemed ready to receive the same. The innermost Teaching is never written or printed, and is passed from mouth to ear—from teacher to student—from hierophant to neophyte—as in the old days. Much of this inner Teaching is of a nature that renders it most advisable that it be reserved for the few, for it contains instruction of a nature that would cause it to be most dangerous were it to fall into unworthy hands. Even as it is, bits of it have leaked out, from time to time, and falling into the hands of unworthy persons have been used improperly. Every student of occultism is aware of the danger of which we speak. But the general principles of the Arcane Teachings have always been offered freely to those who felt attracted to them, and by them. Portions of them may be found in the various schools of the Hermetic Philosophy, and among the Rosicrucian and similar teachings.

In Freemasonry, there are hints of the ancient teachings, carefully disguised and unrecognized by the ordinary members of the order. The exception to the rule regarding written or printed Teaching, is to be found in what the Arcanes know as "The Arcane Scroll," which contains many Arcane Aphorisms, or statements of Teaching, and which are written and renewed from time to time. The authorized copies are in the hands of special persons, high in the Arcane councils, who are known as "The Custodians of The Scroll," and who are to be found in every country of the globe, unknown and working silently. These persons belong to all walks of life, and society, and carefully avoid notoriety or public attention, in order to escape the sensational exploitation of the press, and the idle curiosity of the "wonder-seekers" who are to be found everywhere.

While many of these Arcane Aphorisms have to do with the special branches of the Teachings, and are not allowed to be printed and distributed generally, still the Custodians have always been willing that the fundamental Aphorisms be quoted from in writings and books on the subject. Accordingly, we shall embody a number of the Arcane Aphorisms in this series of lessons, always quoting them as such, and printing them in darker type, that they may be distinguished from our own comments and explanations and personal interpretations. These Aphorisms contain the highest occult truths, and principles, and we are very glad to have been accorded the privilege of presenting them to our students.

The Arcane Teaching is based upon the fundamental principle of the existence of an Absolute Supreme Power, which is the Cause and Reason of the Cosmos and all the manifestations contained therein—all that men call "the universe." This Absolute Supreme

Power is known in the Arcane Teaching as "The Law," and is represented in the symbols by the word "Lex."

The Law is regarded as an Abstract Principle of Power, impossible of being represented by words or even by symbols. It is not a Pantheistic Deity, or Being—It is an Absolute Principle, beyond definition or description. It does not manifest Itself in a universe of shapes and forms, by separating Itself into the Many as the Pantheistic Being is held to do in certain philosophies. Instead of this It causes Universal Being to proceed from Infinite Not-Being—causes the Cosmos to arise from Chaos—causes Manifestation to arise from the Unmanifest—causes Everything to arise from Infinite Nothing. The Law is not Being—but the Cause of Being. It cannot be said to "Be," in the ordinary sense It causes the verb "To Be" to have a meaning.

The Arcane Teaching is not Pantheism, either expressed or implied—either frankly stated, or subtly concealed behind words. The Absolute can never become the Relative. The Law can never separate Itself into bits of "You and I." Nor is the Cosmos to be regarded as a nightmare dream; meditation; illusion; delusion; or imagination; of the Absolute, as some of the philosophical schools of India, and the pessimistic schools of the West, would have men believe, against all the natural intuition of the race. The Law does not dream, meditate, imagine, or "think"—neither is it deluded, or subject to illusion, delusion or "ignorance," as some have taught. These are but qualities belonging to beings—the Law is above beings, and even above Being. To hold otherwise is to degrade It, and to deny Its Absoluteness.

The Arcane Teaching holds that other than The Law there is but Infinity, which is Nothingness. The Teaching distinguishes between the Absolute Law and Infinity, in which it differs from the majority of other philosophies which holds them to be identical. But this daring conception is defended and proven to be logical by the Arcane Teachers, and in this teaching is to be found the only rational explanation of the Cause and Manifestation of the Cosmos. The Nothingness of Infinity, is not a condition of "Not-ness," but a condition or state of "No-Thingness." Infinity is an Infinite No-Thing, in which, however, sleeps the latency, possibility, potency, and promise, of Everything, past, present, and future. In its Infinite Nothingness, no thing is in actuality, but every thing is in latency and possibility, under The Law. The Arcane Teaching on the subject of the Infinity of Nothingness, is a startling revelation to those who have been searching for the Truth in other philosophies, but who have found themselves wandering 'round and 'round in a mental circle—never arriving anywhere.

The Infinity of Nothingness is capable of logical and rational proof. This doctrine flies squarely in the face of the current philosophical dogmas of "From Nothing, no thing comes," or "Ex Nihilo, nihil fit." On the contrary it boldly asserts "From Nothing, Everything comes," or "Ex Nihilo, Omnis fit." But, it must be remembered, that this Nothing contains within itself the possibility, latency, and promise of Everything. It is a No-Thing, instead of a "Not." The Arcane Teachings hold that at the expiration of the great cycle of time—after aeons of Cosmic Night, or Period of Infinite Nothingness, The Law moves over the emptiness of Infinity, and the first activities of a new Cosmic Day, or Manifest Cosmos, begin to show themselves. The first manifestation is the Cosmic Will, or Life Principle.

This Cosmic Will is the One Life of the Cosmos, which many philosophies mistakenly claim to be the Absolute Itself. It is the Universal Being, but it is under The Law, and relative to It, and is not absolute. From this Cosmic Will, Logos, Demiurge, World-Spirit, or Universal Life Principle, is manifested the Cosmos or Manifested Universe of life, shape and form. The Cosmos is alive in every part, and its real nature vests in the Cosmic Will, which is ever behind, under, and in, all manifestations of the universal activities, from lowest to highest. Here is the World Spirit, or Pantheistic One –All—but it is under The Law!

In the Cosmos is contained "The Three Principles"—of Substance, Motion, and Consciousness; respectively. From the Three Principles arise all the infinite variety of combinations of mind, energy and matter, which go to make up the varieties of manifestation in the universe. The Arcane Teaching includes the doctrine of Perpetual Evolution of Substance, Energy, and Consciousness, respectively, on all the various planes of activity.

The Teaching is that there are infinite planes of evolution, in groups of seven, which are sub-divided in seven, and so on. The Arcane Teaching holds that the Cosmos is regulated by "The Seven Laws," which are superimposed by The Law upon the Cosmic Will, and thus upon all that is manifested. These Seven Cosmic Laws are as follows:

I. The Law of Orderly Trend. Under this law there is always manifested law and order in the Cosmos, from suns to atoms; from highest to lowest; matter, energy, and mind. There is no Disorder, In harmony, or Chance in the Cosmos.

II. The Law of Analogy. Under this law, there is found a correspondence and agreement between all of the various forms of manifestation. What is true of the atom, is true of the sun. What is true of the amoeba is true of man, and beings above man. What is true of matter, is true of energy and mind. To know one is to know all. "As above, so below," as the Hermetists express it. "Ex Uno disce Omnes"—"From One Know All," as the Arcane axiom says. This law is applied in studying the higher planes—they may be known by the lower, just as solar systems may be known by studying the atoms and molecules.

III. The Law of Sequence. Under this Law, there is included the activities of what is generally known as "Cause and Effect." Nothing happens by chance. Nothing happens without a precedent manifestation, and a subsequent manifestation. Everything has its "before and after" things. Nothing stands alone, and independent of what has gone before, nor can it escape from acting upon that which comes after. Everything proceeds from something, and is succeeded by something.

IV. The Law of Rhythm. Under this law falls a variety of phenomena, among which is the important phenomenon of Vibration. Everything is in constant vibration—everything material, mental or of energy. Upon this fact depends the variety, degrees, states and conditions of the manifestations of the Cosmos. All is in vibration—physical, mental and spiritual. Vibration is the key of relative power, and relative activities. To control Vibration is to control all forces in the universe. The control of Vibrations forms an important part of the Arcane formulas.

V. The Law of Balance. Under this law there is to be found an explanation for the universal equilibrium, compensation and balance, observed in all of the manifestations of the Cosmos. One thing balances another, in the physical, mental and spiritual. Everything has something set opposite it, to balance it. Everything has its compensation. Everything has its Cosmic price. In an understanding of the Law of Balance, there is to be found the Secret of Power and Poise. The Arcane Teaching contain formulas for Balance.

VI. The Law of Cyclicity. Under this law is found the cyclic, or circular trend of all things, physical, mental and spiritual. Everything moves in circles. The wise and strong convert the circles into spirals. Instead of traveling around in an eternal circle, the wise and strong rise in spirals to attainment and advancement. Worlds and atoms; Cosmos and Man; all are under this law, and move in accordance therewith. To convert the Circle into the Spiral, is one of the Arcane Secrets, conveyed in its formulas.

VII. The Law of Opposites. Under this law is to be found the explanation of that wonderful fact in nature—the fact that everything has its opposite; everything is, and is not, at the same time; everything has its other side; every truth is but a half-truth; everything is a paradox; every thesis has its anti-thesis; every truth contains a bit of untruth, and every untruth a bit of truth; every male contains female—every female contains male. Also, the fact that opposite things are alike, in the end; that extremes meet; the contradictions may be reconciled. In this great Cosmic law is found the fact that diametrically opposite things, physical, mental and spiritual, are in reality but the different poles of the same thing. In this law is found the Mystery of Polarity—in it vests the Secret of Sex-Generation and Regeneration—the Arcane Teaching embraces all these.

The Arcane Teaching, as presented in these Lessons, will include the Arcane Formulas whereby the Seven Laws may be applied under the mind and will of the individual, enabling him to take advantage of the flood-tide of Rhythm, and to neutralize the ebb-tide; to enable him to neutralize the Opposites; to find and hold the Balance and Poise; to convert the Cycles into Rising Spirals; to take advantage of the Law of Sequence—thus to Master Fate, instead of being her Slave; to conquer laws by laws; to oppose principle to principle; to acquire the Art of Mental Alchemy, or Transmutation of Metal States and Conditions. These and many other fields of occult knowledge will the Arcane Teaching open out to the earnest seeker. To those who are ready, this Teaching will appeal. Do you feel attracted to it—then follow the leading of your intuition. If not, pass it by for the present, for you are not prepared—instead call the attention of some person more ready, to it, and thus be an instrument of The Law.

Lesson II.

Absolute Law.

The Arcane Scroll contains the following Aphorisms regarding this Supreme Power, which in the Arcane Teaching is known as "The Law." Aphorism i. "The Law is." Aphorism ii. "Beyond The Law there is Not. Higher than The Law there is Not. Elder than the Law there is Not." Aphorism iii. "The Law is the Absolute. Existing beyond Time, and Space, and Change; transcending the Three Principles and the Seven Laws; It ever hath been, ever is, and ever shall be. Ever Unique; Unconditioned; Immutable; Self-Existent; Self-Sufficient; Independent; Abstract; It dwelleth Unknowable, Unthinkable, Ineffable." Aphorism iv. "The Law is the Efficient Reason of All-Things; and is the Supreme Power and Causer."

A consideration of the above four Aphorisms will throw light on the inner meanings contained within them. Let us now consider them in detail: Aphorism i. "The Law Is." In this Aphorism the word "is" denotes "present, actual existence." It is as strong a term denoting actual existence as the English language supplies. But, in the ancient Arcane terminology its Grecian equivalent was used in a still stronger sense than the ordinary use of the word "is" indicates. In the English language, the word "is" is used as the third person singular of the verb "Be," in the indicative mood, present tense.

But the words "is" and "be" have two entirely different original meanings, particularly when considered from the point of view of the ancient arcane schools. To explain further: The word "Be" is derived from the Greek word "phuo," meaning: "to bring forth; to produce; to be born;" etc., the original meaning signifying beginning in time; existence of a preceding cause; relativity, etc. And, accordingly, the ancient Greek philosophers, especially those of the Arcane schools, used the term "be" and "being" to denote the relative existence of the phenomenal or manifested universe, and not in the sense of absolute existence. The word "is," on the contrary, is desired from the word, "esti," which in turn was derived from the Sanscrit word "asti," both of which denote "existence," in its absolute sense, without reference to birth, bringing forth, or production. In its true and Arcane significance, the word "is" is analogous to "am," which had its origin in the Sanscrit "asmi," signifying absolute existence, which significance was also imparted to analogous words in the Hebrew, Egyptian and other Oriental languages. The word "Is" has the significance of the word "Am" in the following quotation from Exodus, iii. 14, in the Hebrew Sacred Books: "And God said unto Moses, 'I am That I am'; and he said, Thus shalt thou say unto the children of Israel: I am hath sent me unto you." This then is the sense in which the Arcane Aphorism employs the term "is"—in the sense of Absolute Existence. We have taken the pains to explain this to you at length, not for the purpose of verbal hair-splitting, but in order to bring out the true occult meaning of the term.

This, particularly, because we shall use the term "Being" in its relative sense in connection with the Cosmos, as we proceed. Remember that there is no "is-ness" other than that of The Law—all other "is-ness" is but "Being" which is relative, created, and phenomenal. In the true sense, there is no is other than the Absolute Law.

For this reason, we shall always print the word in capital letters when we use it in its arcane significance. Aphorism ii. "Beyond The Law there is Not. Higher than The Law there is Not. Elder than The Law there is Not." In these three sentences is taught the Absolute Omnipresence; the Absolute Supremacy; the Eternity; and the Self-Existence of The Law. There is naught beyond It, for there is no beyond; there is naught elder than It, for it is eternal and self-existent, there being nothing precedent to It to have caused or created It. We must here ask you to consider the fact that the Aphorism uses the term "Not," instead of "Nothing," for the reason that the Arcane meaning of the two terms is different. In the Arcane sense, the word "Not" means absolute negation—that is it denotes the absence of "is-ness," or "am-ness," and also the absence of even relative "being." "Not" means absolute not-ness—a condition of non-existence past, present, or future; absolute or relative. It is a positive denial of any existence whatsoever, of any kind, character, or degree, past, present or future. Further than this, language cannot go. But, the words: "Nothing," and "Nothingness," although generally used as meaning "not-ness" in the sense just mentioned, have an entirely different Arcane significance and meaning. In the Aphorisms, and in all of the Arcane Teaching these words are used in a relative sense, a capital "N" being employed to denote the said use of the word.

We shall consider this "'Nothingness," a little later on. Aphorism iii. The first sentence is: "The Law is Absolute." In this sentence is stated the highest truth capable of being expressed in words. Let us examine the term and see what it really means. "Absolute" means, in its original and essential significance: "Unbound; Free; Unfettered; Unrestrained." There are a number of derivative meanings, but the above definition gives the essential meaning of the term—and that meaning may be reduced to one word: "free." In other words, Absoluteness means Perfect Freedom—Sovereignty—Supremacy. There can be nothing higher than Absoluteness. There can be nothing over Absoluteness. There can be no Power beyond Absoluteness.

The "Law" of a thing, or things, is the sovereign power that exercises a control over it. And an Absolute Law is the supreme, highest and unqualified Power over all things. Therefore, is the Absolute called Law—therefore is The Law called Absolute. The term, Absolute Law is the highest and most positive term in the language, expressing Power and Control. There can be nothing that can oppose such Power; or run contrary to It, or overrule It, or "break" It. It is Power Absolutely Supreme.

The Absolute Law must not only be Self-Governed and Uncontrolled, but must also be Self-Existent and Causeless, for if there were aught else to have created It, or to have caused It to exist, then that "other" would be the Absolute. The very meaning of the term precludes any outside Cause affecting It. It is Causeless; and It exists of, and because of, Itself. To speak of aught causing, governing, or binding the Absolute, is to utter words that have no meaning. And even if we postulate a Supreme Being, governed by the "laws of His own inner nature," then these "inner laws," rather than the Supreme Being are the Absolute. So, you see that at the last the Law and the Absolute must be the one and the same.

The Aphorism continues: Existing beyond, Time, and Space and Change transcending the Three Principles and the Seven Laws; It hath ever been, ever is, and ever shall be. The words: "Is, hath, ever been, and ever shall be," denotes the Eternality of The Law," for a Self-Existent, Causeless, Absolute, must be Eternal—for naught could have caused it, nor could aught ever terminate it. "Beyond Time and Space" expresses Its Omnipresence and Eternality—Time and Space belong to the Infinite Nothingness, which is subject to the Absolute Law. "Transcending the Three Principles and the Seven Laws"—by this is meant the Three Principles of the Cosmos, and the Seven Laws by which The Law manifests Itself through the Cosmos, when the latter emerges in Manifestation from the Unmanifest, Infinity of Nothingness.

"Transcending," means, of course: "surpassing; surmounting; being above"; "being beyond"; etc. As the Three Principles are aspects of the Cosmos; and the Seven Laws are caused by The Absolute Law, it follows that the latter is superior and over them. "Ever Unique; Unconditioned; Immutable; Self-Existent; Self-Sufficient; Independent; and Abstract"—let us consider the meaning of each of the words composing this remarkable sentence:

Ever: "Always; forever; continually; without cessation." Unique: "Without a like or equal; unmatched; Unparalleled; sole."

Unconditioned: "Not subject to conditions or limitations; hence, inconceivable; incognitable."

Immutable: "Unchangeable; invariable; changeless."

Self-Existent: "Free from Cause; existing independent of aught else."

Self-Sufficient: "Sufficient for self, without aid or co-operation."

Independent: "Not dependent; not subject to control; not relying on aught; not subordinate or coordinate."

Abstract: "Apart from aught else; separate from aught else; existing apart and in Itself"; etc.

The above definitions need no further explanation or comment—they tell their own tale, and convey the meaning of the Aphorism clearly, when thus defined. The Aphorism closes with the following words: "It dwelleth Unknowable; Unthinkable; Ineffable." These three words have the following meaning: Unknowable: "That which cannot be known, being too difficult or subtle for the human intellect"; etc.

Unthinkable: "That which cannot be made an object of thought; incapable of being thought; incognitable; eluding the understanding"; etc.

Ineffable: "Incapable of being expressed in words; inexpressible; indescribable"; etc.

The combined idea of the three terms is well expressed by Herbert Spencer in his famous sentence; "By continually seeking to know, and being continually thrown back with a deepened conviction of the impossibility of knowing, we may keep alive the consciousness that it is alike our highest wisdom and our highest duty to regard that through which all things exist as The Unknowable." Or, as Edwin Arnold in his "Light of Asia" voices the beginning of the teachings of the Buddha: "Om, Amitaya! Measure not with words Th' Immeasurable: nor sink the string of thought Into the Fathomless, who asks doth err, who answers, errs. Say naught!

Shall any gazer see with mortal eyes; Or any searcher know with mortal mind? Veil after veil will lift—but there must be Veil upon veil behind." But, it may be asked: If The Law is Unknowable,

Unthinkable, and Ineffable, then why do you attempt to inform us regarding It; why do you attempt to teach us about It? The answer, O Neophyte, is this: We seek not to explain the unexplainable Law to you—we strive not to describe its nature to you, for that would be impossible, there being no words to express It, and no minds capable of understanding It were It explained.

The Aphorism expresses this truth fully and emphatically. But we do desire to impress upon your minds and understanding, the fact that It is. Not only do we ask you to believe this because the Arcane Teaching is the repository of the reports of the highest minds of the race—the illumined of all ages—but also because the intellect and intuition of every advanced man reports to him this truth, and informs him that back of, beyond, over and under, and in All, there is the Supreme Law. No matter what may be his religion, ancient or modern; or his lack of religion—no matter what may be his philosophy, metaphysics or theology, named or unnamed—no matter upon what lines he may have thought, if he has thought at all—Man must ever recognize the report of his reason, and his intuition, which informs him of the existence of a Supreme and Universal Law, governing all things. To deny this, is to deny reason. Faith is not required—reason suffices and fully informs that The Law is. And with that is-ness, the report ceases—the knowledge is then known, to low and high alike. While advanced beings on higher planes have reported great knowledge regarding the Cosmos, they state positively that they know no more regarding the nature of The Law than does the humble thinker on our own plane. But from the highest comes the same report as that which informs the mind of the lowest—The Law IS.

Therefore, in asking you to accept this report of the illumined, the highest of the race, including those whom we call the Elder Brethren, we ask you to accept only that which your own reason informs you to be a basic truth—The Law is. It is true that the race has built around the conception of the Absolute Law, the varying conceptions of personal deities, and pantheistic beings, but analyze them all and you will find that the reason for the activities of these deities, personal or pantheistic, has been the desire; will; want; inclination or "inner-laws" which are supposed to actuate their manifestations, or incite their activities, either consciously, unconsciously; or according to some of the Hindu schools, because of ignorance, illusion, or self-deception. In short, all of these conceptions of deity are Beings who are actuated by motives, feelings, desires of "inner-laws," just as are men, and other manifested or created things.

The anthropomorphic idea is evidenced not only in the crude conceptions of deity held by the savages, but also in the higher concepts; and even in the conceptions of a Pantheistic Being, or Absolute Being held by some of the philosophers and religious teachers of East and West. The pantheistic conception is utterly illogical, for as Schopenhauer says: "When we think of Nature as God, we show God to the door." And as the Arcane Teachers point out, even admitting any of these conceptions The Arcane Teaching of Being, the mind must see that in the "inner law" that moves Being to activity—the Law of Itself—there alone is to be found the Absolute. In such case the Law not the Being, is the Absolute, for it is the causer, and controller, and mover, and reason of the universe.

It is true that some of the philosophers and teachers try to explain away this fact, by saying that "Being and Law" are One. But this is no solution, for even if that be admitted, then the Law within the Being is the Efficient Reason and Causer of Action, and the rest of the Being is controlled, acted upon and moved by the Law within it. The whole idea of Being must be discarded in considering the Absolute. The Absolute is, and can be, only Law. For in all conceptions, The Law is, and must be, seen to be the Ultimate Cause of all activity. The advocates of Absolute Being, object that they are unable to conceive of Law without a Law giving Being.

But, considering this answer, we soon see that in order for the Lawgiving Being to proceed to give or promulgate Law, it must be moved by some inner law, desire, want, or will of its own nature—and that simply pushes back the question one step further. Try as we may, we cannot escape the conviction that Law is the First, and Last Cause—the Beginning and the Ending—the Efficient Reason of All-Things.

Law is not a Being—not a Mind—not a Spirit—not a Thing—It is Law, and naught else. We must accept It as Absolute Power, and as the Aphorisms present It to us. Beyond this we cannot go. Examine the Aphorisms carefully, and you will find that they agree fully with the highest reports of your reason, and in no way run contrary to it. The Law is the Efficient Reason of All-Things, and is the Supreme Power and Causer of the Cosmos. In this Aphorism is stated plainly and clearly the truth that The Law is the Supreme Power of the Cosmos, and the Causer thereof. The term "Efficient Reason" conveys the entire truth regarding the creation of or evolution of the Cosmos.

Let us consider the definition of the two words composing the term, in order to see the meaning still more clearly:

Efficient: "Causing or producing effects or results; acting as the cause of effects; a prime mover; actively operative; etc."

Reason: "An efficient cause; a final cause; explanation; that which explains or accounts for anything; motive of action; etc."

The Cosmos is explainable only by The Law. Without The Law there could be no Cosmos. The Law is the cause of the Cosmos, and of every manifestation within it. The very word "Cosmos" is derived from the Greek word meaning: "the universe as governed by law." Not only the Arcane Teaching, but modern science states as its first axiom: "The Cosmos is Governed by Law." To those who prefer the idea of an anthropomorphic Being, or a World-Spirit, as the Absolute, we have to say that, unfortunately for their idea, the facts of the Cosmos are all against them—Law is everywhere seen to be dominant and sovereign, even in its relative manifestations. We cannot escape it, and should not desire to; and will not desire to, when we understand its meaning. The explanation of this must wait until its proper place in these lessons is reached.

Enough for the present to state that in all human ideas of Law there is to be found the correlated ideas of Justice and Equity. Know then that this relative idea, when transformed to the absolute plane, results in the identification of Absolute Justice and Absolute Equity, with the Absolute Law. Could mortal ask more? Has he aught to fear of Absolute Equity and Justice? Can he not postulate in the Absolute all the highest conceptions of Fair Play that he finds in himself? The Cosmos is Governed by Law!

Lesson III.

Infinity of Nothingness.

We now invite you to consider the correlative principle of Truth, in which is set forth the Infinity of Nothingness—Chaos—the Unmanifest; from which, under The Law, emerges Everything—the Cosmos—the Manifest. We have informed you that The Law is not a Pantheistic Being, either breaking Itself into bits, or parts, in order to create Universes; neither does It imagine, mentally create, dream, or meditate into existence a false and fictitious Universe "all in its mind," as pseudo-occultism and pessimistic philosophies would have you believe. Listen to the Aphorism: Aphorism v. "Other than The Law, there is but Infinity, which is Nothingness. But in that Infinity of Nothingness, there is Unmanifest, the Latency, Possibility, Futurity, Potentiality, and Promise of Manifest Everythingness. It is the Chaos from which, under The Law, emerges the Cosmos. It is the Womb of the Cosmos."

Postponing for the moment the consideration of the distinction between the Absolute and Infinity, which is uncommon in ordinary modern thought, we wish to call your attention to the fact that Infinity is not designated as "Not," or as partaking of "not-ness," but is spoken of as "Nothingness," which is a state of Nothing. In the Arcane Teaching the words: "Nothing" and "Nothingness," signify "No-Thing," and "No-Thingness," respectively. This may seem like metaphysical hair-splitting, but it is not. Not having common words to express uncommon ideas, philosophers must need split common words into shades of meaning and significance, or else remain silent with their thoughts unexpressed. In order to understand "No-Thingness," and a "No-Thing," you must understand the meaning of the word "Thing" to which these words are opposed.

A "Thing" is "whatever exists as a separate object of sense or thought," in the sense of being and having apparent qualities which can be thought of in terms of sense-perception, such as size, shape, form, etc.—something connected directly or indirectly with physical appearance—something of the relative universe—something having a correspondence in experience.

And No-thingness must be the opposite of Thingness. Therefore, the Aphorism practically says that Infinity is a "Latency" that is No-Thing in reality, but yet has an existence of some kind, at least potentially. It can contain naught actually apparent to the senses; naught that can be experienced; naught that can be sensed; naught that can be thought of by the intellect, nor pictured in the imagination—in short, nothing that is capable of inducing a mental image in your mind. And yet it exists (if the word can be used) as a state or condition in which all is in Latency, Possibility, Futurity, Potentiality, and Promise. In short, it is The Unmanifest containing All Manifestation within it in latency, possibility and futurity, awaiting the force of The Law to bid it conceive, produce, and bring forth Being.

We shall learn about this Infinite Nothingness shortly, in connection with another Aphorism. Enough for the present to realize the words of the Aphorism before us, which informs us that other than The Law there is Not, with the exception of the Infinity of Nothingness which exists in latency. Other than The Law, there is Not in the absolute sense. Philosophies and schools of metaphysics have generally confused the meaning of the two terms "absolute" and "relative," and have used them as identical in meaning. The Arcane Teaching makes a sharp distinction between the two terms, however—not a difference based upon a metaphysical hair-splitting tendency, but because there are two entirely different ideas which must be expressed in these two words, and, in spite of the customs of the metaphysicians the distinction must be made. We do not wish to lead you into an extended metaphysical discussion, but we think that you should be taught to make this important distinction in the true meaning of these terms.

The term "absolute," in its true sense and essential meaning, implies an apartness; separation; independence; self-existence; self-sufficiency; supreme; unfettered; free. The "essence of the essence" of its meaning is to be found in the words "free, independent, self-sufficient." And when used in connection with the word "law," it represents the Supreme Power, depending upon no other power; its own sovereign; and the ruler of all else, without restriction. This conception we have in The Absolute Law which is the Independent, Free, Sovereign Lord of All.

The term "infinite" has an entirely different meaning, in its true sense, although the philosophers and metaphysicians often add to it the attributes of the Absolute, which is a mistake. The word "infinite" in its true sense and essential meaning, implies a state of boundlessness; limitlessness; not circumscribed; as to time, space, variety, possibilities, combination, shape, form, etc. Its essence may be understood by referring to the words from which it sprung, i.e., the Latin words "in," meaning "not"; and "finitus" meaning "finished." In short, the word "infinite" means "not finished; not complete; capable of unlimited manifestation, and possibilities." So, you see, while the idea of "Absolute" means fixed, complete independent state or condition; "Infinite" means a state of endless and unlimited possibilities of manifestation and expression.

The true philosophical idea of Infinity, consists of the conception of any sort of mental object as having the quality of quantity which cannot be exhausted by any succession of experiences, however prolonged or extended, in time, space, variety, or number. By holding this idea in mind, you will never make the mistake of confounding infinity with absoluteness, hereafter. The chief cause of the confusion arises from the unauthorized use of the term "infinite" in relation to "power." Power belongs to the Absolute, and is not one of the attributes of Infinity. "Infinite Power" would mean an infinite possibility of the manifestation and expression of unlimited power; while Absolute Power means all the Power there is, fixed, independent and sovereign, unvarying and immutable, and not subject to changes of degree, etc. Absolute Law is not an infinite capacity for expression of power—It is Power-in-Itself.

All the great thinkers of all times, esoteric and exoteric, have agreed in this idea of the Infinite being the Unlimited Possibility. The best of the ancient Greek philosophers, from Aristotle down, held to this idea. As Schopenhauer says: "It is already a doctrine of Aristotle, that Infinity can never be actu (actual, given, fixed) but only potential (in possibility, latency, promise, potentiality)." And as Lewes says: "If Zero is the sign of a vanished quantity, the Infinite is the sign of continuity." We trust that you now see that the Absolute could never become Relative or Many—and that the Infinite alone is capable of endless changes in shape, form, variety, in time, space, and number; and contains within itself the promise, possibility, latency, and potentiality of Everything.

The Arcane Teachers, in the olden time, illustrated this to their pupils by the following symbols: The figure "1" standing for the Absolute, and being fixed, independent, sovereign, and alone. By itself, and in itself it is incapable of multiplying or dividing—multiply anything by "1"; or divide anything by "1," and the thing remains unchanged. Multiply or divide "1" by itself, and the answer still is "1," showing that the Absolute cannot be increased or divided, even by itself. Subtract "1" from Infinity of itself, and the result is "0," showing that if the Absolute were subtracted from it would cease to exist, and there would be naught left but the Infinite Nothingness. Then the Teachers called the attention of the pupil to the Zero, or "Infinite Nothing" symbol, i.e., "0." In itself, "0" means Nothing. Multiply or divide anything by "0," and the answer is always "0." Multiply "0" by itself, and "0" remains—the Infinite cannot increase itself, for in its circle it includes All Possibility. But divide "0" by itself— and lo! "0 into 0 goes 1 time": the answer is "1," showing that if the Infinite be divided by itself, the Absolute is found to be at its center, undisturbed, independent, self-existent. The symbol of Infinity, in mathematics, however, is not "0" or Unmanifest Infinity, but ∞ which indicates Manifest Infinity, the symbol always indicating endless continuation of action. Now the symbol of the Infinite Nothing, becoming Place a string of "0's," as follows: 000,000,000,000,000—you see that they still mean "Nothing."

Now place "1" (the symbol of the Absolute), before the string and we have 1,000,000,000,000,000, which we may enlarge to infinite number by the addition of "0's." Or place the Absolute "1," behind the string, and we have 000,000,000.000,000, 1, a very small decimal, which may be carried to infinitesimal smallness by the addition of "0's." Thus, we see, by symbols, that the action of the Absolute Law on the Infinite Nothingness produces Infinite Greatness, or Infinite Smallness.

Now that you understand that Infinity means the Infinite Possibility of Things, rather than an Infinite Manifest Thing, you may be able to see that the Infinity of Nothingness of the Arcane Teaching is not quite so irrational as it appeared at first sight. In order to realize the truth of the Aphorism still more forcibly, let us consider what Infinity (even in the ordinary use of the term) really is. You will find that all thought if analyzed, implies the Nothingness of Infinity.

Non-Being, or Nothingness, was always regarded by certain schools of the ancient Greek philosophy, as existent in a philosophical sense. Empty space was considered as truly existent as the atoms which afterward appeared in space. Plato regarded Empty Space as the matrix, or mold, in which the universe was formed. He held that there was possible an abstract realization of pure empty space, which is Nothing; the Void, which is the all-containing receptacle of creative energy, and in which being, first distinguished into geometrical figures, becomes the framework of the physical world. Scotus held that since Deity creates the world out of Nothing, then Nothing must exist as an emanation of Deity. Hegel distinguished between a "nicht," or "Not"; and a "nichts," or "Nothing."

Theology has always held that Deity "created the universe from Nothing," thereby implying at least a quasi-existence of Infinite Nothingness. Spinoza recognized an "infinitely infinite" which is practically an Infinite Nothing. Plato said that "Space as a Thing is incredible, difficult of explanation, most difficult to comprehend." And Zeno, the Eleatic, said: "If Space is a Thing, it must be in Something, and so in Space; for everything that is, is in Something, and so in Space; and so, on ad infinitum. Therefore, Space is not a Thing." So much for the philosophers. Let us see what our own reason informs us. Let us first examine the idea of Space.

Space is the mental symbol for Infinity. Consider yourself as standing at a fixed point in Space—then you must realize that there exists an infinite distance or extension in Space, from that point, in an infinite number of directions. Leaving out of consideration all objects in space—considering Pure Empty Space—and you must see that there is an endless extension possible, in innumerable directions—extension without end. Imagine a number of miles represented in a row of figures extending from earth to the most distant star; then multiply that number by itself; and then the product by itself; and so on, for a time equal to the number of years since the Cosmic Day began.

Then you would have a number of miles, the written figures of which would fill all the space that your mind is able of even conceiving. Then think of a Being traveling to the extent of that measurement—would he then be near the end of space? No! the distance traveled by him would be as a mathematical "Nothing" or Zero, compared with Infinite Space. No mathematician could have figured out the infinitesimal smallness of the fraction denoting the comparison, were he to have worked continually since the dawn of the Cosmic day. The calculation would be endless, because the result would be infinitesimal, and at the end, he would have to place the sign of "infinity" back of it.

Just think! To be able to travel for all Eternity through Space without coming to an end! You cannot come to an end of Space, even in thought or imagination—try it! You will find that think as far as you will into Space, there must always be Infinite Space beyond that imagined point. There is "no up or down" in Space. Space is something with its center everywhere, and its circumference nowhere. At the last, philosophy and science are compelled to hold that "Space is merely the possibility of infinite extension; or the infinite possibility of extension"—to the Universal Ether.

In the end, Ether is called the Great Mystery of Science. It must be considered as a Nothing that is a Something. A leading scientific lecturer said, and wrote, recently: "The Ether is unconditioned, an entity of no properties but of all possibilities, or, more exactly, not an entity at all, but an infinite possibility." And, so we find, even Matter and Things themselves, arising from and being resolved into an Infinite Nothingness that is also Infinite Possibility.

Now, for a moment, let us endeavor to imagine the condition or state of the Infinity of Nothingness—the Unmanifest Cosmos—during the Cosmic Night, and before the faintest dawn of the new Cosmic Day. The Three Cosmic Principles are resolved into the condition of the Unmanifest, but are not destroyed—there are Nothing, but not "Not!" The Three Cosmic Principles are Substance; Motion; and Consciousness, respectively. Substance has assumed its most subtle form, infinitely rarer and finer than the finest ether—it is practically Nothing, but yet exists in latency, possibility, and promise. Motion has assumed a rate of vibration so high that it is practically at Rest, although not destroyed —it is still Motion in latency.

Consciousness has assumed the condition of a deep unconsciousness—a profound dreamless sleep; a swoon following upon the infinite ecstasy of the Supreme Cosmic Consciousness of the previous Cosmic Day. It knows Nothing; is conscious of Nothing—for there is but Nothing of which it could be conscious, or could know, for all manifestation has ceased until the dawn of the new Cosmic Day. It is even unconscious of the presence and power of The Law, although The Law still reigns over it, and will awaken it once more, as it has many times before, in the Eternal Chain of Cosmic Days and Nights.

The Cosmos sleeps in the condition of Infinite Nothingness—the Unmanifest! The Abyssmal Abyss—the Eternal Deep—the Face of the Waters—the Void—the Cosmic Womb! The Mother Sleeps! The Laws of Cyclic Rhythm have brought to Her the Rest of the Cosmic Night! But she will awaken and greet her Supreme Lord at the dawn of the Cosmic Day. From the Cosmic Womb will proceed The Cosmic Will, which will manifest the universe of universes; infinitudes of infinitudes of shape, form, and variety, of things, life, and beings. In her Existence is the Promise of all that Shall Be throughout the Ages and Aeons of Eternities of Eternities. The Mother sleeps, sleeps, sleeps! But, through the Night, as through the Day, The Law is, immutable, unchanged, Absolute.

A MANUAL ON THE PATH OF KNOWLEDGE

By JNANA MARGA - 1928 - 1997

THE human mind naturally reasons about Truth. In its unremitting operations, wittingly or unwittingly, it is always seeking Truth. To find Truth is to see Truth, therefore, in proportion as the mind is able to recognize and distinguish what is true from what is false, so it may be said to find Truth, or at least an aspect of Truth. All things express or represent, in some manner, aspects of Truth. In fact, in this sense, Truth itself is the very Reason of their existence objectively and subjectively.

Hence, since the Mind cannot conceive of anything that has no existence, it follows that whatever the human mind reasons about, is, in this same sense, an aspect of truth, however far removed from the final and absolute Truth. But the full significance of any aspect of truth is to be understood only when seen in its correct perspective and proper relationship with all other aspects.

Therefore, a living consciousness of Truth is dependent upon the integrity and comprehensiveness of the human reason. In like manner, universal and integral aspects of truth are more easily recognized and accepted than particularized and partial expressions. But, in every case, the clearness of perception is modified by the pre-conceptions or prejudices already in the mind, and, likewise, by the objects or motives for which Truth is sought. For instance, the object may be to collect and classify countless expressions of finite truth in order to formulate generalized laws for practical ends personal or impersonal. Such conceptions are scientific, in the common acceptance of the term.

On the other hand, the object may be for the sake of Truth itself, in order to attain, through It, a consciousness of the ultimate Reality. Such conceptions are philosophical in the original and best application of the term. Philosophy, in contradistinction to Science, deals with the essential, universal and abstract nature of things, more than with their apparent, particularized and concrete characteristics.

Philosophy, as its name signifies, is wisdom rather than knowledge, and is more unitive and synthetic, while Science is more partitive and analytical. Moreover, among Systems of Philosophy, those that are the most universal in world-view and most adequate in expression, are also the most self-evident and harmonious, both in themselves and in their relationships with other systems.

The Hermetic System of Philosophy may be defined as the Wisdom concerning God, the Universe and Man. As the Wisdom concerning God it presents a most exalted conception of Deity and is characterized by a tone of profoundest sanctity. As the Wisdom concerning the Universe, or Macrocosm, it brings the Sensible World into the light of the Intelligible Sphere, and reveals the underlying unity sub standing all duality.

As the Wisdom concerning Man, or the Microcosm, it is characterized at once by the principle of unity and universality, extensively unfolding all his principles, powers, vehicles and relationships, and intensively indicating his assimilation to the type and pattern of Perfect Man. The principal Hermetic conceptions under these three headings are conveniently summarized thus:

I. GOD.

(1) The Divine Unity.

(2) The Divine Trinity.

(3) The Divine Plurality.

II. THE MACROCOSM.

(1) The Intelligible Universe Above.

(2) The Sensible Universe Below.

Many of these aspects are so self-evident that they hardly need expression, but by considering them in their hierarchical order, they not only become more luminous but also shed additional light upon other less obvious conceptions.

I. GOD.

(1) The Divine Unity.

What could be more simple and yet, at the same time, more profound in ultimate implication than that Name for the Supreme which seems to ring reverberatingly through all the works of the Platonists and Neoplatonists? They spoke of Him Whom they knew to be wholly ineffable as THE ONE, sometimes, however, supplementing that Name by another, as if to confer a title which in some measure might be faintly applicable.

THE ONE AND THE GOOD

For not only is HE, Who is so denominated, the ONE prior to all, and THE ONE superior to all, but HE is also THE ONE within Whom all things have their Being and without Whom nothing could possibly be. But besides being in such an exempt transcendental sense THE INEFFABLE ONE, He is also denominated THE GOOD, because the whole of existence thirsts to partake of His Perfect Plenitude and Infinite Goodness.

Simple, Reverent, and Ineffably Occult is this beautiful appellation of the Most High, Who must always remain transcendentally beyond the highest conception of the highest philosophy.

The Divine Trinity.

Although GOD is essentially ONE and the Unity of all Unities, yet He cannot be conceived without immediately introducing the Idea of a Trinity. Philosophically, this Root Trinity is conceivable as: The Divine Essence, abiding immanent in all, the cause of all being; The Divine Life, proceeding providentially through all, the cause of all activity; The Divine Mind, transcendentally converting all things to Itself, the cause of all intelligence.

The Divine Essence is the Logos of Being, Light, and Love the All-Father.

The Divine Life is the Logos of Life and Providence the All-Mother.

The Divine Mind is the Logos of Power, the Creator Lord, and Great Architect.

This triadic conception beautifully unfolds the inconceivable Unity of the Supreme, revealing the Three Hypostatic Principles upon which the whole of manifestation fundamentally depends, and providing the human intelligence with a key to the understanding of the true nature of all things.

It has its analogies everywhere, in all realms inner and outer in the great and in the small, in science, religion, mysticism and in every field of activity.

The Divine Plurality.

The Three become the Many, and the Many are held subjectively within the Three; for, from and by and through each of the Three Logoi, a multitude of Divine Powers, Principles and Perfections proceed. In the Platonic terminology these Divine Processions are celebrated under the appropriate title of The Immortal High Gods Immortal because They are stable and eternal in essence and energy; and Gods, because They are the immediate Progeny of the One Only Supreme God. The primal emanations of Deity must necessarily be most like unto It, therefore are They truly Divine and Their proper appellation is The Gods.

Although They are a multitude of self-perfect Unities, They do not constitute a plurality of God-heads, but rather by magnifying the mystery of the One Godhead, They raise In other systems they receive other names. Our conceptions of the Absolute to the most exalted point possible. To deny the existence of the High Gods is to deny the existence of the universe, for They are those Powers, Principles and Perfections which sustain the Universe.

And to doubt the Power of the Supreme to produce the Gods is to doubt His Omnipotence and to place a limit to His Unfathomable Prolificness. Without His Plurality and Divine Irradiations, the Supreme would be like a rayless sun. But the Gods, Who are God in His manifestations, bring Him near to man, for They all perpetually proceed from and return to Him as Unities from and to One Primal Monad.

They distribute, regulate and make manifest the Divine Essence and Life, and, as God s Eternal Ministers, are the support, guidance and up liftment of all that is, was or ever will be.

II. THE MACROCOSM

In philosophy it is customary to consider the universe as composed of a number of different planes of existence, consciousness and action. These are said to inter-penetrate each other and are difficult to conceive of from a purely finite standpoint.

But, more obviously, the Macrocosm is twofold, when considered apart from the Divine. For example, its dual aspects are known as: the Above and the Below; the Eternal and the Transient; the Subjective and the Objective; the Spiritual and the Corporeal; the Intelligible and the Sensible. The lower is symbolical of the higher; the outer is an expression of the inner; the objective is a projection of the subjective. Each, in turn, has various sub-divisions or sub-planes, but an intimate parallelism may be traced throughout, and for this reason their relative characteristics may be hypothetically postulated by means of the Hermetic Law of Correspondences, and, by taking them as a basis, a more or less complete cosmological scheme may be outlined.

The Spiritual Universe is the Field of Divine Operations and is characterized by Intelligible Essence and Eternal Life, of which the Sensible Universe is the outer, lower and transient expression. It subjectively comprehends the archetypes or Ideas of all things that have been or ever will be expressed. These Ideas are unitary, fontal and productive; preserving, elevating and perfecting. Hence, the Spiritual Universe is not only potentially but likewise actually perfect. It is the Kingdom where all Ideals are realized.

The Sensible Universe embraces the objective life and corporeal existences by which the archetypes of the Intelligible Universe are made manifest under the limited conditions of time and space. It includes all kingdoms of nature.

III. THE MICROCOSM

Archetypal Man

According to the Hermetic Philosophy Man is called the Microcosm of the Macrocosm. The Macrocosm below analogically expresses the Spiritual Macrocosm above. In a corresponding manner, the human Microcosm below is an expression of the Spiritual Archetype Above. The Archetype is essentially Monadic, Perfect and Eternal. From It all Microcosms may be said to proceed, and, inasmuch as they are potentially one with It, they inherit the right to participate and manifest Its attributes in varying degrees of glory. The Archetypal Microcosm stands in the same relation to the Spiritual Sphere as Humanity holds in regard to the Sensible Universe, for the Supreme Microcosm, as the Universal Christos, is not only the Head of Humanity, but also the Lord of the Universe.

Threefold Man

The One, the Three and the Many are repeated in the Microcosm, Man. The Mystery of the Trinity is reflected in each of the three root principles of Spirit, Soul and Body. Of these, the first and the last, with their several aspects, correspond to the dual Macrocosm, while the Soul stands, metaphorically, between, with a twofold vision, power and purpose.

Above the Soul is the Spirit, the Ideal Principle, in and by and through which the Soul participates in the Divine Unity, Trinity and Plurality, and without which it can never enter consciously the Kingdom of spiritual realities and perfections. Below the Soul, the Body Principle is suspended, in and by and through which the Soul expresses itself and without which it could not enter into conscious relationship with the Sensible Universe.

When united to Spirit the Soul is assumed into Its likeness, and when identified with Body it becomes subject to the laws of the Sensible World. The Soul, infinitely receptive, is destined to hold, on the one hand, the infinite plenitude of Spirit, and on the other, to manifest that plenitude through the principles of Order, Harmony and Beauty.

Pan-Humanity

Pan-Humanity is essentially one, just as the Immortal High Gods are essentially one. Its apparent multiplicity is due to the numerous attributes possessed and manifested by each Microcosm in multifarious ways. For example: The Intellectual Activity, with its objective and subjective expressions; the Affectional or Vital Principle, with its lower and higher activities; the Volitional Faculty, with its free and determined aspects. The action, inter-action, and re-action of these attributes, with their numberless phases in individual and collective Microcosms, result in the infinite diversity by which Pan-Humanity is characterized.

The destiny of each Microcosm is to manifest harmoniously all its attributes to the utmost on all planes of consciousness. This is partially to be achieved by various processes but finally it depends for its consummation upon conscious identification with the One Perfect Spiritual Arche type, Who, while transcending all multiplicity and diversity, is Himself the unification and co-ordination of all.

Through Him, Pan-Humanity, following the Divine Plan, is converted from its manyness to its basic triune nature, and from that to its Unity or One-ness with the Supreme.

HERMETIC SYMBOLOGY

THE PRINCIPLE.

THE principle of Hermetic Symbology, and indeed of all symbology, is the hypothesis that the manifested expresses, in some manner, the unmanifested. The Divine Manifestor is the Great Symbolist. It is He who expresses in the panorama of the universe the Supernal Wisdom of the Inconceivable Supreme. It is He who unfolds ideation into substantiality, and potentiality into actuality, and it is He indeed who causes the manifested to spring into being from the unmanifested.

This principle underlies the Laws of Expression, Correspondence and Affinity, whereby the Thoughts of God are so written in the world of form that whoso desires to read, may read. The world of form is a vast symbolic code in which is concealed God s Idea of all things of the Cosmos, of Nature, and of Man himself. The outer objects have their inner significance, even as that which is below is in some way a reflected type of that which is above.

Man, as a symbol, is God s masterpiece, for, hidden within him is to be found the key to every mystery. He is not a fleeting chimera of a few years, for, beyond, behind and above his transient nature is an eternal ideal archetype which it is his sublime destiny to realize. Extrinsically man is human; intrinsically he is divine. The intrinsic value of a symbol is determined by the dignity of the idea represented, the degree to which that idea may be realized and the adequacy of its expression. The extrinsic value of a symbol is proportionate to the depth and dignity of the mind that uses it. To one mind a symbol might be meaningless but to another fraught with unutterable secrets.

A true symbol is a living emblem of Truth. It speaks to all who hear and understand. Nature is a gigantic system of symbolism and its voice is a living and intelligent voice. The lore of Nature is the Book of God, which grows more and more legible in the light of the Hermetic Law of Correspondence. The symbol Man, is set in the midst of a stupendous and mysterious mosaic of symbols with which he has countless hidden but intimate affinities. The more he realizes this the nearer he comes to a knowledge of himself. Metaphysics alone mean little to the mind until amplified symbolically either by metaphors, allegories, personifications or other means. The memory and recognition of phenomenal and concrete objects depend upon the faculty of symbolizing them mentally. The objects themselves cannot, concretely, enter our minds, but by substituting appropriate symbols or impressions for the objects contemplated we give them a place within the horizon of our consciousness. In this way our store of knowledge is said to increase, for by reproducing the idea of a thing we make it our own.

Conscious thought is impossible without symbols and when so employed symbols constitute a species of language whereby thoughts are rendered expressible. This language may verge towards abstractions or it may be quite concrete, according to the penetrative depth and power of the mind using it. All language, necessarily, is composed of symbolic ideas, images, or characters; hence the study of symbology becomes, in reality, the study of those counters of thought used by man throughout the ages.

THE CLASSIFICATION

I. Symbols may be classified in many ways. For example, there are symbols corresponding to all the activities and accomplishments of man, falling naturally under those titles with which we are so familiar Science, Art, Philosophy, Religion, Mysticism, Occultism, Mathesis, Technology, Music, Commerce, Sociology, etc.

II. A more comprehensive classification is the following:

(1) Universal Symbols.

(2) Arbitrary Symbols.

Universal Symbols are more or less self-evident and immutable in basic significance. Arbitrary Symbols are subject to modification and mutability according to the manner of their use. Numerical Symbology is a good instance of the class that is universal, such as the number three, or the triangle, which reveals the root triplicity of all phases of existence and the triadic nature of all things.

Arbitrary Symbols are extremely diverse in nature and significance, for example the greetings used in conventionality or the chosen emblems in the symbology of the artistic. But even Arbitrary Symbols are connected with universal ones, however apparently remote the relationship may be.

III. The quaternary classification of symbols is an excel
lent one.

(1) Formal Symbols.

(2) Sound Symbology.

(3) Symbols of Colors, Odors, Tastes.

(4) Symbols of Motion.

Each of these is twofold Natural and Human.

Natural Symbols are those we perceive in Nature; they make up the stupendous mysterious Symbology of the Great Architect. Human Symbols are those made by man in all his works. The World of Art makes up Human Symbology, just as the World of Nature figures the Symbolism of God. The Sun is a splendid example of a Formal Symbol, revealing the vast center of our System from which flows ceaselessly the Light, Heat and Force that sustains our Universe. Figures, numbers, letters, whether graphical, geometrical or hieroglyphical belong to formal symbology.

The astronomical symbols comprise the alphabet of the stars and are profoundly significant. Of Sound Symbols there are: the voices of Nature and of man; the music of the spheres; the sounds of the Great Mother and of all Her children. Spoken words or names are symbols of ideas. Man is an incarnation of a word a name. The language used and the sound of the voice is an index of the dispositions of the speaker. All languages are symbolical. Some are elegant, some dignified, some mystical, some mantric.

Words are vehicles of thoughts and symbols of feeling. There are words of love, words of wisdom, words of power, words of fire; winged words, sacramental words, and traditional words pregnant with power and mystery. As examples of Color Symbols there are the prismatic colors and their correlation in the septenary scheme; and the pigments used in art.

The odoriferous and gustatory properties also have symbolical correspondences. The cosmic movements and periodic revolutions of the orbs in space, the flowing of a river, the flight of a bird, the attitudes and gestures of man are instances of Symbols of Motion.

THE APPLICATION

Some indication of the extent to which symbols are to be applied is opened out by considering the symbolical significance of the ten Aristotelian categories which can be predicated of all things.

(1) Substance. Substantial symbols provide the basis or groundwork of manifestation. In Neoplatonism there are spiritual as well as material substances.

(2) Quality. The qualifications or attributes of all things are appreciable only through the medium of symbols. The qualities themselves in here in things, whether recognized or not, but they are the more exactly estimated the nearer the symbols employed approximate to those qualities. For example, gold is an appropriate symbol of purity because it is the purest metal.

(3) Quantity. Mathematical theorems, as well as quantitative measurements, depend essentially upon suitable symbols. (Euclid was a great Symbolist as well as a Platonist.) Numerical Symbology is perhaps the most profound and scientific of all.

(4) Relation. Self-consciousness implies, and is indigent of, the clear perception of relations between the knower and the thing known. In its expansion, this consciousness enters into wider and also closer symbolical relationships with all beings, and, at last, with the Infinite Itself.

(5) Place. That which is placed Here symbolizes that which is placed Yonder; All localities or planes have their analogical symbology. Heaven and Hell as places are, symbolical.

(6) Time. The past and the future exist only as simple or compound symbols in consciousness, human or cosmic. The present symbolizes the Everlasting Now. All chronological orders, sequences, and successions are symbolical.

(7) Condition. Symbols are applied to denote dispositions, the permanence or impermanence of qualities, the changes of properties chemical, alchemical, or otherwise.

(8) Situation. The hierarchical order indicates symbolically where everything is situated.

(9) Activity. The symbolics of forces, functions, energies, etc.

(10) Passivity. All things are both positive and negative, symbolically and actually. They are positive to those less active, but negative or passive to those more active. The Sun is a passive symbol to God but a positive symbol to the planets.

II. In the Interpretation of any symbol there are at least three stages, leading from the outer and finite meaning to the inner and infinite significance.

(1) Concrete Significance. The consideration and predication of the extrinsic, explicit, particular and obvious properties, e.g., the Sun, its subsistence, quality, activity, etc.

(2) Transitional Stage. The extension of the concrete significance by inference, deduction or induction; treating the symbol as a theorem to be explained by a chain of reasoning leading to axioms, e.g., the characteristics of the Sun, the significance of its shape and position, its triple activity or manifestation, its numberless rays, its prior and causal relationships with the lesser orbs of its system, etc.

(3) Abstract Significance. The intrinsic, implicit, and more inner meaning, revealing the innate, essential and universal idea, when by analogy, correspondence, affinity and association, we penetrate beyond the visible and apparent; e.g., the Sun, its spiritual significance as an emblem of Deity, having its three primal characteristics, its numberless irradiations, its prior causality, etc. The above method utilizes the concrete to interpret the abstract, the phenomenal to express the nominal, the sensible to unfold the intelligible, the relative to sense the absolute, the outward to open the inward.

It must be recognized that in itself alone this method is incomplete. For the finite does not represent the infinite, nor need a labyrinth of particulars necessarily lead to a universal truth. Nevertheless, since that which is below bears witness to that which is above, it may take us a few rungs up the ladder of Truth.

III. Example. As an illustrative application the front cover of our Quarterly is suggestive, for instance: The Circle is symbolical of the Supreme Source and Goal of all, beginningless and endless. The Triangle within the Circle denotes the three primal manifestations of the One Supreme. The Two Ankhs and

Columns suggest, among other things, the two streams of Life the proceeding and the returning. The Gammadion at the base of each column suggests the four-fold whirling's of the streams of life upon the Cross of Manifestation.

A true symbol has many applications however. It is a key that can be turned again and again. It may be 3-fold, 7-fold, 10-fold or even 12-fold. Its significance on one plane may reveal its meaning on another. By the application of symbols, thoughts may be coordinated, ideas may be unified, vague conceptions may be clarified. Symbolism is concentrated ideation. The vividness of a thought depends upon the ability to create a true and clear symbol of it, separated from all extraneous elements.

Symbols portray ideas and ideals too deep and sublime for mere words; they evoke exalted and inexpressible thoughts and feelings. What wondrous varieties and combinations of forms and figures and colors can be adapted to express that which the human voice could never utter. What ineffable emotions, infinite reminiscences and majestic ideals can, by the use of symbols, be called forth from the unmanifest into manifestation.

HERMETIC MYTHOLOGY PURPOSE

THERE are three main modes by which great teachers have presented Truth to mankind, Dogmatically, Scientifically and Mystically. These methods are, more or less, interdependent, but nevertheless, there are occasions when, for special reasons, one may be predominant. To affirm that the Kingdom of Heaven is within, is a dogmatic truth. To explain the affirmation if this be possible by philosophy or other means, and then present it in terms of these, is to change it into a scientific truth. But if the statement, although positively asserted, is considered to have more than a literal significance and is to be understood symbolically or metaphorically, then it is a mystical truth.

Absolute Truth is, of course, infinite and therefore never to be fathomed by finite means. Faith may accept Its dogmas. Reason may perceive Its science. Intuition may receive Its mystery.

But Absolute Truth Itself remains, ineffable, although the whole universe is fashioned to unfold It. The acceptance or perception of truth avail nothing unless productive of effect. A dogmatic truth may be acted upon because of its moral influence on the will. A scientific truth may be made practical because of its rational influence upon the mind. But, as an impelling power, a mystical truth, when intuitively perceived, is more potent and productive than either of these, because it sheds its own intrinsic, irresistible beauty on the Soul and lifts up all things to higher and more effective levels.

Myths and Allegories are, in this respect, important means for presenting mystical aspects of truth. They are tales of wonder and beauty, containing images of what the Soul longs for and thirsts for Their beauty is the most unforgettable thing in the world. And, because of the Immortal Ideals they contain, these legends of the old ancient days; still retain their hold upon all lovers of beauty. They have fulfilled, and continue to fulfil, at least a threefold purpose viz., to veil, to preserve and to reveal mystical aspects of truth as presented in sacred legends and traditions. Hermetic Mythology is that which pertains particularly to the Hermetic Tradition, which, emanating originally from Egypt flowed from thence through Chaldea to Greece.

Therefore, it embraces the pre-eminent mythological systems of the Egyptian and Grecian mysteries. A myth is a veil that may be lifted, little by little, as its allegorical and inner significance is perceived. Because the meaning of a myth is not self-evident, there is sometimes a tendency to regard it as an enigma purposely devised to hide truth. But this, although to some extent incidental, is not the primal purpose. Truth is not self-evident save when suitably presented to faculties that are capable of perceiving it. When the true vision is attained, Truth is perceived however much it may be veiled.

Therefore, although myths veil truth, they do not exactly conceal it but rather are they the means of gradually preparing the eyes of the Soul to behold that which would blind by excess of light, if seen without meet preparation. The mythological systems of antiquity constitute an immense repository of truth, which is the common heritage of humanity. Considered collectively, they form a universal tradition in which the inspired utterances of the Great Ones are preserved. For almost without exception the mythical or fabulous element enters into every philosophic and religious system. Invariably, too, the basic principles of a tradition are embodied in the myths belonging to it.

Therefore, even if such a tradition should ever become corrupt, the characteristic preservative power of its myths will enable it to be periodically purified and revived. Furthermore, they are more readily handed down through the generations or translated from one language into another than are philosophical or metaphysical treatises. It is difficult to transmit the full significance of a philosophical principle in its original purity, but the story of a myth is easily conveyed even by those who do not understand it, and its significance is retained.

As the accumulated myths, fables, legends, allegories, and sacred traditions are more and more widely disseminated in many languages, so they grow more and more in universality and thus provide criteria of Truth of increasing value. They have an inherent vitality and perennial freshness although their beginnings may be lost in the remote past. It is not without reason that myths have been called the truest things ever written, for they can reveal deep truths that would, in all probability, remain hidden if presented through other media.

Moreover, the truth in them is to be seen rather than to be reasoned about or accepted blindly. The Hermetic Myths tell of the Irradiations of the One Supreme, i.e., the Eternal High Gods; of the Incarnation of the Logos or Christos-Osiris Principle; of the descent of the Soul into manifestation and of its final redemption and perfection. They repeat in varied forms, the divine macrocosmic and microcosmic history fabulous and yet true.

Interwoven with these magical mystery tales are ideas of almost fathomless significance. And the view-points from which they may be approached are without limit. Their influence is all-comprehensive. Religion draws upon them for the personifying of its divine principles, through which, in worship, concrete and finite conceptions may lead to the abstract and infinite. Philosophy adopts mythical terminology as soon as it leaves the concrete and practical and enters the realms of the Ideal. Plato, the Master Idealist, continually alludes to the Orphic and Homeric fables. His own allegories, too, are masterly examples of the mythic art. Art, in turn, could not well dispense with mythology.

Poets, painters, sculptors and musicians all have recourse to mythology as the fount of their inspiration. The day for myths and allegories is by no means past. Long will they serve useful purposes while mankind continues to speak in figures and metaphors. Indeed, bereft of these products of imagination, language would be shorn of those elements that give to it, not only its strength and beauty, but also much of its power of appeal to the intuition and that innate sense of truth and taste for beauty.

A true myth is a narrative, complete in itself, as a story, but having a veiled meaning. The visible world is complete in itself but it too holds its veiled mysteries. An ancient writer truly said: We might call the whole world a myth, which contains visible bodies and things, but souls and spirits in a hidden manner (Sallust on The Gods and the World.

II. EXEGESIS

The principles underlying Hermetic Symbology enter largely in the exegesis or interpretation of myths. Certain general guiding principles, however, may be laid down, embracing their construction, significance and application. (a) Construction. There is a similarity in nearly all myths inasmuch as the localities historical or purely fabulous usually denote not only places but also states or realms of existence; the personages, proper names and terms also are employed, as a rule, symbolically; and the events narrated are often extraordinary and permit of more than one interpretation. (b) Significance. Here again, similar stages can be remarked in lifting the veils of nearly all myths.

The first veil is lifted by obtaining the literal explanation and derivation of the proper names and principal terms used. The second veil is raised by reconstructing the narrative in the light of these literal and suggestive meanings.

The third veil is gradually removed by the aid of reflection, when the symbolical and allegorical significance is applied and developed. This process may be extended, and intuitional flashes obtained, in which there may be glimpses of the infinite truth behind. (c) Application and development. To apply myths is to use them to present and explain aspects of truth. The majority of true myths are applicable from many stand points natural and artistic, moral and ethical, philosophical and metaphysical, religious and theological, mystical and occult. Moreover, they may be treated macrocosmically or microcosmically, and correspondences may be traced between them all. Thus, from a simple story, with a literal and finite meaning, we are led stage by stage, to the apprehension of an infinite truth with its application in all realms of consciousness.

These mystery tales are inexhaustible sources of suggestiveness. At different times they hold different messages, and, likewise, different eyes see different messages at the same time. And, even as the vision of exterior beauty is intensified by the realization of interior beauty, so the beauty embedded in myths is more and more perceived as the Soul s own beauty unfolds.

A myth does not reveal the same mystery to all. It reflects only as much as the eye of the Soul can receive and understand, even as the secrets of Nature, although laid bare, are seen only by the eyes that can behold them with veneration and love.

THE MYTH OF OSIRIS & ISIS

BRIEF OUTLINE OF NARRATIVE.

In the legendary Golden Age of Egypt, Osiris and Isis reigned as King and Queen. They were not only the rulers but also the teachers of their subjects. They were not as their people but were said to have come direct from the Gods; their parents, according to some, being the Divinities Seb and Nut. For a time, all was peace. Then, while Osiris was away in a distant part of his kingdom, his brother Typhon arose to usurp his place.

Eventually, when Osiris returned, Typhon, by cunning, slew him and cut his body into 14 pieces which were scattered over the sacred land of Egypt. Then began the lamentations and search of Isis for her lost lord. Long did she wander, and as she found fragments of his holy body, so did she bury them and cause tombs and sanctuaries to appear. At last, a son is born to her, named Horus, who becomes the conqueror of Typhon. Osiris rises again from the dead, ascends into Heaven, and, through his resurrection, becomes the redemption of all who identify themselves with him.

This is but a very cursive story of the myth and does not reveal its beauty, but nevertheless it will be found that in the full narrative there is much of that indescribable beauty which is the special characteristic of the Grand Egyptian Mysteries. (2) RELIGIO-MYSTICAL SIGNIFICANCE (Suggestive). Egypt may be regarded as symbolical of the field of the Divine operations, in which the mysteries of God are hidden and yet revealed. The Egyptians may be taken as symbolizing Pan-Humanity. Nut and Seb represent Heaven and Earth respectively. As such they constitute that principle of duality through which all things proceed from and return to Unity.

Osiris is the Divine Incarnation. God s Idea or Archetype of Man: Potential Perfection. Isis is the Divine Mother Incarnate. Typhon is comparable to material darkness, that which is below, where the universal essence and life of Osiris and Isis are slain, in a mystical sense. Horus is comparable to spiritual light, that which is above, the re-born or risen Osiris, also called, Osiris-Horus

Actualized Perfection

This bare outline, which is given merely as an example, may suggest a multitude of interpretations, especially when other details not given here are added. Osiris, the central figure of the myth, may be considered as personifying the Divine Immanence, the Indwelling Spirit, slain from the foundation of the world. He is God and also Man. Son of Heaven and Child of Earth.

To be identified with Him, as Osiris-Horus was, according to the Priest-Hierophants of the Pyramid, to become Osirified, divinized in the Hall of Seb. Without Osiris there was no regeneration, no resurrection, no perfection, but with Him there was, and is, Life Everlasting.

HERMETIC MYSTICAL SCIENCE
AND ART DEFINITIONS MYSTICAL

Science is the precise delineation of the principles, and the exact formulation of the laws underlying mysticism and mystical concerns. Mystical Art is the application of these scientific principles and laws to mystical purposes. Religion is inseparably connected with Mystical Science and Art and cannot properly be divorced therefrom. For Mystical Science is the culmination of that phase of Religion which aims at the correlation of the outer to the inner and of the partitive to the integral.

While Mystical Art is the consummation of that aspect of Religion which ordinates the human nature to the divine. It is a process by which Spiritual Ideals and Types of Divine Science are expressed in the Worlds of Form. Science should precede Art even as Knowledge should go before Practice; for Science explores the means and Art applies them to the end in view. True Science is therefore essentially illuminative, and true Art essentially perfective.

Special and particular Sciences investigate external causes and effects: Hermetic Science reveals their inner analogy and intelligibility. Practical Arts put into application that which Special Sciences explain, directing them to useful ends.

Absolute Science is the revelation of True Being: Perfect Art is conscious active union with True Being. Indeed, from the human standpoint, Perfection is the fullest possible expression of Real Being.

II. THE PRINCIPLES

The principles sub standing Mystical Science and Art are there is an intimate correspondence between the microcosm and the macrocosm, the intelligible and the sensible, the inner and the outer.

There is a profound affinity not only between the Divine Unity and the Divine Trinity in Man and in the All, but also between the

Divine Plurality and the many faculties of Pan-Humanity. By Hermetic Mystical Science the principles and laws of the Universe are brought into correspondence and relationship while their mutual interactions and affinities human and divine are revealed.

By Hermetic Mystical Art these same principles and laws, thus intimately integrated, are brought forth perfectly expressed. The light of Hermetic Mystical Science penetrates the veil of multiplicity, explores the deep metaphysical recesses of the Universe, and sheds its luminous rays over all things so that at last the Perfect Divine Order itself is to be seen.

Hermetic Mystical Art, established in the Divine Order, traverses the path opened by the light of Hermetic Science, bringing into perfect ordination and expression all that was latent and unmanifested before. This alternate ingoing and outgoing, constitutes the life of Mystical Science and Art; the former disclosing the treasures concealed within the center of the Cosmos and the latter beautifully unfolding them into the Orb of the Circumference in plenary manifestation.

III. THE APPLICATION

It is the Soul universal and human that is forever putting into application the principles of Hermetic Science, because, since it subsists midway between primary and secondary natures, the Soul has affinity with both, and can, not only enter into correspondence with every Order of being in the hierarchy of existence, but also give actual expression to what is potentially inherent. Therefore, it may be said that the Soul contains all sciences and arts and that its purpose is to realize and apply them. The Soul s affinity with primary natures is dependent upon the Spirit, i.e., the Logos or Nous, through which the Soul is potentially united (1) by its being to the Divine Unity and Trinity; and (2) by its life and activities to the Divine Plurality, i.e., the Eternal High Gods; while (3) by its secondary natures and instruments of expression the Soul is united to the universe and humanity. In the Divine Unity is the Supreme Science of the Soul.

In the Gods is the Pure Art of the Soul, for pure art springs from divine inspiration which, in reality, is the activity of the Gods within the Soul. In the universe all sciences are applied by the Art of the Gods operating in and through the Soul s secondary natures.

The perfection of the human Soul s Art depends upon its conscious living union with God and the Gods, through the Spirit. This perfective-union is to be attained by three processes in which the Soul s Art is gradually unfolded, consciously or unconsciously. (1) The free expression of the Soul s faculties as they emerge from potentiality into actuality by evolutionary processes; this alone will not accomplish the desired end for it only leads to a certain point. (2) The assimilation of these faculties to their divine affinities, which is to be accomplished by the action of the personal will when it serves or tries to serve the Divine and is thus converted from self-seeking to the light and life of the Gods. (3) The elevation and transformation of the Souls faculties or secondary principles to their primary archetypes by fuller and fuller participation in the Divine.

These three means are summarized as the processes of Evolution, Redemption and Participation all of which have a deep significance when considered in the light of Hermetic Science and Art. (1) Evolution, regarded mystically, has a more profound meaning than when explained solely from a material point of view; not that the latter is untrue but rather that it is only a partial truth which is not always seen in its correct relationship with the universe.

The Soul s essential nature is not subject to evolutionary laws because it is rooted in Spirit, and Spirit cannot truly be said to evolve. Therefore, evolutionary processes refer to the Soul s activities and secondary natures. As a result of these activities and by means of the Art of the Gods, the Soul follows the Divine Plan and produces or evolves three instruments of expression, each of which, in turn, is a plural-unity, or a multiplicity in a unity.

These are called the Volitional, Vital and Intellectual Instruments. The will to exist evolves vehicles of manifestation; the vital principle generates life and stimulates activity, and the intellectual principle develops new contents of consciousness. All these, in the first place, spring from the deep fontal impulses in the Soul to move, to stand forth, to open out, to unfold, to express, to create and to make manifest. But as a natural consequence of these evolutionary impulses, the Soul changes its center, and, in a mystical sense, is said to depart from its summit, losing knowledge of its Real Being, and forgetting its allegiance to its Source.

Hence it lapses, so to speak, from the Above to the Be Below, there to gain experience and knowledge. This is what is implied by the fall and descent of the Soul, The evolution alone of the Souls secondary principles cannot restore the Soul to a consciousness of its original but innocent state, because, since these principles are secondary and subsidiary to the Soul, they can neither change the Souls essential nature nor cause it to be united to that from which it proceeds.

Therefore, it is evident why evolution alone neither changes humanity s essential nature nor leads the Soul of Man to its goal. Moreover, if the attainment of the goal depended solely upon an infallible natural evolutionary law, then there would be no need for individual effort nor would there be any intrinsic value in it. Mystical Science and Art would have no place in the affairs of mankind. All Souls would be subject, voluntarily or involuntarily, to one General Law and Cosmic Process which they could never transcend.

But purely natural evolutionary processes apply only to humanity s natural principles and cannot affect in any way the Eternal Spiritual Principles, which must necessarily subsist above the transient and mutable conditions of Nature. Therefore, in order that the Soul may be introduced consciously to its spiritual principles, further processes must be super imposed upon those of evolution. (2) Redemption is the means for restoring the proper relationship between the human and the Divine natures. It is an inner process more than an outer one.

When applied to the Soul, redemptive processes do not necessarily imply any inherent change of nature, but only a conversion of activity by which its secondary principles are redeemed. Evolution has more to do with leading out from the potential into the actual, while redemption is more concerned with leading out of the actual into the ideal. The Soul cannot freely and consciously exercise its potential lordship over Nature until it is liberated from the limitations imposed upon it by Nature s conditions and no longer entangled in Matter.

The redemption of the Soul is the removal of its false and illusory alliances; while the redemption of the Soul secondary principles is their orderly orientation to the Pure Art of the Gods.

Redemption is conversional, i.e., it is the turning away from that which is inordinate, negative and disintegrating. It is Purgatorial, i.e., the elimination of the effects of this departure from Real Being by the substitution of that which is orderly, positive and integrating or re-integrating.

Redemption is also Regenerational, i.e., the generating anew of the Souls instruments on higher planes so that they may be used to contact that which is above Nature. The conversion of the Mind, Heart and Will from ignorance and darkness, selfishness and attachments, and inertia and aimless drifting tendencies, prepares the human nature for the reception of Divine Light, Grace and Strength.

The Purgation of the Souls secondary vehicles is the dissolution, separation and purification of their impure elements by the Spiritual Life which opens them to the influence of Divine Art through which the whole being is ennobled.

Regeneration is an awakening of the inner life, a quickening and a re-birth of the Souls vehicles, elevating them to the participation of Divine Goodness, Truth and Beauty. Each of the redemptive processes has a beginning in the realms of Time, but each may be continued perpetually, leading to more and more perfect art and to fuller and fuller life and consciousness in all realms of existence and activity. Mystical Participation is communion with the Divine. It is a growing conscious response to the Being, Life and Mind of God by the spiritualization of the Souls instruments of contact. From another standpoint it is the action of the Gods upon the Soul, the mystical and magical operations of the Art of the Gods producing in the Soul supernal representations and revelations of Their Glory and Greatness.

Participation attunes the instruments of the Soul to the music of the Gods, and in the enjoyment of Their Inspiration the Soul responds and corresponds to the Divine Harmony. This is the ultimate function of mystical and religious Art or Spiritual Alchemy. There are various theories concerning Participation or Divine Inspiration, e.g., that it is by Divine Right, or that it is by Divine Grace, or that it is self-determined. Each of these is partially true.

When the Soul is united to God through its divine principle, Spirit, it may participate in Him by Divine Right.

When the Soul becomes immersed in Matter as a natural result of evolution and bound to the activities of its secondary principles, it becomes subject to the decrees of Fate and is obliged to wait for what appears to be the intervention of Divine Grace for the removal of its limitations.

Again, the Soul, by entering into intimate relationship with the manifested universe may be said to fall. But it retains its essential inherent purity and can always exercise its Elective Power or Freewill, although it cannot always immediately accomplish what it wills. Hence its conversion to Heaven and to mystical participation is self-determined, because even the Gods cannot redeem the Soul unless it becomes receptive to Their Inspiration or Supernal Breath.

There are four distinct modes by which the Soul may be conjoined to the Gods in mystic participation. These correspond to the four Inspirations distinguished by Plato in the dialogue Phaedrus, viz., the Musical, the Telestic, the Prophetic and the inspiration of Mystical Love. When under the influence of any of these Divine Breaths, the Soul is for the time being transported from the world of the Actual into the Realms of the Ideal.

These Inspirations provide subject matter for subsequent treatment, but each of them has its place in the three principal pathways of Perfective Union, i.e., the Path of Union by Good Works (Telestic), the Path of Union by Knowledge in which the Prophetic Inspiration is especially a requisite, and the Path of Union by Devotion, or Mystic Love, in which Music or Harmony also has its place. However, the four inspirations are not limited to any one particular pathway, but may enter into all in varying degrees. The most important, of course, is Mystical Love.

THE EFFECTS

The consummation of Hermetic Mystical Science is in the realization of the True even as the consummation of Hermetic mystical Art is in the attainment of the Beautiful. Each of the three great processes of Evolution, Redemption and Participation has manifold effects. Evolution tends to the production of finer and finer vehicles of expression and to a more and more perfect subjugation of Matter to the Formative Principle of the Soul.

Redemption not only purifies and sublimates the Souls vehicles of expression by purgation, preparing them for the supranatural action of the Gods, but also opens the whole being, by regeneration, to an altogether fuller and deeper realization of Real Being. Participation, which is the natural fruition of purgation and regeneration, is a re-ascent to the Divine Likeness, a return of the Soul to its Sovereign Source. By it the Souls vehicles are transformed, re-ordinated and revivified and brought, Mystically by Sacred Sympathy, into the hands of the Master Artist whose Art is Perfect and whose Acts are absolutely Just. Sanctification, Transformation and Justification are therefore the three primal effects of the Hermetic Mystical Science and Art.

It is evident from these considerations that there is a clear distinction between the purely natural process of Evolution and the altogether supranatural process of Participation. Man, naturally inherits the Kingdom of Earth, but it is only by an awakening to a realization of his true relationships with the Above and his true destiny in regard to the Below, that Man inherits the Kingdom of Heaven.

Not only is Hermetic Mystical Science necessary the pursuit and perception of the True, but also Hermetic Mystical Art the manifestation and perpetuation of the Beautiful; not only Realization but also Attainment.

By the natural progression of Nature towards higher and higher manifestations of the Formative Principle and finer and finer manifestations of the Material Principle, Man evolves he secondary vehicles of his Soul, but it is not until the Soul begins to look above and to be converted to its Principle, the Shining Spirit, that the reception of the Art of the Gods becomes possible. For it is only by and through the Spirit, that Man can participate in that which is above, even as it is only by and through his secondary principles that he can participate in that which is below.

The culture of the Souls vehicles is very different from their Sanctification, for the way of Participation is not the seeking to attain this goodness or that virtue, but rather the pursuit of the Good Itself. It is indeed the consecration of all things to God, so that all acts become sacramental and all the vehicles of the Soul are sanctified, i.e., made holy. Again, how different is the sublime transfigurations in the lives of the Great Ones, to the merely natural growth and improvement witnessed in the lives of the unawakened. Evolution may change a man s habits, his thoughts, his actions, but only a Participation in the Divine Art of the Gods can change the tenor of his Soul and give a sublimity and sanctity to his life.

And lastly, the awakened man is justified; his purpose in life is in course of fulfilment, of conscious fulfilment. A holy peace pervades him in the realization of all that can be accomplished under the wise guidance of the Inner Master Artist, Who brings all acts within the Divine Circle of Accord, con firming and strengthening them and imbuing them with Light and Life and Love.

Hermetic Mystical Science is ultimately the finding and knowing of God, even as Hermetic Mystical Art is ultimately the loving and serving of God. And by the unification of the two processes in the Soul of the awakened man, his secondary principles are woven into the pattern of perfection as the Divine Wisdom gradually unfolds within his Mind, the Divine Life within his Heart and the Divine Power within his Will.

Such a one is justified, for his is the life Eternal.

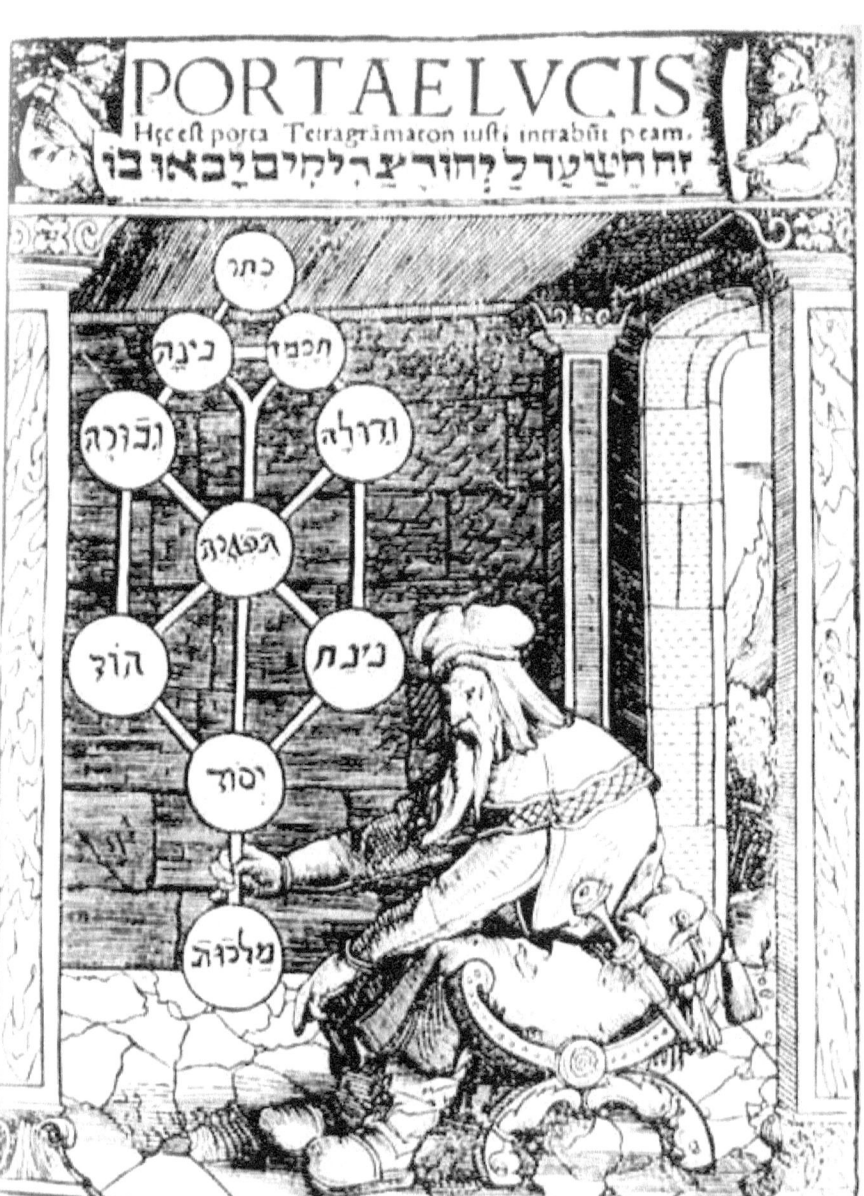

SECRETS OF THE ROSICRUCIAN'S

by a Frater of the Rosy Cross

Is this work is written principally for the students of the Rosicrucian Order, Crotona Fellowship, much of the subject matter herein may be unfamiliar to those outside the Order. Yet to those unacquainted with the subject of Occultism this little work will introduce the study of that which has been known and practiced for all ages.

Should any reader wish to further his search into the subject of Practical Occultism, application through the publisher will receive consideration. Many are the vexed questions concerning Life and destiny which man would seek to answer. Have I lived this life before? Does this life continue after that which is called death? Is mind and thought independent of the human organism? Does man possess higher faculties than those he is in the habit of using day after day, and if so, how can those faculties be unfolded?

Such questions every man of intelligence asks himself. It is the purpose of this work to answer these questions in a clear and logical manner and in the light of the experience of the Rosicrucian's. Let us first of all survey, briefly, the history of the Rosicrucian Fraternity. The Fraternity owes its origin to the archaic teachings of the Atlanteans who passed on their knowledge to the early Egyptians. By tradition and in some instances by writings, the knowledge has been passed on to the present time.

The Fraternity bearing the name Rosicrucian was founded as such in Europe during the mediaeval Ages and its purpose was to teach the esoteric side of Christianity, and in addition to promulgate Eastern Mystery Science and Philosophy in a form adaptable to the minds of European people. During the centuries which have elapsed since the Medieval Age a vast amount of knowledge has been accumulated, furthermore, the accumulated knowledge has proved to be practicable. That which could not be applied to practice has been archived as "Mystery Teaching" and treated in a manner more philosophic than scientific. The Rosicrucian Order, Crotona Fellowship, is divided into two sections: The Fraternity and the Order.

The Fraternity consists exclusively of Occultists who have applied to practice the Teachings of the Fraternity and have satisfied themselves as to the verity of all Teachings passed down through the centuries. Members of the Fraternity constitute the Magistii and Adeptii. The Order or Fellowship is made up of students devoted to the studies of the Rosicrucian's, students who hope after application and practice of the studies to enter the Fraternity.

In a short work of this description, it is not possible to give in detail the full history of the Fraternity, much regarding the history has been written by others, and many of these have forgotten or do not know that the Order does not advertise itself and that all writings for the outside world and for the purposes of tradition are written in symbolic form. Occasionally the Fraternity sends out a work dealing with its Philosophy or Science for the purpose of enhancing discoveries made by the layman during any particular century, but the bulk of its Teachings are reserved for the accredited members or given out in the form of novels or plays.

Usually, a cipher or code is concealed in the work and by means of that cipher or code any member may know which particular Brother is responsible for the work. We shall now in a brief manner deal with various sides of the Conceptions of the Rosicrucian's for the benefit of all who gam possession of this book. Like the Freemasons, the Rosicrucian's believe in a Supreme Architect of the Universe, though the term "Universe," in the Rosicrucian sense, refers only to a Sun with its attendant planets. The Rosicrucian's use the term "Kosmos" for the millions of Universes extant in space, and the Ruler and Guide of all these is a Supreme Architect or Absolute Consciousness.

That this Supreme Ruler gives ear unto every individual being who asks for favors is not the belief of the Fraternity, realizing as it does that the Supreme has endowed man with faculties and powers (inherent within himself) by means of which he may overcome the difficulties which wait upon his ignorance. To be able to contact the Supreme Architect means that the being possesses an unfolded consciousness equivalent to that of Kosmos. Such a being would have no need to manifest in a physical body or world. That a physical being may contact in his consciousness a higher being than himself, though infinitely lower than the Absolute, is the belief of all Rosicrucian's.

Space is peopled by entities of all degrees of consciousness, some of these have been embodied in physical vehicles and others have not. That these entities irrespective of whether they have been embodied in the flesh or not, can help mankind, is the knowledge of all true Rosicrucian's. Man possesses a consciousness by means of which he may know himself and the world about him. As to how much he may know depends upon the degree to which his consciousness has unfolded. In Rosicrucian Philosophy, Mind is considered to function in three ways, as follows:

Mind Objective.

Mind Subjective.

Mind Super-Conscious.

The mind objective is that which rules the voluntary acts of the organism and works through the cerebro-spinal nervous system. The mind subjective is that which rules the involuntary acts of the organism and works through the sympathetic nervous system. The Super-conscious mind is that which manifests as a result of the workings of the objective and subjective minds. The three minds respectively have their location in the three brains, the Cerebrum, Cerebellum and Medulla Oblongata. The Cerebrum concerns itself with the present state of affairs, the Cerebellum with the past, and the Medulla Oblongata with the past, present and future.

The Super-conscious mind may be considered the acme consciousness. The Objective and Subjective minds are the body and soul, the Super-conscious mind is the avenue for the Spirit's expression. The Rosicrucian's know that man is constituted as body, soul and Spirit. In the right understanding and unfoldment of the three minds as one, lies the key to the solving of the problems of life and destiny. Nature is constantly revealing her secrets to man but man will never know those secrets unless he seeks for them. Before disease manifests in the human body, nature always gives warning, and if man does not heed the warning he will suffer.

In mental diseases there is one which gives the key to the functions of the three minds mentioned above. The disease is known as General Paralysis of the Insane, or to put it briefly, G.P.I. In this disease the unfortunate sufferer slowly, but surely, loses his consciousness, and passes from a fully conscious man to the state of an infant incapable of controlling the voluntary function of the body. In the last stages consciousness withdraws completely from the cerebrum, cerebellum and medulla oblongata. The great secret of Practical Occultism is to be able to function at will in any of the three brains. The infant, when it comes into the world, manifests and from the Medulla Oblongata. As it grows and takes experiences of life, it functions through the cerebellum - finally the cerebrum.

During the latter functioning, its forehead broadens as well as the crown of the head, and slowly but surely the infant becomes a conscious thinker. In practical occultism, as known to the Rosicrucian this process is reversed, and as the consciousness is centered in the different brains by an effort of will, the experiences of the present and the past are reviewed. The result of this is not only the acquirement of a long memory, but also a checking of those tendencies which retard unfoldment (in the occult sense). Man thinks to-day because minds have thought in the past and as a result of that he thinks into his own life and world for his own specific purposes.

That which brings about unfoldment of higher faculties is new thinking and new grooving of the brain as a result of efforts of the will to penetrate into the three brains. There are in the head and throat three centers or glands which play an important part in this unfoldment. They are known as the Pineal Gland the Pituitary Body and the Thyroid Gland. These glands have a special function of their own but their functions may be blended and linked up with the functions of the three brains and states of consciousness. It is the will which determines all this.

The right use of the will and the method of controlling the glands, brain and mind is the great secret of the Rosicrucian's. The reader of this work will have noticed how everything works in a threefold manner, as examples: three states of consciousness, three brains, three glands and man constituted as a threefold being—body, soul and spirit. The mystery of the Trinity need not be sought any further than the Physical Organism for the Kingdom of God is found within the human being.

In the science of Alchemy, three terms are used as Salt, Sulphur and Mercury. Nature functions in a threefold' manner and the work of the Practical Occultist or Rosicrucian is to link his unfolded powers with those of the greater nature, by so doing he learns the secret of life, and to him there comes the knowledge that there is no death in God's great Kosmos but progress from one state of matter to another. He learns that mind can exist outside of a physical organism and that by means of that mind he can link up with other entities, either in or out of Physical bodies.

Time becomes to him only an illusion for he perceives that there is naught but Duration—infinite life everywhere from the meanest microbe to the mightiest of worlds. A world of magic opens up to the Occultist's when mind he has rightly unfolded the faculties which lie slumbering within himself, then he sees how he can consciously cause changes within himself or outside of himself as hen desires or wills. The way to this unfoldment is not easy, but it is possible to those who are willing to undergo the training necessary.

There are many unbelievers in the world, but this little book have been written especially for those who do believe to those who do it we say, "Learn more about your own brain, there is much in it. Do not imprison that which seeks for an outer expression."

A ROSICRUCIAN PROBLEM

By MANLY HALL - 1901 - 1990

For several years we have been investigating the secret societies of the ancient and mediaeval worlds. These organizations may be divided into three general classes—political, philosophical, and religious. During the last three centuries a fourth type of secret order has appeared, namely, the fraternal. All secret societies were originally priestly institutions created to perpetuate the mystery religion which had been revealed to the first of humanity by the gods.

"Knowledge is power" declares the Egyptian, but knowledge in the possession of such as have not yet mastered the animal soul is dangerous. The Mystery Schools were created in order that divine wisdom should neither perish from the earth, nor yet fall into the hands of the profane. The great truths discovered by the illumined were therefore carefully concealed under abstruse symbols and allegories, and a man desiring to know them was compelled to pass through a number of tests to prove that he as entitled to this honor.

Christianity, like all the wisdom religions, is a threefold structure, consisting of a spirit, a soul, and a body. Ante-Nicene Christianity was a school of the Mysteries, and as such promulgated a secret teaching concerning which the modern church knows practically nothing. The first Christian mystics were the Gnostics, but nothing now remains of their cult except a few inscribed gems and an occasional literary fragment mutilated almost beyond recognition.

The Middle Ages found Europe struggling to free herself from the limitations of religious intolerance, philosophic despotism, and scientific ignorance. The doctrines promulgated by Galen, Avicenna, and Aristotle held the minds of the learned in intellectual bondage. It was against this bigotry that the great Paracelsus directed his hammer blows, liberating the medical profession from the dogmas of Avicenna.

Centuries after him came Sir Frances Bacon, who with the sheer transcendency of his genius brought down, Samson-like, the pillars of Galen and Aristotle, and with their fall the house of arbitrary notions collapsed. We shall probably never fully appreciate the part played by the Rosicrucian's in the reconstruction periods of European thought. The Rosicrucian's constitute the most remarkable organization of the modern world. During the seventeenth century their name was upon every man's lips, but none knew who or what they were. In their manifestoes, published between 1610 and 1620, the Rosicrucian's declare that their purpose was to promulgate the secret teachings which they had received from their illustrious founder, Father C. R. C. (Christian Rose-Cross), and to heal the sick without pay. They were deeply concerned with alchemy and astrology, and their ranks included several great Kabbalists and transcendental magicians.

Elias Ashmole, one of the Order, declares that two Rosicrucian physicians cured Queen Elizabeth of smallpox, and a young duke of leprosy. There are also records that the Rosicrucian chemists manufactured gold and furnished it to the British mint. Raymond Lully, (probably a member of the fraternity) is said to have transmuted thousands of pounds of base metals into gold in the Tower of London. Lully did this in order that the English might finance a crusade against the Mohammedans.

After describing the purposes of their organization, the Rosicrucian's in their first manifestoes recount the adventures of their leader and how he came to establish the society. The story is briefly as follows: Father C. R. C. was the son of poor but noble parents, and was placed in a cloister when but five years of age; but several years later finding the instructions unsatisfactory he associated himself with a monk who was about to start on a pilgrimage for the Holy Land. This brother died at Cyprus, and C. R. C. continued alone to Damascus.

Here poor health detained him, and he remained some time studying with the physicians and astrologers. Hearing by chance of a group of wise men abiding in Damcar, a mysterious city in Arabia, C. R. C. made arrangements to visit them, and arrived in Damcar in the sixteenth year of his life. Here he was received by the wise men as one long expected, and remained with them for a considerable time, during which he learned the Arabian tongue, and translated the mysterious book "M" into Latin. From Damcar C. R. C. journeyed to Fez, where he was instructed concerning the creatures existing in the elements. From Fez the young Initiate took boat to Spain, carrying with him many rare medicines, curious animals, and wonderful books. He conferred with the learned at Madrid, but they dared not accept his teaching because it would reveal their previous ignorance; so, deeply discouraged, he went to Germany, where he built himself a house on the brow of a little hill and devoted his life to study and experimentation.

After a silence of five years C. R. C. gathered about him a few faithful friends, and they began to arrange and classify the great knowledge which he possessed. Thus, the Rosicrucian Fraternity was founded. New members were later accepted, and the brethren traveled into various parts of the world to give their knowledge to those who were worthy and willing to receive such a boon. The first of the Order to die passed out in England, and it was after this that Father C. R. C. prepared his own tomb in perfect Miniature reproduction of the universe. None of the Order knew when their founder passed on, but 120 years after his death they discovered his tomb with an ever-burning lamp suspended from the ceiling. The room had seven sides, and in the center of it was a circular stone under which they found the body of their founder in perfect condition, clasping in one hand a mysterious paper containing the arcana of the Order.

Many efforts have been made to interpret the symbolism of this allegory, for it is undoubtedly a myth symbolically setting forth the deepest secrets of the Rosicrucian's. Father C. R. C. is to be considered not only as a personality but also as the personification of a power or principle in Nature. This practice of using an individual to set forth the workings of divine power was frequently resorted to by the ancients. The Masonic legend of Hiram Abiff, the Chaldean myth of Ishtar, the Greek allegory of Bacchus, and the Egyptian account of Osiris are all examples of this type of symbolism. It is not improbable that the entire mystery of Rosicrucianism could be cleared up if the story of Father C. R. C. were properly interpreted.

During the sixteenth century many pseudo-organizations sprang up claiming to represent the Rosicrucian Brotherhood, but the very nature of the teachings they promulgated proved beyond all doubt that they were fraudulent. One of these groups after exacting the most terrible oaths from those joining the society gave each one of the new members a black rope with which he was supposed to strangle himself if he broke any of the laws of the order.

The pseudo-Rosicrucian's were short-lived; for, after passing through all the degrees of the elaborate rituals and spending considerable sums of money, the unfortunate "initiates" discovered that these organizations did not possess the knowledge they claimed to disseminate. Many false claims were made by charlatans who attempted to capitalize the name of Rosicrucianism, but in some mysterious way these dishonest parties were exposed and their plans came to naught.

Several years ago, Arthur Edward Waite, an English Masonic writer of note, published a work in two volumes entitled, The Secret Tradition in Freemasonry. Among a large number of plates, he reproduced was one he declared to be the supposed portrait of Father C. R. C. We examined the reproduction with great interest but with a certain amount of skepticism, in view of the vast number of false claims and documents that have appeared in recent years. We had a feeling that somewhere we had seen that picture before, and the general appearance of it made us suspect that it was a copy of a more ancient painting.

At last, after considerable pains, we discovered what we believe to be the original of the picture. In the Lisbon Museum there is a famous painting by Albert Durer. The resemblance to Waite's picture is very marked. The position of the head, the linger touching the temple of the skull, the hat, the reading table, the beard, and the folds of the cloak are all nearly identical. The reader may say that Durer copied the painting from the supposed portrait of Father C. R. C., but this is most unlikely, as Durer was a truly great artist and great artists seldom copy the paintings of other men. Furthermore, the Durer painting was made about A.D. 1500 and is apparently much older than the other picture. The Durer painting is an idealistic conception of St. Jerome, and Durer has in several other pictures shown this saint with the same reading table, and a skull is always placed near him.

In the Harding collection in Chicago is also a portrait of St. Jerome by the Master of the Life of the Virgin, which resembles the C. R. C. picture even more closely. The only natural presumption is that the picture supposed to be that of Father C. R. C. is in reality a copy of St. Jerome and not an overly good copy at that. Mr. Waite was careful to make no committal regarding the authenticity of the painting, but others more enthusiastic have accepted the picture as real. This is an occurrence which should deter any person not acquainted with the real issues of Rosicrucianism from accepting the wholesale accounts now circulated concerning the historicity of the Order.

The bona-fide Rosicrucian's are an organization of Initiates and Adepts, and only through development of the internal spiritual faculties can the true purpose of the Order be recognized. Only when the disciple lives the Rosicrucian life can he know that sublime Fraternity whose members—so the ancients declare—inhabit the suburbs of heaven.

DVOS CAPVTIS MELIOR QUAM VNVS EST

HOW IS KNOWLEDGE OF THE HIGHER WORLDS ATTAINED?

By RUDOLF STEINER – 1861-1925

Conditions

THERE slumber in every human being faculties by means of which he can acquire for himself a knowledge of higher worlds. Mystics, Gnostics, Theosophists—all speak of a world of soul and spirit which for them is just as real as the world we see with our physical eyes and touch with our physical hands. At every moment the listener may say to himself: that, of which they speak, I too can learn, if I develop within myself certain powers which today still slumber within me. There remains only one question—how to set to work to develop such faculties. For this purpose, they only can give advice who already possess such powers.

As long as the human race has existed there has always been a method of training, in the course of which individuals possessing these higher faculties gave instruction to others who were in search of them. Such training is called occult (esoteric) training, and the instruction received therefrom is called occult (esoteric) teaching, or spiritual science.

This designation naturally awakens misunderstanding. The one who hears it may very easily be misled into the belief that this training is the concern of a special, privileged class, withholding its knowledge arbitrarily from its fellow-creatures. He may even think that nothing of real importance lies behind such knowledge, for if it were a true knowledge—he is tempted to think—there would be no need of making a secret of it; it might be publicly imparted and its advantages made accessible to all.

Those who have been initiated into the nature of this higher knowledge are not in the least surprised that the uninitiated should so think, for the secret of initiation can only be understood by those who have to a certain degree experienced this initiation into the higher knowledge of existence. The question may be raised: how, then, under these circumstances, are the uninitiated to develop any human interest in this so-called esoteric knowledge?

How and why are they to seek for something of whose nature they can form no idea? Such a question is based upon an entirely erroneous conception of the real nature of esoteric knowledge. There is, in truth, no difference between esoteric knowledge and all the rest of man's knowledge and proficiency. This esoteric knowledge is no more of a secret for the average human being than writing is a secret for those who have never learned it. And just as all can learn to write who choose the correct method, so, too, can all who seek the right way become esoteric students and even teachers.

In one respect only do the conditions here differ from those that apply to external knowledge and proficiency. The possibility of acquiring the art of writing may be withheld from someone through poverty, or through the conditions of civilization into which he is born; but for the attainment of knowledge and proficiency in the higher worlds, there is no obstacle for those who earnestly seek them.

Many believe that they must seek, at one place or another, the masters of higher knowledge in order to receive enlightenment. Now in the first place, whoever strives earnestly after higher knowledge will shun no exertion and fear no obstacle in his search for an initiate who can lead him to the higher knowledge of the world. On the other hand, everyone may be certain that initiation will find him under all circumstances if he gives proof of an earnest and worthy endeavor to attain this knowledge. It is a natural law among all initiates to withhold from no man the knowledge that is due him but there is an equally natural law which lays down that no word of esoteric knowledge shall be imparted to anyone not qualified to receive it. And the more strictly he observes these laws, the more perfect is an initiate.

The bond of union embracing all initiates is spiritual and not external, but the two laws here mentioned form, as it were, strong clasps by which the component parts of this bond are held together. You may live in intimate friendship with an initiate, and yet a gap severs you from his essential self, so long as you have not become an initiate yourself. You may enjoy in the fullest sense the heart, the love of an initiate, yet he will only confide his knowledge to you when you are ripe for it. You may flatter him; you may torture him; nothing can induce him to betray anything to you as long as you, at the present stage of your evolution, are not competent to receive it into your soul in the right way.

The methods by which a student is prepared for the reception of higher knowledge are minutely prescribed. The direction he is to take is traced with unfading, everlasting letters in the worlds of the spirit where the initiates guard the higher secrets. In ancient times, anterior to our history, the temples of the spirit were also outwardly visible; today, because our life has become so unspiritual, they are not to be found in the world visible to external sight; yet they are present spiritually everywhere, and all who seek may find them. Only within his own soul can a man find the means to unseal the lips of an initiate. He must develop within himself certain faculties to a definite degree, and then the highest treasures of the spirit can become his own.

He must begin with a certain fundamental attitude of soul. In spiritual science this fundamental attitude is called the path of veneration, of devotion to truth and knowledge. Without this attitude no one can become a student. The disposition shown in their childhood by subsequent students of higher knowledge is well known to the experienced in these matters. There are children who look up with religious awe to those whom they venerate. For such people they have a respect which forbids them, even in the deepest recess of their heart, to harbor any thought of criticism or opposition. Such children grow up into young men and women who feel happy when they are able to look up to anything that fills them with veneration. From the ranks of such children are recruited many students of higher knowledge.

Have you ever paused outside the door of some venerated person, and have you, on this your first visit, felt a religious awe as you pressed on the handle to enter the room which for you is a holy place? If so, a feeling has been manifested within you which may be the germ of your future adherence to the path of knowledge. It is a blessing for every human being in process of development to have such feelings upon which to build. Only it must not be thought that this disposition leads to submissiveness and slavery. What was once a childlike veneration for persons becomes, later, a veneration for truth and knowledge. Experience teaches that they can best hold their heads erect who have learnt to venerate where veneration is due; and veneration is always fitting when it flows from the depths of the heart.

If we do not develop within ourselves this deeply rooted feeling that there is something higher than ourselves, we shall never find the strength to evolve to something higher. The initiate has only acquired the strength to lift his head to the heights of knowledge by guiding his heart to the depths of veneration and devotion. The heights of the spirit can only be climbed by passing through the portals of humility. You can only acquire right knowledge when you have learnt to esteem it. Man has certainly the right to turn his eyes to the light, but he must first acquire this right. There are laws in the spiritual life, as in the physical life. Rub a glass rod with an appropriate material and it will become electric, that is, it will receive the power of attracting small bodies. This is in keeping with a law of nature. It is known to all who have learnt a little physics. Similarly, acquaintance with the first principles of spiritual science shows that every feeling of true devotion harbored in the soul develops a power which may, sooner or later, lead further on the path of knowledge.

The student who is gifted with this feeling, or who is fortunate enough to have had it inculcated in a suitable education, brings a great deal along with him when, later in life, he seeks admittance to higher knowledge. Failing such preparation, he will encounter difficulties at the very first step, unless he undertakes, by rigorous self-education, to create within himself this inner life of devotion. In our time it is especially important that full attention be paid to this point. Our civilization tends more toward critical judgment and condemnation than toward devotion and selfless veneration.

Our children already criticize far more than they worship. But every criticism, every adverse judgment passed, disperses the powers of the soul for the attainment of higher knowledge in the same measure that all veneration and reverence develops them. In this we do not wish to say anything against our civilization. There is no question here of leveling criticism against it. To this critical faculty, this self-conscious human judgment, this "test all things and hold fast what is best," we owe the greatness of our civilization. Man could never have attained to the science, the industry, the commerce, the rights relationships of our time, had he not applied to all things the standard of his critical judgment. But what we have thereby gained in external culture we have had to pay for with a corresponding loss of higher knowledge of spiritual life. It must be emphasized that higher knowledge is not concerned with the veneration of persons but the veneration of truth and knowledge.

Now, the one thing that everyone must acknowledge is the difficulty for those involved in the external civilization of our time to advance to the knowledge of the higher worlds. They can only do so if they work energetically at themselves. At a time when the conditions of material life were simpler, the attainment of spiritual knowledge was also easier. Objects of veneration and worship stood out in clearer relief from the ordinary things of the world. In an epoch of criticism ideals are lowered; other feelings take the place of veneration, respect, adoration, and wonder.

Our own age thrusts these feelings further and further into the background, so that they can only be conveyed to man through his every-day life in a very small degree. Whoever seeks higher knowledge must create it for himself. He must instill it into his soul. It cannot be done by study; it can only be done through life. Whoever, therefore, wishes to become a student of higher knowledge must assiduously cultivate this inner life of devotion. Everywhere in his environment and his experiences he must seek motives of admiration and homage.

If I meet a man and blame him for his shortcomings, I rob myself of power to attain higher knowledge; but if I try to enter lovingly into his merits, I gather such power. The student must continually be intent upon following this advice. The spiritually experienced know how much they owe to the circumstance that in face of all things they ever again turn to the good, and withhold adverse judgment. But this must not remain an external rule of life; rather it must take possession of our innermost soul. Man has it in his power to perfect himself and, in time, completely to transform himself. But this transformation must take place in his innermost self, in his thought-life.

It is not enough that I show respect only in my outward bearing; I must have this respect in my thoughts. The student must begin by absorbing this devotion into this thought-life. He must be wary of thoughts of disrespect, of adverse criticism, existing in his consciousness, and he must endeavor straightaway to cultivate thoughts of devotion.

Every moment that we set ourselves to discover in our consciousness whatever there remains in it of adverse, disparaging and critical judgement of the world and of life; every such moment brings us nearer to higher knowledge. And we rise rapidly when we fill our consciousness in such moments with thoughts evoking in us admiration, respect and veneration for the world and for life. It is well known to those experienced in these matters that in every such moment powers are awakened which otherwise remain dormant. In this way the spiritual eyes of man are opened. He begins to see things around him which he could not have seen before. He begins to understand that hitherto he had only seen a part of the world around him.

A human being standing before him now presents a new and different aspect. Of course, this rule of life alone will not yet enable him to see, for instance, what is described as the human aura, because for this still higher training is necessary. But he can rise to this higher training if he has previously undergone a rigorous training in devotion. (In the last chapter of his book Theosophy, the author describes fully the Path of Knowledge; here it is intended to give some practical details.)

Noiseless and unnoticed by the outer world is the treading of the Path of Knowledge. No change need be noticed in the student. He performs his duties as hitherto; he attends to his business as before. The transformation goes on only in the inner part of the soul hidden from outward sight. At first his entire inner life is flooded by this basic feeling of devotion for everything which is truly venerable. His entire soul-life finds in this fundamental feeling its pivot. Just as the sun's rays vivify everything living, so does reverence in the student vivify all feelings of the soul.

It is not easy, at first, to believe that feelings like reverence and respect have anything to do with cognition. This is due to the fact that we are inclined to set cognition aside as a faculty by itself—one that stands in no relation to what otherwise occurs in the soul. In so thinking we do not bear in mind that it is the soul which exercises the faculty of cognition; and feelings are for the soul what food is for the body.

If we give the body stones in place of bread, its activity will cease. It is the same with the soul. Veneration, homage, devotion are like nutriment making it healthy and strong, especially strong for the activity of cognition. Disrespect, antipathy, underestimation of what deserves recognition, all exert a paralyzing and withering effect on this faculty of cognition. For the spiritually experienced this fact is visible in the aura. A soul which harbors feelings of reverence and devotion produces a change in its aura. Certain spiritual colorings, as they may be called, yellow-red and brown-red in tone, vanish and are replaced by blue-red tints. Thereby the cognitional faculty is ripened; it receives intelligence of facts in its environment of which it had hitherto no idea. Reverence awakens in the soul a sympathetic power through which we attract qualities in the beings around us, which would otherwise remain concealed.

The power obtained through devotion can be rendered still more effective when the life of feeling is enriched by yet another quality. This consists in giving oneself up less and less to impressions of the outer world, and to develop instead a vivid inner life. A person who darts from one impression of the outer world to another, who constantly seeks distraction, cannot find the way to higher knowledge. The student must not blunt himself to the outer world, but while lending himself to its impressions, he should be directed by his rich inner life. When passing through a beautiful mountain district, the traveler with depth of soul and wealth of feeling has different experiences from one who is poor in feeling. Only what we experience within ourselves unlocks for us the beauties of the outer world.

One person sails across the ocean, and only a few inward experiences pass through his soul; another will hear the eternal language of the cosmic spirit; for him are unveiled the mysterious riddles of existence. We must learn to remain in touch with our own feelings and ideas if we wish to develop any intimate relationship with the outer world. The outer world with all its phenomena is filled with splendor, but we must have experienced the divine within ourselves before we can hope to discover it in our environment.

The student is told to set apart moments in his daily life in which to withdraw into himself, quietly and alone. He is not to occupy himself at such moments with the affairs of his own ego. This would result in the contrary of what is intended. He should rather let his experiences and the messages from the outer world re-echo within his own completely silent self. At such silent moments every flower, every animal, every action will unveil to him secrets undreamt of.

And thus, he will prepare himself to receive quite new impressions of the outer world through quite different eyes.

The desire to enjoy impression after impression merely blunts the faculty of cognition; the latter, however, is nurtured and cultivated if the enjoyment once experienced is allowed to reveal its message. Thus, the student must accustom himself not merely to let the enjoyment reverberate, as it were, but rather to renounce any further enjoyment, and work upon the past experience. The peril here is very great. Instead of working inwardly, it is very easy to fall into the opposite habit of trying to exploit the enjoyment. Let no one underestimate the fact that immense sources of error here confront the student. He must pass through a host of tempters of his soul. They would all harden his ego and imprison it within itself. He should rather open it wide to all the world. It is necessary that he should seek enjoyment, for only through enjoyment can the outer world reach him. If he blunts himself to enjoyment, he is like a plant which cannot any longer draw nourishment from its environment.

Yet if he stops short at the enjoyment, he shuts himself up within himself. He will only be something to himself and nothing to the world. However much he may live within himself, however intensely he may cultivate his ego—the world will reject him. To the world he is dead. The student of higher knowledge considers enjoyment only as a means of ennobling himself for the world. Enjoyment is to him like a scout informing him about the world; but once instructed, by enjoyment, he passes on to work. He does not learn in order to accumulate learning as his own treasure, but in order that he may devote his learning to the service of the world.

In all spiritual science there is a fundamental principle which cannot be transgressed without sacrificing success, and it should be impressed on the student in every form of esoteric training. It runs as follows: All knowledge pursued merely for the enrichment of personal learning and the accumulation of personal treasure leads you away from the path; but all knowledge pursued for growth to ripeness within the process of human ennoblement and cosmic development brings you a step forward. This law must be strictly observed, and no student is genuine until he has adopted it as a guide for his whole life. This truth can be expressed in the following short sentence: Every idea which does not become your ideal slays a force in your soul; every idea which becomes your ideal creates within you, life-forces.

Inner Tranquility

At the very beginning of his course, the student is directed to the path of veneration and the development of the inner life. Spiritual science now also gives him practical rules by observing which he may tread that path and develop that inner life. These practical rules have no arbitrary origin. They rest upon ancient experience and ancient wisdom, and are given out in the same manner, wheresoever the ways to higher knowledge are indicated. All true teachers of the spiritual life are in agreement as to the substance of these rules, even though they do not always clothe them in the same words. This difference, which is of a minor character and is more apparent than real, is due to circumstances which need not be dwelt upon here.

No teacher of the spiritual life wishes to establish a mastery over other persons by means of such rules. He would not tamper with anyone's independence. Indeed, none respect and cherish human independence more than the spiritually experienced. It was stated in the preceding pages that the bond of union embracing all initiates is spiritual, and that two laws form, as it were, clasps by which the component parts of this bond are held together. Whenever the initiate leaves his enclosed spiritual sphere and steps forth before the world, he must immediately take a third law into account.

It is this: Adapt each one of your actions, and frame each one of your words in such a way that you infringe upon no one's free-will. The recognition that all true teachers of the spiritual life are permeated through and through with this principle will convince all who follow the practical rules proffered to them that they need sacrifice none of their independence. One of the first of these rules can be expressed somewhat in the following words of our language: Provide for yourself moments of inner tranquility, and in these moments learn to distinguish between the essential and the non-essential. It is said advisedly: "expressed in the words of our language." Originally all rules and teachings of spiritual science were expressed in a symbolical sign-language, some understanding of which must be acquired before its whole meaning and scope can be realized. This understanding is dependent on the first steps toward higher knowledge, and these steps result from the exact observation of such rules as are here given. For all who earnestly will, the path stands open to tread.

Simple, in truth, is the above rule concerning moments of inner tranquility; equally simple is its observation. But it only achieves its purpose when it is observed in as earnest and strict a manner as it is, in itself, simple. How this rule is to be observed will, therefore, be explained without digression. The student must set aside a small part of his daily life in which to concern himself with something quite different from the objects of his daily occupation. The way, also, in which he occupies himself at such a time must differ entirely from the way in which he performs the rest of his daily duties. But this does not mean that what he does in the time thus set apart has no connection with his daily work. On the contrary, he will soon find that just these secluded moments, when sought in the right way, give him full power to perform his daily task. Nor must it be supposed that the observance of this rule will really encroach upon the time needed for the performance of his duties. Should anyone really have no more time at his disposal, five minutes a day will suffice. It all depends on the manner in which these five minutes are spent.

During these periods the student should wrest himself entirely free from his work-a-day life. His thoughts and feelings should take on a different coloring. His joys and sorrows, his cares, experiences and actions must pass in review before his soul; and he must adopt such a position that he may regard all his sundry experiences from a higher point of view. We need only bear in mind how, in ordinary life, we regard the experiences and actions of others quite differently from our own.

This cannot be otherwise, for we are interwoven with our own actions and experiences, whereas those of others we only contemplate. Our aim in these moments of seclusion must be so to contemplate and judge our own actions and experiences as though they applied not to ourselves but to some other person. Suppose, for example, a heavy misfortune befalls us. How different would be our attitude toward a similar misfortune had it befallen our neighbor. This attitude cannot be blamed as unjustifiable; it is part of human nature, and applies equally to exceptional circumstances and to the daily affairs of life.

The student must seek the power of confronting himself, at certain times, as a stranger. He must stand before himself with the inner tranquility of a judge. When this is attained, our own experiences present themselves in a new light. As long as we are interwoven with them and stand, as it were, within them, we cling to the non-essential just as much as to the essential. If we attain the calm inner survey, the essential is severed from the non-essential. Sorrow and joy, every thought, every resolve, appear different when we confront ourselves in this way. It is as though we had spent the whole day in a place where we beheld the smallest objects at the same close range as the largest, and in the evening climbed a neighboring hill and surveyed the whole scene at a glance. Then the various parts appear related to each other in different proportions from those they bore when seen from within.

This exercise will not and need not succeed with present occurrences of destiny, but it should be attempted by the student in connection with the events of destiny already experienced in the past. The value of such inner tranquil self-contemplation depends far less on what is actually contemplated than on our finding within ourselves the power which such inner tranquility develops.

For every human being bears a higher man within himself besides what we may call the work-a-day man. This higher man remains hidden until he is awakened. And each human being can himself alone awaken this higher being within himself. As long as this higher being is not awakened, the higher faculties slumbering in every human being, and leading to supersensible knowledge, will remain concealed. The student must resolve to persevere in the strict and earnest observation of the rule here given, so long as he does not feel within himself the fruits of this inner tranquility. To all who thus persevere the day will come when spiritual light will envelop them, and a new world will be revealed to an organ of sight of whose presence within them they were never aware.

And no change need take place in the outward life of the student in consequence of this new rule. He performs his duties and, at first, feels the same joys, sorrows, and experiences as before. In no way can it estrange him from life; he can rather devote himself the more thoroughly to this life for the remainder of the day, having gained a higher life in the moments set apart. Little by little this higher life will make its influence felt on his ordinary life. The tranquility of the moments set apart will also affect everyday existence. In his whole being he will grow calmer; he will attain firm assurance in all his actions, and cease to be put out of countenance by all manner of incidents. By thus advancing he will gradually become more and more his own guide, and allow himself less and less to be led by circumstances and external influences. He will soon discover how great a source of strength is available to him in these moments thus set apart. He will begin no longer to get angry at things which formerly annoyed him; countless things he formerly feared cease to alarm him. He acquires a new outlook on life.

Formerly he may have approached some occupation in a fainthearted way. He would say: "Oh, I lack the power to do this as well as I could wish." Now this thought does not occur to him, but rather a quite different thought. Henceforth he says to himself: "I will summon all my strength to do my work as well as I possibly can." And he suppresses the thought which makes him fainthearted; for he knows that this very thought might be the cause of a worse performance on his part, and that in any case it cannot contribute to the improvement of his work. And thus, thought after thought, each fraught with advantage to his whole life, flows into the student's outlook. They take the place of those that had a hampering, weakening effect. He begins to steer his own ship on a secure course through the waves of life, whereas it was formerly battered to and fro by these waves.

This calm and serenity react on the whole being. They assist the growth of the inner man, and, with the inner man, those faculties also grow which lead to higher knowledge. For it is by his progress in this direction that the student gradually reaches the point where he himself determines the manner in which the impressions of the outer world shall affect him. Thus, he may hear a word spoken with the object of wounding or vexing him. Formerly it would indeed have wounded or vexed him, but now that he treads the path to higher knowledge, he is able—before the word has found its way to his inner self—to take from it the sting which gives it the power to wound or vex. Take another example. We easily become impatient when we are kept waiting, but—if we tread the path to higher knowledge—we so steep ourselves in our moments of calm with the feeling of the uselessness of impatience that henceforth, on every occasion of impatience, this feeling is immediately present within us. The impatience that was about to make itself felt vanishes, and an interval which would otherwise have been wasted in expressions of impatience will be filled by useful observations, which can be made while waiting.

Now, the scope and significance of these facts must be realized. We must bear in mind that the higher man within us is in constant development. But only the state of calm and serenity here described renders an orderly development possible. The waves of outward life constrain the inner man from all sides if, instead of mastering this outward life, it masters him. Such a man is like a plant which tries to expand in a cleft in the rock and is stunted in growth until new space is given it. No outward forces can supply space to the inner man. It can only be supplied by the inner calm which man himself gives to his soul. Outward circumstances can only alter the course of his outward life; they can never awaken the inner spiritual man. The student must himself give birth to a new and higher man within himself.

This higher man now becomes the inner ruler who directs the circumstances of the outer man with sure guidance. As long as the outer man has the upper hand and control, this inner man is his slave and therefore cannot unfold his powers. If it depends on something other than myself whether I should get angry or not, I am not master of myself, or, to put it better, I have not yet found the ruler within myself. I must develop the faculty of letting the impressions of the outer world approach me only in the way in which I myself determine; then only do I become in the real sense a student. And only in as far as the student earnestly seeks this power can he reach the goal. It is of no importance how far anyone can go in a given time; the point is that he should earnestly seek. Many have striven for years without noticing any appreciable progress; but many of those who did not despair, but remained unshaken, have then quite suddenly achieved the inner victory.

No doubt a great effort is required in many stations of life to provide these moments of inner calm; but the greater the effort needed, the more important is the achievement. In spiritual science everything depends upon energy, inward truthfulness, and uncompromising sincerity with which we confront our own selves, with all our deeds and actions, as a complete stranger.

But only one side of the student's inner activity is characterized by this birth of his own higher being. Something else is needed in addition. Even if he confronts himself as a stranger, it is only himself that he contemplates; he looks on those experiences and actions with which he is connected through his particular station of life. He must now disengage himself from it and rise beyond to a purely human level, which no longer has anything to do with his own special situation. He must pass on to the contemplation of those things which would concern him as a human being, even if he lived under quite different circumstances and in quite a different situation. In this way something begins to live within him which ranges above the purely personal. His gaze is directed to worlds higher than those with which every-day life connects him. And thus, he begins to feel and realize, as an inner experience, that he belongs to those higher worlds.

These are worlds concerning which his senses and his daily occupation can tell him nothing. Thus, he now shifts the central point of his being to the inner part of his nature. He listens to the voices within him which speak to him in his moments of tranquility; he cultivates an intercourse with the spiritual world. He is removed from the every-day world. Its noise is silenced. All around him there is silence. He puts away everything that reminds him of such impressions from without.

Calm inward contemplation and converse with the purely spiritual world fill his soul. Such tranquil contemplation must become a natural necessity in the life of the student. He is now plunged in a world of thought. He must develop a living feeling for this silent thought-activity. He must learn to love what the spirit pours into him. He will soon cease to feel that this thought-world is less real than the every-day things which surround him.

He begins to deal with his thoughts as with things in space, and the moment approaches when he begins to feel that which reveals itself in the silent inward thought-work to be much higher, much more real, than the things in space. He discovers that something living expresses itself in this thought-world. He sees that his thoughts do not merely harbor shadow-pictures, but that through them hidden beings speak to him. Out of the silence, speech becomes audible to him. Formerly sound only reached him through his ear; now it resounds through his soul. An inner language, an inner word is revealed to him. This moment, when first experienced, is one of greatest rapture for the student. An inner light is shed over the whole external world, and a second life begins for him. Through his being there pours a divine stream from a world of divine rapture.

This life of the soul in thought, which gradually widens into a life in spiritual being, is called by Gnosis, and by Spiritual Science, Meditation (contemplative reflection). This meditation is the means to supersensible knowledge. But the student in such moments must not merely indulge in feelings; he must not have indefinite sensations in his soul. That would only hinder him from reaching true spiritual knowledge. His thoughts must be clear, sharp and definite, and he will be helped in this if he does not cling blindly to the thoughts that rise within him. Rather must he permeate himself with the lofty thoughts by which men already advanced and possessed of the spirit were inspired at such moments.

He should start with the writings which themselves had their origin in just such revelation during meditation. In the mystic, gnostic and spiritual scientific literature of today the student will find such writings, and in them the material for his meditation. The seekers of the spirit have themselves set down in such writings the thoughts of the divine science which the Spirit has directed his messengers to proclaim to the world.

Through such meditation a complete transformation takes place in the student. He begins to form quite new conceptions of reality. All things acquire a fresh value for him. It cannot be repeated too often that this transformation does not alienate him from the world. He will in no way be estranged from his daily tasks and duties, for he comes to realize that the most insignificant action he has to accomplish, the most insignificant experience which offers itself to him, stands in connection with cosmic beings and cosmic events. When once this connection is revealed to him in his moments of contemplation, he comes to his daily activities with a new, fuller power. For now, he knows that his labor and his suffering are given and endured for the sake of a great, spiritual, cosmic whole. Not weariness, but strength to live springs from meditation.

With firm step the student passes through life. No matter what it may bring him, he goes forward erect. In the past he knew not why he labored and suffered, but now he knows. It is obvious that such meditation leads more surely to the goal if conducted under the direction of experienced persons who know of themselves how everything may best be done; and their advice and guidance should be sought. Truly, no one loses his freedom thereby.

What would otherwise be mere uncertain groping in the dark becomes under this direction purposeful work. All who apply to those possessing knowledge and experience in these matters will never apply in vain, only they must realize that what they seek is the advice of a friend, not the domination of a would-be ruler. It will always be found that they who really know are the most modest of men, and that nothing is further from their nature than what is called the lust for power.

When, by means of meditation, a man rises to union with the spirit, he brings to life the eternal in him, which is limited by neither birth nor death. The existence of this eternal being can only be doubted by those who have not themselves experienced it. Thus, meditation is the way which also leads man to the knowledge, to the contemplation of his eternal, indestructible, essential being; and it is only through meditation that man can attain to such knowledge.

Gnosis and Spiritual Science tell of the eternal nature of this being and of its reincarnation. The question is often asked: Why does a man know nothing of his experiences beyond the borders of life and death? Not thus should we ask, but rather: How can we attain such knowledge? In right meditation the path is opened. This alone can revive the memory of experiences beyond the border of life and death.

Everyone can attain this knowledge; in each one of us lies the faculty of recognizing and contemplating for ourselves what genuine Mysticism, Spiritual Science, Anthroposophy, and Gnosis teach. Only the right means must be chosen. Only a being with ears and eyes can apprehend sounds and colors; nor can the eye perceive if the light which makes things visible is wanting. Spiritual Science gives the means of developing the spiritual ears and eyes, and of kindling the spiritual light; and this method of spiritual training: (1) Preparation; this develops the spiritual senses. (2) Enlightenment; this kindles the spiritual light. (3) Initiation; this establishes intercourse with the higher spiritual beings.

THE STAGES OF INITIATION

THE information given in the following chapters constitutes steps in an esoteric training, the name and character of which will be understood by all who apply this information in the right way. It refers to the three stages through which the training of the spiritual life leads to a certain degree of initiation. But only so much will here be explained as can be publicly imparted. These are merely indications extracted from a still deeper and more intimate doctrine. In esoteric training itself a quite definite course of instruction is followed.

Certain exercises enable the soul to attain to a conscious intercourse with the spiritual world. These exercises bear about the same relation to what will be imparted in the following pages, as the instruction given in a higher strictly disciplined school bears to the incidental training. But impatient dabbling, devoid of earnest perseverance, can lead to nothing at all. The study of Spiritual Science can only be successful if the student retains what has already been indicated in the preceding chapter, and on the basis of this proceed further.

The three stages which the above-mentioned tradition specifies, are as follows: (1) preparation; (2) enlightenment; (3) initiation. It is not altogether necessary that the first of these three stages should be completed before the second can be begun, nor that the second, in turn, be completed before the third be started. In certain respects, it is possible to partake of enlightenment, and even of initiation, and in other respects still be in the preparatory stage. Yet it will be necessary to spend a certain time in the stage of preparation before any enlightenment can begin; and, at least in some respects, enlightenment must be completed before it is even possible to enter upon the stage of initiation. But in describing them it is necessary, for the sake of clarity, that the three stages be made to follow in order.

Preparation

Preparation consists in a strict and definite cultivation of the life of thought and feeling, through which the psycho-spiritual body becomes equipped with higher senses and organs of activity in the same way that natural forces have fitted the physical body with organs built out of indeterminate living matter. To begin with, the attention of the soul is directed to certain events in the world that surrounds us. Such events are, on the one hand, life that is budding, growing, and flourishing, and on the other hand, all phenomena connected with fading, decaying, and withering. The student can observe these events simultaneously, wherever he turns his eyes and, on every occasion, they naturally evoke in him feelings and thoughts; but in ordinary circumstances he does not devote himself sufficiently to them. He hurries on too quickly from impression to impression.

It is necessary, therefore, that he should fix his attention intently and consciously upon these phenomena. Wherever he observes a definite kind of blooming and flourishing, he must banish everything else from his soul, and entirely surrender himself, for a short time, to this one impression. He will soon convince himself that a feeling which heretofore in a similar case, would merely have flitted through his soul, now swells out and assumes a powerful and energetic form. He must now allow this feeling to reverberate quietly within himself while keeping inwardly quite still. He must cut himself off from the outer world, and simply and solely follow what his soul tells him of this blossoming and flourishing.

Yet it must not be thought that much progress can be made if the senses are blunted to the world. First look at the things as keenly and as intently as you possibly can; then only let the feeling which expands to life, and the thought which arises in the soul, take possession of you. The point is that the attention should be directed with perfect inner balance upon both phenomena. If the necessary tranquility be attained and you surrender yourself to the feeling which expands to life in the soul, then, in due time, the following experience will ensue. Thoughts and feelings of a new kind and unknown before will be noticed uprising in the soul. Indeed, the more often the attention be fixed alternately upon something growing, blossoming and flourishing, and upon something else that is fading and decaying, the more vivid will these feelings become.

And just as the eyes and ears of the physical body are built by natural forces out of living matter, so will the organs of clairvoyance build themselves out of the feelings and thoughts thus evoked.

A quite definite form of feeling is connected with growth and expansion, and another equally definite with all that is fading and decaying. But this is only the case if the effort be made to cultivate these feelings in the way indicated. It is possible to describe approximately what these feelings are like. A full conception of them is within the reach of all who undergo these inner experiences.

If the attention be frequently fixed on the phenomena of growing, blooming and flourishing, a feeling remotely allied to the sensation of a sunrise will ensue, while the phenomena of fading and decaying will produce an experience comparable, in the same way, to the slow rising of the moon on the horizon. Both these feelings are forces which, when duly cultivated and developed to ever increasing intensity, lead to the most significant spiritual results. A new world is opened to the student if he systematically and deliberately surrenders himself to such feelings. The soul-world, the so-called astral plane, begins to dawn upon him. Growth and decay are no longer facts which make indefinite impressions on him as of old, but rather they form themselves into spiritual lines and figures of which he had previously suspected nothing. And these lines and figures have, for the different phenomena, different forms.

A blooming flower, an animal in the process of growth, a tree that is decaying, evoke in his soul different lines. The soul world (astral plane) broadens out slowly before him. These lines and figures are in no sense arbitrary. Two students who have reached the corresponding stage of development will always see the same lines and figures under the same conditions. Just as a round table will be seen as round by two normal persons, and not as round by one and square by the other, so too, at the sight of a flower, the same spiritual figure is presented to the soul. And just as the forms of animals and plants are described in ordinary natural history, so too, the spiritual scientist describes or draws the spiritual forms of the process of growth and decay, according to species and kind.

If the student has progressed so far that he can perceive the spiritual forms of those phenomena which are physically visible to his external sight, he is then not far from the stage where he will behold things which have no physical existence, and which therefore remain entirely hidden (occult) from those who have not received suitable instruction and training. It should be emphasized that the student must never lose himself in speculations on the meaning of one thing or another. Such intellectualizing will only draw him away from the right road. He should look out on the world with keen, healthy senses and quickened power of observation, and then give himself up to the feeling that arises within him. He should not try to make out, through intellectual speculation, the meaning of things, but rather allow the things to disclose themselves. It should be remarked that artistic feeling, when coupled with a quiet introspective nature, forms the best preliminary condition for the development of spiritual faculties. This feeling pierces through the superficial aspect of things, and in so doing touches their secrets.

A further point of importance is what spiritual science calls orientation in the higher worlds. This is attained when the student is permeated, through and through, with the conscious realization that feelings and thoughts are just as much veritable realities as are tables and chairs in the world of the physical senses. In the soul and thought world, feelings and thoughts react upon each other just as do physical objects in the physical world. As long as the student is not vividly permeated with this consciousness, he will not believe that a wrong thought in his mind may have as devastating an effect upon other thoughts that spread life in the thought world as the effect wrought by a bullet fired at random upon the physical objects it hits. He will perhaps never allow himself to perform a physically visible action which he considers to be wrong, though he will not shrink from harboring wrong thoughts and feelings, for these appear harmless to the rest of the world. There can be no progress, however, on the path to higher knowledge unless we guard our thoughts and feelings in just the same way we guard out steps in the physical world. If we see a wall before us, we do not attempt to dash right through it, but turn aside. In other words, we guide ourselves by the laws of the physical world.

There are such laws, too, for the soul and thought world, only they cannot impose themselves on us from without. They must flow out of the life of the soul itself. This can be attained if we forbid ourselves to harbor wrong thoughts and feelings. All arbitrary flitting to and fro in thought, all accidental ebbing and flowing of emotion must be forbidden in the same way. In so doing we do not become deficient in feeling.

On the contrary, if we regulate our inner life in this way, we shall soon find ourselves becoming rich in feelings and creative with genuine imagination. In the place of petty emotionalism and capricious flights of thought, there appear significant emotions and thoughts that are fruitful. Feelings and thoughts of this kind lead the student to orientation in the spiritual world. He gains a right position in relation to the things of the spiritual world; a distinct and definite result comes into effect in his favor.

Just as he, as a physical man, finds his way among physical things, so, too, his path now leads him between growth and decay, which he has already come to know in the way described above. On the one hand, he follows all processes of growing and flourishing and, on the other, of withering and decaying in a way that is necessary for his own and the world's advancement.

The student has also to bestow a further care on the world of sound. He must discriminate between sounds that are produced by the so-called inert (lifeless) bodies, for instance, a bell, or a musical instrument, or a falling mass, and those which proceed from a living creature (an animal or a human being.) When a bell is struck, we hear the sound and connect a pleasant feeling with it; but when we hear the cry of an animal, we can, besides our own feeling, detect through it the manifestation of an inward experience of the animal, whether of pleasure or pain.

It is with the latter kind of sound that the student sets to work. He must concentrate his whole attention on the fact that the sound tells him of something that lies outside his own soul. He must immerse himself in this foreign thing. He must closely unite his own feeling with the pleasure or pain of which the sound tells him. He must get beyond the point of caring whether, for him, the sound is pleasant or unpleasant, agreeable or disagreeable, and his soul must be filled with whatever is occurring in the being from which the sound proceeds. Through such exercises, if systematically and deliberately performed, the student will develop within himself the faculty of intermingling, as it were, with the being from which the sound proceeds.

A person sensitive to music will find it easier than one who is unmusical to cultivate his inner life in this way; but no one should suppose that a mere sense for music can take the place of this inner activity. The student must learn to feel in this way in the face of the whole of nature. This implants a new faculty in his world of thought and feeling. Through her resounding tones, the whole of nature begins to whisper her secrets to the student. What was hitherto merely incomprehensible noise to his soul becomes by this means a coherent language of nature. And whereas hitherto he only heard sound from the so-called inanimate objects, he now is aware of a new language of the soul. Should he advance further in this inner culture, he will soon learn that he can hear what hitherto he did not even surmise. He begins to hear with the soul.

To this, one thing more must be added before the highest point in this region can be attained. Of very great importance for the development of the student is the way in which he listens to others when they speak. He must accustom himself to do this in such a way that, while listening, his inner self is absolutely silent. If someone expresses an opinion and another listens, assent or dissent will, generally speaking, stir in the inner self of the listener. Many people in such cases feel themselves impelled to an expression of their assent, or more especially, of their dissent. In the student, all such assent or dissent must be silenced. It is not imperative that he should suddenly alter his way of living by trying to attain at all times to this complete inner silence. He will have to begin by doing so in special cases, deliberately selected by himself. Then quite slowly and by degrees, this new way of listening will creep into his habits, as of itself. In spiritual research this is systematically practiced. The student feels it his duty to listen, by way of practice, at certain times to the most contradictory views and, at the same time, bring entirely to silence all assent, and more especially, all adverse criticism. The point is that in so doing, not only all purely intellectual judgment be silenced, but also all feelings of displeasure, denial, or even assent. The student must at all times be particularly watchful lest such feelings, even when not on the surface, should still lurk in the innermost recess of the soul. He must listen, for example, to the statements of people who are, in some respects, far beneath him, and yet while doing so suppress every feeling of greater knowledge or superiority.

It is useful for everyone to listen in this way to children, for even the wisest can learn incalculably much from children. The student can thus train himself to listen to the words of others quite selflessly, completely shutting down his own person and his opinions and way of feeling. When he practices listening without criticism, even when a completely contradictory opinion is advanced, when the most hopeless mistake is committed before him, he then learns, little by little, to blend himself with the being of another and become identified with it. Then he hears through the words into the soul of the other. Through continued exercise of this kind, sound becomes the right medium for the perception of soul and spirit.

Of course, it implies the very strictest self-discipline, but the latter leads to a high goal. When these exercises are practiced in connection with the other already given, dealing with the sounds of nature, the soul develops a new sense of hearing. She is now able to perceive manifestations from the spiritual world which do not find their expression in sounds perceptible to the physical ear. The perception of the "inner word" awakens. Gradually truths reveal themselves to the student from the spiritual world. He hears speech uttered to him in a spiritual way. Only to those who, by selfless listening, train themselves to be really receptive from within, in stillness, unmoved by personal opinion or feeling only to such can the higher beings speak of whom spiritual science tells. As long as one hurls any personal opinion or feeling against the speaker to whom one must listen, the beings of the spiritual world remain silent.

All higher truths are attained through such inwardly instilled speech, and what we hear from the lips of a true spiritual teacher has been experienced by him in this manner. But this does not mean that it is unimportant for us to acquaint ourselves with the writings of spiritual science before we can ourselves hear such inwardly instilled speech. On the contrary, the reading of such writings and the listening to the teachings of spiritual science are themselves means of attaining personal knowledge. Every sentence of spiritual science we hear is of a nature to direct the mind to the point which must be reached before the soul can experience real progress. To the practice of all that has here been indicated must be added the ardent study of what the spiritual researchers impart to the world. In all esoteric training such study belongs to the preparatory period, and all other methods will prove ineffective if due receptivity for the teachings of the spiritual researcher is lacking. For since these instructions are culled from the living inner word, from the living inwardly instilled speech, they are themselves gifted with spiritual life. They are not mere words; they are living powers. And while you follow the words of one who knows, while you read a book that springs from real inner experience, powers are at work in your soul which make you clairvoyant, just as natural forces have created out of living matter your eyes and your ears.

Enlightenment

Enlightenment proceeds from very simple processes. Here, too, it is a matter of developing certain feelings and thoughts which slumber in every human being and must be awakened. It is only when these simple processes are carried out with unfailing patience, continuously and conscientiously, that they can lead to the perception of the inner light-forms. The first step is taken by observing different natural objects in a particular way; for instance, a transparent and beautifully formed stone (a crystal), a plant, and an animal. The student should endeavor, at first, to direct his whole attention to a comparison of the stone with the animal in the following manner. The thoughts here mentioned should pass through his soul accompanied by vivid feelings, and no other thought, no other feeling, must mingle with them and disturb what should be an intensely attentive observation.

The student says to himself: "The stone has a form; the animal also has a form. The stone remains motionless in its place. The animal changes its place. It is instinct (desire) which causes the animal to change its place. Instincts, too, are served by the form of the animal. Its organs and limbs are fashioned in accordance with these instincts. The form of the stone is not fashioned in accordance with desires, but in accordance with desireless force." (The fact here mentioned, in its bearing on the contemplation of crystals, is in many ways distorted by those who have only heard of it in an outward, exoteric manner, and in this way such practices as crystal-gazing have their origin Such manipulations are based on a misunderstanding. They have been described in many books, but they never form the subject of genuine esoteric teaching.)

By sinking deeply into such thoughts, and while doing so, observing the stone and the animal with rapt attention, there arise in the soul two quite separate kinds of feelings. From the stone there flows into the soul the one kind of feeling, and from the animal the other kind. The attempt will probably not succeed at first, but little by little, with genuine and patient practice, these feelings ensue. Only, this exercise must be practiced over and over again. At first the feelings are only present as long as the observation lasts. Later on they continue, and then they grow to something which remains living in the soul. The student has then but to reflect, and both feelings will always arise, even without the contemplation of an external object.

Out of these feelings and the thoughts that are bound up with them, the organs of clairvoyance are formed. If the plant should then be included in this observation, it will be noticed that the feeling flowing from it lies between the feelings derived from the stone and the animal, in both quality and degree. The organs thus formed are spiritual eyes. The students gradually learn, by their means, to see something like soul and spirit colors. The spiritual world with its lines and figures remains dark as long as he has only attained what has been described as preparation; through enlightenment this world becomes light. Here it must also be noted that the words "dark" and "light," as well as the other expressions used, only approximately describe what is meant. This cannot be otherwise if ordinary language is used, for this language was created to suit physical conditions. Spiritual science describes that which, for clairvoyant organs, flows from the stone, as blue, or blue-red; and that which is felt as coming from the animal as red or red-yellow. In reality, colors of a spiritual kind are seen. The color proceeding the plant is green which little by little turns into a light ethereal pink. The plant is actually that product of nature which in higher worlds resembles, in certain respects, its constitution in the physical world. The same does not apply to the stone and the animal.

It must now be clearly understood that the above-mentioned colors only represent the principal shades in the stone, plant and animal kingdom. In reality, all possible intermediate shades are present. Every stone, every plant, every animal has its own particular shade of color. In addition to these there are also the beings of the higher worlds who never incarnate physically, but who have their colors, often wonderful, often horrible. Indeed, the wealth of color in these higher worlds is immeasurably greater than in the physical world.

Once the faculty of seeing with spiritual eyes has been acquired, one then encounters sooner or later the beings here mentioned, some of them higher, some lower than man himself—beings that never enter physical reality. If this point has been reached, the way to a great deal lies open. But it is inadvisable to proceed further without paying careful heed to what is said or otherwise imparted by the spiritual researcher. And for that, too, which has been described, attention paid to such experienced guidance is the very best thing. Moreover, if a man has the strength and the endurance to travel so far that he fulfills the elementary conditions of enlightenment, he will assuredly seek and find the right guidance.

But in any circumstances, one precaution is necessary, failing which it were better to leave untrodden all steps on the path to higher knowledge. It is necessary that the student should lose none of his qualities as a good and noble man, or his receptivity for all physical reality. Indeed, throughout his training he must continually increase his moral strength, his inner purity, and his power of observation. To give an example: during the elementary exercises on enlightenment, the student must take care always to enlarge his sympathy for the animal and the human worlds, and his sense for the beauty of nature. Failing this care, such exercises would continually blunt that feeling and that sense; the heart would become hardened, and the senses blunted, and that could only lead to perilous results. How enlightenment proceeds if the student rises, in the sense of the foregoing exercises, from the stone, the plant, and the animal, up to man, and how, after enlightenment, under all circumstances the union of the soul with the spiritual world is effected, leading to initiation—with these things the following chapters will deal, in as far as they can and may do so.

In our time the path to spiritual science is sought by many. It is sought in many ways, and many dangerous and even despicable practices are attempted. It is for this reason that they who claim to know something of the truth in these matters place before others the possibility of learning something of esoteric training. Only so much is here imparted as accords with this possibility. It is necessary that something of the truth should become known, in order to prevent error causing great harm. No harm can come to anyone following the way here described, so long as he does not force matters.

Only, one thing should be noted: no student should spend more time and strength upon these exercises than he can spare with due regard to his station in life and to his duties; nor should he change anything, for the time being, in the external conditions of his life through taking this path. Without patience no genuine results can be attained. After doing an exercise for a few minutes, the student must be able to stop and continue quietly his daily work, and no thought of these exercises should mingle with the day's work. No one is of use as an esoteric student or will ever attain results of real value who has not learned to wait in the highest and best sense of the word.

The Control of Thoughts and Feelings

When the student seeks the path leading to higher knowledge in the way described in the preceding chapter, he should not omit to fortify himself; throughout his work, with one ever present thought. He must never cease repeating to himself that he may have made quite considerable progress after a certain interval of time, though it may not be apparent to him in the way he perhaps expected; otherwise, he can easily lose heart and abandon all attempts after a short time. The powers and faculties to be developed are of a most subtle kind, and differ entirely in their nature from the conceptions previously formed by the student. He had been accustomed to occupy himself exclusively with the physical world; the world of spirit and soul had been concealed from his vision and concepts. It is therefore not surprising if he does not immediately notice the powers of soul and spirit now developing in him. In this respect there is a possibility of discouragement for those setting out on the path to higher knowledge, if they ignore the experience gathered by responsible investigators.

The teacher is aware of the progress made by his pupil long before the latter is conscious of it, He knows how the delicate spiritual eyes begin to form themselves long before the pupil is aware of this, and a great part of what he has to say is couched in such terms as to prevent the pupil from losing patience and perseverance before he can himself gain knowledge of his own progress. The teacher, as we know, can confer upon the pupil no powers which are not already latent within him, and his sole function is to assist in the awakening of slumbering faculties. But what he imparts out of his own experience is a pillar of strength for the one wishing to penetrate through darkness to light. Many abandon the path to higher knowledge soon after having set foot upon it, because their progress is not immediately apparent to them. And even when the first experiences begin to dawn upon the pupil, he is apt to regard them as illusions, because he had formed quite different conceptions of what he was going to experience. He loses courage, either because he regards these first experiences as being of no value, or because they appear to him to be so insignificant that he cannot believe they will lead him to any appreciable results within a measurable time.

Courage and self-confidence are two beacons which must never be extinguished on the path to higher knowledge. No one will ever travel far who cannot bring himself to repeat, over and over again, an exercise which has failed, apparently, for a countless number of times. Long before any distinct perception of progress, there rises in the student, from the hidden depths of the soul, a feeling that he is on the right path. This feeling should be cherished and fostered, for it can develop into a trustworthy guide. Above all, it is imperative to extirpate the idea that any fantastic, mysterious practices are required for the attainment of higher knowledge. It must be clearly realized that a start has to be made with the thoughts and feelings with which we continually live, and that these feelings and thoughts must merely be given a new direction.

Everyone must say to himself: "In my own world of thought and feeling the deepest mysteries lie hidden, only hitherto I have been unable to perceive them." In the end it all resolves itself into the fact that man ordinarily carries body, soul and spirit about with him, and yet is conscious in a true sense only of his body, and not of his soul and spirit. The student becomes conscious of soul and spirit, just as the ordinary person is conscious of his body. Hence it is highly important to give the proper direction to thoughts and feelings, for then only can the perception be developed of all that is invisible in ordinary life. One of the ways by which this development may be carried out will now be indicated. Again, like almost everything else so far explained, it is quite a simple matter. Yet its results are of the greatest consequence, if the necessary devotion and sympathy be applied.

Let the student place before himself the small seed of a plant, and while contemplating this insignificant object, form with intensity the right kind of thoughts, and through these thoughts develop certain feelings. In the first place let him clearly grasp what he really sees with his eyes. Let him describe to himself the shape, color and all other qualities of the seed. Then let his mind dwell upon the following train of thought: "Out of the seed, if planted in the soil, a plant of complex structure will grow." Let him build up this plant in his imagination, and reflect as follows: "What I am now picturing to myself in my imagination will later on be enticed from the seed by the forces of earth and light. If I had before me an artificial object which imitated the seed to such a deceptive degree that my eyes could not distinguish it from a real seed, no forces of earth or light could avail to produce from it a plant."

If the student thoroughly grasps this thought so that it becomes an inward experience, he will also be able to form the following thought and couple it with the right feeling: "All that will ultimately grow out of the seed is now secretly enfolded within it as the force of the whole plant. In the artificial imitation of the seed there is no such force present. And yet both appear alike to my eyes. The real seed, therefore, contains something invisible which is not present in the imitation." It is on this invisible something that thought and feeling are to be concentrated. (Anyone objecting that a microscopical examination would reveal the difference between the real seed and the imitation would only show that he had failed to grasp the point. The intention is not to investigate the physical nature of the object, but to use it for the development of psycho-spiritual forces.)

Let the student fully realize that this invisible something will transmute itself later on into a visible plant, which he will have before him in its shape and color. Let him ponder on the thought: "The invisible will become visible. If I could not think, then that which will only become visible later on could not already make its presence felt to me." Particular stress must be laid on the following point: what the student thinks he must also feel with intensity. In inner tranquility, the thought mentioned above must become a conscious inner experience, to the exclusion of all other thoughts and disturbances. And sufficient time must be taken to allow the thought and the feeling which is coupled with it to bore themselves into the soul, as it were. If this be accomplished in the right way, then after a time—possibly not until after numerous attempts—an inner force will make itself felt. This force will create new powers of perception. The grain of seed will appear as if enveloped in a small luminous cloud. In a sensible-supersensible way, it will be felt as a kind of flame. The center of this flame evokes the same feeling that one has when under the impression of the color lilac, and the edges as when under the impression of a bluish tone. What was formerly invisible now becomes visible, for it is created by the power of the thoughts and feelings we have stirred to life within ourselves. The plant itself will not become visible until later, so that the physically invisible now reveals itself in a spiritually visible way.

It is not surprising that all this appears to many as illusion. "What is the use of such visions," they ask, "and such hallucinations?" And many will thus fall away and abandon the path. But this is precisely the important point: not to confuse spiritual reality with imagination at this difficult stage of human evolution, and furthermore, to have the courage to press onward and not become timorous and faint-hearted. On the other hand, however, the necessity must be emphasized of maintaining unimpaired and of perpetually cultivating that healthy sound sense which distinguishes truth from illusion. Fully conscious self-control must never be lost during all these exercises, and they must be accompanied by the same sane, sound thinking which is applied to the details of every-day life. To lapse into reveries would be fatal. The intellectual clarity, not to say the sobriety of thought, must never for a moment be dulled.

The greatest mistake would be made if the student's mental balance were disturbed through such exercises, if he were hampered in judging the matters of his daily life as sanely and as soundly as before. He should examine himself again and again to find out if he has remained unaltered in relation to the circumstances among which he lives, or whether he may perhaps have become unbalanced. Above all, strict care must be taken not to drift at random into vague reveries, or to experiment with all kinds of exercises. The trains of thought here indicated have been tested and practiced in esoteric training since the earliest times, and only such are given in these pages. Anyone attempting to use others devised by himself, or of which he may have heard or read at one place or another, will inevitably go astray and find himself on the path of boundless chimera.

As a further exercise to succeed the one just described, the following may be taken: Let the student place before him a plant which has attained the stage of full development. Now let him fill his mind with the thought that the time will come when this plant will wither and die. "Nothing will be left of what I now see before me. But this plant will have developed seeds which, in their turn, will develop to new plants. I again become aware that in what I see, something lies hidden which I cannot see. I fill my mind entirely with the thought: this plant with its form and colors, will in time be no more. But the reflection that it produces seeds teaches me that it will not disappear into nothing.

I cannot at present see with my eyes that which guards it from disappearance, any more than I previously could discern the plant in the grain of seed. Thus, there is something in the plant which my eyes cannot see. If I let this thought live within me, and if the corresponding feeling be coupled with it, then, in due time, there will again develop in my soul a force which will ripen into a new perception. Out of the plant there again grows a kind of spiritual flame-form, which is, of course, correspondingly larger than the one previously described. The flame can be felt as being greenish-blue in the center, and yellowish-red at the outer edge.

It must be explicitly emphasized that the colors here described are not seen as the physical eyes see colors, but that through spiritual perception the same feeling is experienced as in the case of a physical color-impression. To apprehend blue spiritually means to have a sensation similar to the one experienced when the physical eye rests on the color blue. This fact must be noted by all who intend to rise to spiritual perception. Otherwise, they will expect a mere repetition of the physical in the spiritual. This could only lead to the bitterest deception.

Anyone having reached this point of spiritual vision is the richer by a great deal, for he can perceive things not only in their present state of being but also in their process of growth and decay. He begins to see in all things the spirit, of which physical eyes can know nothing. And therewith he has taken the first step toward the gradual solution, through personal vision, of the secret of birth and death. For the outer senses a being comes into existence through birth, and passes away through death. This, however, is only because these senses cannot perceive the concealed spirit of the being. For the spirit, birth and death are merely a transformation, just as the unfolding of the flower from the bud is a transformation enacted before our physical eyes. But if we desire to learn this through personal vision, we must first awaken the requisite spiritual sense in the way here indicated.

In order to meet another objection, which may be raised by certain people who have some psychic experience, let it at once be admitted that there are shorter and simpler ways, and that there are persons who have acquired knowledge of the phenomena of birth and death through personal vision, without first going through all that has here been described. There are, in fact, people with considerable psychic gifts who need but a slight impulse in order to find themselves already developed. But they are the exceptions, and the methods described above are safer and apply equally to all. It is possible to acquire some knowledge of chemistry in an exceptional way, but if you wish to become a chemist you must follow the recognized and reliable course.

An error fraught with serious consequences would ensue if it were assumed that the desired result could be reached more easily if the grain of seed or the plant mentioned above were merely imagined, were merely pictured in the imagination. This might lead to results, but not so surely as the method here. The vision thus attained would, in most cases, be a mere fragment of the imagination, the transformation of which into genuine spiritual vision would still remain to be accomplished. It is not intended arbitrarily to create visions, but to allow reality to create them within oneself. The truth must well up from the depths of our own soul; it must not be conjured forth by our ordinary ego, but by the beings themselves whose spiritual truth we are to contemplate.

Once the student has found the beginnings of spiritual vision by means of such exercises, he may proceed to the contemplation of man himself. Simple phenomena of human life must first be chosen. But before making any attempt in this direction it is imperative for the student to strive for the absolute purity of his moral character. He must banish all through of ever using knowledge gained in this way for his own personal benefit. He must be convinced that he would never, under any circumstances, avail himself in an evil sense of any power he may gain over his fellow-creatures.

For this reason, all who seek to discover through personal vision the secrets in human nature must follow the golden rule of true spiritual science. This golden rule is as follows: For every one step that you take in the pursuit of higher knowledge, take three steps in the perfection of your own character. If this rule is observed, such exercise as the following may be attempted: Recall to mind some person whom you may have observed when he was filled with desire for some object.

Direct your attention to this desire. It is best to recall to memory that moment when the desire was at its height, and it was still uncertain whether the object of the desire would be attained. And now fill your mind with this recollection, and reflect on what you can thus observe. Maintain the utmost inner tranquility. Make the greatest possible effort to be blind and deaf to everything that may be going on around you, and take special heed that through the conception thus evoked a feeling should awaken in your soul. Allow this feeling to rise in your soul like a cloud on the cloudless horizon. As a rule, of course, your reflection will be interrupted, because the person whom it concerns was not observed in this particular state of soul for a sufficient length of time.

The attempt will most likely fail hundreds and hundreds of times. It is just a question of not losing patience. After many attempts you will succeed in experiencing a feeling In your soul corresponding to the state of soul of the person observed, and you will begin to notice that through this feeling a power grows in your soul that leads to spiritual insight into the state of soul of the other. A picture experienced as luminous appears in your field of vision. This spiritually luminous picture is the so-called astral embodiment of the desire observed in that soul. Again, the impression of this picture may be described as flame-like, yellowish-red in the center, and reddish-blue or lilac at the edges. Much depends on treating such spiritual experiences with great delicacy. The best thing is not to speak to anyone about them except to your teacher, if you have one. Attempted descriptions of such experiences in inappropriate words usually only lead to gross self-deception. Ordinary terms are employed which are not intended for such things, and are therefore too gross and clumsy. The consequence is that in the attempt to clothe the experience in words we are misled into blending the actual experience with all kinds of fantastic delusions. Here again is another important rule for the student: know how to observe silence concerning your spiritual experiences. Yes, observe silence even toward yourself.

Do not attempt to clothe in words what you contemplate in the spirit, or to pore over it with clumsy intellect. Lend yourself freely and without reservation to these spiritual impressions, and do not disturb them by reflecting and pondering over them too much. For you must remember that your reasoning faculties are, to begin with, by no means equal to your new experience. You have acquired these reasoning faculties in a life hitherto confined to the physical world of the senses; the faculties you are not acquiring transcend this world. Do not try, therefore, to apply to the new and higher perceptions the standard of the old. Only he who has gained some certainty and steadiness in the observation of inner experiences can speak about them, and thereby stimulate his fellow-men.

The exercise just described may be supplemented by the following: Direct your attention in the same way upon a person to whom the fulfillment of some wish, the gratification of some desire, has been granted. If the same rules and precautions be adopted as in the previous instance, spiritual insight will once more be attained. A spiritual insight will once more be attained. A spiritual flame-form will be distinguished, creating an impression of yellow in the center and green at the edges.

By such observation of his fellow-creatures, the student may easily lapse into a moral fault. He may become cold-hearted. Every conceivable effort must be made to prevent this. Such observation should only be practiced by one who has already risen to the level on which complete certainty is found that thoughts are real things. He will then no longer allow himself to think of his fellow-men in a way that is incompatible with the highest reverence for human dignity and human liberty. The thought that a human being could be merely an object of observation must never for a moment be entertained. Self-education must see to it that this insight into human nature should go hand in hand with an unlimited respect for the personal privilege of each individual, and with the recognition of the sacred and inviolable nature of that which dwells in each human being. A feeling of reverential awe must fill us, even in our recollections.

For the present, only these two examples can be given to show how enlightened insight into human nature may be achieved; they will at least serve to point out the way to be taken. By gaining the inner tranquility and repose indispensable for such observation, the student will have undergone a great inner transformation. He will then soon reach the point where this enrichment of his inner self will lend confidence and composure to his outward demeanor. And this transformation of his outward demeanor will again react favorably on his soul. Thus, he will be able to help himself further along the road.

He will find ways and means of penetrating more and more into the secrets of human nature which are hidden from our external senses, and he will then also become ripe for a deeper insight into the mysterious connections between human nature and all else that exists in the universe. By following this path, the student approaches closer and closer to the moment when he can effectively take the first steps of initiation. But before these can be taken, one thing more is necessary, though at first its need will be least of all apparent; later on, however, the student will be convinced of it.

The would-be initiate must bring with him a certain measure of courage and fearlessness. He must positively go out of his way to find opportunities for developing these virtues. His training should provide for their systematic cultivation. In this respect, life itself is a good school—possibly the best school. The student must learn to look danger calmly in the face and try to overcome difficulties unswervingly. For instance, when in the presence of some peril, he must swiftly come to the conviction that fear is of no possible use; I must not feel afraid; I must only think of what is to be done. And he must improve to the extent of feeling, upon occasions which formerly inspired him with fear, that to be frightened, to be disheartened, are things that are out of the question as far as his own inmost self is concerned.

By self-discipline in this direction, quite definite qualities are developed which are necessary for initiation into the higher mysteries. Just as man requires nervous force in his physical being in order to use his physical sense, so also, he requires in his soul nature the force which is only developed in the courageous and the fearless. For in penetrating to the higher mysteries he will see things which are concealed from ordinary humanity by the illusion of the senses. If the physical senses do not allow us to perceive the higher truth, they are for this very reason our benefactors. Things are thereby hidden from us which, if realized without due preparation, would throw us into unutterable consternation, and the sight of which would be unendurable. The student must be fit to endure this sight. He loses certain supports in the outer world which he owes to the very illusion surrounding him. It is truly and literally as if the attention of someone were called to a danger which had threatened him for a long time, but of which he knew nothing. Hitherto he felt no fear, but now that he knows, he is overcome by fear, though the danger has not been rendered greater by his knowing it.

The forces at work in the world are both destructive and constructive; the destiny of manifested beings is birth and death. The seer is to behold the working of these forces and the march of destiny. The veil enshrouding the spiritual eyes in ordinary life is to be removed. But man is interwoven with these forces and with this destiny. His own nature harbors destructive and constructive forces. His own soul reveals itself to the seer as undisguised as the other objects. He must not lose strength in the face of this self-knowledge; but strength will fail him unless he brings a surplus on which to draw. For this purpose, he must learn to maintain inner calm and steadiness in the face of difficult circumstances; he must cultivate a strong trust in the beneficent powers of existence. He must be prepared to find that many motives which had actuated him hitherto will do so no longer. He will have to recognize that previously he thought and acted in a certain way only because he was still in the throes of ignorance. Reasons that influenced him formerly will now disappear. He often acted out of vanity; he will now see how utterly futile all vanity is for the seer. He often acted out of greed; he will now become aware how destructive all greed is. He will have to develop quite new motives for his thoughts and actions, and it is just for this purpose that courage and fearlessness are required.

It is pre-eminently a question of cultivating this courage and this fearlessness in the inmost depths of thought-life. The student must learn never to despair over failure. He must be equal to the thought: I shall forget that I have failed in this matter, and I shall try once more as though this had not happened. Thus, he will struggle through to the firm conviction that the fountain-head of strength from which he may draw is inexhaustible. He struggles ever onward to the spirit which will uplift him and support him, however weak and impotent his earthly self may have proved. He must be capable of pressing on to the future undismayed by any experiences of the past.

If the student has acquired these faculties up to a certain point, he is then ripe to hear the real names of things, which are the key to higher knowledge. For initiation consists in this very act of learning to call the things of the world by those names which they bear in the spirit of their divine authors. In these, their names, lies the mystery of things. It is for this reason that the initiates speak a different language from the uninitiated, for the former know the names by which the beings themselves are called into existence. In as far as initiation itself can be discussed, this will be done in the following chapter.

Initiation

Initiation is the highest stage in an esoteric training concerning which it is possible to give some indications in a book intended for the genuine public. Whatever lies beyond forms a subject difficult to understand, yet the way to it can be found by all who have passed through preparation, enlightenment, and initiation as far as the lesser mysteries. The knowledge and proficiency conferred by initiation cannot be obtained in any other manner, except in some far distant future, after many incarnations, by quite different means and in quite a different form. The initiate of today undergoes experiences which would otherwise come to him much later, under quite different circumstances.

The secrets of existence are only accessible to an extent corresponding to man's own degree of maturity. For this reason alone, the path to the higher stages of knowledge and power is beset with obstacles. A firearm should not be used until sufficient experience has been gained to avoid disaster, caused by its use. A person initiated today without further ado would lack the experience which he will gain during his future incarnations before he can attain to higher knowledge in the normal course of his development. At the portal of initiation, therefore, this experience must be supplied in some other way. Thus, the first instructions given to the candidate for initiation serve as a substitute for these future experiences. These are the so-called trials, which he has to undergo, and which constitute a normal course of inner development resulting from due application to such exercises as are described in the preceding chapters.

These trials are often discussed in books, but it is only natural that such discussions should as a rule give quite false impressions of their nature; for without passing through preparation and enlightenment no one can know anything of these tests and appropriately describe them. The would-be initiate must come into contact with certain things and facts belonging to the higher worlds, but he can only see and hear them if his feeling is ripe for the perception of the spiritual forms, colors and tones described in the chapters on Preparation and Enlightenment.

The first trial consists in obtaining a truer vision than the average man has of the corporeal attributes of lifeless things, and later of plants, animals and human beings. This does not mean what at present is called scientific knowledge, for it is a question not of science but of vision. As a rule, the would-be initiate proceeds to learn how the objects of nature and the beings gifted with life manifest themselves to the spiritual ear and the spiritual eye. In a certain way these things then lie stripped—naked—before the beholder. The qualities which can then be seen and heard are hidden from the physical eyes and ears. For physical perception they are concealed as if by a veil, and the falling away of this veil for the would-be initiate consists in a process designated as the process of Purification by Fire. The first trial is therefore known as the Fire-Trial.

For many people, ordinary life is itself a more or less unconscious process of initiation through the Fire-Trial. Such people have passed through a wealth of experience, so that their self-confidence, courage and fortitude have been greatly strengthened in a normal manner while learning to bear sorrow, disappointment and failure in their undertakings with greatness of soul, and especially with equanimity and unbroken strength. Thus, they are often initiates without knowing it, and it then needs but little to unseal their spiritual hearing and sight so that they become clairvoyant. For it must be noted that a genuine fire-trial is not intended to satisfy the curiosity of the candidate.

It is true that he learns many uncommon things of which others can have no inkling, but this acquisition of knowledge is not the end, but the means to the end; the end consists in the attainment, thanks to this knowledge of the higher worlds, of greater and truer self-confidence, a higher degree of courage, and a magnanimity and perseverance such as cannot, as a rule, be acquired in the lower world.

The candidate may always turn back after the fire-trial. He will then resume his life, strengthened in body and soul, and wait for a future incarnation to continue his initiation. In his present incarnation he will prove himself a more useful member of society and of humanity than he was before. In whatever position he may find himself, his firmness, prudence, resoluteness, and his beneficent influence over his fellows will have greatly increased. But if, after completing the fire-trial, he should wish to continue the path, a certain writing-system generally adopted in esoteric training must now be revealed to him. The actual teachings manifest themselves in this writing, because the hidden (occult) qualities of things cannot be directly expressed in the words of ordinary writing. The pupils of the initiates translate the teachings into ordinary language as best they can. The occult script reveals itself to the soul when the latter has attained spiritual perception, for it is traced in the spiritual world and remains there for all time.

It cannot be learned as an artificial writing is learned and read. The candidate grows into clairvoyant knowledge in an appropriate way, and during this growth a new strength is developed in his soul, as a new faculty, through which he feels himself impelled to decipher the occurrences and the beings of the spiritual world like the characters of a writing. This strength, with the experience it brings of the corresponding trial, might possibly awaken in the soul as though of its own accord, as the soul continually develops, but it will be found safer to follow the instructions of those who are spiritually experienced, and who have some proficiency in deciphering the occult script.

The signs of the occult script are not arbitrarily invented; they correspond to the forces actively engaged in the world. They teach us the language of things. It becomes immediately apparent to the candidate that the signs he is now learning correspond to the forms, colors, and tones which he learned to perceive during his preparation and enlightenment. He realizes that all he learned previously was only like learning to spell, and that he is only now beginning to read in the higher worlds.

All the isolated figures, tones, and colors reveal themselves to him now in one great connected whole. Now for the first time he attains complete certainty in observing the higher worlds. Hitherto he could never know positively whether the things he saw were rightly seen. A regular understanding, too, is now at last possible between the candidate and the initiate in the spheres of higher knowledge. For whatever form the intercourse between an initiate and another person may take in ordinary life, the higher knowledge in its immediate form can only be imparted by the initiate in the above-mentioned sign-language.

Thanks to this language the student also learns certain rules of conduct and certain duties of which he formerly knew nothing. Having learned these, he is able to perform actions endowed with a significance and a meaning such as the actions of one not initiated can never possess. He acts out of the higher worlds. Instructions concerning such action can only be read and understood in the writing in question. Yet it must be emphasized that there are people unconsciously gifted with the ability and faculty of performing such actions, though they have never undergone an esoteric training. Such helpers of the world and of humanity pass through life bestowing blessings and performing good deeds. For reasons here not to be discussed, gifts have been bestowed on them which appear supernatural. What distinguishes them from the candidate for initiation is only that the latter acts consciously and with full insight into the entire situation. He acquires by training the gifts bestowed on others by higher powers for the good of humanity. We can sincerely revere these favored of God; but we should not for this reason regard the work of esoteric training as superfluous.

Once the student has learned the sign-language there awaits him yet another trial, to prove whether he can move with freedom and assurance in the higher worlds. In ordinary life he is impelled to action by exterior motives. He works at one occupation or another because one duty or another is imposed on him by outward circumstances. It need hardly be mentioned that the student must in no way neglect any of his duties in ordinary life because he is living and working in higher worlds.

There is no duty in a higher world that can force a person to neglect any single one of his duties in the ordinary world. The father will remain just as good a father to his family, the mother just as good a mother, and neither the official nor the soldier, nor anyone else will be diverted from his work by becoming an esoteric student. On the contrary, all the qualities which make a human being capable and efficient are enhanced in the student to a degree incomprehensible to the uninitiated. If, in the eyes of the uninitiated, this does not always appear to be the case, it is simply because he often lacks the ability to judge the initiate correctly. The deeds of the latter are not always intelligible to the former. But this only happens in special cases.

At this stage of initiation there are duties to be performed for which no outward stimulus is given. The candidate will not be moved to action by external pressure, but only through adherence to the rules of conduct revealed to him in the occult script. He must now show in this second trial that, led by such rules, he can act with the same firmness and precision with which, for instance, an official performs the duties that belong to him. For this purpose, and in the course of his further training, he will find himself faced by a certain definite task. He must perform some action in consequence of observations made on the basis of what he has learned during preparation and enlightenment.

The nature of this action can be understood by means of the occult script with which he is now familiar. If he recognizes his duty and acts rightly, his trial has been successful. The success can be recognized in the alteration produced by his action in the figures, colors, and tones apprehended by his spiritual eyes and ears. Exact indications are given, as the training progresses, showing how these figures appear and are experienced after the action has been performed, and the candidate must know how to produce this change. This trial is known as the Water-Trial, because in his activity in these higher worlds the candidate is deprived of the support derived from outward circumstances, as a swimmer is without support when swimming in water that is beyond his depth.

This activity must be repeated until the candidate attains absolute poise and assurance.

The importance of this trial lies again in the acquisition of a quality. Through his experiences in the higher worlds, the candidate develops this quality in a short time to such a high degree that he would otherwise have to go through many incarnations, in the ordinary course of his development, before he could acquire it to the same extent. It all centers around the fact that he must be guided only by the results of his higher perception and reading of the occult script, in order to produce the changes in question in these higher regions of existence. Should he, in the course of his activity, introduce any of his own opinions and desires, or should he diverge for one moment from the laws which he has recognized to be right, in order to follow his own willful inclination, then the result produced would differ entirely from what was intended. He would lose sight of the goal to which his action tended, and confusion would result.

Hence ample opportunity is given him in the course of this trial to develop self-control. This is the object in view. Here again, this trial can be more easily passed by those whose life, before initiation, has led them to acquire self-control. Anyone having acquired the faculty of following high principles and ideals, while putting into the background all personal predilection; anyone capable of always performing his duty, even though inclinations and sympathies would like to seduce him from this duty—such a person is unconsciously an initiate in the midst of ordinary life. He will need but little to succeed in this particular trial. Indeed, a certain measure of initiation thus unconsciously acquired in life will, as a rule, be indispensable for success in this second trial.

For even as it is difficult for those who have not learned to spell correctly in their childhood to make good this deficiency when fully grown up, so too it is difficult to develop the necessary degree of self-control at the moment of looking into the higher worlds, if this ability has not been acquired to a certain degree in ordinary life. The objects of the physical world do not alter, whatever the nature of our wishes, desires, and inclinations. In the higher worlds, however, our wishes, desires, and inclinations are causes that produce effects. If we wish to produce a particular effect in these worlds, we must strictly follow the right rules and subdue every arbitrary impulse.

One human quality is of very special importance at this stage of initiation, namely, an unquestionably sound judgment. Attention should be paid to the training of this faculty during all the previous stages; for it now remains to be proved whether the candidate is shaping in a way that shows him to be fit for the truth path of knowledge.

Further progress is now only possible if he is able to distinguish illusion, superstition, and everything fantastic, from true reality. This is, at first, more difficult to accomplish in the higher stages of existence than in the lower. Every prejudice, every cherished opinion with regard to the things in question, must vanish; truth alone must guide. There must be perfect readiness to abandon at once any idea, opinion, or inclination when logical thought demands it. Certainty in higher worlds is only likely to be attained when personal opinion is never considered.

People whose mode of thought tends to fancifulness and superstition can never make progress on the path to higher knowledge. It is indeed a precious treasure that the student is to acquire. All doubt regarding the higher worlds is removed from him. With all their laws they reveal themselves to his gaze. But he cannot acquire this treasure so long as he is the prey of fancies and illusions. It would indeed be fatal if his imagination and his prejudices ran away with his intellect. Dreamers and fantastical people are as unfit for the path to higher knowledge as superstitious people.

This cannot be over-emphasized. For the most dangerous enemies on the way to knowledge of the higher worlds lurk in such fantastical reveries and superstitions. Yet no one need to believe that the student loses all sense of poetry in life, all power of enthusiasm because the words: You must be rid of all prejudice, are written over the portal leading to the second trial of initiation, and because over the portal at the entrance to the first trial he read: Without normal common sense all thine efforts are in vain. If the candidate is in this way sufficiently advanced, a third trial awaits him. He finds here no definite goal to be reached. All is left in his own hands. He finds himself in a situation where nothing impels him to act. He must find his way all alone and out of himself. Things or people to stimulate him to action are non-existent. Nothing and nobody can give him the strength he needs but he himself alone. Failure to find this inner strength will leave him standing where he was. Few of those, however, who have successfully passed the previous trials, will fail to find the necessary strength at this point. Either they will have turned back already or they succeed at this point also. All that the candidate requires is the ability to come quickly to terms with himself, for he must here find his higher self in the truest sense of the word. He must rapidly decide in all things to listen to the inspiration of the spirit.

There is no time for doubt or hesitation. Every moment of hesitation would prove that he was still unfit. Whatever prevents him from listening to the voice of the spirit must be courageously overcome. It is a question of showing presence of mind in this situation, and the training at this stage is concerned with the perfect development of this quality. All the accustomed inducements to act or even to think now cease. In order not to remain inactive he must not lose himself, for only within himself can he find the one central point of vantage where he can gain a firm hold. No one on reading this, without further acquaintance with these matters, should feel an antipathy for this principle of being thrown back on oneself, for success in this trial brings with it a moment of supreme happiness.

At this stage, no less than at the others, ordinary life is itself an esoteric training for many. For anyone having reached the point of being able, when suddenly confronted with some task or problem in life, to come to a swift decision without hesitation or delay, for him life itself has been a training in this sense. Such situations are here meant in which success is instantly lost if action is not rapid. A person who is quick to act when a misfortune is imminent, whereas a few moments of hesitation would have seen the misfortune an accomplished fact, and who has turned this ability into a permanent personal quality, has unconsciously acquired the degree of maturity necessary for the third trial.

For at this stage everything centers round the development of absolute presence of mind. This trial is known as the Air-Trial, because while undergoing it the candidate can support himself neither upon the firm basis of external incentive nor upon the figures, tones, and colors which he has learned at the stages of preparation and enlightenment, but exclusively upon himself. Upon successfully passing this trial the student is permitted to enter the temple of higher wisdom. All that is here said on this subject can only be the slenderest allusion. The task now to be performed is often expressed in the statement that the student must take an oath never to betray anything he has learned. These expressions, however, "oath" and "betray", are inappropriate and actually misleading. There is no question of an oath in the ordinary sense of the word, but rather of an experience that comes at this stage of development. The candidate learns how to apply the higher knowledge, how to place it at the service of humanity. He then begins really and truly to understand the world. It is not so much a question of withholding the higher truths, but far more of serving them in the right way and with the necessary tact. The silence he is to keep refers to something quite different.

He acquires this fine quality with regard to things he had previously spoken, and especially with regard to the manner in which they were spoken. He would be a poor initiate who did not place all the higher knowledge he had acquired at the service of humanity, as well and as far as this is possible. The only obstacle to giving information in these matters is the lack of understanding on the part of the recipients. It is true, of course, that the higher knowledge does not lend itself to promiscuous talk; but no one having reached the stage of development described above is actually forbidden to say anything. No other person, no being exacts an oath from him with this intent. Everything is left to his own responsibility, and he learns in every situation to discover within himself what he has to do, and an oath means nothing more than that he has been found qualified to be entrusted with such a responsibility.

If the candidate is found fit for the foregoing experiences, he is then given what is called symbolically the draught of forgetfulness. This means that he is initiated into the secret knowledge that enables him to act without being continually disturbed by the lower memory. This is necessary for the initiate, for he must have full faith in the immediate present. He must be able to destroy the veil of memory which envelops man every moment of his life. If we judge something that happens to us today according to the experience of yesterday, we are exposed to a multitude of errors. Of course, this does not mean that experience gained in life should be renounced. It should always be kept in mind as clearly as possible. But the initiate must have the ability to judge every new experience wholly according to what is inherent in it, and let it react upon him, unobscured by the past.

We must be prepared at every moment that every object and every being can bring to us some new revelation. If we judge the new by the standard of the old, we are liable to error. The memory of past experiences will be of greatest use for the very reason that it enables us to perceive the new. Had we not gone through a definite experience we should perhaps be blind to the qualities of the object or being that comes before us. Thus, experience should serve the purpose of perceiving the new and not of judging it by the standard of the old. In this respect the initiate acquires certain definite qualities, and thereby many things are revealed to him which remain concealed from the uninitiated.

The second draught presented to the initiate is the draught of remembrance. Through its agency he acquires the faculty of retaining the knowledge of the higher truths ever present in his soul. Ordinary memory would be unequal to this task. We must unite ourselves and become as one with the higher truths. We must not only know them, but be able, quite as a matter of course, to manifest and administer them in living actions, even as we ordinarily eat and drink.

They must become our practice, our habit, our inclination. There must be no need to keep thinking about them in the ordinary sense; they must come to living expression through man himself; they must flow through him as the functions of life through his organism.

Thus, doth man ever raise himself, in a spiritual sense, to that same stature to which nature raised him in a physical sense.

FROM THE MASTER TEACHER TO HIS NEOPHYTE

By R. S. CLYMER -1878 - 1966

You have enrolled in the Oldest Arcane Fraternity in existence today. We can easily trace our lineage from India to Egypt, from Egypt to the Essenes, then the Gnostics, and to the August Fraternity.

Study these recommendations well until they are burned upon your memory in letters of fire: By enrolling you have set yourself entirely apart from your fellow men, though you still remain part and parcel of them. The identical Laws which bind them also constrain you. The difference is this: You are SEEKING FOR THE TRUTH, YOUR SOUL, FREEDOM FROM BONDAGE.

You differ from others in that you accept the Divine Law, having taken the solemn Vow, you will not be free from it until you have fulfilled the Law, to yourself, your God and your fellow man. This is the Mystery. Almost from the beginning of formal churchism and throughout the centuries, the emphasis has not been on what men should do, but what they should believe. Furthermore, all the effort has been to convert their fellow man instead of themselves. This has meant universal interference with the Will and the freedom of men, setting up defiance, ill will and revolt.

You ARE BOUND by A new law. That Law is that you must make a new life for yourself. You will become your own savior and your salvation will be in changing the carnal passions into Godly ones. You will learn to be conscious that within yourself is the Christos who, awakened and BROUGHT INTO CONSCIOUSNESS WILL BE YOUR lord and master. The animalistic forces that have held you in bondage to all the world will be transmuted BY YOUR WILL AND DESIRES, AND BRING YOU THE KINGDOM OF HEAVEN—that is, ALL THAT IS DESIRABLE AND TO YOUR BENEFIT. IT IS FOLLY TO ATTEMPT TO CHANGE OTHERS

No more will you try to change others because you will recognize that they have the same opportunities you have, the same freedom of action, the same Free Will. Your duty is to yourself and to prevent others from interfering with your actions so long as that action is not to their detriment. You will not interfere with others in their habits, their policies, their business and, above all, not in their religion and religious practice. You will not permit either friend or foe, either loved one or enemy, to interfere with your affairs. You will live for yourself and your own Soul's sake, for God and to help others in their need.

Having enrolled for the Great Work of the August Fraternity, you have decided that life as you have known it, conditions you have had to meet, are not the type you would choose for yourself and you resolve to change it all by the power of your desire and efforts.

You will recognize sanely and sensibly that you, as a Neophyte, will not be able to change environments and circumstances all at once.

A SLOW CONSISTENT DEVELOPMENT ASSURES SUCCESS

You will realize that all progress must necessarily be slow, by a gradual procedure, felt rather than manifested. The first essential is that you become thoroughly con versant with the underlying philosophy of the Work, the Divine and Natural Law, and do this as thoroughly as you would subjects were you a student in a first-class college.

This is to be followed by a regular, systematic practice necessary to the awakening of the latent talents within YOURSELF. It demands the arrangement of your affairs, as you would were you attending College, so that you will have certain periods for the practice of methods to develop your now latent physical, mental and Spiritual forces. These forces are to be directed in the accomplishment of the work, business or profession, you have planned for yourself. Having gone this far it is of the utmost importance that you keep in mind the Master Teacher's command: "No man, having put his hand to the plow, and looking back, is fit for the Kingdom of God."—

Luke 9:62.

In these few words are contained the Law and the Prophets; the Law which has governed the actions of those Neophytes who entered the August Fraternity and achieved ultimate success and freedom in all affairs of life. They are simple words, spoken by a simple man who had climbed to the highest achievement of which men are capable. If you fail in this one thing, which, simply stated is: Regularity IN YOUR EFFORTS, PERMITTING NO INTERFERENCE EXCEPT for duty, you will have failed in everything. If you attended College, you would not dare to permit friends, foes, loved ones or family to interfere with your study periods. There is no excuse for you to permit them to interfere with your present efforts. You may not be arbitrary in your actions. You must proceed calmly, slowly, silently and without the "blare of trumpets"—i.e., much talking.

EXCUSES ARE THE DEVIL'S INVENTION

Consider the statement of Luke further and realize its implications as it concerns every one. What would happen to the student in music, or singing, if he or she made the excuse that they were unable to practice because someone interfered. Having let go of the "plow," would they become artists of world renown?

This, the work you have entered, is of the Soul. As such it is Work of God, because your Spirit, your Soul, came from God with a mission and, an obligation. It is still in mortgage to God and will not be yours, you will not be free, until such time as you have fulfilled the Law. To fail, is to fail God, and this is to bring upon you the greater penalty, because you can succeed if you will. You have inherited in total all that is essential to reaching the highest on all planes OF BEING, THE PHYSICAL AND MATERIAL, AS WELL AS THE spiritual.

If you will "follow through," on the advantage given you, then it is certain you will succeed. Referring again to "putting your hand to the plow," this cannot be understood too thoroughly. If your desire was to become a Physician, a Minister or an Attorney, it would require you to attend College Day after day for years. It would require you to study day and night. It would take you away from family, and friends. It would prevent you from engaging in any business or occupation, and in the end, you would NOT achieve as great a status as you will if you will follow through until Initiation or Soul Consciousness is attained. The Great Work demands a short period each day for study and practice. This should not conflict with duty nor sever you from friends, relatives, business or occupation. By obedience to the Divine Law, you will be able, in addition to your Spiritual attainment, to succeed in your worldly affairs beyond any and all ordinary expectations.

This demands of course, that your mind be single. You must follow the straight and narrow path, Biblically and Occultly speaking, inferring that your studies must be along A SINGLE line. You may not mix your studies with the teachings of any other than the chosen one. This is not an arbitrary rule, but it is based on sound practice. If you were to attend a Medical College or a Seminary for religious training, you would not be permitted to study the texts of another school. Why not? Because being different in theory, though perhaps just as true, it would result in confusion, and you would soon be unable to judge what is right. As a result of this confusion, you would lose faith. Confidence would be lost, and both faith and confidence are essential to success.

"LET THINE EYES BE SINGLE"

It is not basically a question of who is right or who is wrong, or who is most nearly correct, but of agreement. No two persons, though of equal training and attainment, will see eye to eye; to teach the philosophy in the same words. Reading the writings of two persons would be to be confronted by two concepts. Shortly the question would arise in your mind: Which is right? Even though both might be right, but stating the principles differently. Failure would be the result of this doubt and questioning. The Arcane commands: "Let thine eye be single."

A Spanish philosopher has said: "One must have an iron Will, a superior Spirit and be unshackled from the tentacles of others so as to be free from the fear of ridicule or discouragement."

TRANSMUTE THE UNDESIRABLE INTO THE DESIRABLE

Change, Arcanely known a Transmutation, is the art of the Alchemists and Occultists. In the Great Work, when ill thoughts arise, such as hatred, bitterness, malice, resentment and jealousy, they must be acted upon immediately, changing them into desires for Spiritual achievement. Time and effort may be necessary to accomplish this, but it is part of the Work.

Improvement and advancement in the Great Work can in part be measured by the ability to meet undesirable experiences calmly, by the ability to meet and transmute the hates, passions, resentment, disappointments, failures, ill feeling and all carnal thoughts and desires into feelings OF GOOD WILL AND THE DESIRE FOR GREATER ADVANCEMENT.

These changes also bring to the fore a different personality, one that draws others to you and helps to assure SUCCESS IN ANY FIELD IN WHICH YOU MAY BE ENGAGED. Enemies become friends; abhorrence changes into respect. In the Climb upwards it is certain, aye, necessary, that many discouraging factors are confronted, and it will appear that as each problem is solved, another presents itself. The climb upwards is like climbing a ladder or staircase. To reach the top, one must climb one step or one rung at a time. This is the Biblical climb to the Divine.

Mistakes rightly accepted, are a way stepping stones to success, and not a cause for disappointment. Lincoln failed thirteen times, but was wise enough to examine each failure, find the cause, and avoid it in the next effort. Man cannot fail who truly tries and keeps on trying. There is so much more reason for success within man as a part of his destiny, than there is reason for failure, that failure is impossible for one who continues to try. This is Illustrated in the motto of the Rosy Cross: "Try and try again, again and again and you will succeed at last." One of the great Laws that even those on the Path would like to evade, but which brings benefits otherwise impossible, is that the greater the difficulties met and overcome, the more important will be the benefits or returns received. The Divine Law clearly assures us of this. The Immortals prove it. Read the history of the truly great who became such because of their sterling honesty and manhood, their willingness to meet all

conditions, however heart breaking, and you will have the proof.
FAILURE IS OFTEN THE STEPPING STONE TO SUCCESS

Edison failed one hundred times in the invention of the electric light. Instead of being discouraged, he used the failure as a field of exploration, seeking the cause of each failure, and avoiding it in the next experiment. Discouragement is for the timid or weak. Weaklings never become successful or free men.

Problems are essential to achievement. They try the strength and the caliber of the person. When accepted in the right spirit, they build strength for greater trials and future success. Accept each problem willingly, and with alacrity, and in the spirit that the prizefighter meets the sparring partner; the football player the opponent. That is the Spirit of achievement and directly affects the physical self, the mind and the Soul. Learn to recognize and evaluate conditions and circumstances calmly and logically; NOT emotionally, and then like the contractor viewing the mountain to be removed, proceed calmly to the task.

Love is the Key to all real success in every avenue of achievement. In the past those who loved what THEY WERE DOING, WERE WILLING TO DIE FOR IT IF necessary. Nothing else mattered to them. This thought little of compensation. They frequently were willing to work without remuneration, asking only that they might be permitted to continue with their efforts on the work they were engaged in. With love in the heart for a work to be done, it becomes a pleasure. Without that love simple tasks become drudgery. Learn to love your work, whatever it may be, do it with all your might and to the best of your ability, and the law will soon provide you with A BETTER FIELD OF ACTIVITY. Failure to succeed in any effort, irrespective of what it may be, all too frequently is due to lack of preparation and application. It is often an unwillingness to be regular in WHAT MUST BE DONE IN COMPLIANCE WITH THE LAW.

This is due to instability of character—a mercurous temperament the Alchemists said. It is a mental attitude that must be corrected if you are its victim. ABSTINENCE—Abstinence in act, desirable as it is, is useless in Spiritual development unless it is accompanied by abstinence in thought and desire. The Nazarene made this most plain in his statement: "He who looks upon woman with lust in his heart has already committed lust."—Math. 5:28.

Substitute any other word for lust and IT WILL BE equally true. THE INFLUENCES OF THE SPHERES.

Always bear in mind that whenever you permit yourself TO THINK UNKIND, VICIOUS, DEGRADING THOUGHTS, THE INFLUENCE OF THE SPIRITUAL SPHERES WILL BE LOCKED OUT, NO MATTER WHAT YOU SAY, PRAY OR WHAT MANTRAM'S YOU REPEAT. The Spiritual beings will know what you think AND FEEL, AS WELL AS WHAT YOU SAY. It IS of utmost importance that you ever bear this in mind in making your efforts toward the goal.

UNDERSTANDING

In developing understanding, so essential to all success, you will gradually learn to distinguish quickly when you make a mistake and why you made it. Likewise, you will recognize how to avoid mistakes by acting differently.

Always be frank with yourself and freely admit to yourself when you are guilty of error, as also the why fore of it. Gradually the Subconscious will warn you when knowingly or unknowingly you are about to make a mistake.

A MIGHTY LAW

It is a part of the fundamental philosophy of the Great Work of the August Fraternity that whatever you can conceive in mind or imagination, you will have the capability and the power to achieve or bring into manifestation, providing the desire to do so IS STRONG ENOUGH TO AROUSE YOUR WILL TO MAKE THE NECESSARY EFFORT, AND CONSISTENTLY REFUSE TO PERMIT ANYTHING TO INTER FERE. This offers you the secret of success in any avenue of activity.

IMPATIENCE

All progress should be by a slow, gradual procedure. The first essential being that you become thoroughly conversant with the underlying philosophy of the work, and the Laws of operation. You should be as thoroughly informed on the subject as the student in College who is prepared to write the necessary thesis. This is then to be followed by a regular, systematic practice essential to the awakening of the latent forces within you, it being assumed that you know just what you seek to become or achieve. This likewise includes the arrangement of your affairs so that you will have a certain free period for those practices which will, if faithfully carried out, develop your mental and Spiritual forces, and their direction in the accomplishment of the work you have planned for yourself.

Having proceeded thus far, it is of utmost importance that you keep in mind the Master Teacher's command already stated but of importance to repeat: "No man, having put his hand to the plow, and looking back, [halting or permitting something to interfere] is FIT for the kingdom of God."—Luke 9:62. In these few words are contained the Law. They are simple words, easily understood. If you fail in this one thing, all else that follows will work toward failure, and you alone will be to blame.

OF UTMOST IMPORTANCE

The Soul, you're Soul, being feminine (the Divine Sophia) demands regular, though not constant devotion, except in case of duty. Woman-like, she knows and will accept no excuse. She is just, and does not demand the impossible from you, but she will not be neglected for the lesser of your interests.

ACCOUNTING TO YOURSELF

Each evening devote some little time giving an account of your day's activity to yourself. Analyze your actions of the day. Ask yourself the questions:

Did I do anything today of which I am not proud?

Did I do anything that was dishonest? Why?

Did I do my best in the position I am in?

Did I do anything that I would not want my friends, my wife, my loved children to know?

What direction did my thoughts and desires take?

Did I weaken in my objects in life?

Question yourself daily: Have I been guilty of any thought or act that one seeking to become an Initiate should not do, that was not done by those who became Soul Conscious. Have my actions been such as to make of me a light for others to follow?

As you question yourself, remember that t hose spiritual FORCES WHICH YOU MUST HAVE TO HELP YOU AND WHICH YOU WILL LATER (gradually) CONTACT, KNOW EVERYTHING YOU THINK, desire and do (even if you were not engaged in the Work), and will credit or debit you accordingly. Remember likewise, that it pays to be honest, the REaction of acts, compensate you fully for righteousness sake or demanding of you payment "to the utmost farthing."

ALWAYS EXPECT THE BEST

It is essential that in all things you look for, and expect only the best. If in need of anything for yourself, or family if married, and there is need of a thing never look for how cheaply you can obtain it. To do so is to attract to yourself those forces which will draw to you always the less desirable. If there is something needed, buy the best you possibly can. If there is no actual immediate need, wait until you can buy the best, though possibly not the costliest. This is the Law to opulence.

OBLIGATIONS

Do not ever obligate yourself to anything, no matter what it may be, unless you feel that you will be able to meet the obligation. If you should find later that you cannot do so, do not wait until the last moment, but as soon as you know, consult those to whom you are obligated, and explain (never make excuses) the conditions and circumstances and come to a fair, honest agreement. Do not, however, permit yourself to be imposed upon. This includes making your reports in the Great Work.

DO NOT BE A BRAGGARD

Never brag, be overbearing in your attitude, or attempt to appear what you are not. Do not try to seemingly be better than anyone else. Let your efforts and calm demeanor impress others rather than your words. Do not, in common parlance, be a "show off," as that will impress no one. Be yourself and even so, be reserved.

ARGUMENTS

Never engage in arguments, more especially not in relation to religion, politics, philosophy, or Spiritual things. Remember always: He who talks does not know; He who knows, will not talk. Discussions between those seriously interested may be of benefit, but even then, do not be impressed by what they think, or what they claim to know. They may not be of your grade of development, and what they know by experience may be, not at all suitable upon your plane.

BE NEUTRAL

Learn to be neutral, in thought and feeling, in order that you will not be affected by anything people may do or say. This requires that you learn to more or less live within yourself, yet not allow yourself to become anti-social or an introvert.

DO NOT BE RADICAL IN ANYTHING

Any changes you make should be done in a way that you can give yourself a logical reason for doing so. Do not offend by rendering judgment or because it does not agree with your opinions. Remember that each one has free Will and a right to his own beliefs and opinions. To try to change such opinions is to confirm them. Proceed slowly and diligently in all things you do for yourself that it may be within reason, and in the process of rebuilding your human structure. Be a reasonable per son, bot h with yourself AND IN DEALING WITH OTHERS.

LABOR-EFFORT

Whatever be your station in life at the moment, get away from the erroneous and destructive idea that manual labor is a curse. Labor (hard work) is the fat her of health and well-being. Unless there is sufficient effort either as a result of exercise or labor during the day to become tired of body, there will be lack of preparation for sound sleep so essential for the reconstruction necessary to health. There ARE NO EXCEPTIONS TO THIS RULE.

THE MIGHTIEST OF ALL LAWS

Only those will fully accept it who earnestly seek to become Soul Conscious Initiates, members of the August Fraternity, and of the select of the New Dispensation. The Nazarene's statement: "As ye sow, so shall ye reap," is so simple that only the very few become conscious of its universal application and its positiveness. Stated differently: You will be able to RECEIVE ONLY THAT WHICH YOU PAY OR EXCHANGE FOR. YOU MUST PAY FOR EVERYTHING YOU seek OR obtain.

The more ready you are to give, or exchange for that which you desire, bet his spiritual or material, the quicker you will receive it, and the greater good it will do you. If you desire something, NEVER falsely make the excuse that you cannot afford it, when in truth you possess the wherewith to obtain it. If you do, you FALSIFY THE

SPIRIT THAT IS THE REAL YOU; YOU BLIND YOUR SELF WITH THE IDEA THAT YOU CAN MISLEAD THE SPIRITUAL BEINGS WHO ALONE CAN HELP YOU IN EVERY WALK OF LIFE, MORE ESPECIALLY THE spiritual. "Bread cast upon the waters, etc.," the more you give to that which the heart seeks, the more you will receive in exchange. Study this time and time again until it is finally impressed upon your consciousness wherein is hidden the Christos.

YOUR RESPONSIBILITY

By enrolling—and you did so—otherwise you would not possess this text—you have assumed the greatest responsibility of which the human creature is capable. It is the obligation that you, created in the image of God, given all potentialities of a god and the ability to become an Initiate, will follow all instructions to the best of your ability, because it will enable you, by your own humble efforts, to attain the highest achievement any human Soul can reach, and to help you to find that Kingdom of God which offers you God's highest gift—peace—a gift beyond compare and without THE SACRIFICE OF A SINGLE THING THAT IS TO YOUR BENEFIT.

Education—The Foundation of True Success "And every one that heareth these sayings of mine, and doeth them not, shall be likened unto a foolish man which built his house upon the sand: "And the rain descended, the floods came, and the winds blew, and beat upon that house; and it fell: and great was the fall of it."—Matt. 7:26-27. Education, a thorough understanding of that WHICH YOU DESIRE TO ACCOMPLISH, OR BY MEANS OF WHICH YOU SEEK TO ACHIEVE, IS ESSENTIAL TO YOUR SUCCESS.

One of the most successful of all systems of education was that which Lincoln's teacher followed. This is a method which has never been improved upon and which you as a Neophyte should follow in your study of the Great Work in order that you may attain the highest from every point of view: physical, mental and Spiritual.

This method is outlined in a book lately issued and entitled Lincoln's Teacher, by Kunigunde Duncan, Advance Publishing Co.,

Great Barrington, Mass. Our excerpts or outline from it are not always verbatim.

IN LINCOLN'S TIME

The method followed by Mentor Graham, Lincoln's teacher, was more or less in vogue in all schools of the period. It was during this period that the greatest men, whether in the little red or log school houses, received their education. Writers, public speakers and Statesmen were the result of the system. You, a Neophyte who has entered the Great Work, can do no better than follow the plan in your study of the text books and the lessons, so that you will be thoroughly conversant with the philosophy. Your first text books should be Soul Consciousness and the present work.

FOLLOW THE WISE MAN

None but the foolish would attempt to build a mansion or a palace upon the sand. The wise man will build a firm foundation. You, if you are wise, will do likewise. The foundation for your Spiritual edifice should be a thorough knowledge of the subject, lest you become bewildered and fail. The method of your study should be identical with that employed by Mentor Graham: "First, open your book and read the first sentence of the lesson. Now shut your book and in mind—without pronouncing any words, either aloud or silent—tell yourself what that sentence meant."

You should follow this procedure not only in the study of the lessons of instructions, but of the texts, including the present, also. By doing this the knowledge gained is built on firm ground—the impression upon the Conscious which in time will Subconsciously direct you in your action away from the weakening, undesirable and debasing; acting as an Angel of Light to you. "Do the same with each sentence until you have completed the first paragraph. Then tell yourself what the paragraph means. "Open your book, and reread the paragraph, one sentence at a time to see if you have all of it. If you missed something or if it is not clear to you, find out what it is. Study until you understand the entire paragraph or sentence.

Finish the assignment, paragraph by paragraph, in this fashion. Then read the entire lesson from start to finish and explain to yourself what it all means. Then read it again to see if you missed anything, and what that was, and then tell yourself what the entire assignment means—all of it."

Undoubtedly you who read this have a better education than had Lincoln, and it may not be as difficult for you as it was for him. Always bear in mind what he had to do and what he accomplished. Rest in the assurance that in your choice for achievement of attainment you will have a much greater opportunity to succeed than he had if you will follow in his footsteps in the gaining of the essential knowledge necessary for your accomplishment.

THE BASIC PHILOSOPHY

You are now to attain to INDIVIDUALIZATION, which is just another term for godhood. The individual is one who has, by desire and effort, freed himself of his weaknesses and passions, and replaced them with strength and courage, and has BECOME THE MASTER OF HIMSELF AND THE SLAVE OF none. In accomplishing this task, you will replace every passion by an ability, uppermost of which will be the ability of doing as did Michelangelo in that which he most desired. Admittedly, this is no mean task, but again you need not accept the Occult concept for confirmation, but refer to the

Biblical story of the "talents" which assure you that you were born with an innate, though undeveloped ability to ACHIEVE THAT FOR WHICH YOU FIND LOVE WITHIN YOUR INNER SELF. Men have suffered all the evils of the REactions of the carnal nature. This is because they lacked knowledge of the TRUTH, the eternal verity. This truth which is also the Divine Law as well as the Natural Law, is not readily found because, for untold centuries falsehoods have been IMPRESSED UPON THE MIND OF MAN INSTEAD OF TRUTH.

You must begin by first living up to one of the things you feel is right, because in its REaction there is no accusation of conscience.

To the first obedience of the Law is added a second, then a third, and thence ad infinitum. As you proceed in this change of life's activity, if you are not wise and talk too much of what you are about, there may be sneers, perhaps vilification and even persecution. You will remember the promise that "he who suffers for my sake [that of righteousness] will be repaid many fold," by reason of the REaction of the Law as the result of wisely acting, as also the feeling of moral and Spiritual strength and wellbeing. Step by step the "ladder to heaven" is climbed until your weaknesses as a novice have been overcome and you are as one of the "select."

THE MYSTERY WITHIN YOURSELF

The Divine and Natural Laws you may learn from the texts, but the knowledge—the knowing—can come to you only from within the self; from the subconscious where all the knowledge gained throughout the ages is stored, to be drawn upon as you progress in your development and pre pare yourself for it.

"Seek ye within." Yes, within yourself you will find that which was hidden from the angels and can be yours only by trying. A price MUST be paid. This is true in all things, even for the things that destroy the Soul. One offers eternal peace, including that which we know as happiness, while the other degrades, leading to Gehenna with all its horrors and the universal suffering and afflictions of mankind, all because man is unwilling to obey the Law which governs him WHETHER HE WILL OR NOT.

This state of being, fortunately while selective, is not arbitrary. It IS selective, as selective as the tree of the fruit it bears. It is accorded to those who comply with the law. This Law demands that you change the thoughts, de sires and actions which are not conducive to your welfare or that of others, until you come within the action of the Law and "bear" the "fruit" for which you were originally ordained.

AROUSE THE SLEEPING GIANT

The Spiritual forces or forces of the Spirit of the eternal are never for those who refuse to recognize and abide with the Divine Law. This Law is not selective as to personality to begin with. You as a person possess Free Will with the right of choice. It recognizes only desire, or the aspiration of the real self, though this self may still be almost dormant. It does, however, demand: "Arouse that which sleepeth" so that the Spirit which is the Divine Self, may manifest in the sleeper. Never permit yourself to be misled by the Will o' the Wisp or illusion known as happiness. At most the feeling of happiness is only for fleeting moments. Your thought and effort should be for the eternal verity—peace. Peace is possible only as a result of a free conscience.

A free conscience is possible only by rooting out all that is destructive or degrading in thought and desire; by dealing justly by one's fellow man. The ultimate of man's existence is the peace that begins here on earth now, and the first step is found in knowledge. Educating the self in what is right and what is wrong; knowing that any wrong against the self or others is the destroyer of peace. Biblically and Occultly, peace is "heaven" and simply stated: "Seek ye first the kingdom of God and His righteousness [peace] and all these things shall be added unto you."—Matt. 6:33.

A SLEEPING GOD WITHIN YOUR SOUL

There is another enLiGHTening statement in the Scriptures that has much to do with your ultimate goal—peace: "Behold, the Kingdom of God is within you."—Luke 17:21. This is the same truth differently stated: God is eternal peace. God cannot dwell within your being until you first find the Kingdom of God. That kingdom is a free conscience, a state of peace, and that peace may be present even when you are persecuted, tortured or shunned by your fellow men.

Where there is peace there also is God. God dwells within the Soul that has found peace. Another potent thought connected with this Law: "Man was created in the Image of God," but man does not symbolize God until he has found the kingdom. Then man also has become the Son of God, knowing good and evil, having experienced both, and having overcome evil. To add a mundane note to this sublime subject, this freeing of the conscience and finding peace is also the way to success in all phases of life. It is said that Lincoln made the remark that: "God is with me when I do His Will, and there is no evil in me, my conscience is free." Whether or not Lincoln said this, it is based on a truth that is eternal.

Material success and Spiritual attainment proceed hand in hand if you first seek the kingdom where peace dwells and you are free from an accusing conscience.

YOUR FEELING IS A RELIABLE GUIDE

The illusive something, which will follow in the wake of your efforts to free yourself from the bondage of the flesh and the carnal self, cannot be uncovered by the mind or the senses. It must be felt, and it can be felt only as it becomes a part of your sensing or feeling, a part of your Spiritual, emotional nature.

Feeling is a sensing, and in the ultimate is the only reality. Your feelings or sensing will at all times place you either in heaven or hell, whatever the physical conditions may be. As a sense of feeling you find yourself in complete peace of mind, or heaven, or suffer the tortures of hell, even though you have all your wants fulfilled. You are more or less now in either one of these states according to the state of your conscience. Conscience stands at the gate of both; the one key opens both doors or gates.

THE LAW MUST ALWAYS GOVERN

In seeking for the ultimate, which will become the immediate in time, bringing you both peace and success in the affairs of life, it is essential that you obey the Divine Law.

God called this Law into activity at the same time He permitted the first Soul, or Divine Spark, part of Himself, to incarnate, and in conjunction with the edict that the Divine Law should govern. Natural Law likewise must be obeyed because they work conjointly. This may appear as a Herculean task, but it demands ONLY THAT WHICH IN THE ULTIMATE IS TO YOUR benefit. Whether we are willing to admit it or not, we DO GET PAID FOR BEING WHAT IS TERMED "good" and punished by what is known as evil. You begin with faith as an essential and as an urge to TRY. It is a faith which is accompanied by effort.

This Faith permits you no rest until there is effort; constant effort as part of life's activities, until there is fulfillment of the inborn desire. As an extreme example we can cite Michelangelo who loved his art so well that he was not happy unless he was wielding his brush. He was happy in doing so though he was both cold and hungry. The result: The world's greatest art and Immortality for himself. You are held in bondage by your thoughts and this restricts you to their limits. By means of the study of the texts of The Great Work, and the actual practice of the instructions that will be given you as a Neophyte by the August Fraternity, new thoughts will come to your mind and these will replace the old. These thoughts will awaken you to new and constructive ideas.

This in turn will give birth to desires of a different nature than those which bound you heretofore. As these desires grow stronger, they will be followed by efforts different by far from the former ones; resulting in awakening into a new plane of life and activity. This is the pathway to success ON all planes. Admittedly this will be cause for travail, because all birth is in pain.

The activities of the new life will be far different than the old, though there may be no outward show of this for a time, with the result that former friends and associates will possibly turn their back on you. This is the price to be paid for advancement. Something, whether good or ill, cannot be had for nothing. The Law is exchange; but that which is received in turn will be well worth the price paid.

YOUR THREE-FOLD LIFE

The Great Work and the August Fraternity does not consider you merely a physical being to be born to toil; to suffer and grow old for the mere sake of living. It visions for you a three-fold life, each of a different nature, yet all working in harmony. First of all, it sees you beginning as a weak creature, buffeted about by many things which control you. It sees your body as a machine that must be perfected in detail and engineered.

Then there is the mind which will require much training so as to coordinate it with the governing Law. This mind, very gradually, will become the engineer of the machine, the body, and direct it just as the trained engineer controls the machine in his charge.

This will not be an easy matter because this mind has formed habits and will not readily respond to direction. Gradually, step by step, the mind will fall in line as a result OF THE IMPRESSIONS MADE UPON IT BY YOUR STUDY AND practice. Then, in harmony with the more controlled body and a mind that responds, the desires become aroused in harmony with the new concepts which the mind accepted. In conjunction with this new state of the mind the Will also come into play. The body, mind, desire and Will begin to work together in harmony and all in an upward trend.

TRUTH IS RESERVED FOR THOSE WHO ARE READY

This is not a new idea. It is almost as old as is thinking man. The August Fraternity existed ages ago in India, then in Egypt and on down the ages. It has not been necessary for it to change these fundamentals in a single instance, because they are based on the recognition of forces Spiritual in nature, but hidden from all but those who have not as yet entered the gates toward this new life. The blending of the awakened mind with Spiritual aspirations (desires) will lead you, as it has others, to the ultimate of attainment. You must never forget that your future depends on an inner urge which is Spiritual in nature and therefore unchangeable throughout eternity.

You have heard or read the Biblical injunction: "Do not put new wine into old bottles." You are directly concerned. This new wine is the new Spirit which your efforts will awaken within you. For lo, how long has it been dormant? With the very first practice of the instructions of the Great Work, if YOUR FEELINGS ARE IN THE EFFORT, you will begin to arouse this Spirit and slowly bring it into activity.

This naturally requires the cooperation of the mind because the mind will be the director of your action. It is the feeling aroused in you by your effort that will cause the mind to gradually change, take another track as it were, and as a result both mind and the Spirit, or feeling, will begin to function in the newly opened channel.

THE WHOLE MAN MUST BE REGENERATED

This gradual change will also be the beginning of the establishment of the Kingdom of God within you. This change is not, as has long been taught, a wholly religious matter. On the contrary, it includes all of man, and ALL THINGS THAT concern him. It is for the whole of you. It appears to be a simple matter to find the kingdom of heaven, the changing of the body for the new wine. It is simple, but you will soon be confronted with difficulties, once you begin to TRY to control your thoughts. This also is not merely of the mind, but involves the whole of you and you will find all the forces of your carnal nature pitted against you.

The old self, this old wine, is formidable because it is yourself as you now are, but the "wages of the laborer" that is, the results of every effort, and every sacrifice, will rebuild this OLD self, the old bottle, and bring you, its benefits. Oh, yes, there are sacrifices to be made because it is the giving up of much that you are, and making the replacements.

Once you get into the Spirit you will no longer feel that it is a sacrifice, because you will get a vision of what it is to be to have found this kingdom within, and to be able to be living in it. You will also take notice that whatever occupies your thought, will return measure for measure; measure to overflowing as a REaction to whatever you are engaged in, be this the most menial of tasks.

WITHIN YOURSELF THERE IS A SLEEPING GIANT

Nothing of this inner self can come from the outside, nor be given to you. It is already present. All that you do is to arouse the inner self, the Christos, the God-self placed within from the beginning of time. The beginning of this change within yourself will be at the very moment you become conscious that the old thoughts are undesirable and degrading, whether they be of hate, envy, resentment, or any one of the many other Degenerative thoughts.

By your desire and effort, you replace the undesirable with their opposite. At that very moment you will have sown the "seed" that will in time create the new self; bringing into manifestation the being that had been asleep within, lo, these many years.

THE OLD SELFISHNESS MUST DIE

It is simple, all so very simple, but because it is so simple it does not make the work any easier. The old self will be constantly on the alert to save its own existence and you must be prepared to do battle. This also is simple because it only requires that you replace the old thoughts with the new constructive, exalting thoughts until the old has been entirely eliminated. You must be on the alert because the old self has long experience and is firmly established, while you are travelling the new route toward a newer, greater self; toward freedom and success on all planes.

As this awakening of the new self within you and the elimination of the old takes place, you will be changing the old worldly personal and limited self into an individuality, and this individual is the son of God which has been reborn out of the son of man; the Spiritual self out of the limited mortal self; mortality will have been changed into Immortality.

YOU ARE CREATED IN GOD'S IMAGE

The August fraternity has a firm belief in good based on experience and that all of man's attributes called "good" are part of Him, or different manifestations. You, being created in God's image possess all the qualities He possesses, though in lesser degree. These are in embryo. They are in a dormant, unawakened state, soundly asleep, and you live entirely on the husks of physical existence.

The Biblical story of the "talents" indicates this truth clearly, and that all that is necessary for you to reap the "harvest" is to dig deep down within yourself. By MEANS OF DESIRE, FORTIFIED BY WILL, YOU AWAKEN THE TALENT OR TALENTS INTO MANIFESTATION. YOU WILL BECOME A CREATOR IN YOUR OWN RIGHT—THE CREATION THE CREATOR INTENDED YOU TO BE. THAT WHICH YOU WILL RECEIVE, OR BECOME, WILL BE IN EXCHANGE FOR YOUR DESIRE AND EFFORT. IT IS THEN YOURS BECAUSE YOU HAVE HONESTLY EARNED IT, AND NO MAN, OR NATION OF MEN, CAN TAKE IT FROM YOU. THE SLEEPING CREATIVE SPIRIT MUST BE AWAKENED.

The Father, whom we speak of, but few know, is God the eternal in Spirit. He is the Creator by force of his creation. He does not need mind, nor will, desire is the essence of His being as it should be of yours, because He is an eternal Creator. Man is not so because he fails to fulfill the Law, THOUGH HE HAS THE DIVINE SPARK OF GOD WITHIN HIMSELF.

This creative Spirit will never awaken of its own accord. The mind must first be brought into constructive activity as a result of some experience, to the fact that there is something more to life than mortality and the hate nature. You must awaken to the assurance that you possess something you as yet know not what, and that you have the ABILITY TO AROUSE AND AWAKEN THIS GREATER SOME THING within. When this occurs your work actually begins. You, the Neophyte, now stand before the gate, and it is your privilege to enter in, and in due time partake of the "Bread" which is a full life here, and Eternal life in the future.

In the texts of the Great Work much is written of the greatness of the Initiates of the August Fraternity in the time of India and Egypt. While your problems of today, differ greatly from those of that far time, neither the divine LAW, NOR THE NATURAL LAW, HAVE CHANGED IN ANY INSTANCE.

Your path is not in the slightest different from what it was for the men of long ago. Your body is the same as was theirs, requires exactly the same care, the same nourishment and the same training. Your mind is as was theirs. Your mortal desires are the same. The same stubbornness, conceit and desires, which led towards failure and decay, are present. The same Will that has never been trained toward an upward trend, is yours.

You have an advantage. You may learn from their experiences and begin practically where they left off, but you must make the same beginning in awakening your mind. Your desires must be aimed toward the end sought. You must study the Law that you may apply it in your efforts and "follow through" by refusing to give up the effort, or be swayed by the influences of others. Just as these of the past were derided by their fellow men, their associates, their families in the beginning, so may it be with you, especially if you talk too much, while the same honors will be yours as were theirs, if you are steadfast in your efforts.

Ever bear in mind that the man who refused to deviate from set principles is always honored even though he be hated. It is truthfully said that Lincoln was the most hated man who ever lived. It is equally true that he was also, still is, the most honored, and even those of his day who saw him only as a stubborn man handed him the laurel.

"I AM THE WAY"

It is said that the Nazarene taught: "I am the way, the truth and the life." It would be more in harmony with the Law if this were changed to "I am the truth, the way and the life," because the Neophyte does not enter the "way" until he has become mentally awakened to the existence of a truth that is new to him, a way of life leading away from death and all this implies; to the new wine that will be in the new bottle. Some shreds of truth at least must be learned before there is an awakening of the mind to desire; desire to be on the path, and this path followed as it leads into the new life and all that it promises.

TRUTH IS OFTEN MOST DIFFICULT TO FIND

Develop a deep yearning for the truth and the way. This will create a desire to attain, and arouse you to action. If the desire is intense enough it will arouse a Spiritual Fire that will fortify you against the "old devil," your former weaknesses and habits, and those, who, having no knowledge of a different life, will do all they can to distract you, discourage you, and win you away from your newly chosen path. Keep in mind constantly the promises of this new life; vision the Gold that is at the end of the rainbow; the arising of the once sleeping Spiritual self.

"I am the way." These are the words that are spoken constantly by the awakening hidden self within to every human being possessed of a Soul. It is the cry of the Christos, the Spiritual self-seeking to be released that it may truly live, and lead you onward and upward—instead of the dead self-leading you downward—to the lower depths of mortal life which offers no more at best than questionable joys and empty honors; possessions that leave you when most needed; passions that corrode the Real self within.

THE OLD SELF MUST GIVE WAY TO THE NEW

This Spiritual self once fully aroused within cannot remain confined within the old self. It must and will find outward expression. This expression is first of all a feeling of well-being, then the winning of friends, success in your chosen avocation, greatest of all perhaps, the deep respect and affection of your loved one, who perhaps in the beginning of your Novitiate sneered at you for your "peculiar" way, made fun of you because you would not accept anything degrading. You would not cheat in the affairs of life but kept every promise made even though it might be a loss to the gateway in to yourself, having the inner assurance that a loss through honesty would return to you tenfold with the addition of blessings in the form of great peace of mind and approval of conscience.

"Seek ye first the kingdom that is within you," find it by effort, and all things else will be added unto you. This is a promise never repudiated because it is made by the activating, governing Law itself.

FORWARD-EVER

FORWARD-TOWARD SUCCESS

This it is also to become one in the New Age, a "selected" one of the citizens of that Dispensation. The path from the moment you enter it is continuous. It is step by step onward and forward from the present into the future, and, as the song would have it: "For evermore." This is the promise of St. John in Revelation. For the present, it is the blessing of such a life in the material world, an unexplainable peace, a love that is eternal. The falling away of one you thought a friend, the turning away from one you thought of as a "loved one," all these things will hurt deeply until you become aware that they were not actually real friends, that the love professed was artificial and selfish.

OVERCOMING EVIL BRINGS MASTERSHIP

Finally, the evils of the world in which you live are multitudinous. As you free yourself from the purely temporal, carnal nature, you will at the same time free yourself from the effects of these worldly evils. The evils rampant on the world are no worse than the reflections from the hearts of men. All of them are temporary as are those who give way to them. To become the victim of the carnal is to "be of a few days to be known no more." Think not evil and you will become a free man, conscious free. The most evil things in the world can affect you only to the degree and to the extent that your Spiritual self is not itself free from these carnal things.

All evils in as far as you are concerned, are from within yourself. Your freedom from them must likewise come from within yourself, as the RESULT OF YOUR DESIRES AND EFFORTS. You ARE what you think you are if you will act accordingly. Any bondage or failure is your own weaving. Unthread the tie that binds you. This is the Great Work of the August Fraternity. It will help you to achieve your destiny and become a Living Soul.

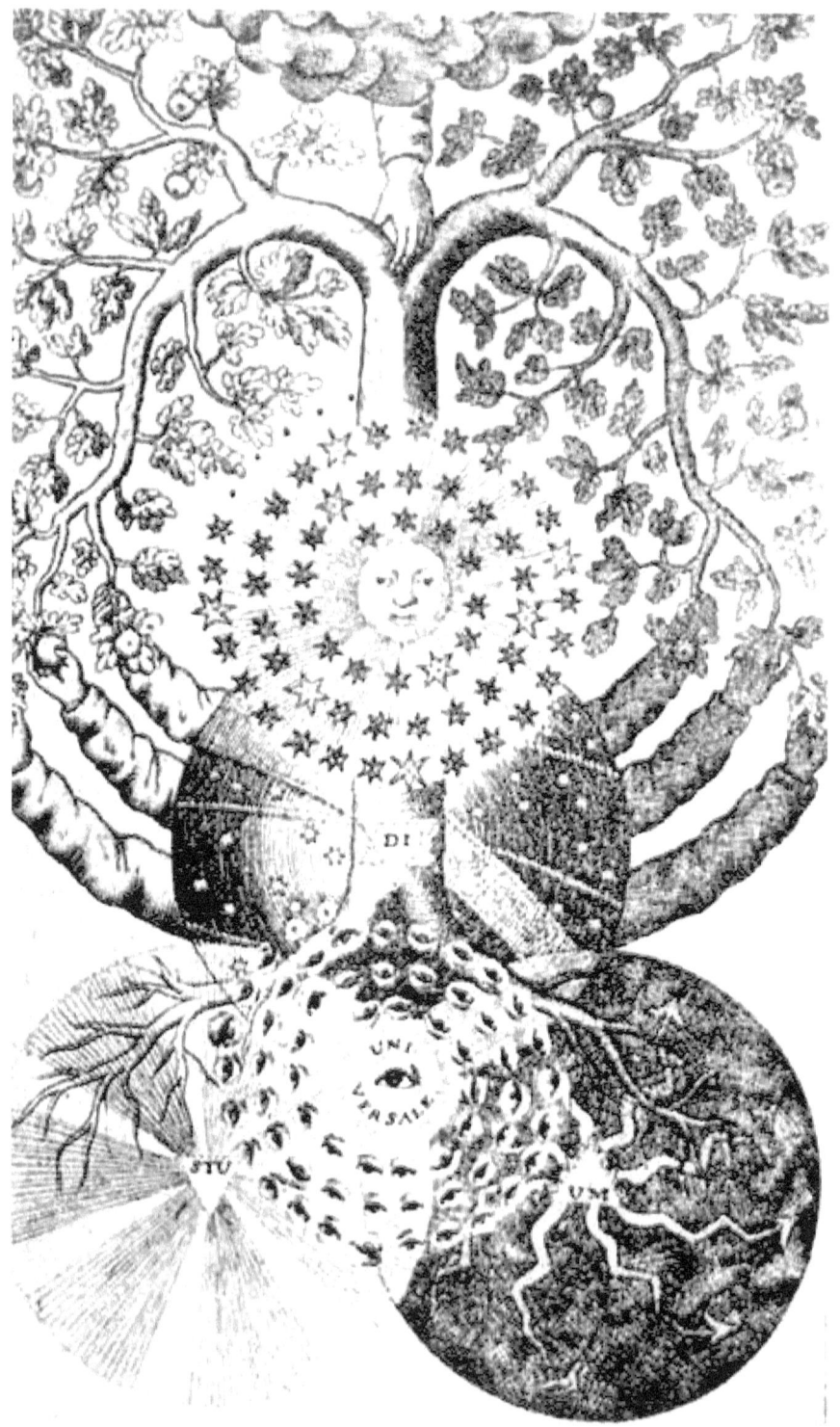

JOHN

By CHARLES FILLMORE - 1854 - 1948

In the beginning was the Word, and the Word was with God, and the Word was God. 2 The same was in the beginning with God. 3 All things were made through him; and without him was not anything made that hath been made. 4 In him was life; and the life was the light of men. And the light shineth in the darkness, and the darkness apprehended it not.

IN PURE METAPHYSICS there is but one word, the word of God. This is the original creative Word or thought of Being. It is the "God said" of Genesis. The Greek original refers to it in the 1st chapter of John as the logos. The Greek word cannot be adequately translated into English. In the original it denotes wisdom, judgment, power, and in fact all the inherent potentialities of Being. This divine Logos was and always is in God; in fact, it is God as creative power. The Divine Mind creates under law; that is, spiritual law. Man may get a comprehension of the creative process of Being by analyzing the action of his own mind. First is mind, then the idea in mind of what the act is to be, then the act itself. Thus, the Word and the divine process of creating are identical. Apart from mind nothing can be made.

Even man, in his forming and bringing anything into manifestation, uses the same creative process that God used; to the degree that the qualities of the one Mind enter into man's thought in the process his work will be enduring. The divine idea the Christ or Word of God is always everywhere present.

Among the four Gospels that of John is readily discerned by metaphysicians as a symbolical life of Jesus Christ and should appear first in the New Testament, corresponding to the first chapters of Genesis. Quite a few Bible critics so consider it, among them Ferrar Fenton, who gives it first place in his "Complete Bible in Modern English" John explains that all existence is spiritual, that it comes to man as a gift, and that Christ is its fulfillment.

"In the beginning was the Word, and the Word was with God, and the Word was God "The Word" is the English translation of the Greek logos, which means a thought or concept and also the word that is an expression or utterance of the same. It also involves the logical relation between idea and expression; hence our word logic, which also derives from logos. Our attention is called to the 1st chapter of Genesis: "And the Spirit of God moved upon the face of the waters. And God said, Let there be light: and there was light' Here in detail, day by day, or period by period, creation is ideated. The parallel between Genesis and John is shown by the manifestation of the ideal man. In Genesis dam appears first.

In John it is John the Baptist, who is said to "bear witness" to the coming man, Jesus Christ. In Genesis man was given dominion over all things; in John "all things were made through him." John the Baptist represents the natural man, the physical man, who is the nucleus around which the spiritual man builds. Man may be compared to a house, the foundation being rock, the superstructure lighter material. The rock upon which Jesus built was not material: it was mental; its symbol, Peter, was a mind receptive to spiritual Truth and spiritual substance.

The first Adam was formed of the "dust of the ground," representing radiant substance instead of gross earth. So, John the Baptist was more than the perfect physical man. He was the illumined natural man. He preached and baptized his disciples and with spiritual vision saw the unfoldment of the natural man into the Christ man.

Spiritual man is the true light "which lighteth every man, coming into the world." The world was made by him and yet "knew him not." There is a creative force constantly at work in man and all creation, but it is not recognized. It is Spirit-mind shining consciously in the minds and hearts of those who recognize it. Those who ignore this light do not "apprehend" it, and to them it is nonexistent.

"But as many as received him, to them gave he the right to become children of God, even to them that believe on his name." There came a man, sent from God, whose name was John. The same came for witness, that he might bear witness of the light, that all might believe through him. He was not the light, but came that he might bear witness of the light. Man in his darkened, ignorant state dwells in a realm of material thoughts and perceives nothing higher until he arrives at the point in his unfoldment where he is ready to receive understanding of the Christ Truth. Then he enters into the John the Baptist or intellectual perception of Truth. The intellectual perception of Truth by the natural man (John the Baptist) is not the true light (the Christ) but bears witness to the light and prepares the way for its dawning in consciousness.

There was the true light, even the light which lighteth every man, coming into the world. He was in the world, and the world was made through him, and the world knew him not. He came unto his own, and they that were his own received him not. The true light (the Christ or Word) that lights every man coming into the world is and ever has been in man. Even the outer man was formed and came into existence through it. Up to a certain stage in his unfolding man does not recognize this truth; now however this mystery, which is "Christ in you, the hope of glory" is being revealed to the race with more and more clarity and with greatly increased power.

But as many as received him, to them gave he the right to become children of God, even to them that believe on his name: who were born, not of blood, nor of the will of the flesh, nor of the will of man, but of God. According to the 12th and 13th verses, the same truth that held good for Jesus will hold good for as many as receive Him (the Christ) and believe in His resurrecting power as Jesus believed in it.

And the Word became flesh, and dwelt among us (and we beheld his glory, glory as of the only begotten from the Father), full of grace and truth. Jesus recognized this truth that the Christ, the divine-idea man or Word of God, was His true self and that He was consequently the Son of God. Because Jesus held to this perfect image of the divine man, the Christ or Word entered consciously into every atom of His being, even to the very cells of His outer organism, and transformed all His body into pure, immortal, spiritual substance and life. Thus "the Word became flesh" The resurrecting of His whole being included His body. Jesus entered alive and entire into the spiritual realm.

John beareth witness of him, and crieth, saying, This was He of whom I said, He that cometh after me is become before me; for He was before me. For of his fulness we all received, and grace for grace. For the law was given through Moses; grace and truth came through Jesus Christ. No man hath seen God at any time; the only begotten Son, who is in the bosom of the Father, he hath declared him. "The law was given through Moses." Moses represents a phase of the evolutionary process in man. "The law" the outer commandments cannot redeem." Grace and truth came through Jesus Christ; that is, the real saving, redeeming, transforming power came to man through the work that Jesus Christ did in establishing for the race a new and higher consciousness in the earth.

We can enter into that consciousness by faith in Him and by means of the inner spirit of the law that He taught and practiced. The 18th verse teaches that through the Christ in us we come into an understanding of the Father, since the Son (the Word) ever exists in God, and Father and Son are one and are omnipresent in man and in the universe. Spirit Truth is discerned through Spirit only; not in outer ways or through intellectual perception do we come to know God.

And this is the witness of John, when the Jews sent unto him from Jerusalem priests and Levites to ask him, Who art thou? And he confessed, and denied not; and he confessed, I am not the Christ. And they asked him, What then? Art thou Elijah? And he saith, I am not. Art thou the prophet? And he answered, No. They said therefore unto him, Who art thou? that we may give an answer to them that sent us. What sayest thou of thyself? He said, I am the voice of one crying in the wilderness, Make straight the way of the Lord, as said Isaiah the prophet. And they had been sent from the Pharisees. And they asked him, and said unto him, Why then baptizest thou, if thou art not the Christ, neither Elijah, neither the prophet? John answered them, saying, I baptize in water: in the midst of you standeth one whom ye know not, even he that cometh after me, the latchet of whose shoe I am not worthy to unloose.

These things were done in Bethany beyond the Jordan, where John was baptizing. In the regeneration two states of mind are constantly at work. First comes the cleansing or denial state, in which all the error thoughts are eliminated. This includes forgiveness for sins committed and a general clearing up of the whole consciousness. The idea is to get back into the pure, natural consciousness of Spirit. This state of mind is typified by John the Baptist, who came out of the wilderness a child of nature whose mission it was to make straight the way for One who was to follow. This putting away of sin from the consciousness (baptism through denial, plus forgiveness) is very closely allied to the deeper work that is to follow; so much so that to the observer it seems the same. Hence the followers of John, when they saw the works he did, asked if he was the Messiah. His answer was that the One who followed him was to baptize with Holy Spirit. From this we discern that mental cleansing and the reforms that put the conscious mind in order are designed to prepare the way for that larger and more permanent consciousness which is to follow.

This is the denial of "self" or personality. Jesus said, "If any man would come after me, let him deny himself" We are all guilty in a way of undue devotion to personal aims, which are always narrow and selfish. So long as these exist and take the place of the rightful One there is no room for the higher self, the Christ of God. The recorded "This is the Son of God" is a reference to a matter of first importance in the regeneration. The recognition of man as the Son of God and the establishment in the mind of the new relations between the divine Father and the Son are essential to the process.

If we do not affirm our sonship, with all its privileges and powers, we are sure to belittle ourselves and make limitations that prevent us from entering into the fullness of the Godhead. "Be perfect, as your heavenly Father is perfect" On the morrow he seeth Jesus coming unto him, and saith, Behold, the Lamb of God, that taketh away the sin of the world! This is he of whom I said, After me cometh a man, who is become before me: for he was before me. And I knew him not; but that he should be made manifest to Israel, for this cause came I baptizing in water. And John bare witness, saying, I have beheld the Spirit descending as a dove out of heaven; and it abode upon, him. And I knew him not; but he that sent me to baptize in water, he said unto me, Upon whomsoever thou shalt see the Spirit descending, and abiding upon him, the same is he that baptizeth in the Holy Spirit.

And I have seen, and have borne witness that this is the Son of God. Metaphysically interpreted, John the Baptist symbolizes in each individual the natural man, but with an illumined intellect. His face is turned toward the light in the measure that he recognizes and pays homage to the higher self within the individual. John baptized with water all those who believed that Jesus Christ was soon to make His appearance. This is a cleansing, purifying process, preparing the individual to see spiritually and to discern spiritually. The Father-Mind is the living principle, the absolute, the unlimited. The Son is the living Word. "Word" is used to designate man's I AM identity.

The Holy Spirit is the action or outpouring or activity of the living Word. This activity produces what may be termed the light of Spirit, the breath of God, the "personality" of Being. The outpouring of the Holy Spirit is the sign by which the natural man recognizes the divine. Jesus, who became the "Lamb of God" or perfect expression of God, baptized in the Holy Spirit.

Again, on the morrow John was standing, and two of his disciples; and he looked upon Jesus as he walked, and saith, Behold, the Lamb of God! By cultivation the spiritual mind becomes an active factor in consciousness. It has to be desired and sought before it becomes a part of one's conscious life. John the Baptist (the natural conscious mind) is expecting, looking for, and earnestly desiring a greater realization of Spirit. He knows that he is not fulfilling the Christ ideal of manhood; hence his prophecy of One who is to come, "the latchet of whose shoe" he is not worthy to loose. This willingness to give up the natural man to the divine is a most propitious sign in one who is in the regenerative process. Many persons are ambitious to put on Christ, but are not willing to give up the present man in order to do so. John the Baptist had a following, yet he was willing that his disciples should go to Jesus. He openly acknowledged Him as the "Lamb of God." This was his acknowledgment of the Christ mind. That mind has no personal ambition; it is innocent, loving, and obedient to the call of God.

And the two disciples heard him speak, and they followed Jesus. And Jesus turned, and beheld them following, and saith unto them, What seek ye? And they said unto him, Rabbi (which is to say, being interpreted, Teacher), where abidest thou? He saith unto them, Come, and ye shall see. They came therefore and saw where he abode; and they abode with him that day: it was about the tenth hour. One of the two that heard John speak, and followed him, was Andrew, Simon Peter's brother. He findeth first his own brother Simon, and saith unto him, We have found the Messiah (which is, being interpreted, Christ).

He brought him unto Jesus. Jesus looked upon him, and said, Thou art Simon the son of John: thou shalt be called Cephas *(which is by interpretation, Peter)*. When the conscious mind recognizes the Chris mind, the various faculties gradually awaken and attach themselves to it. Andrew is the first disciple mentioned, and with him was one whose name is not given here but who is supposed to have been John (love). Love is modest and retiring, "seeketh not its own" Andrew represents the strength of the mind, which, greatly rejoiced when it finds the inexhaustible source of all strength, exclaims, "We have found the Messiah:" Strength is clearly related to substance (Simon), which in spirit we call faith. "Faith is the substance of things hoped for" (A. V.). What we hope for and mentally see as a possibility in our life comes into visibility, and we call it substantial.

On the morrow he was minded to go forth into Galilee, and he findeth Philip: and Jesus saith unto him, Follow me. 44 Now Philip was from Bethsaida, of the city of Andrew and Peter. Philip findeth Nathanael, and saith unto him, We have found him, of whom Moses in the law, and the prophets, wrote, Jesus of Nazareth, the son of Joseph. And Nathanael said unto him, Can any good thing come out of Nazareth? Philip saith unto him, Come and see. Jesus saw Nathanael coming to him, and saith of him, Behold, an Israelite indeed, in whom is no guile! Nathanael saith unto him, Whence knowest thou me? Jesus answered and said unto him, Before Philip called thee, when thou wast under the fig tree, I saw thee. Nathanael answered him, Rabbi, thou art the Son of God; thou art King of Israel. Jesus answered and said unto him, Because I said unto thee, I saw thee underneath the fig tree, believest thou? thou shalt see greater things than these.

And he saith unto him, Verily, verily, I say unto you, Ye shall see the heaven opened, and the angels of God ascending and descending upon the Son of man. The name Philip means "lover of horses," and Philip is symbolic of the vigor, power, vitality, and energy of the mind. Philip, Andrew, and Peter are of the same "city," Bethsaida. The name Bethsaida means "house of fishing," and Bethsaida signifies a group of thoughts in consciousness that have as their central idea a belief in the increase of ideas and their expression and manifestation in outer form. Nathanael (representing the imagination) is also called Bartholomew. In the realm of the real (Israel) the imaging power of the mind is guileless, innocent of error images. It is open and receptive to the beauty and perfection of Being.

It is the faculty of imagination that makes the great artist and the great poet. It is the guileless innocence of the Nathanael state of mind that causes the religious enthusiast to believe all things about Spirit and the world invisible. Exercised without Christ understanding, the imagination becomes delusory. It is the image maker in the psychic; the clairvoyant may be deceived by its conjuring power. In itself it is not error, but it may, like all the other faculties, be used in erroneous ways. When the mind of Spirit uses it, as in the case of Jesus' discerning Nathanael when he was under the fig tree, it is without guile; and in God's communication with man this faculty plays an important part. Among the disciples, Bartholomew represents the imagination. He is called Nathanael in the 1st chapter of John, where it is recorded that Jesus saw him under the fig tree, the inference being that He discerned Nathanael's presence before the latter came into visibility. This would indicate that images of people and things are projected into the imaging chamber of the mind and that by giving them attention one can understand their relation to outer things.

Mind readers, clairvoyants, and dreamers have developed this capacity in varying degree. Consciousness is what is concerned with soul unfoldment both primarily, and secondarily and all the way! Forms are always manifestations of ideas. Whoever understands this can interpret the symbols shown him in dreams and visions, but lack of understanding of this law makes one a psychic without discernment. With this spiritual faculty it is possible for man to penetrate into the "fourth dimension" or what is usually called the "kingdom of the heavens" and to discern the trend of the spiritual forces. The angels of God are spiritual forces active in the Sons of God, the spiritually quickened. The open and receptive and believing mind can see the things that take place in the Christ mind, thus transcending the capacity of the unillumined natural man.

VOYAGE TO THE LAND OF THE ROSICRUCIAN'S

A. E. WAITE Collection - 1857 - 1942

(This extract was in old English spelling which has been converted to modern spelling for ease of reading.)

We travelled from Sydmouth for London and Spain by the south sea, taking with us victuals for twelve months, and had good winds from the East, though soft and weak, for five months' space and more. But then the winds came about into the West, so as we could make little way, and were sometimes in purpose to turn back. Then again here arose strong and great winds from the South, with a point East, which carried us up towards the North, by which time our victuals failed us, and we gave ourselves for lost men, and prepared for death. We did lift up our hearts and voices to God, beseeching Him of His mercy that He would discover land to us, that we might not perish.

The next day about evening we saw before us, towards the North, as it were thick clouds, which did put us in hope of land, knowing that part of the south sea was utterly unknown, and might have islands or continents hitherto not come to light. We bent our course thither all that evening, and in the dawning of the next day discerned a land flat and full of boscage. After an hour and a half's sailing, we entered into a good haven, the port of a faire city, not great indeed, but well built, and that gave a pleasant view from sea. We came close to shore, and offered to land, but straightaways we saw divers people with bastons in their hands forbidding us, yet without any cry's or fierceness, but only warning us off by signs that they made, whereupon, being not a little discomfited, we were advising with ourselves what we should do, during which there made forth to us a small boat, with about eight persons in it, whereof one had in his hand a tipstaff of yellow cane, tipped at both ends with green, who came aboard without any shew of distrust, and drew forth a little scroll of parchment, somewhat yellower than our parchment, and shining like the leaves of writing tables, but otherwise soft and flexible, and delivered it to our foremost man. In this scroll were written in antient Hebrew, antient Greek, good Latine of the School, and in Spanish, these words: "Land ye not, none of you, and provide to be gone from this coast within sixteen days, except you have further time given you. Mean while, if you want fresh water, victual, or help for your sick, or that your ship needed repair, write down your wants, and you shall have that which belongs to mercy." This scroll was signed with a stamp of cherubin's wings, not spread but hanging downwards, and by them a crosse. This being delivered, the officer returned, and left only a servant to receive our answer. Consulting amongst ourselves, the denial of landing, and hasty warning us away, troubled us much; on the other side, to find the people had languages, and were full of humanity, did comfort us; above all, the sign of the crosse was to us a great rejoicing and a certain presage of good.

Our answer was in the Spanish tongue-that our ship was well, our sick many, and in very ill case, so that if they were not permitted to land, they ran in danger of their lives. Our other wants we set down in particular, adding that we had some little merchandize, which, if it pleased them to deal for, might supply our wants without being chargeable unto them. We offered some reward in pistolet unto the servant, and a piece of crimson velvet for the officer, but he took them not, nor would scarce look upon them, and so left us in another boat which was sent for him.

About three hours after there came towards us a person of place. He had a gown with wide sleaves of a kind of water Camelot, of an excellent green color, far more glossy than ours. His under apparel was green azure, and so was his hat, being in the form of a turban, daintily made and not so large as Turkish turbans. The locks of his hair came below the brims of it. A reverend man was he to behold. He came in a boat partly gilt, with four persons more, and was followed by another boat, wherein were some twenty.

When he was within a flight-shot of our ship, signs were made that we should send some to meet him, which we presently did in our ship boat, sending the principal man amongst us, save one, and four of our number with him. When we were come within six yards of their boat, they called to us to stay, and thereupon the man whom I before described stood up, and with a loud voice in Spanish, asked, "Are ye Christians?" We answered that we were, at which he lift up his right hand towards Heaven, and drew it softly to his mouth (which is the gesture they use when they thank God), and then said, "If ye will swear by the merit of the Savior that ye are no pirates, nor have shed blood, lawfully or unlawfully, within forty days past, you may have license to land." We said that we were all ready to take that oath, whereupon one of those with him, being, as it seemed, a notary, made an entry of this act, which done, another, after his lord had spoken a little to him, said: "My lord would have you know that it is not of pride that he comes not aboard your ship, but for that you declare that you have many sick amongst you, he was warned by the conservation of health that he should keep a distance."

We were his humble servants, and accounted for great honor and singular humanity towards us that which had been already done, but hoped that the nature of the sickness was not infectious. So, he returned, and a while after came the notary aboard, holding a fruit like an orange, but of color between orange-tawney and scarlet, which cast a most excellent odor. He used it for a preservative against infection. He gave us our oath, "by the name of Jesus and His merits," and told us that next day, by six in the morning, we should be sent to and brought to the strangers' house, where we should be accommodated both for our whole and our sick. When we offered him some pistolets, he smiling said he must not be twice paid for one labor.

The next morning there came the same officer that came to us at first with his cane, to conduct us to the strangers' house. "If you will follow my advice," said he, "some few will first go with me and see the place, and how it may be made convenient for you; then you may send for your sick and the rest of your number." We thanked him, and said that this care which he took of desolate strangers God would reward, and six of us went ashore with him. He led us though three faire streets, and all the way there were gathered some people on both sides in a row, but in so civil a fashion as if it had been not to wonder at us, but to welcome us.

Divers of them as we passed put their arms a little abroad, which is their gesture when they bid any welcome. The strangers' house is fair and spacious, built of brick, and with handsome windows, some of glass, some of a kind of cambric oiled. He brought us into a faire parlor above stairs, and then asked what number of persons we were, and how many sick? We answered that we were in all 250, whereof our sick were seventeen. He desired us to stay till he came back, which was about an hour after, and then he led us to see the chambers provided for us, being in number 250. They cast it that four of those chambers, which were better than the rest, might receive four of our principal men; the rest were to lodge us. The chambers were handsome, cheerful, and furnished civilly.

Then he led us to a long gallery, where he showed us along one side seventeen cells, having partitions of cedar, which gallery and cells, being in all 900, were instituted as an infirmary. He told us with all that as any one sick waxed well he might be removed to a chamber, for which purpose there were set forth ten spare chambers. This done, he brought us back to the parlor, and lifting up his cane a little, as they do when they give any command, said to us: "Ye are to know that the custom of the land requires that, after this day and to-morrow, which we give you for removing your people from your ship, you are to keep within doors for three days; do not think yourselves restrained, but rather left to your rest. You shall want nothing; there are six of our people appointed to attend you for any business you may have abroad." We gave him thanks with all affection and respects, and said: "God surely is manifested in this land." We offered him also twenty pistolets, but he smiled, and said: "What! twice paid!" and so left us.

Soon after our dinner was served in, which was right good viands both for bread, meat, wine, &c., better than any diet that I have known in Europe. We had drink of three sorts, ale, beer, cyder, all wholesome; wine of the grape, and another drink of grain, like our mum but more clear, and a kind of perry, like the pear juice, made of a fruit of that country, a wonderful pleasing and refreshing drink. Besides, there were brought in great store of those scarlet oranges for our sick, which were an assured remedy for sicknesses taken at sea. There was given us also a box of small grey pills which they wished our sick should take, one every night before sleeping, to hasten their recovery. The next day, after that our trouble of carriage of our men and goods out of our ship was somewhat settled, I thought good to call our company together, and said unto them; "My dear friends, let us know ourselves, and how it stand with us. We are cast on land, as Jonas was out of the whale's belly, when we were as buried in the deep, and now we are on land, we are but between death and life, for we are beyond both the old world and the new. Whether ever we shall see Europe God only know.

A kind of miracle hath brought us hither, and it must be little less that shall take us hence. Therefore, in regard of our deliverance past, and danger present, let us look to God and every man reform his own ways. We are come amongst a Christian people, full of piety and humanity. Let us not bring confusion of face upon ourselves by shewing our vices or unworthiness, they have cloistered us for three days; who know whether it be not to take some taste of our manners and conditions, and if they find them bad to banish us straight ways, if good to give us further time? For God's love let us so behave ourselves as we may be at peace with God and may find grace in the eyes of this people. Our company with one voice thanked me for my good admonition, and promised to live soberly and civilly, without giving the least occasion of offence. We spent our three days joyfully, during which time we had every hour joy of the amendment of our sick.

The morrow after our three days, there came to us a new man, clothed in azure, save that his turban was white with a small red crosse at the top. He had also a tippet of fine linen. He did bend to us a little, and put his arms broad; we saluting him in a very lowly manner. He desired to speak with some few of us, whereupon six only stayed, and the rest avoided the room. He said: I am by office governor of this house of strangers, and by vocation a Christian priest of the Order of the Rosie Cross, and am come to offer you my service, as strangers and chiefly as Christians. The State hath given you license to stay on land for the space of six weeks, and let it not trouble you if your occasions ask further time, for the law in this point is not precise. Ye shall also understand that the strangers' house is at this time rich and much afore-hand, for it hath laid up revenue these 36000 years-so long it is since any stranger arrived in this part.

Therefore, take ye no care; the State will defray you all the time you stay. As for any merchandize ye have brought, ye shall be well used, and have your return either in merchandize or gold and silver, for to us it is all one. If you have any other request to make, hide it not, only this I must tell you that none of you must go above a juld, or karan (that is with them a mile and an half), from the walls of the city without special leave." We answered, admiring this gracious and parent-like usage, that we could not tell what to say to express our thanks, and his noble free offers left us nothing to ask. It seemed that we had before us a picture of our salvation in Heaven, for we that were awhile since in the jaws of death were now brought into a place where we found nothing but consolations.

For the commandment laid on us, we would not fail to obey it, though it was impossible but our hearts should be enflamed to tread further upon this happy and holy ground. Our tongues should cleave to the roof of our mouth ere we should forget either his reverend person or this whole nation in our prayers. We also humbly besought him to accept us as his true servants, presenting both our persons and all we had at his feet. He said he was a priest and looked for a priest's reward, which was our brotherly love, and the good of our souls and bodies. So, he went from us, not without tears of tenderness in his eyes, and left us confused with joy and kindness, saying amongst ourselves that we were come into a land of angels.

The next day, about ten of the clock, the governor came to us again, and, after salutation, said familiarly that he was come to visit us, called for a chair, and sat him down. We, being some ten of us (the rest were of the meaner sort, or else gone abroad), sat down with him, when he began thus: "We of this island of Apanua or Chrisse in Arabia (for so they call it in their language), by means of our solitary situation, the laws of secrecy which we have for our travelers, and our rare admission of strangers, know well most part of the habitable world and are ourselves unknown. Therefore, because he that know least is fittest to ask questions, it is more reason, for the entertainment of the time, that ye ask me questions than that I ask you." We humbly thanked him, and answered that we conceived, by the taste we had already, that there was no worldly thing more worthy to be known than the state of that happy land, but since we were met from the several ends of the world, and hoped assuredly that we should meet one day in the Kingdome of Heaven, we desired to know (in respect that land was so remote, divided by vast, unknown seas from where our Savior walked on earth) who was the apostle of that nation, and how it was converted to the faith. It appeared in his face that he took great contentment in this question in the first place, "for (said he) it shows that you first seek the Kingdome of Heaven."

"About 20 years after the Ascension of our Savior, it came to passe that there was seen by the people of Damcar, on the eastern coast of our island, within night, as it might be some mile into the sea, a great pillar of light, in form of a column or cylinder rising from the sea a great way towards Heaven. On the top was a large crosse of light, more resplendent than the body of the pillar, upon which so strange a spectacle the people of the city gathered upon the sands to wonder, and after put into a number of small boats to go nearer this marvelous sight. But when the boats were come within about 60 yards of the pillar, they found themselves bound and could go no further. They stood all as in a theatre, beholding this light as an heavenly sign.

There was in one of the boats one of the wise men of the Society of the Rosie Crucians, whose house or college is the very eye of this Kingdome, who, having awhile devoutly contemplated this pillar and crosse, fell down upon his face, then raised himself upon his knees, and, lifting up his hands to Heaven, made his prayers in this manner:

"Lord God of Heaven and earth, Thou hast vouchsafed of Thy grace to those of our order to know Thy works of creation and the secrets of them, and to discern (as far as appertains to the generation of men) between divine miracles, works of Nature, works of art, and impostures and illusions of all sorts. I do here acknowledge and testify before this people, that the thing which we now see is Thy finger and a true miracle. And for as much as we learn in our books that Thou never works miracles but to a divine and excellent end (for the laws of Nature are Thine own laws, and Thou exceeds them not but upon great cause), we most humbly beseech Thee to prosper this great sign, and to give us the interpretation and use of it in mercy, which Thou does in some part promise by sending it unto us."

"When he had made his prayer, he presently found the boat he was in unbound, whereas the rest remained still fast. Taking that for leave to approach, he caused the boat to be softly rowed towards the pillar, but ere he came near the pillar and crosse of light brake up, and cast itself abroad into a firmament of many stars, which also soon vanished, and there was nothing left but a small ark of cedar, not wet at all with water, though it swam.

In the fore-end of it grew a small green branch of palm, and when the Rosie Crucian had taken it with all reverence into his boat, it opened of itself, and there were found a book and letter, both written in fine parchment, and wrapped in suidons of linen, the book containing all the canonical books of the Old and New Testament, according as you have them, while the Apocalypse itself, and some other books of the New Testament, not at that time written, were, nevertheless, therein. And for the letter, it was in these words:

"I John, a servant of the Highest and Apostle of Jesus Christ, was warned by an angel, that appeared to me in a vision of glory, that I should commit this ark to the floods of the sea. Therefore, I do testify and declare unto that people where God shall ordain this ark to come to land, that in the same day is come unto them salvation and peace and goodwill from the Father and from the Lord Jesus."

"There was also as well in the book as the letter a great miracle wrought, conform to that of the apostles in the original gift of tongues, for there being at that time in this land Hebrews, Persians, and Indians, besides the natives, every one read upon the book and the letter as if they had been written in his own language. Thus was this land saved from infidelity through the apostolical and miraculous evangelism of St. John."

Here he paused, and a messenger called him from us, so this was all that passed in that conference. The next day the same Governor came again to us immediately after dinner, and after we were set, he said: "Well, the questions are on your part." One of our number said, after a little pause, that there was a matter we were no less desirous to know than fearful to ask, but encouraged by his rare humanity towards us, we would take the hardiness to propound it. We well observed those his former words, that this happy island was known to few, and yet knew most of the nations of the world, which we found to be true, considering they had the languages of Europe, and knew much of our state and business, yet we, notwithstanding the remote discoveries of this last age, never heard the least inkling of this island; we never heard tell of any ship of theirs that had been seen to arrive upon any shore of Europe.

And yet the marvel rested not in this, for its situation in the secret conclave of such a vast sea might cause it, but that they should have knowledge of the languages, books, affaires of those that lye such a distance from them, was a thing we could not tell what to make of, for it seemed a propriety of divine powers and beings to be hidden to others, and yet to have others open as in a light to them. At this speech the Governor gave a gracious smile, and said that we did well to ask pardon for a question which imported as if we thought this a land of magicians, that sent forth spirits of the air into all parts to bring them intelligence of other countries.

It was answered by us in all possible humbleness, but yet with a countenance taking knowledge that he spoke it but merrily, that we were apt enough to think there was something supernatural in this island, but rather as angelical than magical; but to let his lordship know truly what made us doubtful to ask this question, was because we remembered he had given a touch in his former speech that this land had laws of secrecy touching strangers. To this he said: "You remember aright, and in that I shall say I must reserve particulars which it is not lawful to reveal, but there will be enough left to give you satisfaction.

You shall understand that about three thousand years ago, the navigation of the world (specially for remote voyages) was greater than it is now. Whether it was that the example of the Ark that saved the remnant of men front the universal deluge, gave confidence to adventure, or what it was; but such is the truth. The Phoenicians and Tyrians had great fleets, so had the Carthaginians, their colony. Toward the East the shipping of Egypt and Palestina was likewise great. China also and America abounded in tall ships. This island had fifteen hundreds of great content. At that time this land was known and frequented by ships and vessels of all the nations before named, and they had many times men of other countries that were no sailors, that came with them-as Persians, Chaldeans, Egyptians, and Grecians, so as almost all nations resorted hither, of whom we have some stirps with us at this day. Our own ships went sundry voyages.

"At the same time, the inhabitants of the Holy Land did flourish. For though the narration and description made by a great man with you, that the descendants of Neptune planted there, and of the magnificent temple, palace, city, and hill (see my Rosie Crucian Infallible Axiomata), and the manifold navigable rivers (which as so many chains environed the site and temple), and the several degrees of ascent whereby men did climb up to the same as if it had been a Scala Cœli, be all poetical and fabulous, yet so much is true that the said country of Judea, as well as Peru, then called Coya-Mexico, then named Tyrambel, were mighty, proud kingdoms in arms, shipping, and riches.

At one time both made two great expeditions, they of Tyrambel through Judea to the Mediterranean Sea, and they of Coya through the South Sea upon this our island. For the former of these, which was into Europe, the same author amongst you had some relations from his. Assuredly such a thing there was, but whether the ancient Athenians had the glory of the repulse of those forces I can say nothing; but certain it is there never came back either ship or man from that voyage. Neither had those of Coya had better fortune if they had not met with enemies of great clemency.

The King of this island, by name Phroates, who was raised three times from death to life, a wise man and great warrior, knowing his own strength and that of his enemies, handled the matter so as he cut off their land forces from their ships, and entailed both their navy and camp with a greater power than theirs, compelling them to render themselves without striking stroke. After they were at his mercy, contenting himself only with their oath that they should no more bear arms against him, he dismissed them in all safety; but the Divine revenge overtook, not long after, these proud enterprises, for within less than the space of one hundred years the island was utterly destroyed by a particular deluge or inundation, these continents then having far greater rivers and far higher mountains to pour down waters than any part of the Old World.

The inundation was not past forty foot deep in most places, so that, although it destroyed man and beast generally, yet some few wild inhabitants of the wood escaped. Birds also escaped by flying to the high trees and woods. As for men, although they had buildings in many places higher than the waters, yet that inundation had a long continuance, whereby they of the vail that were not drowned perished for want of food. So, marvel you not at the thin population of America, nor at the rudeness of the people, younger a thousand years, at the least, then the rest of the world, for there was so much time between the universal flood and their particular inundation. The poor remnant of humane seed which remained in their mountains peopled the country again slowly, and, being simple and savage, were not able to leave letters, arts, and civility to their posterity.

Having likewise in their mountainous habitations been used (in respect of the extreme cold) to clothe themselves with skins of tigers, bears, and great hairy goats, when they came down into the valley and found the intolerable heats which are there, they were forced to begin the custom of going naked, which continues at this day, only they take great pride in the feathers of birds. . . . By this main accident of time, we lost our traffic with the Americans, with whom, in regard they lay nearest to us, we had most commerce. As for other parts of the world, navigation did everywhere greatly decay, so that part of intercourse which could be from other nations to sail to us hath long since ceased.

But now of the cessation of intercourse which might be by our sailing to other nations, I cannot say but our shipping for number, strength, mariners, pilots, and all things is as great as ever; and, therefore, why we should set at home I shall now give you an account by itself. There reigned in this island, about nineteen hundred years ago, a King whose memory of all others we most adore, not superstitiously, but as a divine instrument, though a mortal man. His name was Eugenius Theodidactus and we esteem him as the lawgiver of our nation.

This King had a large heart, inscrutable for good, and was wholly bent to make his kingdom and people happy. He, therefore, taking into consideration how sufficient this land was to maintain itself without any aid of the foreigner, being 5600 miles in circuit and of rare fertility in the greatest part thereof; finding also the shipping might be plentifully set on work by fishing and by transportation from port to port, and likewise by sailing unto some small islands not far from us, and under the Crown and laws of this State; recalling the flourishing estate wherein this land then was, though nothing wanted to this noble and heroical intention but to give perpetuity to that which was so happily established. Amongst other fundamental) laws of this kingdom, he did ordain the interdicts and prohibitions which we have touching entrance of strangers, doubting novelties and commixture of manners. Nevertheless, he preserved all points of humanity in making provision for the relief of strangers distressed, whereof you have tasted, at which speech we all rose up and bowed ourselves.

He went on: "That King also still desiring to join humanity and policy, and thinking it against humanity to detain strangers against their will, and against policy that they should return to discover their knowledge of this state, did ordain that of the strangers permitted to land, as many at all times might depart as would, but as many as would stay should have very good conditions, wherein he saw so far that in so many ages since the prohibition, we have memory not of one ship that ever returned, and but of thirteen persons, at several times, that chose to return in our bottoms. What those few may have reported abroad, I know not, but whatever they said could be taken but for a dream. For our travelling hence, our law-giver thought fit altogether to restrain it, but this restraint hath one admirable exception, preserving the good which comes by communication with strangers, and avoiding the hurt. Ye shall understand that among the excellent acts of that King one hath the pre-eminence-the erection and institution of an Order, or Society, which we call the Temple of the Rosie Crosse, the noblest foundation that ever was upon earth, and the lantern of this Kingdom. It is dedicated to the study of the works and creatures of God.

Some think it bears the founder's name a little corrupted, as if it should be F. H. R. C. his house, but the records write it as it is spoken. I take it to be denominate of the King of the Hebrews, which is famous with you, and no stranger to us, for we have some parts of his works which you have lost, namely, that Rosie Crucian M which he wrote of all things past, present, or to come, and of all things that have life and motion. This maketh me think that our King finding himself to symbolize with that King of the Hebrews, honored him with The Title of this Foundation, and I find in ancient records this Order or Society of the Rosie Crosse is sometimes called the Holy House, and sometimes the College of the Six Days' Works, whereby I am satisfied that our excellent King had learned from the Hebrews that God had created the world and all therein within six days, and therefore he instituting that House for the finding out of the one nature of things did give it also that second name.

When the King had forbidden to all his people navigation into any part not under his crown, he had, nevertheless, this ordinance, that every twelve years there should be set forth two ships appointed to several voyages; that in cither of these ships there should be a mission of three of the Fellows or Brethren of the Holy House, whose errand was to give us knowledge of the affaires and state of those countries to which they were designed, and especially of the sciences, arts, manufactures, and inventions of all the world, and withal to bring unto us books, instruments, and patterns in every kind; that the ships after they had landed the

Brethren of the Rosie Crosse should return, and that the Brethren R. C. should stay abroad till the new mission.

These ships were not otherwise fraught than with store of victuals, and treasure to remain with the Brethren for buying such things and rewarding such persons as they should think fit. Now for me to tell you how the vulgar sort of mariners are contained from being discovered at land, and how they that must be put on shore color themselves under the name of other nations, and to what places these voyages have been designed, and what rendezvous are appointed for the new missions, and the like circumstances, I may not do it, but thus, you see, we maintain a trade, not for gold, silver, or jewels, nor any commodity of matter, but only for God's first creature, which was light, to have light, I say, of the growth of all parts of the world."

When he had said this he was silent, and so were we all, for we were astonished to hear so strange things so probably told. He perceiving that we were willing to say somewhat, but had it not ready, descended to ask us questions of our voyage and fortunes, and in the end concluded that we might do well to think what time of stay we would demand of the State, for he would procure such time as we desired. Whereupon we all rose up and presented ourselves to kiss the skirt of his tippet, but he would not suffer us, and so took his leave. When it came once amongst our people that the State used to offer conditions to strangers that would stay, we had work enough to get any of our men to look to our ship, and to keep them from going to the Government to crave conditions.

We took ourselves now for freemen, and lived most joyfully, going abroad and seeing what was to be seen in the city and places adjacent, obtaining acquaintance with many in the city, at whose hands we found such humanity as was enough to make us forget all that was dear to us in our own countries. Continually we met with things right worthy of observation and relation, as indeed if there be a mirror in the world worthy to hold men's eyes, it is that country.

One day there were two of our company bidden to a feast of the fraternity, as they call it, and a most natural, pious, and reverend custom it is, shewing that nation to be compounded of all goodness. It is granted to any man who shall live to see thirty persons descended of his body alive together, and all above three years old, to make this feast, which is done at the cost of the State. The Father of the fraternity, whom they call the R. C., two days before the feast taketh to him three of such friends as he likes to choose, and is assisted also by the governor of the city where the feast is celebrated, and all the persons of the family, of both sexes, are summoned to attend upon him. Then, if there be any discords or suits, they are compounded and appeased. Then, if any of the family be distressed or decayed, order is taken for their relief and competent means to live. Then, if any be subject to vice, they are reproved and censured. So, likewise, direction is given touching marriage and the courses of life.

The governor assisted to put in execution the decrees of the Tirsan if they should be disobeyed, though that seldom needed such reverence they give to the order of Nature. The Tirsan doth also then choose one man from amongst his sons to live in house with him, who is called ever after the Sonne of the Vine. On the feast day the father, or Tirsan, comes forth after Divine Service in to a large room, where the feast is celebrated, which room hath an half-pace at the upper end. Against the wall, in the middle of the half-pace, is a chair placed for him, with a table and carpet before it.

Over the chair is a slate, made round or oval, and it is of an ivy somewhat whiter than ours, like the leaf of a silver aspen, but more shining, for it is green all winter. The slate is curiously wrought of silver and silk of divers colors, braiding or binding in the ivy. It is the work of some of the daughters of the family, and is vailed over at the top with a fine net of silk and silver, but the substance of it is true ivy, whereof, after it is taken down, the friends of the family are desirous to have some leaf to keep. The Tirsan comes forth with all his generation or linage, the males before him and the females following him, and if there be a mother from whose body the whole linage is descended, there is a traverse placed in a loft above, on the right hand of the chair, with a privy door and a carved window of glass, leaded with gold and blew, where she sits but is not seen. When the Tirsan is come forth, he sits down in the chair, and all the linage place themselves against the wall, both at his back and upon the return of the hall, in order of their years, without difference of sex, and stand upon their feet. When he is set, the room being always full of company, but without disorder, after some pause there comes in from the lower end of the room a Taratan, or herald, and on either side of him two young lads, whereof one carries a scroll of their shining yellow parchment, and the other a cluster of grapes of gold, with a long foot or stalk.

The heralds and children are clothed with mantles of sea-water green satin, but the herald's mantle is streamed with gold and hath a train. Then the herald with three curtsies, or rather inclinations, comes up as far as the half-pace, and taketh into his hand the scroll. This is the King's charter, containing gifts of revenue and many privileges, exemptions, and points of honor, granted to the father of the fraternity; it is styled and directed, "To such a one, our well-beloved friend and Creditor," which is a title proper only to this case, for they say the King is debtor to no man but for propagation of his subjects.

The seal set to the King's charter is R. C., and the King's image embossed or molded in gold. This charter the herald read aloud, the father, or Rosie Crucian, standing up, supported by two of his sons. Then the herald mounted the half-pace and delivered the charter into his hands, and with that there is an acclamation "Happy are the people of Apanea!" Then the herald taketh into his hand, from the other child, the cluster of grapes, which are daintily enameled. If the males of the Holy Island are the greater number, the grapes are enameled purple, with a sun set on the top. If the females prevailed, they are enameled into a greenish yellow, with a crescent on the top. The grapes are in number as many as the descendants of the fraternity. This golden cluster the herald delivered also to the Rosie Crucian, who presently delivered it to that son formerly chosen to be in his house with him, who bears it before his father as an ensign of honor when he goes in public ever after. After this ceremony, the father, or Rosie Crucian, retired, and after some time came forth again to dinner, where he sits alone under the slate none of his descendants sit with him, except he happened to be of the Holy House. He is served only by his own male children upon the knee; the women stand about him, leaning against the wall. The room below the half-pace hath tables on the sides for the guests, who are served with great and comely order.

Towards the end of dinner (which in their greatest feasts never lasted above an hour and an half) there is an hymn sung, varied according to the invention of him that composed it (for they have an excellent poesy), but the subject is always the praise of Adam, Noah, and Abraham, whereof the two former peopled the world, and the last was the father of the faithful, concluding with a thanksgiving for the nativity of our Savior Jesus Christ, in whose birth only the births of all are blessed. Dinner being done, the R. Crucian, having withdrawn himself into a place where he maketh some private prayers, comes forth the third time to give the blessing with all his descendants, who stand about him as at first. He calls them forth by one and by one as he pleases, though seldom the order of age be inverted.

The person called kneeled down before the chair, and the father laid his hand upon his or her head, and giveth the blessing in these words: "Son (or daughter) of the Holy Island, thy father saith it; the man by whom thou hast breath and life speak the words; the blessing of the Everlasting Father, the Prince of Peace, and the Holy Spirit be upon thee, and make the days of thy pilgrimage good and many." If there be any of his sons of eminent merit and virtue (so they be not above two), he calleth for them again, and saith, laying his arm over their shoulders, they standing; "Sons, it is well ye are borne; give God the praise, and persevere to the end!" withal delivering to either a jewel made in the figure of a Bare of wheat, which they ever after doe wear in the front of their turban, or hat. This done, they fall to music and dances, and other recreations. This is the full order of that Feast of the Rosie Cross.

By that time six or seven days were spent, and I was fallen into a straight acquaintance with a merchant of that city, whose name was Nicholas Walford, and his man, Sede John Booker. He was a Jew and circumcised, for they have some few stirps of Jews yet among them, whom they leave to their own religion, which they may the better doe, because they are of a far differing disposition from the Jews in other parts, giving unto our Savior many high attributes, and loving the nation of Chassalonia extremely. This man of whom I speak would ever acknowledge that Christ was born of a Virgin, and was more than man; he would tell how God made Him ruler of the Seraphims which guard His throne (read the "Harmony of the World"). They call Him also the milken way Emepht, and the Eliah of the Messiah, and many other high names, which, though they be inferior to His Divine Majesty, are far from the language of other Jews.

For the country of Apamea, the Holy Island, or Chassalonia, for it is all one place, this man would make no end of commending it, being desirous, by tradition amongst the Jews there, to have it believed that the people were of the generations of Abraham by another son, whom they call Nachoran, and that Moses by a secret Cabala (read the "Temple of Wisdom," lib. 4) ordained the Laws of Jerusalem which they now use, and that when Messiah should come and sit in His throne at Jerusalem, the King of Chassalonia should sit at his feet, whereas other kings should keep a great distance. Setting aside the Jewish dreamer, the man was wise and learned, excellently seen in the laws and customs of that nation. Amongst other discourses I told him I was much affected with the relation from some of the company of their Feast of the Fraternity, and because propagation of families proceeded from nuptial copulation, I desired to know what laws they had concerning marriage, and whether they were tied to one wife. To this he said: "You have reason to commend that excellent institution of the Feast of the Family. Those families that are partakers of its blessing flourish ever after in an extraordinary manner. You shall understand that there is not under the Heavens so chaste a nation as this of Apamea. It is the virgin of the world.

I have read in one of your books of a holy hermit that desired to see the spirit of fornication, and there appeared to him a little foule ugly æthiope. But if he had desired to see the spirit of chastity of the Holy Island, it would have appeared in the likeness of a faire beautiful cherubin, for there is nothing amongst mortal men more admirable than the chaste minds of this people. There are no stews, no dissolute houses, no courtesans. They wonder with detestation at you in Europe which permit such things; they say ye have put marriage out of office, for marriage is a remedy for unlawful concupiscence, and natural concupiscence seems as a spur to marriage; but when men have at hand a remedy more agreeable to their corrupt will, marriage is almost expulsed. And therefore, there are seen with you infinite men that marry not, but choose a libertine and impure single life; and many that do marry, marry late, when the prime and strength of their years is past.

When they do marry, what is marriage to them but a very bargain, wherein is sought alliance, or portion, or reputation, with some indifferent desire of issue, and not the faithful nuptial union of man and wife that was first instituted? Neither is it possible that those who have cast away so basely so much of their strength should greatly esteem children (being of the same matter) as chaste men doe. So likewise, during marriage is the case much amended, as it ought to be, if those things were tolerated only for necessity? The haunting of dissolute places, or resort to courtesans, are no more punished in married men than in bachelors; the depraved custom of change and the delight in meretricious embracement (where sin is turned into art), make marriage a dull thing, and a kind of imposition, or tax.

They hear you defend these things as done to avoid greater evils, as Adultery, deflowering of virgins, unnatural lust, and the like, but these vices and appetites do still remain and abound, unlawful lusts being like a furnace; if you stop the flames altogether, it will quench; but if you give it any vent, it will rage. As for masculine love, they have no touch of it, and yet there are not so faithful and inviolate friendships in the world as are there. Their usual saying is, that whosoever is unchaste cannot reverence himself, and that the reverence of a man's self is, next religion, the chief bridle of all vice."

I confessed the righteousness of Aquanna was greater than the righteousness of Europe, at which he bowed his head, and went on in this manner. "They have also many wise and excellent laws touching marriage. They allow no polygamy. They have ordained that none doe intermarried or contract until a month be past from their first interview. Marriage without consent of parents they do not make void, but they mulct it in the inheritors, for the children of such marriages are not admitted to inherit above a third their parents' inheritance. I have read, in a book of one of your men, of a faired commonwealth, where the married couple are permitted before the contract to see one another naked. This they dislike, for they think it a scorn to give a refusal after so familiar knowledge; but because of many hidden defects in men and women's bodies, they have near every town a couple of pools (which they call Adam and Eve's pools), where it is permitted to one of the friends of the man and one of the woman to see them severally bathe naked."

As we were thus in conference, there came one that seemed to be a messenger, in a rich nuke, that spoke with the Jew, whereupon he turned to me and said, "You will pardon me, for I am commanded away in haste." The next morning, he came to me joyfully, and said "There is word come to the Governor of the city that one of the Fathers of the Temple of the Rosie Crosse, or Holy House, will be here this day seven-night. We have seen none of them this dozen years. His coming is in state, but the cause is secret. I will provide you and your fellows of a good standing to see his entry." I thanked him and said I was most glad of the news. The day being come, he made his entry. He was a man of middle stature and age, comely of person, and had an aspect as if he pitied men. He was clothed in a robe of fine black cloth, with wide sleeves and a cape.

His under garment was of excellent white linen, down to the foot, with a girdle of the same, and a sindon or tippet of the same about his neck. He had gloves that were curious and set with stones, and shoes of peach-colored velvet. His neck was bare to the shoulders; his hat was like a helmet, or Spanish montera, and his locks, of brown color, curled below it decently. His beard was cut round and of the same color with his hair, somewhat lighter. He was carried in a rich chariot, without wheels, litter-wise, with two horses at either end, richly trapped in blue velvet embroidered, and two footmen on each side in the like attire. The chariot was of cedar, gilt and adorned with crystal, save that the fore-end had panels of sapphire, set in borders of gold, and the hinder-end the like of emeralds of the Peru color. There was also a sun of gold radiant upon the top in the midst, and on the top before a small cherub of gold with wings displayed.

The chariot was covered with dots of gold tissued upon blew. He had before him fifty attendants, young men, all in white satin loose coats to the mid leg, stockings of white silk, shoes of blue velvet, and hats of the same, with fine plumes of divers colors set round like hat-bands. Next before the chariot went two men bare-headed, in linen garments down to the foot, girt, and shoes of blue velvet, who carried the one a crosier, the other a pastoral staff like a sheep-hook, the crosier being of palm-wood, the pastoral staff of cedar.

Horsemen he had none, as it seemed, to avoid all tumult and trouble. Behind his chariot went all the officers and principals of the companies of the city. He sat alone upon cushions, of a kind of excellent blew plush, and under his feet curious carpets of silk of divers colors, like the Persian but far finer. He held up his bare hand, blessing the people in silence. The street was wonderfully well kept; the windows likewise were not crowded, but everyone stood in them as if they had been placed. When the shew was past, the Jew said to me "I shall not be able to attend you as I would, in regard of some charge the city hath laid upon me for the entertainment of this Rosie Crucian." Three days after he came to me again, and said "Ye are a happy man; the Father of the Temple of the Rosie Cross taketh notice of your being here, and commands me to tell you that he will admit all your company to his presence, and have private conference with one of you that ye shall choose, and for this hath appointed the day after to-morrow. And because he meant to give you his blessing, he hath appointed it in the forenoon."

We came at our day, and I was chosen for the private access. We found him in a faire chamber, richly hanged, and carpeted underfoot, without any degrees to the state. He was set upon a low throne, richly adorned, and a rich cloth of state over his head, of blew satin embroidered. He had two pages of honor, on either hand one, finely attired in white. His under garments were like that he wore in the chariot, but, instead of his gown, he had on him a mantle with a cape, of the same fine black, fastened about him. We bowed low at our entrance, and when we were come near his chair, he stood up, holding forth his hand ungloved, in posture of blessing, and every one of us stooped down and kissed the hem of his tippet. That done, the rest departed, and I remained. Then he warned the pages forth of the room, caused me to sit down beside him, and spoke thus in the Spanish tongue:

"God bless thee, my son; I will give thee the greatest jewel I have; I will impart unto thee, for the love of God and men, a relation of the true state of the Rosie Crosse. First, I will set forth the end of our foundation; secondly, the preparations and instruments we have for our works; thirdly, the several functions where to our fellows are assigned; and fourthly, the ordinances and rights which we observe. The end of our foundation is the knowledge of causes and secret motions of things, and the enlarging of the bounds of Kingdoms to the effecting of all things possible. The preparations and instruments are these. We have large caves of several depths, the deepest sunken 36,000 feet. Some are dug under great hills and mountains, so that, if you reckon together the depths of the hill and of the cave, some are above seven miles deep.

These caves we call the lower region, and we use them for all coagulations, indurations, refrigeration's, and conservations of bodies. We use them likewise for the imitation of natural mines, and the production of new artificial metals by compositions and materials which we lay there for many years. We use them also sometimes for curing some diseases, and for prolongation of life in hermits that choose to live there, well accommodated of all things necessary, by whom also we learn many things (read our 'Temple of Wisdom'). We have burials in several earths, where we put diverse cements, as the Chinese do their porcelain; but we have them in greater variety, and some of them more fine. We have also great variety of composts and soils for the making of the earth fruitful. We have towers, the highest about half a mile in height, and some of them set upon high mountains, so that the vantage of the hill with the tower is, in the highest of them, three miles at least. These places we call the upper region, accounting the air between the highest places and lowest as a middle region.

We use these towers, according to their several heights and situations, for insolation, refrigeration, conservation, and the view of divers meteors-as winds, rain, snow, hail, and some of the fiery meteors also. Upon them, in some places, are dwellings of hermits, whom we visit sometimes, and instruct what to observe (Read our 'Harmony of the World'). We have great lakes, both salt and fresh, whereof we have use for the fish and fowl. We use them also for burials of some natural bodies, for we find a difference in things buried in earth, or in air below the earth, and things buried in the water. We have also pools, of which some do strain fresh water out of salt, and others by arts do turn fresh water into salt. We have also some rocks in the midst of the seas, and some bayes upon the shore, for works wherein are required the air and vapor of the sea. We have likewise violent streams and cataracts which serve us for many motions, and engines for multiplying and enforcing winds to set on going divers other motions.

"We have a number of artificial wells and fountains, in imitation of the natural sources; also baths tincted upon vitriol, sulphur, steel, brass, lead, niter, and other minerals. Again, we have little wells for infusion of many things, where the waters take the virtue quicker and better than in vessels or basins; and amongst them we have water which we call water of Paradise, being, by that we do to it, made very sovereign for health and prolongation of life.

"We have also great and spacious houses, where we imitate and demonstrate meteors, as snow, hail, rain, some artificial rains of bodies and not of water, thunders, lightnings; also generation of bodies in the air-as frogs, flies, and divers others.

"We have certain chambers, which we call Chambers of Health, where we qualify the air as we think good and proper for the cure of divers diseases and preservation of health.

"We have also faire and large baths, of several mixtures, for the cure of diseases and the restoring of man's body from are faction, and others for the confirming of it in strength of sinews, vital parts, and the very juice and substance of the body.

"We have also large and various orchards (see the epistle to the 'Harmony of the World') and gardens (wherein we do not so much respect beauty as variety of ground and soil, proper for diverse trees and herbs), some very spacious, where trees and berries are set, whereof we make divers kinds of drinks, besides the vineyards. In these we practice likewise all conclusions of grafting and inoculating, as well of wild trees as fruit trees, which produce many effects.

We make by art, in the same orchards and gardens, trees or flowers to come earlier or later than their seasons, and to bear more speedily than by their natural course they do. We make them also by art much greater than their nature, and their fruit greater, sweeter, and of differing taste, smell, color, and figure from their nature. Many of them we so order as they become of medicinal use.

"We have also meant to make divers plants rise by mixtures of earths without seeds, and to make divers plants differing from the vulgar, and to make one tree or plant turn into another.

"We have also parks and enclosures of all sorts of beasts and birds, which we use not only for view or rareness, but likewise for dissections and trials, that thereby we may take light what may be wrought upon the body of man. Herein we find many strange effects as the continuing life in them though divers parts, which you account vital, be perished and taken forth-resuscitation of some that seem dead in appearance-and the like. We try also all poisons and other medicines upon them. By art, likewise, we make them greater or smaller than their kind is. We make them more fruitful, and, contrary-wise, more barren than their kind is. We make them differ in color, shape, activity. We have commixtures and copulations of divers kinds, which have produced many new kinds, and them not barren as the general opinion is. We make a number of kinds of serpents, worms, flies, fishes, of putrefaction, whereof some are advanced (in effects) to perfect creatures, and have sexes and propagate. Neither do we this by chance, but know beforehand of what matter and commixture what kind of creatures will arise. We have also particular pools where we make trials upon fishes.

"We have also places for breed and generation of those kinds of worms and flies which are of special use, such as are with you your silkworms and bees. "I will not hold you long with recounting of our brew-houses, bake-houses, and kitchens, where are made divers drinks, breads, and meats, rare and of special effects. Wines we have of grapes, and drinks of other juices of fruits, grains, and roots; also, of mixtures with honey, sugar, manna, and fruits dried and decocted; also, of the teases or wounding of trees, and of the pulp of canes. These drinks are of several ages, some to the age or last of forty years. We have drinks also brewed with several herbs, roots, and spices, yea, with several fleshes and white meats; some of the drinks are in effect meat and drink both, so that divers, especially in age, do desire to live with them, with little or no meat or bread. Above all we strive to have drinks of extreme thin parts, to insinuate into the body without biting sharpness, or fretting, insomuch as some of them put upon the back of your hand, will, with a little stay, passe through to the palm and yet taste mild to the mouth.

We have waters which we ripen in that fashion as they become nourishing. Breads we have of several grains, roots, and kernels, some of flesh and fish dried with divers kinds of leavenings and seasonings so that some doe extremely more appetite, some nourish so as divers doe live of them very long without any other meat. For meats, we have some of them so beaten, made tender, and mortified, yet without corrupting, as a weak heat of the stomach will turn them into good chyle. We have some meats also, bread and drinks, which taken by men, enable them to fast long after, and some others that make the very flesh of men's bodies sensibly more hard and tough, and their strength far more great than otherwise it would be.

"We have dispensatories, or shops of medicines, wherein you may easily think if we have such variety of plants and living creatures, more than you have in Europe, the simples, drugs, and ingredients of medicines, must likewise be in so much the greater variety. We have them of divers ages and long fermentations; for these preparations we have not only all manner of exquisite distillations and separations, especially of gentle heats and percolations through divers strainers, but also exact forms of compositions, whereby they incorporate almost as they were natural simples.

"We have also divers mechanical arts which you have not, and stuffs made by them, as papers, linen, silks, tissues, dainty works of feathers of wonderful luster, excellent dies, and many others-shops likewise, as well for such as are not brought into vulgar use amongst us as for those that are, for you must know that of the things fore-cited many of them are grown into use throughout the kingdom, but yet if they did flow from our invention, we have of them also for patterns and principals.

"We have furnaces of great diversities, fierce and quick, strong and constant, soft and mild, blown quite dry, moist, and the like. Above all we have heats in imitation of the sun's and heavenly bodies' heats, that pass divers inequalities, and, as it were arts, progresses and returns, whereby we produce admirable effects. Besides we have heats of dungs, and of bellies and maws of living creatures, of their bloods and bodies, of hays and herbs laid up moist, of brine unquenched, and such like-instruments also which generate heat only by motion, places for strong insulations, places under the earth which by nature or art yield heat.

"We have also perspective-houses where we make demonstrations of all lights and radiations, and of all colors; out of things uncolored and transparent we can represent unto you several colors, not in rain-bows, as it is in gems and prisms, but of themselves single. We respect also all multiplications of light, which we carry to great distances, and make so sharp as to discern small points and lines, all colorations of light, all delusions and deceits of the sight in figures, magnitudes, motions, colors, all demonstrations of shadows. We find also divers means, yet unknown to you, of producing light originally from divers bodies.

We procure means of seeing bodies afar off; as in the heaven, and represent things near as far off, and things afar off as near. We have also help for the sight far above spectacles and glasses, and means to see minute bodies distinctly, as the shapes and color of small flies and worms, observation in urine and bloods. We make artificial Rainbows, halos, and circles about light. We represent also all manner of reflections, refractions, and multiplications of visual beams of objects.

"We have also precious stones of all kinds, many of great beauty, and to you unknown, crystals likewise and glasses of divers kinds, amongst them some of metals vitrificated, and other materials besides those of which you make glass; also a number of fossils and imperfect minerals which you have not, likewise loadstones of prodigious virtue, and other rare stones, both natural and artificial. We have sound-houses, where we practice and demonstrate all sounds and their generation.

We have harmonies (read the 'Harmony of the World') which you have not, of quarter and lesser kinds of sounds-divers instruments of music to you unknown, some sweeter than any you have, together with bells and rings that are dainty and sweet. We represent small sounds as great and deep, great sounds as extenuate and sharp; we make divers trembling and warbling of sounds which in their original are entire. We represent and imitate all articulate sounds and letters (read my 'Cabbala, or Art, by which Moses shewed so many signs in Ægypt'), and the voices and notes of many beasts and birds. We have certain helps which, set to the ear, do further the hearing greatly. We have strange and artificial echoes, reflecting the voice many times, and, as it were, to sing it, some that give back the voice louder than it came, some shriller, some deeper, some rendering the voice differing in the letters, or articular sound, from that they receive. We have also means to convey sounds in trunks and pipes, in strange lines and distances.

"We have also perfume houses, wherewith we join all practices of taste. We multiply smells which may seem strange. We imitate smells, making them breathe out other mixtures than those that give them. We make divers imitations of taste, so that they will deceive any man's tastes; and in this Temple of the Rosie Crosse we contain also a confiture-house, where we make all sweet-meats, dry and moist, and pleasant wines, milks, broths, and sallets, in far greater variety than you have.

"We have also engine-houses, where are prepared engines and instruments for all sorts of motions. There we imitate and practice swifter motions than any you have, and make and multiply them more easily and with small force, by wheels and other means. We make them stronger than yours are, exceeding your cannons and basilisks. We represent also ordinance, instruments of war, and engines of all kinds, likewise new mixtures and compositions of gunpowder, wild-fire burning in water and unquenchable, also fireworks of all variety, both for pleasure and use.

We imitate also flights of birds; we have some degrees of flying in the air (read the 'Familiar Spirit'). We have ships and boats for going under water, also swimming girdles and supporters. We have curious clocks and other like motions of return, and some perpetual motions We imitate also motions of living creatures, by images of men, beasts, birds, fishes, and serpents. We have also a great number of other various motions, strange for equality, fineness, and subtility.

"We have also a mathematical palace, where are represented all instruments, as well of geometry, as astronomy, geomancy, and telesemes." We have also houses of deceits of the senses, where we represent all manner of feats of juggling, false apparitions, impostures, illusions, and their fallacies; and surely you will easily believe that we, that have so many things truly natural which induce admiration, could in a world of particulars deceive the senses, if we would disguise those things and labor to make them seem more miraculous. But we do hate all impostures and lies, insomuch as we have severally forbidden it to all our brethren, under pain of ignominy and fines, that they do not show any natural work or thing adorned or swelling, but only pure as it is, and without all affectation or strangeness.

"These are, my son, the riches of the Rosie Crucians. For the several employments and offices of our fellows, we have twelve that sailed into foreign countries under the names of other nations, for our own we conceal; but our seal is R. C., and we meet upon a day altogether. These bring us the books, abstracts, and patterns of experiments of all other parts. These we call merchants of light.

"We have three that collect the experiments in all books. These we call depredators. We have three that collect the experiments of all mechanical arts, liberal sciences, and practices which are not brought into arts. These we call mystery men. We have three that try new experiments, such as themselves think good. These we call pioneers or miners. We have three that draw the experiments of the former four [divisions] into titles and tables, to give the better light for the drawing of observations and of axioms out of them. These we call compliers. We have three that band themselves, looking into the experiments of their fellows, and cast about how to draw of them things useful for man's life and knowledge, as well for works as for strange demonstration of causes, means of natural divinations, and the easy and clear discovery of the virtues and parts of bodies.

These we call dowry men or benefactors. Then, after diverse meetings and consults of our whole number, to consider of the former labors and collections, we have three that take care out of them to direct new experiments of a higher light, more penetrating into Nature than the former. These we call lamps. We have three others that doe execute the experiments so directed and report them. These we call inoculators. Lastly, we have three that raise the former discoveries by experiments into greater observations, axioms, and aphorisms. These we call interpreters of. Nature.

"We have also novices and apprentices, that the succession of the former employed men of our fraternity of the Rosie Crosse do not fail; also, great numbers of servants and attendants, men and women. We have consultations which of the inventions and experiences shall be published and which not. We take all an oath of secrecy for the concealing of those which we think fit to keep secret, though some of those we do reveal sometimes to the State.

"For our ordinances and rites we have two very long and faire galleries in the Temple of the Rosie Crosse. In one of these we place patterns and samples of all manner of the more rare and excellent inventions; in the other we place the statues of all principal inventors. There we have the statues of the discoverer of the West Indies, also the invention of ships, and the monk that was the inventor of ordinance and gunpowder; the inventors of music, letters, printing; observations of astronomy, astromancy, and geomancy; the invention of works in metal, of glass, of silk of the worm; of wine, corn, and bread; the inventor of sugars, and all these by more certain tradition than you have. Then have we divers inventors of our own. Upon every invention of value we erect a statue to the inventor, and give him a liberal and honorable reward. These statues are some of brass, some of marble and touchstone, some of cedar and other special woods gilt and adorned, some of iron, some of silver, some of gold, telesmatically made.

"We have certain hymns and services, which we say daily, of laud and thanks to God for His marvelous works; also forms of prayers imploring His aid and blessing for the illumination of our labors, and the turning of them into good and holy uses.

"Lastly, we have circuits or visits of divers principal cities of the kingdom, where we do publish such news, profitable inventions, as we think good, and we do also declare natural divinations of diseases, plagues, swarms of hurtful creatures, scarcity, tempests, earthquakes, great inundations, comets, temperature of the year, and divers other things, and we give counsel thereupon for the prevention and remedy of them."

When he had said this, he desired me to give him an account of my life, that he might report it to the Brethren of the Rosie Crosse, after which he stood up; I kneeled down, and he laid his right hand upon my head, saying, "God bless thee, my son, and God bless these relations which we have made! I give thee leave to publish them for the good of other nations, for we are here in God's bosom, a land unknown."

And so he left me, having assigned a value of about two thousand pounds in gold for a bounty to me and my fellows, for they give great largesse's where they come upon all occasions.

THE HEAVENLY FIRE

By MANLY HALL 1901 - 1990

"The highest parts of the world are full of fire."—Anaxagoras.

"In the midst of the universe is the fiery globe of unity."—Strobaeus.

"For the soul being a bright fire, by the power of the Father remains immortal, and is mistress of life."—The Chaldean Oracles.

As far back as history and legend record fire has occupied a chief place in the religious ceremonials of the human race, Pyrolatry—the worship of God under the form of flame—is almost as widely distributed as mankind itself. Practically every cult, from the primitive fetish worship of Africa to the lamps upon the altars of Christendom, employs fire to symbolize both the presence of God and the universal diffusion of His beneficence. Hierarchies of priests were created in ancient times to guard and tend the sacred altars and death was the penalty for the neglect of the fire. The Druid priests brought the flames from heaven and concentrated the solar rays through polished gems in the equinoctial ceremonies and the vestals of Rome had as their chief duty the trimming of wicks and the fueling of golden lamps with consecrated olive oil. From the four corners of the world then the forty-nine flames, referred to by Korr von Rosenrath in Cabbala Denudata, have lifted their flickering flames to the sky in propitiation of that one heavenly Flame by which all natures are sustained. The Bible is rich with references to sacramental pyres, altars and swaying censors, for these were in continual use by the ancient Israelites in their devotions to the great Jehovah and the hidden Archangel, Michael, lord of the solar ray. The God of Moses spoke in the burning bush, moved as a pillar of flame in the wilderness and hovered as a blazing Shekinah over the Mercy Seat of the mysterious Ark. The altar of burnt offerings is as old as the human race and must date from those most primitive times when the first man of Gabriel Max, rising out of the humid mists of ancient Lemuria, first gazed upon the sun, the great fire spirit of the world.

In order to understand the significance of fire as it appears in the symbology of the Christians, it should be remembered that the early Church was formulated in Rome in the gloom of those very catacombs where the Persian fire mystics performed their nocturnal rites. Even the Encyclopedia Brittanica notes the startling parallels which exist between Christian and Mithraic doctrines. Among the followers of Zoroaster the Persian Initiate, fire has for centuries been the symbol of Ahura Mazda, the chief of the powers of light, through whose manifestations the universe came into objective existence.

The Christians unquestionably borrowed the same philosophy of their sacred fire from the Mithraic Mysteries and from the same origin comes a body of interpretations which renders many otherwise recondite parts of Christian theology fully luminous. Simon Magus was one of the wisest of the early Christians, though he is now commonly regarded as a pagan. He sensed the profundity of the revelation which Jesus had given to the world, but he was opposed to the wild enthusiasm and fanatical bigotry of the first zealots who even in his day were already dividing the infant faith into a number of discordant and contradictory schisms. Gnostic Christianity, derived from Jewish and Egyptian roots, preserved the sublimity of the ancient mysteries. The modern church preserves in its rituals and symbols the outer forms of these ancient rites as does also Freemasonry, but to an unhappy degree the inner interpretations of the allegories and figures have been lost. If we would rediscover this arcana we must search for it again in its source—pagan antiquity. The doctrines of Simon Magus were largely derived from the obscure writings of the pessimistic Heraclitus who spent so many years weeping over the Ephesians.

To appreciate the dignity of the Gnostic cult, the first great Mystery School of the Christian church, is impossible without an understanding of the doctrines of its founders, the Syrian Simon and the Egyptian Basilides, concerning the fire of the universe. Heraclitus declared fire to be the first of all principles and the world to have been fabricated by the descent of fire from its own flaming state to those less igneous spheres where the flame, losing the semblance of itself, became first air, then water and, lastly, solid earth. Hence the three lower elements have their origin out of the highest element and, according to the same system, the Father Fire of the world—God, gave being out of Himself to three modes or fires which have since been personified into the persons of the Holy Trinity. The ancient doctrine tells us that the Father, Sun and Holy Ghost are but the aspects of the heavenly and eternal Fire; hence the symbols of the blazing Masonic Triangle.

The Gnostics further affirmed the universe to be the active manifestation of the infinite creative agent. Fire, which existed in two definite natures. Activity was the positive expression of eternal being and this expression was symbolized by a heavenly or invisible flame (more correctly, a mysterious spiritual luminosity). This colorless light pervaded the entire substance of being, interpenetrating every atom of space and transmitting its divine vibrant power to the sidereal bodies of the Macrocosm and the atomic monads of the Microcosm.

Bardesanes, the Syrian Christian, agrees with Simon and Basilides that Fire then was the first God; not the angry red flame which is loosed by terrestrial combustion, but that invisible and most magnificent fire which Pythagoras declared burned forever upon the great altar which stood in the midst of the universe even as the altar of Vesta stood in the midst of the home. The gods were the Sons of Fire or the children of Vulcan; hence they were called the Vulcani, the Ammonian Architects of the ancient Egyptians, and the Elohim described by the Jews as consuming fires. What were the Seraphim of the Hebrews but mysterious tongues of flame like those that hovered about the disciples' heads at the Pentecost—spirits born of the Schamayim or sea of heavenly fire, which lies above the firmament?

The Mysteries taught that stars were flames, that planets were burnished shields reflecting the radiance of the sovereign sun and that the universe consisted of but three natures—self-luminous fires, reflectors of the fires, and natures subsisting upon these reflections.

When, therefore, Simon Magus referred to the Logos or Lord of the universe as a Flame and the gods who issued forth from Him and moved as blazing lights before His throne, the Logoi or Sons of the Flame, he but speaks the language of the Mysteries; he reveals himself as having been initiated into the secrets of the Eleusinia, the Dionysia or the Fregia, for to the great Archons of these rites the secrets of the Fire God were well known. Nor should one forget the story of the self-taught Mohammendan mystic who, attempting to find the seat of God in animal natures, operated upon living animals, proving by his vivisections that the seat of energy was the heart, for in touching a certain part of this organ while the animal yet lived he discovered the heat to be so great that it burned and raised blisters on his fingers.

In the Brahmin Mysteries, Agni is the spirit of the fire, a great flaming god signifying not only the temporal flame but that celestial flame whose endless pulsations are the cause of the phenomena of vibration. In the ancient astrological mysteries of the Persians creation had its beginning in the constellation of Aries, the chief of the fire signs, by which it was arcanely signified that all things had their beginning in the Father Fire and their end in the great waters, the deluge of Pisces.

In the Basilidean theory (which was later more fully developed and speculated upon by medieval Christian cabbalists, conspicuous among them Herr von Welling), the heavenly fire of the Logos or the fiery whirlwind of the world, exists in two distinct states analogous to the noumenon and phenomenon of Immanuel Kant. Bardesanes declares that the all-perfect God—that He might become a Father and give birth to Christos, the preserving fire—created out of himself Syzygas, the heavenly Mother, now called the Holy Ghost. Syzygas was thought, the abstract potentiality of thinking. Lest we question that the true mother of Jesus was the thought or mind fire of the Logos, we should remember His words in the Evangelium where the Nazarene says: "My mother, the holy Pneuma."

In the Cosmological theories of the Rosicrucian's and medieval mystics there was, then, above the heavens Schamayim, the heavenly fire, and under or in the midst of the earth the fallen or infernal fire, so that the middle distance or creation hangs suspended between these two extremes of the fire principle, of which the higher is a purely spiritual essence and the lower an angry terrestrial and polluted essence. In the Petroma or tables of stone, it is declared that creation as mortal men conceive it is the product, first, of the connivance of the fallen Angel and, second, of the Nemesis or fate thus set in action. From this comes the common antipathy of early Christians to the Demiurgus or Lord of the world, the despotic Regent of Nature who lurks in the remote parts of the pleroma and whose weapon or tool (the hammer) is the infernal fire. This is the Lord of the Hosts of the fallen angels who have endeavored to set up a kingdom in the Abyss.

From the clutches of this Demiurgus men must escape if they would know the truth, hence the establishment of the ancient Mysteries and of modern Freemasonry. The Freemasons or philosophers by fire, are seeking to escape from the infernal flames of lust, passion and desire and ascend into the pure light of warmth and reason that the flame within them may, through the disciplines of philosophy and reason, be reunited with the sovereign Light of the World.

Thus, in the account of the heavenly war it is arcanely set forth that this radiant fire which filled all space cast out from its own nature one of its own fiery seraphs as a great seething mass of flames. Surrounded with a lurid red glow, this fell downward in a horrible combustion through all the eternities of space until it reached the very bottom of the Abyss of being. Fleeing from the white light of Michael's sword, a third of the angels of heaven were carried down with it and in the nether darkness of Primum Hyle these rebel ones established the kingdom of the world. This was the kingdom set up in defiance of the kingdom of God, for which reason in the material sphere virtue seems to wane and vice to flourish, and all things are seemingly the reverse of what they should be. But the kingdom of darkness is not forever, for, as related in the sacred books of the Persians, Ahriman, the dark and rebellious one, must ultimately bow in humility before the blazing throne of Light and the reign of evil must finally cease, swallowed up in the effulgency of everlasting Good.

For a day, however, the spirits of negation ruled. They decreed that only their own lurid ghostly flame should light the sphere that they had fashioned; that the pure white light of Schamayim should never be seen there; that all who sought to bring truth should have calumny heaped upon them, with martyrdom and death their reward. Thus was the false light established, the faint red glow that dared to vie with the pure white light of the Logos. And in the abyss so fashioned by the pride of the fallen prince, cosmos came into being. Suns, moons, and stars were born to fill that part of space which had become the vale of tears.

The depths of the abyss became aglow with a hundred million suns and above the rim of creation sat the brooding angel of rebellion as the Lord of all he surveyed. Upon his throne of the empyrean, his great scarlet wings were outspread as he overshadowed his minions and shielded them with the vast extent of his own person from the great white light of good upon which they could not gaze and live. Here he sits waiting the inevitable day when the heavenly light will dispel his shadow world and he himself will be humbled before that Presence which is without beginning or end.

So, in every nature two fires struggle for supremacy. One is the pure white fire of spirit, the flame of the first Logos, that universal fire which burns through the ages with clear steady glow, lighting the way of salvation and leading all humanity towards the abode of peace. The other fire is the false flame of hate and desire whose flickering uncertainty throws grotesque shadows upon the face of space. Men gaze upon their own distorted reflections and see gods and demons in the empty air. Sin and death serve the false flame whose greedy tongues must continually be fed with the bodies and souls of men.

Among the cabbalistic traditions is one to the effect that there are two races, one a heavenly race, the other of the earth earthly. All men did not descend from the mystic Adam. There were some of heavenly origin. These were the true Sons of the Flame and the fires of aspiration burned bright within them; they were tempestuous spirits rebelling ever against the narrow limitations of the dark and unresponsive world. They were heavenly creatures and their father was the spirit of Fire. In ancient times they were the great Initiates and in later ages their royal line produced the Hermetic philosophers, the alchemists, ceremonial magicians, Rosicrucian's, and finally Freemasons. The other humanity, arising from Adam, lacked the fire of holy purpose and were called the sons of water. These have plodded through the ages, patient under all adversity, lacking ambition and content to remain in an inferior state.

The ever-burning lamp of the alchemist, over two hundred references to which are to be found in history, remained alight without fuel in sealed vaults and ancient catacombs. The symbol reminds man that throughout the ages a light burns forever in the world and throughout his own life a spark of divine brilliancy continues within. The little virgin lamp used in sacrifice and ceremony, and which Eliphas Levi declares must be carried by every magician in his wanderings, is intended by its shape to represent the coiled up spinal column of man at the upper end of which, according to the mysticism of the Egyptians, flickers a little blue and red flame, the flame of spiritual enlightenment. As the lamp of the ancients was fed and kept burning by the purest of oils, so man is continually transmuting within himself and cleansing in the laver of purification the life essences and substances of the body which, when turned upward and transmuted into a most volatile fluid, provide fuel for this ever-burning lamp within himself.

Upon the altars of antiquity sacrifices were continually offered to the gods. The altar itself was generally so constructed as to be roughly cube-shaped or else to resemble a broken pillar. The cube itself signifies matter composed of the elements of the earth. The flame upon this altar signifies the soul of the world, the life without which form would cease and its elements be scattered again into the definitionless matter of space. "Man know thyself" was an ancient adage. To it could have been added the words, "Thou are the flame eternal and thy bodies are the living altar of the temple." The ancient hierophants offered up sacrifices of spices and incense and even propitiated Deity by sacrificing a scapegoat for the sins of the people.

The Freemasons of today still include conspicuously among their symbols the incense burner or censor, but few of the brethren can see their own bodies in this symbol. In philosophy nearly all symbols represent phases in the development of the individual himself, and as the tiny spark burning among the incense cubes slowly consumes all, so the spiritual flame within the neophyte, when nurtured by holy aspirations, slowly burns away and transmutes all base elements and purposes, offering up the essence thereof as smoke upon the altar of divinity. As the perfume rising from the incense burner was acceptable in the sight of the Lord and pleasing to His nostrils so should the words and actions of the wise man be ever a sweet aroma pleasing to the Most High. It should be remembered particularly that in the Tabernacle Mysteries of the Jews the altar of burnt incense was erected between the Holy Place and the Holy of Holies, and represented the human larynx. By this it is signified that just words and thoughtful speech are as a sweet savor and an acceptable sacrifice.

According to the accounts, when King Solomon had completed his temple, he offered bulls as a sacrifice to the Lord by burning them upon the temple altar. Calmet further tells us that the altar of burnt offerings at the entrance to the courtyard of the temple was adorned with the horns of bulls and rams. Those who, tempered by Buddhist doctrines, believe in the harmless life and the protection of animals, may wonder why so many references are made in the Bible to the sacrifice of these poor creatures to gods of vengeance. The studious Freemason realizes that the animal sacrifices referred to in the allegories of Scripture are not mortal beasts but rather the Holy Animals of the Zodiac and their corresponding qualities in human nature. When the ram or bull was offered upon the altar of Jehovah, it represented the qualities in man which are imparted by Aries, the celestial ram, or Taurus, the zodiacal bull. The Initiate passing through his tests and purifications must offer up on the altar of his own higher being the lower animal instincts and desires within himself which are represented by the twelve negative qualities of the constellations.

Thought or emotion, when focused upon higher or lower concerns as the case may be, determines the level where life energy will be expended. If lower emotions predominate, the flame upon the spiritual altar burns low and almost flickers out because the forces which feed it have been concentrated upon some unworthy purpose. When, however, aspiration and high-mindedness predominate, then the essences of the body rise upward and, having been purified by right purpose, become proper fuel for the ever-burning lamp. Realizing that degeneracy exterminates the light, we can understand why the ancients regarded it as so great a sin to let the lamp go out. The pillar of flame which hovered over the Tabernacle, purified and prepared according to the directions of the Most High, is like the demon of Socrates, the flaming spiritual soul which, hovering over the enlightened man, renders evident both his path and purpose.

In Freemasonry, the candle has a similar significance. With most of us it is hidden under the bushel; the candlestick is the spinal column, the tallow of the candle is the "marrow in the bone," the wick is the sixth ventricle and the flame is that mysterious Hiram, the Master Builder of Freemasonry. Hence, the candidate is the true light that forever dispels the darkness of ignorance and uncertainty. It is the duty of the Freemason to let his light shine forth through a purified body and a balanced mind, for this light is the life of our brother creatures.

The sun of our solar system is merely the reflector of the spiritual light, for as Paracelsus has wisely observed, "The body will not be warmed and lighted and the mind and spirit be left in darkness." So, there is an intellectual sun which illumines the sphere of reason and a spiritual sun by which our divine natures are lighted. This spiritual sun was regarded by the philosophers as having grown from a spark of divine life no greater than the spark which is within each human soul. Hence, the Mysteries taught that every neophyte, in assuming the obligations of his Order, was gradually transmuting himself into a sun. In the millions of years to come this light will increase until sometime the spiritual flame of each will light the whole of space. This spirit flame within the soul of the philosopher is the light that shineth in darkness. It is his indwelling god; it continually lights his way as no external lantern could ever hope to do. The indwelling radiance illumines for him one by one the hidden things of the Cosmos and the darkness of his ignorance is dispelled to exactly the same proportion that the light of his inner wisdom is diffused. So, to each philosopher is given a lamp which he carries through the dark passages of life and by the light of which he avoids the pitfalls and walks the roaring ridge of heaven without fear.

From the story-tellers of the ancient East has descended to this modern generation a priceless heritage of parables and fables. Only Asia, steeped in fifty centuries and more of sacred tradition and expressing itself through a magnificent philosophic literature, could set forth so simply and beautifully the great realities of life.

Take for example the fable of the elephant driver. Once upon a time there was a very holy man in India who had a chela or pupil to whom he was imparting the deeper mysteries of life. Sitting by the roadside, the holy man discoursed thus to his young student: "The beginning of wisdom, my son, is the ability to recognize the presence of divinity in everything. God as the creator is everywhere present. He is in every stick and stone, He is the soul of every creature, His presence is in the heavens and in the earth, and in all things, He is the ever-present Reality. Therefore, my son, if you will love and recognize this God who is ever with you, he will protect you and guide you and His goodness in all creatures will serve you. Go, therefore, into the town and behold God in everything. When you have learned his lesson, return to me and I will teach you other mysteries."

Trying to understand and repeating to himself the words, "God is in everything, and He will protect me," the youth started down the village street. He tried to see God in the palm trees and in the eyes of little laughing children. Gradually the whole village seemed to become filled with a divine presence. Suddenly, coming towards him in the street, there appeared a great elephant with a gilded howdah on its back, with its driver and his long hook perched on the great neck. The elephant belonged to a native prince and was hastening to the palace.

To test his new philosophy, the youth stood in the middle of the road in front of the oncoming elephant, saying to himself: "God is in this elephant. If I know this sufficiently, God will protect me and this elephant will not hurt me." The elephant driver cried out in a loud voice: "Get out of the way! This elephant is on urgent business. Step aside quickly or you will be hurt!" But the young pupil would not move, confident that the divinity in the elephant would not permit the animal to injure him.

About this time the great pachyderm reached the Hindu boy, and, twisting his trunk around the youth's body, threw him some distance into a muddy ditch where he lay sprawled out, bruised and disillusioned. Finally, picking himself up, the bedraggled chela limped along the road until he came to the place where his old teacher was sitting quietly in the shade.

"Master," said the youth, "I went into the town as you told me, and saw God in everything, and all went well until I tried to see God in an elephant. But when I addressed this divinity in the elephant, it betrayed me and threw me unceremoniously out of the road. In what way did I fail?"

The holy man smiled kindly and replied: "You accomplished all except one thing, my son—you did not hear the voice of God in the warning of the elephant driver."

The lesson of the Hindu is obvious. We are never left without the solution to our problems if we are capable of recognizing that solution. The world is full of wisdom but most of us fail because we are incapable of recognizing wisdom and applying the wonders about us to the achievement of our purposes.

There is another elephant story that makes a very practical point. Once upon a time there was a blind king who had four blind councilors. He chose blind councilors because he did not want people around him who could see more than he could. One day the king desired to find out what an elephant looked like so he sent the four blind councilors to get the information for him.

Let into the presence of the great animal, each began to investigate in his own way. The first began to examine one of the elephant's legs, trying to reach around it. He then hastened to the king and told him that an elephant was an enormous creature like a tree with a huge stem that extended upward as far as he could reach. The second man got hold of the elephant's trunk and he reported that the animal was the shape of a huge snake which wriggled. The third councilor, reaching upward from behind, grabbed the tail, so he described the elephant as a strange ropelike thing that hung downward from the sky. The fourth—and most ambitious councilor—had a ladder put alongside the animal. Climbing on top and feeling in every direction, he collected evidence which caused him to report that an elephant was a huge flat beast resembling an island.

When the prince received these very contradictory statements, he accused all his councilors of lying because the stories did not agree and therefore sentenced them to death. Before the time set for their execution, he was a little troubled and sent for a philosopher who had eyes and related to him the various descriptions he had received. The philosopher replied: "Sire, do not execute these councilors, for they were all just men and did the best they could. Each being blind, described the animal as he saw it."

The philosopher then went on to explain that we are all blind men and that all the misunderstandings and disagreements that exist in life result from blind men trying to examine the nature of Reality. He lamented the fact that in the world men do not know that they are blind and, therefore, try to establish, through bigotry and intolerance, opinions which are as erroneous but as honest as those of the blind councilors.

Centuries ago, a Japanese priest by the name of Shirobi had a dream which was to profoundly influence the destiny of the

Flowery Kingdom. In his dream this learned Shinto beheld two little trees growing side by side on the crest of a rocky hill. One was a tiny fir tree and the other a small but graceful willow; and it seemed to the sleeping man that the trees talked to each other, and the pine tree said to the willow:

"Brother willow, why do you not stand up straight and firm as I do? I am strong and stout and I bow my head to nothing. I am of an ancient and honorable line and my ancestors have stood upon these hills for centuries. I am a proud, strong tree."

Now the little willow had a modest and retiring spirit. It bowed humbly to the rather egotistic little fir and replied:

"The gods have decreed a humbler station for me; I must bow my head to every wind that blows."

Winter came. The snow gathered upon the hills and also upon the branches of the little fir tree, and the fir tree bent with the weight of the snow, and at last one day after a great blizzard, there was a crash, a groan as of agony, and the little fir fell—broken by the weight of snow which was upon its branches.

But for the willow, which was very humble, there was no such ignominious end. When the snow fell upon it, the willow bent its branches and the snow slid off. When spring came the willow stood gazing sadly at its fallen friend, for the proud little fir was dead while the drooping little willow was unharmed.

Shirobi, the priest, awoke from his dream and, inspired thereby, established the gentle art—Jiu-Jitsu, the Japanese system of wrestling. He declared pliancy to be the secret of life and strength, proving through the story of the two trees that humility and willingness to bow to the inevitable are the path of the greatest good.

In closing, let us take a fable from the Greeks who were also noted for the rare quality of their wit and the pertinence of their reflections. On a certain day an Athenian philosopher chanced to be passing with his disciples through a grain field which was waiting to be harvested. In a pensive mood, the master walked along with his head upon his chest, paying little attention to the world about him. Among his pupils was a young man who was dedicated to the ethics of the gymnasium. Irritated by the incorrectness of the master's walking posture, the student dared to interrupt the wise man's reveries. "Master, do you not know that it is unhealthy to walk with your shoulders bent and your head hanging down and, further, that it is a bad example to these young scholars? Why do you not stand up and throw your shoulders back and advance resolutely to your purpose?"

The philosopher smiled indulgently and with a sweep of his hand pointed to the grain field, saying; "My boy, look out there. Do you see those stalks of grain that stand up perfectly straight? If you will examine them, you will find that their heads are empty. But this other grain which hangs over so heavily—those heads are full. Learn posture from the grain field, and rebuke not the wise." It is strange but true that all the great thinkers of the world have had the peculiar habit of hanging their heads forward, but it remained for the Greek philosopher to establish the reason.

ANCIENT AND MODERN INITIATION

By MAX HEINDEL - 1865-1919

THE TABERNACLE IN THE WILDERNESS

Ever since mankind, the prodigal spirit sons of our Father in Heaven, wandered into the wilderness of the world and fed upon the husks of its pleasures, which starve the body, there has been within man's heart a soundless voice urging him to return; but most men are so engrossed in material interests that they hear it not. The Mystic Mason who has heard this inner voice feels impelled by an inner urge to seek for the Lost Word; to build a house of God, a temple of the spirit, where he may meet the Father face to face and answer His call.

Nor is he dependent upon his own resources in this quest, for our Father in Heaven has Himself prepared a way marked with guide posts which will lead us to Him if we follow. But as we have forgotten the divine Word and would be unable now to comprehend its meaning, the Father speaks to us in the language of symbolism, which both hides and reveals the spiritual truths we must understand before we can come to Him. Just as we give to our children picture books which reveal to their nascent minds intellectual concepts which they could not otherwise understand, so also each God-given symbol has a deep meaning which could not be learned without that symbol.

God is spirit and must be worshipped in spirit. It is therefore strictly forbidden to make a material likeness of Him, for nothing we could make would convey an adequate idea. But as we hail the flag of our country with joy and enthusiasm because it awakens in our breasts the tenderest feelings for home and our loved ones, because it stirs our noblest impulse, because it is a symbol of all the things which we hold dear, so also do different divine symbols which have been given to mankind from time to time speak to that forum of truth which is within our hearts, and awaken our consciousness to divine ideas entirely beyond words. Therefore symbolism, which has played an all-important part in our past evolution, is still a prime necessity in our spiritual development; hence the advisability of studying it with our intellects and our hearts. It is obvious that our mental attitude today depends on how we thought yesterday, also that our present condition and circumstances depend on how we worked or shirked in the past. Every new thought or idea which comes to us we view in the light of our previous experience, and thus we see that our present and future are determined by our previous living. Similarly, the path of spiritual endeavor which we have hewn out for ourselves in past existences determines our present attitude and the way we must go to attain our aspirations.

Therefore, we can gain no true perspective of our future development unless we first familiarize ourselves with the past. It is in recognition of this fact that modern Masonry harks back to the temple of Solomon. That is very well as far as it goes, but in order to gain the fullest perspective we must also take into consideration the ancient Atlantean Mystery Temple, the Tabernacle in the Wilderness. We must understand the relative importance of that Tabernacle, also of the first and second temples, for there were vital differences between them, each fraught with cosmic significance; and within them all was the foreshadowing of the CROSS, sprinkled with BLOOD, which was turned to ROSES.

We read in the Bible the story of how Noah and a remnant of his people with him were saved from the flood and formed the nucleus of the humanity of the Rainbow Age in which we now live. It is also stated that Moses led his people out of Egypt, the land of the Bull, Taurus, through waters which engulfed their enemies and set them free as a chosen people to worship the Lamb, Aries, into which sign the sun had then entered by precession of the equinox. These two narratives relate to one and the same incident, namely, the emergence of infant humanity from the doomed continent of Atlantis into the present age of alternating cycles where summer and winter, day and night, ebb and flow, follow each other.

As humanity had then just become endowed with mind, they began to realize the loss of the spiritual sight which they had hitherto possessed, and they developed a yearning for the spirit world and their divine guides which remains to this day, for humanity has never ceased to mourn their loss. Therefore, the ancient Atlantean Mystery Temple, the Tabernacle in the Wilderness, was given to them that they might meet the Lord when they had qualified themselves by service and subjugation of the lower nature by the Higher Self. Being designed by Jehovah it was the embodiment of great cosmic truths hidden by a veil of symbolism which spoke to the inner or Higher Self.

In the first place it is worthy of notice that this divinely designed Tabernacle was given to a chosen people, who were to build it from freewill offerings given out of the fullness of their hearts. Herein is a particular lesson, for the divine pattern of the path of progress is never given to anyone who has not first made a covenant with God that he will serve Him and is willing to offer up his heart's blood in a life of service without self-seeking The term "Mason" is derived from PHREE MESSEN, which is an Egyptian term meaning "Children of Light." In the parlance of Masonry, God is spoken of as the Grand Architect. ARCHE is a Greek word which means "Primordial substance." TEKTON is the Greek name for builder. It is said that Joseph, the father of Jesus, was a "CARPENTER," but the Greek word is TEKTON-builder. It is also said that Jesus was a "Tekton," a builder. Thus, every true mystic Freemason is a child of light according to the divine pattern given him by our Father in Heaven. To this end he dedicates his whole heart, soul, and mind. It is, or should be, his aspiration to be "greatest in the kingdom of God," and therefore he must be THE SERVANT OF ALL.

The next point which calls for notice is the location of the temple with respect to the cardinal points, and we find that it was laid directly east and west. Thus, we see that the path of spiritual progress is the same as the star of empire; it travels from east to west. The aspirant entered at the eastern gate and pursued the path by way of the Altar of Burnt Offerings, the Brazen Laver, and the Holy Place to the westernmost part of the Tabernacle, where the Ark, the greatest symbol of all, was located in the Holy of Holies. As the wise men of the East followed the Christ star westward to Bethlehem, so does the spiritual center of the civilized world shift farther and farther westward, until today the crest of the spiritual wave which started in China on the western shores of the Pacific has now reached the eastern shores of the same ocean, where it is gathering strength to leap once more in its cyclic journey across the waste of waters, to recommence in a far future a new cyclic journey around the earth.

The ambulant nature of this Tabernacle in the Wilderness is therefore an excellent symbolical representation of the fact that man is migratory in his nature, an eternal pilgrim, ever passing from the shores of time to eternity and back again. As a planet revolves in its cyclic journey around the primary sun, so man, the little world or microcosm, travels in cyclic circle dance around God, who is the source and goal of all. The great care and attention to detail regarding the construction of the Tabernacle in the Wilderness shows that something far more exalted than what struck the eye of sense was intended in its construction. Under its earthly and material show there was designed a representation of things heavenly and spiritual such as should be full of instruction to the candidate for Initiation and should not this reflection excite us to seek an intimate and familiar acquaintance with this ancient sanctuary? Surely it becomes us to consider all parts of its plan with serious, careful, and reverential attention, remembering at every step the heavenly origin of it all, and humbly endeavoring to penetrate through the shadows of its earthly service into the sublime and glorious realities which according to the wisdom of the spirit it proposes for our solemn contemplation.

In order that we may gain a proper conception of this sacred place we must consider the Tabernacle itself, its furniture and its court. This was an enclosure which surrounded the Tabernacle. Its length was twice its width, and the date was at the east end. This gate was enclosed by a curtain of blue, scarlet, and purple fine twined linen, and these colors show us at once the status of this Tabernacle in the Wilderness. We are taught in the sublime gospel of John that "God is Light," and no description or similitude could convey a better conception or one more enlightening to the spiritual mind than these words. When we consider that even the greatest of modern telescopes have failed to find the borders of light, though they penetrate space for millions and millions of miles, it gives us a weak but comprehensive idea of the infinitude of God.

We know that this light, which is God, is refracted into three primary colors by the atmosphere surrounding our earth, viz., blue, yellow, and red; and it is a fact well known to every occultist that the ray of the Father is blue, while that of the Son is yellow, and the color of the Holy Spirit's ray is red. Only the strongest and most spiritual ray can hope to penetrate to the seat of consciousness of the life wave embodied in our mineral kingdom, and therefore we find about the mountain ranges the blue ray of the Father reflected back from the barren hillsides and hanging as a haze over canyons and gulches.

The yellow ray of the Son mixed with the blue of the Father gives life and vitality to the plant world, which therefore reflects back a green color, for it is incapable of keeping the ray WITHIN. But in the animal kingdom, to which unregenerate man belongs anatomically, the three rays are absorbed, and that of the Holy Spirit gives the red color to his flesh and blood. The mixture of the blue and the red is evident in the purple blood, poisoned because sinful. But the yellow is never evident until it manifests as a soul body, the golden "WEDDING garment" of the mystic Bride of the mystic Christ evolved from within.

Thus, the colors on the veils of the Temple, both at the gate and at the entrance of the Tabernacle, showed that this structure was designed for a period previous to the time of Christ, for it had only the blue and the scarlet colors of the Father and the Holy Spirit together with their mixture, purple. But white is the synthesis of all colors, and therefore the yellow Christ ray was hidden in that part of the veil until in the fullness of time Christ should appear to emancipate us from the ordinances that bind, and initiate us into the full liberty of Sons of God, Sons of Light, Children of Light, Phree Messen or Mystic Masons.

THE BRAZEN ALTAR AND LAVER

THE BRAZEN ALTAR was placed just inside the eastern gate, and it was used for the sacrifice of animals during the temple service. The idea of using bulls and goats as sacrifices seems barbaric to the modern mind, and we cannot realize that they could ever have had any efficacy in that respect. The Bible does indeed hear out this view of the matter, for we are told repeatedly that God desires not sacrifice but a broken spirit and a contrite heart, and that He has no pleasure in sacrifices of blood. In view of this fact, it seems strange that sacrifices should ever have been commanded. But we must realize that no religion can elevate those whom it is designed to help if its teachings are too far above their intellectual or moral level.

To appeal to a barbarian, religion must have certain barbaric traits. A religion of love could not have appealed to those people; therefore, they were given a law which demanded "an eye for an eye, and a tooth for a tooth." There is not in the Old Testament any mention whatever of immortality, for these people could not have understood a heaven nor aspired to it. But they loved material possessions, and therefore they were told that if they did right, they and their seed should dwell in the land forever, that their cattle should be multiplied, et cetera.

They loved material possessions, and they knew that the increases of the flock were due to the Lord's favor and given by Him for merit. Thus, they were taught to do right in the hope of a reward in this present world. They were also deterred from wrongdoing by the swift punishment which was meted out to them in retribution for their sins. This was the only way to reach them. They could not have done right for the sake of right, nor could they have understood the principle of making themselves "living sacrifices," and they probably felt the loss of an animal for sin as we would feel the pangs of conscience because of wrongdoing.

The Altar was made of brass, a metal not found in nature, but made by man from copper and zinc. Thus, it is symbolically shown that sin was not originally contemplated in our scheme of evolution and is an anomaly in nature as well as its consequences, pain and death, symbolized by the sacrificial victims. But while the Altar itself was made from metals artificially compounded, the fire which burned thereon unceasingly was of divine origin, and it was kept alive from year to year with the most jealous care. No other fire was ever used, and we may note with profit that when two presumptuous and rebellious priests dared to disregard this command and use strange fire, they met with an awful retribution and instant death. When we have once taken the oath of allegiance to the mystic Master, the HIGHER SELF, it is extremely dangerous to disregard the precepts then given.

When the candidate appears at the eastern gate he is "poor, naked, and blind." He is at that moment an object of charity, needing to be clothed and brought to the light, but this cannot be done at once in the mystic Temple. During the time of his progress from the condition of nakedness until he has been clothed in the gorgeous robes of the high priest there is a long and difficult path to be traveled.

The first lesson which he is taught is that man advances by sacrifices alone. In the Christian Mystic Initiation when the Christ washes the feet of His disciples, the explanation is given that unless the minerals decomposed and were offered us as embodiments for the plant kingdom, we should have no vegetation; also, did not the plant food furnish sustenance for the animals, these latter beings could not find expression; and so on, the higher is always feeding on the lower. Therefore, man has a duty to them, and so the Master washes the feet of His disciples symbolically performing for them the menial service as a recognition of the fact that they have served Him as stepping-stones to something higher.

Similarly, when the candidate is brought to the Brazen Altar, he learns the lesson that the animal is sacrificed for his sake, giving its body for food and its skin for clothing. Moreover, he sees the dense cloud of smoke hovering over the Altar and perceives within it a light, but that light is too dim, too much enshrouded in smoke, to be of permanent guidance to him. His spiritual eyes are weak, however, and it would not do to expose them at once to the light of greater spiritual truths.

We are told by the apostle Paul that the Tabernacle in the Wilderness was a shadow of greater things to come. It may therefore be of interest and profit to see what is the meaning of this Brazen Altar, with its sacrifices and burning flesh, to the candidate who comes to the Temple in modern times. In order that we may understand this mystery, we must first grasp the one great and absolutely essential idea which underlies all true mysticism, viz., that these things are WITHIN and not without. Angelus Silesius says about the Cross: "Though Christ a thousand times in Bethlehem be born, And not within thyself thy soul will be forlorn."

The Cross on Golgotha thou lookest to in vain, Unless within thyself it be set up again. This idea must be applied to every symbol and phase of mystic experience. It is not the Christ without that saves, but THE CHRIST WITHIN. The Tabernacle was built at one time; it is clearly seen in the Memory of Nature when the interior sight has been developed to a sufficient degree; but no one is ever helped by the outward symbol. We must build the Tabernacle within our own hearts and consciousness.

We must live through, as an actual inner experience, the whole ritual of service there. We must become both the Altar of sacrifice and the sacrificial animal lying upon it. We must become both the priest that slays the animal and the animal that is slain. Later we must learn to identify ourselves with the mystic Laver, and we must learn to wash therein in spirit. Then we must enter behind the first veil, minister in the East Room, and so on through the whole Temple service till we BECOME the greatest of all these ancient symbols, the Shekinah Glory, or it will avail us nothing. In short, before the symbol of the Tabernacle can really help us, we must transfer it from the wilderness of space to a home in our hearts so that when we have become everything that that symbol is, we shall also have become that which it stands for spiritually.

Let us then commence to build within ourselves the Altar of sacrifice, first that we may offer upon it our wrongdoings and then expiate them in the crucible of remorse. This is done under the modern system of preparation for discipleship by an exercise performed in the evening and scientifically designed by the Hierophants of the Western Mystery School for the advancement of the aspirant on the path which leads to discipleship. Other schools have given a similar exercise, but this one differs in one particular point from all previous methods. After explaining the exercises we shall also give the reason for this great and cardinal difference. This special method has such a far-reaching effect that it enables one to learn now not only the lessons which one should ordinarily learn in this life, but also attain a development which otherwise could not be reached until future lives.

After retiring for the night, the body is relaxed. This is very important, for when any part of the body is tense, the blood does not circulate unimpeded; part of it is temporarily imprisoned under pressure. As all spiritual development depends upon the blood, the maximum effort to attain soul growth cannot be made when any part of the body is in tension.

When perfect relaxation has been accomplished, the aspirant to the higher life begins to review the scenes of the day, but he does not start with the occurrences of the morning and finish with the events of the evening. He views them in REVERSE order: first the scenes of the evening, then the events of the afternoon, and lastly the occurrences of the morning. The reason for this is that from the moment of birth when the child draws its first complete breath, the air which is inspired into the lungs carries with it a picture of the outside world and as the blood courses through the left ventricle of the heart, each scene of life is pictured upon a minute atom located there.

Every breath brings with it new pictures, and thus there is engraved upon that little seed atom a record of every scene and act in our whole life from the first breath to the last dying gasp. After death these pictures from the basis of our purgatorial existence. Under the conditions of the spirit world, we suffer pangs of conscience so acute that they are unbelievable for every evil deed we have done, and we are thus discouraged from continuing on the path of wrongdoing. The intensity of the joys which we experience on account of our good deeds acts as a goad to spur us on the path of virtue in future lives. But in the post-mortem existence this panorama of life is reenacted in reverse order for the purpose of showing first the effects and then the causes which generated them that the spirit may learn how the law of cause and effect operates in life.

Therefore, the aspirant who is under the scientific guidance of the Elder Brothers of the Rosicrucian's is taught to perform his evening exercise also in reverse order and to judge himself each day that he may escape the purgatorial suffering after death. But let it be understood that no mere perfunctory review of the scenes of the day will avail. It is not enough when we come to a scene where we have grievously wronged somebody that we just say, "Well, I feel rather sorry that I did it. I wish I had not done it."

At that time, we are the sacrificial animal lying upon the Alter of Burnt Offerings, and unless we can feel in our hearts the divinely enkindled fire of remorse burn to the very marrow of our bones because of our wrongdoings during the day, we are not accomplishing anything. During the ancient dispensation all the sacrifices were rubbed with salt before being placed upon the Altar of Burnt Offerings. We all know how it smarts and burns when we accidentally rub salt into a fresh wound.

This rubbing of salt into the sacrifices in that ancient Mystery Temple symbolized the intensity of the burning which we must feel when we as living sacrifices place ourselves upon the Altar of Burnt Offerings. It is the feeling of remorse, of deep and sincere sorrow for what we have done, which eradicates the picture from the seed atom and leaves it clean and stainless, so that as under the ancient dispensation transgressors were justified when they brought to the

Altar of Burnt Offerings a sacrifice which was there burnt, so we in modern times by scientifically performing the evening exercise of retrospection wipe away the record of our sins.

It is a foregone conclusion that we cannot continue evening after evening to perform this living sacrifice without becoming better in consequence and ceasing, little by little, to do the things for which we are forced to blame ourselves when we have retired for the night. Thus, in addition to cleansing us from our faults this exercise elevates us to a higher level of spirituality than we could otherwise reach in the present life.

It is also noteworthy that when anyone had committed a grievous crime and fled to the sanctuary, he found safety in the shadow of the Altar of sacrifice, for there only the divinely enkindled fire could execute judgment. He escaped the hands of man by putting himself under the hand of God.

Similarly, also, the aspirant who acknowledges his wrongdoing nightly by fleeing to the altar of living judgment thereby obtains sanctuary from the law of cause and effect, and "though his sins be as scarlet they shall be white as snow."

THE BRAZEN LAVER

The Brazen laver was a large basin which was always kept full of water. It is said in the Bible that it was carried on the backs of twelve oxen, also made of brass, and we are told that their hind parts were toward the center of the vessel. It appears from the Memory of Nature, however, that those animals were not oxen but symbolical representations of the twelve signs of the zodiac. Humanity was at that time divided into twelve groups, one group for each zodiacal sign. Each symbolic animal attracted a particular ray, and as the holy water used today in Catholic churches is magnetized by the priest during the ceremony of consecration, so also the water in this Laver was magnetized by the divine Hierarchies who guided humanity.

There can be no doubt concerning the power of holy water prepared by a strong and magnetic personality. It takes on or absorbs the effluvia from his vital body, and the people who use it become amenable to his rule in a degree commensurate to their sensitiveness.

Consequently, the Brazen Lavers in the ancient Atlantean mystery Temples, where the water was magnetized by divine Hierarchs of immeasurable power, were a potent factor in guiding the people in accordance with the wishes of these ruling powers. Thus, the priests were in perfect subjection to the mandates and dictates of their unseen spiritual leaders, and through them the people were made to follow blindly. It was required of the priests that they wash their hands and feet before going into the Tabernacle proper.

If this command was not obeyed, death would follow immediately on the priest entering into the Tabernacle. We may therefore say that as the keyword of the Brazen Altar was "justification" so the central idea of the Brazen Laver was "consecration."

"Many are called but few are chosen." We have the example of the rich young man who came to Christ asking what he must do to be perfect. He asserted that he had kept the law, but when Christ gave the command, "Follow me," he could not, for he had many riches which held him fast as in a vise. Like the great majority he was content if he could only escape condemnation, and like them he was too lukewarm to strive for commendation merited by service.

The Brazen Laver is the symbol of sanctification and consecration of the life to service. As Christ entered upon His three years' ministry through the baptismal waters, so the aspirant to service in the ancient Temple must sanctify himself in the sacred stream which must sanctify himself in the sacred stream which flowed from the Molten Sea. And the mystic Mason endeavoring to build a temple "without sound of hammer" and to serve therein must also consecrate himself and sanctify himself. He must be willing to give up all earthly possessions that he may follow the CHRIST WITHIN.

Though he may retain his material possessions he must regard them as a sacred trust to be used by him as a wise steward would use his master's possessions. And we must be ready in everything to obey this Christ within when he says, "Follow me," even though the shadow of the Cross looms darkly at the end, for without this utter abandonment of the life to the Light, to the higher purposes, there can be no progress.

Even as the Spirit descended upon Jesus when he arose from the baptismal water of consecration, so also the mystic Mason who bathes in the Laver of the Molten Sea begins dimly to hear the voice of the Master within his own heart teaching him the secrets of the Craft that he may use them for the benefit of others.

EAST ROOM OF THE TEMPLE

HAVING MOUNTED the first steps upon the path the aspirant stands in front of the veil which hangs before the mystic Temple. Drawing this aside he enters into the East Room of the sanctuary, which was called the HOLY PLACE. No window or opening of any sort was provided in the Tabernacle to let in the light of day, but this room was never dark. Night and day it was brightly illuminated by burning lamps.

Its furniture was symbolical of the methods whereby the aspirant may make SOUL GROWTH BY SERVICE. It consisted of three principal articles: The ALTER OF INCENSE, the TABLE OF SHEWBREAD, and the GOLDEN CANDLESTICK from which the light proceeded.

It was not allowable for the common Israelite to enter this sacred apartment and behold the furniture. No one but a priest might pass the outer veil and go in even as far as this first room. The Golden Candlestick was placed on the south side of the Holy Place so as to be to the left of any person who stood in the middle of the room. It was made entirely of pure gold, and consisted of a shaft or principal stem, rising upright from a base, together with six branches.

These branches started at three different points on the stem and curved upward in three partial circles of varying diameter, symbolizing the three periods of development (Saturn, Sun, and Moon Periods) which man went through before the Earth period, which was not half spent. This latter period was signified by the seventh light. Each of these seven branches terminated in a lamp, and these lamps were supplied with the purest olive oil, which was made by a special process. The priests were required to take care that the Candlestick was never without a light. Every day the lamps were examined, dressed, and supplied with oil so that they might burn perpetually.

The TABLE OF SHEWBREAD was placed on the north side of the apartment so as to be in THE RIGHT HAND of the priest when he walked up toward the second veil. Twelve loaves of unleavened bread were continually kept upon this table. They were placed in two piles, one loaf upon another, and on top of each pile there was a small quantity of frankincense. These loaves were called shewbread, or bread of the face, because they were set solemnly forth before the presence of the Lord, who dwelt in the Shekinah Glory behind the second veil. Every Sabbath day these loaves were changed by the priests, the old ones being taken away and new ones put in their place. The bread that was taken away was used by the priests to eat, and no one else was allowed to taste it; neither were they suffered to eat it anywhere except within the Court of the Sanctuary, because it was most holy, and therefore might only be taken by sacred persons upon holy ground. THE INCENSE THAT WAS UPON THE TWO PILES OF SHEWBREAD WAS BURNED when the bread was changed, as an offering by fire unto the Lord, as a memorial instead of the bread.

The ALTAR OF INCENSE or the Golden Altar was the third article of furniture in the East Room of the Temple. It was situated in the center of the room, that is to say, halfway between the north and the south walls, in front of the second veil. No flesh was ever burned upon this Altar, nor was it ever touched with blood except on the most solemn occasions, and then its horns alone were marked with the crimson stain. The smoke that arose from its top was never any other than the smoke of burning incense. This went up every morning and evening, filling the sanctuary with a fragrant cloud and sending a refreshing odor out through all the courts and far over the country on every side for miles beyond. Because incense was thus burned every day it was called "A PERPETUAL INCENSE before the Lord."

It was not simple frankincense which was burned, but a compound of this with other sweet spices, made according to the direction of Jehovah for this special purpose and so considered holy, such as no man was allowed to make like unto for common use. THE PRIEST WAS CHARGED NEVER TO OFFER STRANGE INCENSE on the Golden Altar, that is, any other than the sacred composition. This Altar was placed directly before the veil on the outside of it, but before the Mercy Seat, which was within the second veil; for though he that ministered at the Altar of Incense could not see the Mercy Seat because of the interposing veil, yet he must look toward it and direct his incense that way. And it was customary when the cloud of fragrant incense rose above the temple for all the people who were standing without in the Court of the Sanctuary to send up their prayers to God, each one silently by himself.

THE MYSTIC SIGNIFICANCE OF THE EAST ROOM AND ITS FURNITURE THE GOLDEN CANDLESTICK As previously said, when the priest stood in the center of the East Room of the Tabernacle, the Seven-branched Candlestick was ON HIS LEFT toward the SOUTH.

This was symbolical of the fact that the seven light-givers or planets which tread the mystic circle dance around the central orb, the sun, travel in the narrow belt comprising eight degrees on either side of the sun's path, which is called the zodiac. "God is Light," and the "Seven Spirits before the Throne" are God's ministers; therefore, THEY ARE MESSENGERS OF LIGHT to humanity. Furthermore, as the heavens are ablaze with light when the moon in its phases arrives at the "full" in the eastern part of the heavens, so also the East Room of the Tabernacle was filled with LIGHT, indicating VISIBLY the presence there of God and His seven Ministers, the STAR ANGELS.

We may note, in passing, the light of the Golden Candlestick, which was clear and the flame odorless, and compare it with the smoke-enveloped flame on the Altar of Burnt Offerings, which in a certain sense generated darkness rather than dispelled it. But there is a still deeper and more sublime meaning in this fire symbol, which we will not take up for discussion until we come to the SHEKINAH GLORY, whose dazzling brilliance hovered over the Mercy Seat in the WEST ROOM.

Before we can enter into this subject, we must understand all the symbols that lie between the Golden Candlestick and that sublime Father Fire which was the crowning glory of the Holy of Holies, the most sacred part of the Tabernacle in the Wilderness.

THE TABLE OF SHEWBREAD

(Shewbread is twelve loaves of bread placed every Sabbath in the Jewish Temple and eaten by the priests at the end of the week.)

The East Room of the Temple may be called the Hall of Service, for it corresponds to the three years' ministry of Christ, and contains all the paraphernalia for soul growth, though, as said, furnished with only three principal articles. Among the chief of these is the Table of Shewbread.

Upon this table, as we have already seen, there were two piles of shewbread, each containing six loaves, and upon the top of each pile there was a little heap of frankincense. The aspirant who came to the Temple door "poor, naked, and blind" has since been brought to the light of the Seven branched Candlestick, obtaining a certain amount of cosmic knowledge, and THIS HE IS REQUIRED TO USE IN THE SERVICE OF HIS FELLOW MEN; the Table of Shewbread represents this in symbol.

The grain from which this shewbread was made had been originally given by God, but then it was planted by mankind, who had previously plowed and tilled the soil. After planting their grain, they must cultivate and water it; then when the grain had borne fruit according to the nature of the soil and the care bestowed upon it, it had to be harvested, threshed, ground, and baked. Then the ancient

SERVANTS OF GOD had to carry it into the Temple, where it was placed before the Lord as bread to "SHEW" THAT THEY HAD PERFORMED THEIR TOIL AND RENDERED THE NECESSARY SERVICE.

The God-given grains of wheat in the twelve loaves represent the OPPORTUNITIES FOR SOUL GROWTH given by God, which come to all through the twelve departments of life represented by the twelve houses of the horoscope, under the dominion of the twelve divine Hierarchies known through the signs of the zodiac. BUT IT IS THE TASK OF THE MYSTIC MASON, THE TRUE TEMPLE BUILDER, TO EMBRACE THESE OPPORTUNITIES, TO CULTIVATE AND NOURISH THEM SO THAT HE MAY REAP THEREFROM THE LIVING BREAD WHICH NURTURES THE SOUL.

We do not, however, assimilate our physical food IN TOTO; there is a residue, a large proportion of ash, left after we have amalgamated the quintessence into our system. Similarly, the showbread was not burned or consumed before the Lord, but two small heaps of frankincense were placed on the two stacks of shewbread, one on each pile. This was conceived to be the aroma thereof, and was later burned on the Altar of Incense. Likewise, the soul sustenance of service gathered daily by the ardent Mystic Mason is thrown into the mill of retrospection at eventide when he retires to his couch and performs there the scientific exercises given by the Elder Brothers of the Rose Cross.

There is a time each month which is particularly propitious for extracting the frankincense of soul growth and burning it before the lord so that it may be a sweet savor, TO BE AMALGAMATED WITH THE SOUL BODY and form part of that golden, radiant "wedding garment." This as at the time when the moon is at the full. Then she is in the east, and the heavens are ablaze with light as was the East Room of the ancient Atlantean Mystery Temple where the priest garnered the pabulum of the soul, symbolized by the shewbread and the fragrant essence, which delighted our Father in Heaven then as now.

Let the Mystic Mason take particular note, however, that the loaves of shewbread were not the musings of dreamers; they were not the product of speculation upon the nature of God or light. THEY WERE THE PRODUCT OF ACTUAL TOIL, of orderly systematic work, and it behooves us to follow the path of actual service if we would garner treasure in heaven. Unless we really WORK and SERVE humanity, we shall have nothing to bring, no bread to "shew," at the Feast of the Full Moon; and at the mystic marriage of the higher to the lower self we shall find ourselves minus the radiant golden sold body, the mystic wedding garment without which the union with Christ can never be consummated.

THE ALTER OF INCENSE

At the Altar of Incense, as we saw in the general description of the Tabernacle and its furniture, incense was offered before the lord continually, and the priest who stood before the altar ministering was at that time looking toward the mercy Seat over the Ark, though it as impossible for him to see it because of the SECOND VEIL which was interposed between the first and second apartments of the Tabernacle, the Holy Place and the Holy of Holies. We have also seen in the consideration of the "shewbread" that INCENSE symbolizes the extract, THE AROMA OF THE SERVICE we have rendered according to our opportunities; and just as the sacrificial animal upon the Brazen Altar represents the deeds of wrongdoing committed during the day, so the incense burned upon the Golden Altar, which is a sweet savor to the Lord, represents the virtuous deeds of our lives.

THE ARK OF THE COVENANT

It is noteworthy and fraught with great mystic significance that the aroma of VOLUNTARY SERVICE is represented as SWEET-SMELLING, FRAGRANT INCENSE, while the odor of sin, selfishness, and transgression of the law, represented by COMPULSORY SACRIFICE upon the Altar of service, is nauseating; for it needs no great imagination to understand that the cloud of smoke which went up continually from the burning carcasses of the sacrificial animals created a nauseating stench to show the exceeding loathsomeness of it, while the perpetual incense offered upon the Altar before the second veil showed by antithesis the beauty and sublimity of selfless service, thus exhorting the Mystic Mason, as a CHILD OF LIGHT, to shun the one and cleave to the other.

Let it be understood also that SERVICE does not consist in doing great things only. Some of the heroes, so-called were mean and small in their general lives, and rose only to the occasion upon one great and notable day. Martyrs have been put on the calendar of saints because they DIED for a cause; but it is a greater heroism, it is a greater martyrdom sometimes, to do the little things that no one notices and sacrifice self IN SIMPLE SERVICE TO OTHERS.

We have seen previously that the veil at the entrance to the outer court and the veil in front of the East Room of the Tabernacle were both made in four colors, blue, red, purple, and white. But THE

SECOND VEIL, which divided the East Room of the Tabernacle from the West Room, differed with respect to make-up from the other two. It was wrought with the figures of Cherubim. We will not consider, however, the significance of this fact until we take up the subject of the NEW MOON AND INITIATION, but will now look into the second apartment of the Tabernacle, the western room, called the Most Holy or the Holy of Holies.

Beyond the second veil, into this second apartment, no mortal might ever pass save the HIGH PRIEST, and he was only allowed to enter on one occasion in the whole year, namely, Yom Kippur, the Day of Atonement, and then only after the most solemn preparation and with the most reverential care. The Holiest of All was clothed with the solemnity of another world; it was filled with an unearthly grandeur. The whole Tabernacle was the sanctuary of God, but here in this place was the awful abode of His presence, the special dwelling place of the SHEKINAH GLORY, and well might mortal man tremble to present himself within these sacred precincts, as the High Priest must do on the Day of Atonement.

In the westernmost end of this apartment, the western end of the whole Tabernacle, rested the "ARK OF THE COVENANT." It was a hollow receptacle containing the GOLDEN POT OF MANNA, AARON'S ROD THAT BUDDED, AND THE TABLES OF THE LAW which were given to Moses. While this Ark of the Covenant remained in the Tabernacle in the Wilderness, TWO STAVES WERE ALWAYS WITHIN THE FOUR RINGS OF THE ARK so that it could be picked up instantly and moved, but when the Ark as finally taken to Solomon's Temple, the staves were taken out. This is very important in its symbolical significance. Above the Ark hovered the Cherubim, and between them dwelt the uncreated glory of God. "Three," said He to Moses, "I will meet with thee, and I will commune with thee from above the Mercy Seat, from between the two Cherubim which are upon the Ark of the Testimony." The glory of the Lord seen above the Mercy Seat was in the appearance of a cloud. The Lord said to Moses, "Speak unto Aaron they brother that he come not at all time into the Holiest Place within the veil before the Mercy Seat which is upon the Ark, that he die not, for I will appear in the cloud upon the Mercy Seat." This manifestation of the divine presence was called among the Jews the SHEKINAH GLORY. Its appearance was attended no doubt with a wonderful spiritual glory of which it is impossible to form any proper conception. Out of this cloud the voice of God was heard with deep solemnity when He was consulted in behalf of the people.

When the aspirant has qualified to enter into this place behind the second veil, he finds everything DARK to the physical eye, and it is necessary that he should have another light WITHIN. When he first came to the eastern Temple gate, he was "POOR, NAKED, AND BLIND," asking for LIGHT.

He was then shown the dim light which appeared in the smoke above the Altar of sacrifice, and told that in order to advance he must kindle within himself that flame by remorse for wrongdoing. Later on, he was shown the more excellent light in the East Room of the Tabernacle, which proceeded from the Seven- branched Candlestick; in other words, he was given the light of knowledge and of reason that by it he might advance further upon the path. But it was required that BY SERVICE he should evolve within himself and around himself another light, the golden "wedding garment," which is also THE CHRIST LIGHT OF THE SOUL BODY. By lives of service this glorious soul substance gradually pervades his whole aura until it is ablaze with a golden light. Not until he has evolved this INNER illumination can he enter into the darkened precincts of the second Tabernacle, as the Most Holy place is sometimes called.

"GOD IS LIGHT; if we walk in the light as He is in the Light, we have fellowship one with another." This is generally taken to indicate only the fellowship of the Saints, but as a matter of fact it applies also to the fellowship which we have with God. When the disciple enters the second Tabernacle, THE LIGHT WITHIN HIMSELF VIBRATES TO THE LIGHT OF THE SHEKINAH GLORY between the Cherubim, and he realizes the fellowship with his FATHER FIRE.

As the Cherubim and the Father Fire which hover above the Ark represent the divine Hierarchies which overshadow mankind during his pilgrimage through the wilderness, so THE ARK WHICH IS FOUND THERE REPRESENTS MAN IN HIS HIGHEST DEVELOPMENT. Three were, as already said, three things within the Ark: the Golden Pot of Manna, the Budding Rod, and the Tables of the Law. When the aspirant stood at the eastern gate as a child of sin, THE LAW WAS WITHOUT AS A TASKMASTER to bring him to Christ.

It exacted with unrelenting severity an eye for an eye and a tooth for a tooth. Every transgression brought a just recompense, and man was circumscribed on every hand by laws commanding him to do certain things and refrain from doing others. But when THROUGH SACRIFICE AND SERVICE he has finally arrived at the stage of evolution represented by the Ark in the western room of the Tabernacle, the TABLES OF THE LAW ARE WITHIN. He has then become emancipated from all outside interference with his actions; not that he would break any laws, but because HE WORKS WITH THEM. Just as we have learned to respect the property right of others and have therefore become emancipated from the commandment. "Thou shalt not steal," so he who keeps all laws because he wants to do so has on that account no longer need of an exterior taskmaster, but gladly renders obedience in all things because HE IS A SERVANT OF THE LAW AND WORKS WITH IT, FROM CHOICE AND NOT THROUGH NECESSITY.

THE GOLDEN POT OF MANNA

Manas, mensch, mens, or man is readily associated with the MANNA that came down from heaven. it is the HUMAN SPIRIT that descended from our Father above for a pilgrimage through matter, and the Golden Pot wherein it was kept symbolizes the golden aura of the soul body.

Although the Bible story is not in strict accordance with the events, it gives the main facts of the mystic manna which fell from heaven. When we want to learn what is the nature of this so-called BREAD, we may turn to the sixth chapter of the Gospel of John, which relates how Christ fed the multitudes with LOAVES AND FISHES, symbolizing the mystic doctrine of the 2000 years which He was then ushering in, for during that time the sun BY PRECESSION OF THE EQUINOX has been passing through the sign of the fishes, Pisces, and the people have been taught to abstain at least one day during the week (Friday) and at a certain time of the year from the fleshpots which belonged to Egypt or ancient Atlantis. They have been given the Piscean water at the temple door, and the Virginian Wafers at the communion table before the altar when they worshiped the Immaculate Virgin, representing the celestial sign Virgo (which is opposite the sign Pisces), and entered communion with the sun begotten by her.

Christ also explained at that time in mystic but unmistakable language what that LIVING BREAD, or manna, was, namely, the Ego. This explanation will be found in verses thirty-three and thirty-five, where we read: "For the bread of God is he which cometh down from heaven and giveth light unto the world-I am (EGO SUM) THE BREAD OF LIFE." This, then, is the symbol of the golden pot of manna which was found in the Ark. This manna is the Ego or human spirit, which gives life to the organisms that we behold in the physical world. It is hidden within the Ark of each human being, and the Golden pot or soul body or "wedding garment" is also latent within every one. It is made more massive, lustrous, and resplendent by the spiritual alchemy whereby service is transmuted to soul growth. It is THE HOUSE NOT MADE WITH HANDS, eternal in the heavens, wherewith Paul longed to be clothed, as said in the Epistle to the Corinthians. Everyone who is striving to aid his fellow men thereby garners within himself that golden treasure, laid up in heaven, where neither moth nor rust can destroy it.

AARON'S ROD

An ancient legend relates that when Adam was expelled from the Garden of Eden, he took with him three slips of the TREE OF LIFE, which were then planted by Seth. Seth, the second son of Adam, is, according to the Masonic legend, father of the spiritual hierarchy of CHURCHMEN working with humanity through Catholicism, while the sons of Cain are the CRAFTSMEN of the world. The latter are active in Freemasonry, promoting material and industrial progress, as builders of the temple of Solomon, the universe, should be. The three sprouts planted by Seth have had important missions in the spiritual development of humanity, and one of them is said to be the Rod of Aaron.

In the beginning of concrete existence generation was carried on under the wise guidance of the angels, who saw to it that the creative act was accomplished at times when the interplanetary rays of force were propitious; and man was also forbidden to eat of the Tree of Knowledge. The nature of that tree is readily determined from such sentences as "Adam KNEW his wife, and she bore Cain"; "Adam KNEW his wife, and she bore Seth"; "how shall I bear a child seeing that I KNOW not a man?" as said by Mary to the angel Gabriel. In the light of this interpretation the STATEMENT of the Angel (it was not a curse) when he discovered that his precepts had been disobeyed, namely, "dying thou shalt die," is also intelligible, for the bodies generated regardless of cosmic influences could not be expected to persist.

Hence man was exiled from the etheric realms of spiritual force (Eden), where grows the tree of vital power; exiled to concrete existence in the dense physical bodies which he has made for himself by generation.

This was surely a blessing, for who has a body sufficiently good and perfect in his own estimation that he would like to live in it forever? Death, then, is a boon to the spiritual realms for a season, and build better vehicles each time we return to earth life. As Oliver Wendell Holmes says: "Build thee more stately mansions, O my soul! As the swift seasons roll. Leave thy low-vaulted past, Let each new temple, nobler than the last, Shut tree from Heaven with a dome more vast, Till thou at length art free, Leaving thine outgrown shell by life's unresting sea."

In the course of time when we learn to shun the pride of life and the lust of the flesh, generation will cease to sap our vitality. The vital energy will then be used for regeneration, and the spiritual powers, symbolized by Aaron's Rod, will be developed.

The wand of the magician, the holy spear of Parsifal the Grail king, and the budding Rod of Aaron are emblems of this divine creative force, which works wonders of such a nature that we call them miracles. But let it be clearly understood that no one who has evolved to the point in evolution where he is symbolized by the Ark of the Covenant in the West Room of the Tabernacle ever uses this power for selfish ends.

When Parsifal, the hero of the soul myth by that name, had witnessed the temptation of Kundry and proved himself to be emancipated from the greatest sin of all, the sin of lust and unchastity, he recovered the sacred spear taken by the black magician, Klingsor, from the fallen and unchaste rail king, Amfortas. Then for many years he traveled in the world, seeking again the Castle of the Grail, and he said: "Often was I sorely beset by enemies and tempted to use the spear in self-defense, but I knew that THE SACRED SPEAR MUST NEVER BE USED TO HURT, ONLY TO HEAL."

And that is the attitude of everyone who develops within him the budding Rod of Aaron. Though he may turn this spiritual faculty to good account in order to provide bread for a multitude, he would never think of turning a single stone to bread FOR HIMSELF that his hunger might be appeased. Though he were nailed to the cross to die, he would not free himself by spiritual power which he had readily exercised to save others from the grave. Though he were reviled every day of his life as a fraud or charlatan, he would never misuse his spiritual power to show a sign whereby the world might know without the shadow of a doubt that he was regenerate or heaven-born. This was the attitude of Christ Jesus, and its has been and is imitated by everyone who is a Christ-in-the making.

THE SACRED SHEKINAH GLORY

The Western Room of the Tabernacle was as dark as the heavens are at the time when the lesser light, the moon, is in the western portion of sky at eventide with the sun; that is to say, at the new moon, which begins a new cycle in a new sign of the zodiac. In the westernmost part of this darkened sanctuary stood the Ark of the Covenant, with the Cherubim hovering above, and also the fiery Shekinah Glory, out of which the Father of Light communed with His worshipers, but which to the physical vision was invisible and therefore dark.

We do not usually realize that the whole world is afire, that fire is in the water, that it burns continually in plant, animal, and man; yes, there is nothing in the work that is not ensouled by fire.

The reason why we do not perceive this more clearly is that we cannot dissociate fire and flame. But as a matter of fact, FIRE bears the same relation to FLAME as SPIRIT to the BODY; it is the unseen but potent power of manifestation. In other words, the true fire is dark, invisible to the physical sight. IT IS ONLY CLOTHED IN FLAME WHEN CONSUMING PHYSICAL MATTER.

Consider, for illustration, how fire leaps out of the flint when struck, and how a gas flame has the darkened core beneath the light-giving portion; also, how a wire may carry electricity and be perfectly cold, yet it will emit a flame under certain conditions. At this point it may be expedient to mark the difference between the Tabernacle in the Wilderness, Solomon's Temple, and the later Temple built by Herod. There is a very vital difference. Both the MIRACULOUSLY ENKINDLED FIRE on the Brazen Altar in the eastern part of the Tabernacle and the invisible SHEKINAH GLORY in the distant western part of the sanctuary were also present in Solomon's Temple. These were thus sanctuaries in a sense not equaled by the Temple built by Herod.

The latter was, nevertheless, in a sense the most glorious of the three, for IT WAS GRACED BY THE BODILY PRESENCE OF OUR LORD, CHRIST JESUS, IN WHOM DWELT THE GODHEAD. Christ made the first self-sacrifice, thereby abrogating the sacrifice of animals, and finally at the consummation of His work in the visible world RENT THE VEIL and opened a way into the Holy of Holies, not only for the favored few, the priests and Levites, but that WHOSOEVER WILL may come and serve the Deity whom we know as our Father.

Having fulfilled the law and the prophets Christ has done away with the OUTWARD sanctuary, and from henceforth the Altar of Burnt Offerings must be set up WITHIN the heart to atone for wrongdoing; the Golden Candlestick must be lighted WITHIN the heart to guide us upon our way, as the Christ WITHIN, the Shekinah Glory of the Father, must dwell WITHIN the sacred precincts of our own God Consciousness.

THE SHADOW OF THE CROSS

Paul in his letter to the Hebrews gives a description of the Tabernacle and much information about the customs used there which it would benefit the student to know. Among other things note that he calls the Tabernacle "a shadow of good things to come." There is in this ancient Mystery Temple a promise given which has not yet been fulfilled, a promise that holds good today just as well as upon the day it was given. If we visualize in our mind the arrangement of things inside the Tabernacle, we shall readily see the shadow of the Cross.

Commencing at the eastern gate there was the ALTAR OF BURNT OFFERINGS; a little farther along the path to the Tabernacle itself we find the LAVER OF CONSECRATION, the Molten Sea, in which the priests washed. Then upon entering the East Room of the Temple we find an article of furniture, THE GOLDEN CANDLESTICK, at the EXTREME LEFT, and the TABLE OF SHEWBREAD at the EXTREME RIGHT, the two forming a cross with the path we have been pursuing toward and within the Tabernacle.

In the center in front of the second veil we find the ALTAR OF INCENSE, which forms the center of the cross, while the Ark placed in the westernmost part of the West Room, the Holy of Holies, gives the short or upper limb of the cross. In this manner the symbol of spiritual unfoldment which is our particular ideal today was shadowed forth in the ancient Mystery Temple, and that consummation which is attained at the end of the cross, the achievement of getting the law WITHIN as it was within the Ark itself, is the one that we must all concern ourselves with at the present time.

The light that shines over the Mercy Seat in the Holy of Holies at the head of the cross, at the end of the path in this world, is a light or reflection from the invisible world into which the candidate seeks to enter when all the world has grown dark and black about him. Only when we have attained to that stage where we perceive the spiritual light that beckons us on, the light that floats over the Ark, only when we stand in the shadow of the cross, can we really know the meaning, the object, and the goal of life.

At present we may take the opportunities which are offered and perform service more or less efficiently, but it is only when we have by that service evolved the spiritual light WITHIN ourselves, which is the SOUL BODY, and when we have thus gained admission to the West Room, called the Hall of Liberation, that we can really perceive and understand why we are in the world, and what we need in order to make ourselves properly useful. We may not remain, however, when access has been gained.

The High Priest was only allowed to enter ONCE A YEAR; there was a very long interval of time between these glimpses of the real purpose of existence. In the times between it was necessary for the High Priest to go out and function among his brethren, humanity, and serve them to the very best of his ability, also to sin, because he was not yet perfect, and then reenter the Holy of Holies after having made proper amends for his sins.

Similar it is with ourselves at this day. We at times attain glimpses of the things that are in store for us and the things we must do to follow Christ to that place where He went. You remember that He said to His disciples: Ye cannot follow me now, but ye shall follow me later. And so, it is with us. We have to look again and again into the darkened temple, the Holy of Holies, before we are really fit to stay there; before we are really fitted to take the last step and leap to the summit of the cross, THE PLACE OF THE SKULL, that point in our heads where the spirit takes its departure when it finally leaves the body, or off and on as an Invisible Helper.

That Golgotha is the ultimate of human attainment, and we must be prepared to enter the darkened room many times before we are fitted for the final climax.

THE FULL MOON AS A FACTOR IN SOUL GROWTH

Let us now consider the Path of Initiation as symbolically shown in the ancient Temples with the Ark, Fire, and Shekinah, and in the later Temples where Christ taught. Note first that when man was expelled from the Garden of Eden because he had eaten of the Tree of Knowledge, Cherubim guarded the entrance with a flaming sword. Passages like the following, "Adam KNEW Eve, and she bore Abel"; "Adam KNEW Eve, and she bore Seth"; "Elkanah KNEW Hannah, and she bore Samuel"; also, Mary's question to the angel Gabriel, "How shall I conceive seeing that I KNOW not a man?" all show plainly that indulgence of the passions in the creative act was meant by the phrase, "eating the Tree of Knowledge." When the creative act was performed under inauspicious planetary rays it was a sin committed against the laws of nature, which brought pain and death into the world, estranged us from our primal guardians, and forced us to roam the wilderness of the world for ages.

At the gate of the mystic Temple of Solomon we find the Cherubim, but the fiery sword is not longer in their hand; instead, they hold a FLOWER, a symbol full of mystic meaning. Let us compare man with a flower that we may know the great import and significance of this emblem. Man takes his good by way of the head, whence it goes downward. The plant takes nourishment through the root and forces it upward. Man is passionate in love, and he turns the generative organ toward the earth and hides it in shame because of this taint of passion. The plant knows no passion, fertilization is accomplished in the most pure and chaste manner imaginable, therefore it projects its generative organ, the flower, TOWARD THE SUN, a thing of beauty which delights all who behold it. Passionate fallen man exhales THE DEADLY CARBON DIOXIDE; the chaste flower inhales this poison, transmutes it, and gives it back pure, sweet, and scented, a fragrant elixir of life.

This was the mystery of the Grail Cup; this is the emblematic significance of the Cup of Communion, which is called "KELCH" in German "Calix" in Latin, both names signifying the seed pod of the flower. The Communion Cup with its mystic blood cleansed from the passion incident to generation brings to him who truly drinks thereof eternal life, and thus it becomes the vehicle of regeneration, of the mystic birth into a higher sphere, a "foreign country," where he who has served his apprenticeship in Temple building and has mastered the "art and crafts" of this world may learn higher things.

The symbol of the Cherubim with the open flower placed upon the door of Solomon's Temple delivers the message to the aspirant that PURITY IS THE KEY by which alone he can hope to unlock the gate to God; or as Christ expressed it, "Blessed are the pure in heart for they shall see God." The flesh must be consumed on the Altar of self-sacrifice, and the sold must be washed in the Laver of Consecration to the higher life where it may approach the Temple door.

When "naked," "poor," and "blinded" by tears of contrition it gropes in darkness, seeking the Temple door, it shall find entrance to the Hall of Service, the East Room of the Tabernacle, which is ablaze with light from the Seven-branched Candlestick, emblematic of the luminosity of the full moon, the moon changing in cycles of seven days. In this Hall of Service, the aspirant is taught to weave the luminous vesture of flame which Paul called "soma psuchicon," or soul body (1st Cor., 15:44), from the aroma of the shewbread.

When we speak of the soul body, we mean exactly what we say, and this vehicle is in nowise to be confused with the soul that permeates it. The Invisible Helper who uses it on soul flights knows it to be as real and tangible as the dense body of flesh blood. But within that golden "wedding garment" there is an INTANGIBLE SOMETHING cognized by the spirit of introspection. It is unnamable and indescribable; it evades the most persistent efforts to fathom it, yet it is there just as certainly as the vehicle which it fills-yes, and more so. It is not life, love, beauty, wisdom, nor can any other human concept convey an idea of what it is, for it is the sum of all human faculties, attributes, and concepts of good, immeasurably intensified. If everything else were taken from us, that prime reality would still remain, and we should be rich in its possession, for through it we feel the drawing power of our Father in Heaven, that inner urge which all aspirants know so well.

To this inner something Christ referred when He said: No man cometh to me except my Father draw him. Just as the true fire is hidden in the flame that encloses it, so that unnamable, intangible something hides in the soul body and burns up the frankincense extracted from the shewbread; thus, it lights the fire which makes the soul body luminous. And the AROMA OF LOVING SERVICE to others penetrates the veil as a sweet savor to God, who dwells in the Shekinah Glory similar created above the Ark in the innermost sanctuary, the Holy of Holies.

THE NEW MOON AND INITIATION

When the candidate entered at the eastern gate of the Temple looking for light, he was confronted by the fire on the Altar of Burnt Offerings, which emitted a dim light enveloped in clouds of smoke. He was then in the spiritually darkened condition of the ordinary man; he lacked the light within and therefore it was necessary to give him the light without. But when he has arrived at the point when he is ready to have evolved the luminous soul body in the service of humanity. Then he is thought to have the light within himself, "the light that lighteth every man." Unless he has that, he cannot enter the dark room of the Temple.

What takes place secretly in the Temple is shown openly in the heavens. As the moon gathers light from the sun during her passage from the new to the full, so the man who treads the path of holiness by use of his golden opportunities in the East Room of selfless service gathers the materials wherewith to make his luminous "wedding garment," and that material is best amalgamated on the night of the full moon. But conversely, as the moon gradually dissipates the accumulated light and draws nearer the sun in order to make a fresh start upon a new cycle at the time of the new moon, so also according to the law of analogy those who have gathered their treasures and laid them up in heaven by service are at a certain time of the month closer to their Source and their Maker, their Father Fire in the higher spheres, than at any other time.

As the great saviors of mankind are born at the winter solstice on the longest and darkest night of the year, so also the process of Initiation which brings to birth in the invisible world one of the lesser saviors, THE INVISIBLE HELPER, is most easily accomplished on the longest and darkest night of the month, that is to say, on the night of the new moon when the lunar orb is in the westernmost part of the heavens. All occult development begins with the vital body, and the keynote of that vehicle is "repetition."

To get the best out of any subject repetition is necessary. In order to understand the final consummation to which all this has been leading up, let us take a final look from another angle at the three kinds of fire within the Temple. Near the eastern gate was the Altar of Burnt Offering. On that altar smoke was continually generated by the bodies of the sacrifices, and the pillar of smoke was seen far and wide by the multitude who were instructed in the inner mysteries of life.

The flame, the light, hidden in this cloud of smoke was at best but dimly perceived. This showed that the great majority of mankind are taught principally by the immutable laws of nature, which exact from them a sacrifice whether they know it or not. As the flame of purification was then fed by the more coarsely constructed and baser bodies of animal sacrifices, exacted under the Mosaic law, so also today the baser and more passionate mass of humanity is being brought into subjection by fear of punishment by the law in the present world-more than by apprehension of what my follow in the world to come.

A light of a different nature shone in the East Room of the Tabernacle. Instead of drawing its nourishment from the sinful and passionate flesh of the animal sacrifices, it was fed by olive oil procured from the chaste plant kingdom; and its flame was not shrouded in smoke, but was clear and distinct, so that it might illuminate the room and guide the priests, who were the servants of the Temple, in their ministrations. The priests were endeavoring to work in harmony with the divine plan, therefore they saw the light more clearly that the uninstructed and careless multitude.

Today also the mystic light shines for all who are endeavoring to really serve at the shrine of self-sacrifice particularly for the pledged pupils of a Mystery School such as the Rosicrucian Order. They are walking in a light not seen by the multitude, and if they are really serving, they have the true guidance of the Elder Brothers of humanity, who are always ready to help them at the difficult points on the Path.

But the most sacred fire of all was the Shekinah Glory in the West Room of the Tabernacle above the Mercy Seat. As this West Room was dark, we understand that it was an invisible fire, a light from another world. Now mark this, the fire that was shrouded in smoke and flame upon the Altar of Burnt Offerings, consuming the sacrifices brought there in expiation of sins committed under the law, was the symbol of JEHOVAH THE LAWGIVER; and we remember that the law was given to brings us to Christ. The clear and beautiful light which shone in the Hall of Service, the East Room of the Tabernacle, is the golden-hued Christ light, which guides those who endeavor to follow in His steps upon the path of self-forgetting service.

As the Christ said, "I go to my Father," when He was about to be crucified, so also the Servant of the Cross who has made the most of his opportunities in the visible world is allowed to enter the glory of his Father Fire, the invisible Shekinah Glory. He ceases then to see through the dark glass of the body, and beholds his Father face to face in the invisible realms of nature. The church steeple is very broad at the bottom, but gradually it narrows more and more until at the top it is just a point with the cross above it.

So, it is with the path of holiness; at the beginning there are many things which we may permit ourselves, but as we advance, one after another of these digressions must be done away with, and we must devote ourselves more and more exclusively to the service of holiness. At last, there comes a point where this path is as sharp as the razor's edge, and we can then only grasp at the cross. But when we have attained that point, when we can climb this narrowest of all paths, then we are fitted to follow Christ into the beyond and serve there as we have served here.

Thus, this ancient symbol shadowed forth the trial and triumph of the faithful servant, and thought it has been superseded by other and greater symbols holding forth a higher ideal and a greater promise, the basic principles embodied in it are as valid today as ever.

In the Altar of Burnt Offerings we see clearly the nauseating nature of sin and the necessity of expiation and justification. By the Molten Sea we are still taught that we must live the stainless life that of holiness and consecration.

From the East Room we learn today how to make diligent use of our opportunities to grow the golden grain of selfless service and make that "living bread" which feeds the soul, the Christ within. And when we have ascended the steps of Justification, Consecration, and Self-Abnegation, we reach the West Room, which is the threshold of Liberation. Over it we are conducted into greater realms, where greater soul unfoldment may be accomplished.

But through this ancient Temple stands no longer upon the plains where the wandering hosts pitched their camps in the hoary past, it may be made a much more potent factor for soul growth by any aspirant of today that it was by the ancient Israelites provided he will build it according to pattern. Nor need the lack of gold wherewith to build distress anyone, for now the true tabernacle must be built in heaven and "HEAVEN IS WITH YOU." To build well and true, according to the rules of the ancient craft of Mystic Masonry, the aspirant must learn first to build within himself the altar with its sacrifices, then he must watch and pray while patiently waiting for the divine fire to consume offering. Then he must bathe himself with tears of contrition till he has washed away the stains of sin.

Meanwhile he must keep the lamp of divine guidance filled that he may perceive how, when, and where to serve; he must work hard to have abundance of "bread of shew," and the incense of aspiration and prayer must be ever in his heart and on his lips. Then YOM KIPPUR, the Great Day of At-one-ment, will surely find him ready to go to his Father, and learn how better to help his younger brothers to ascent the Path.

THE ANNUNCIATION AND IMMACULATE CONCEPTION

Much is said in certain classes of the Western World about Initiation. This in the minds of most people seems usually to be associated with the occultism taught in the religions of the far East; something that is peculiar to the devotees of Buddhism, Hinduism, and kindred systems of faith, and which in nowise appertains to the religion of the Western World, particularly to the Christian religion. We have shown in the preceding series on "Symbols and Ancient and Modern Initiation": that this idea is entirely gratuitous, and that the ancient Tabernacle in the Wilderness pictures in its symbolism the path of progression from childlike ignorance to superhuman knowledge. As the VEDAS brought light to the devotees who worshiped in faith and fervor on the banks of the Ganges in the sunny South, so the Eddas were a guiding star to the sons of the rugged Northland, who sought the Light of life in ancient Iceland where the sturdy Vikings steered their ships in frozen seas.

"Arjuna," who fights the noble fight in the "Mahabharata," or "Great War," constantly being waged between the higher and the lower self, difference in nowise from the hero of the northern soul myth, "Siegfried," which means, "He who through victory gains peace." Both are representative of the candidate undergoing Initiation. And though their experiences in this great adventure vary in certain respects called for by the temperamental differences of the northern and southern peoples, and provided for in the respective schools to which they are referred for soul growth, the main features are identical, and the end, which is enlightenment, is the same.

Aspiring souls have walked to the Light in the brilliantly illuminated Persian temples where the sun god in his blazing chariot was the symbol of Light, as well as under the mystic magnificence of the iridescence shed abroad by the aurora borealis of the frozen North. That the true Light of the deepest esoteric knowledge has always been present in all ages, even the darkest of the so-called dark, there is ample evidence to show.

Raphael used his wonderful skill with the brush to embody it in two of his great paintings, "The Sistine Madonna" and the "Marriage of the Virgin," which we would advise the interested reader to examine for himself. Copies of these paintings are procurable in almost any art store. In the original there is a peculiar tint of golden haze behind the Madonna and Child, which though exceedingly crude to one gifted with spiritual sight, is nevertheless as close an imitation of the basic color of the first-heaven world as it is possible to make with the pigments of earth. Close inspection of this background will reveal the fact that it is composed of a multitude of what we are used to call "angel" heads and wings.

This again is as literal a pictorial representation of facts concerning the inhabitants of that world as could be given, for during the process of purgation which takes place in the lower regions of the Desire World the lower parts of the body are actually disintegrated so that only the head, containing the intelligence of the man, remains when he enters the first heaven, a fact which has puzzled many who have happened to see the souls there.

The wings of course have no reality outside the picture, but were placed there to show ability to move swiftly, which is inherent in all beings in the invisible worlds. The People is represented as pointing to the Madonna and the Christ Child, and a close examination of the hand wherewith he points will show that it has six fingers. There is not historical evidence to show that the Pontiff actually had such a deformity, neither can that fact be an accident; the six fingers in the painting must therefore have been due to design on the part of the painter.

What its purpose was we shall learn by examination of the "Marriage of the Virgin," where a similar anomaly may be noted. In that picture Mary and Joseph are represented together with the Christ Child under such conditions that it is evident that they are just on the eve of departure for Egypt, and a Rabbi is in the act of joining them in wedlock. The left foot of Joseph is the foremost object in the picture, and if we count, we shall find it represented as having six toes. By the six fingers in the Pope's picture and the six toes of Joseph, Raphael wants to show us that both possessed a sixth sense such as is awakened by Initiation. By this subtle sense the foot of Joseph was guided in its flight to keep secure that sacred things which had been entrusted to his care.

To the other was given a sixth sense that he might not be a blind leader of the blind but might have the "seeing eye" required to point out the Way, the Truth, and the Life. And it is a fact, though not commonly known, that with one or two exceptions when political power was strong enough to corrupt the College of Cardinals, all who have sat upon the so-called throne of Peter have had the spiritual sight in a greater or lesser degree.

We have seen in the articles on "Symbols of Ancient and Modern Initiation," which preceded the present article, that the Atlantean Mystery Temple known as the Tabernacle in the Wilderness was a school of soul growth; and it should not surprise us to learn that the four Gospels containing the life of Christ are also formulae of Initiation, revealing another and a later Path to power.

In the ancient Egyptian Mysteries, Horus was the first fruit whom the aspirant endeavored to imitate, and it is significant that in the Ritual of Initiation which was in vogue in that day and which we now call the "Book of the Dead," the aspirant to Initiation was always addressed Horus so-and-so. Following the same method today we might appropriately address those following the Christian Path of Initiation as Christ so-and-so, for as a matter of fact all who tread this Path are really Christs-in-the-making. Each in his or her turn will reach the different stations of the Via Dolorosa, or Path of Sorrow, which leads to Calvary, and experience in his or her own body the pangs and pains suffered by the Hero of the Gospels. Initiation is a cosmic process of enlightenment and evolution of power; therefore, the experiences of all are similar in the main features.

The Christian Mystic form of Initiation differs radically from the Rosicrucian method, which aims to bring the candidate to compassion through knowledge, and therefore seeks to cultivate in him the latent faculties of spiritual sight and hearing at the very start of his career as an aspirant to the higher life. it teaches him to know the hidden mysteries of being and to perceive intellectually the unity of each with all, so that at last through this knowledge there is awakened within him the feeling that makes him truly realize his oneness with all that lives and moves, which puts him in full and perfect tune with the Infinite, making him a true helper and worker in the divine kingdom of evolution.

The goal attained through the Christian Mystic Initiation is the same, but the method, as said, is entirely different. In the first place, the candidate is usually unconscious of trying to attain any definite object, at least during the first stages of his endeavors, and there is in this noble School of Initiation but no Teacher, the Christ, who is ever before the spiritual vision of the candidate as the Ideal and the Goal of all his striving. The Western world, alas! has become so enmeshed in intellectuality that its aspirants can only enter the Path when their reason has been satisfied; and unfortunately, it is a desire for more knowledge which brings most of the pupils to the Rosicrucian School. It is an arduous task to cultivate in them the compassion which must blend with their knowledge and be the guiding factor in the use of it before they are fitted to enter the Kingdom of Christ. But those who are drawn to the Christian Mystic Path feel no difficulty of that nature.

They have within themselves an all-embracing love, which urges them onward and eventually generates in them a knowledge which the writer believes to be far superior to that attained by any other method. One who follows the intellectual Path of development is apt to sneer superciliously at another whose temperament impels him along the Mystic Path. Such an attitude of mind is not only detrimental to the spiritual development of whomever entertains it, but it is entirely gratuitous, as the works of Jacob Boehme, Thomas a Kempis, and many others who have followed the Mystic Path will show. The more knowledge we possess the greater condemnation also shall we merit if we do not use it right. But love, which is the basic principle in the Christian Mystic's life, can never bring us into condemnation or conflict with the purposes of God. It is infinitely better to be able to FEEL any noble emotion that to have the keenest intellect and one which is able to define all emotions.

Hairsplitting over the constitution and evolution of the atom surely will not promote soul growth as much as humble helpfulness toward our neighbor. There are nine definite steps in the Christian Mystic Initiation, commencing with the Baptism, which is dedicatory. The Annunciation and Immaculate Conception precedes as matters of course for reasons given later. Having prepared our minds by the foregoing consideration, we are now ready to consider each stage separately in this glorious process of spiritual unfoldment.

THE ANNUNCIATION AND IMMACULATE CONCEPTION

The Christian Mystic is emphatically not the product of one life, but the flower of many preparatory existences, during which he has cultivated that sublime compassion which makes him feel the whole world's woe, and conjures up before his spiritual vision the Christ Ideal as the true balm of Gilead, its practice the only palladium against all human grief and sorrow. Such a soul is watched over special care by the divine Hierarchies who have charge of our progression along the path of evolution, and when the time is ripe for him to enter that life in which he is to run the final race to reach the goal and become a Savior of his kind, angels are indeed watching, waiting, and singing hosannas in joyful anticipation of the great event.

Like always seeks like, and naturally the parents are carefully selected for (and by such a noble soul from among the "sons and daughters of the King." They may be in the poorest circumstances from a worldly point of view; it may be necessary to cradle the babe in a manger, but no richer gift ever came to parents that such a noble soul. Among the qualifications necessary to be the parents of such an Ego is that the mother be a "virgin" and the father a "builder."

It is stated in the Bible that Joseph was a CARPENTER, but the Greek word is "tekton" which means "builder." In Mystic Masonry God is called the Grant Architect. ARCHE is the Greek word signifying primordial substance, and a tekton is a builder. Thus, God is the Great Master Builder, who out of primordial substance fashioned the world as an evolutionary field for various grades of beings. He uses in His universe many tektons, or builders, of various grades.

Everyone who follows the Path of spiritual attainment, endeavoring to work constructively with the laws of nature as a servant of humanity, is a TEKTON or builder in the sense that he has the qualifications necessary to aid in giving birth to a great soul. Thus, when it is said that Jesus was a carpenter and the son of a carpenter, we understand that they were both TEKTONS or builders along cosmic lines.

The Immaculate Conception, like all other sublime mysteries, has been dragged down into the gutter of materiality, and being so sublimely spiritual it has perhaps suffered more by this rude treatment than any other of the spiritual teachings. Perhaps it has suffered even more from the clumsy explanation of ignorant supporters that from the jeers and sneers of the cynic. The doctrine of the Immaculate Conception, as popularly understood, is that about two thousand years ago God in a miraculous manner fertilized a certain Mary who was a virgin, as the result she gave birth to Jesus, an individual who is consequence was the Son of God in a sense different from all other men. There is also in the popular mind the idea that this incident is unique in the history of the world.

It is particularly the latter fallacy which has served to distort the beautiful spiritual truth concerning the Immaculate Conception. It is not unique in any sense. Every great soul who has been born into the world to live a life of sublime saintliness, such as required for the Christian Mystic Initiation, has also found entrance through of immaculate virginity who were not besmirched by passion in the performance of the generative act. Men do not gather grapes of thorns. It is an axiomatic truth that like begets like, and before anyone can become a Savior, he must himself be pure and sinless. He, being pure cannot take birth from one who is vile; HE MUST BE BORN OF VIRGIN PARENTS.

But the virginity to which we refer does not comprehend a merely physical condition. There is not inherent virtue in physical virginity, for all possess it at the beginning of life no matter how vile their disposition may be. The virginity of the mother of a Savior is a quality of the soul, which remains unsullied regardless of the physical act of fertilization.

When people perform the first creative act without desire for offspring, merely for gratification of heir animal lusts and propensities, they lose the only (physical) virginity they ever possessed; but when prospective parents unite in a spirit of prayer, offering their bodies upon the altar of sacrifice in order to provide an incoming soul with the physical body needed at the present time to further spiritual development, their purity of purpose preserves their virginity and draws a noble soul to their hearth and home.

Whether a child is conceived in sin or immaculately depends upon its own inherent soul quality, for that will unerringly draw it to parents of a nature like unto its own. To become the son of a virgin predicates a past career of spirituality for the one who is so born.

The "mystic birth" of a "builder" is a cosmic event of great importance, and it is therefore not surprising that it is pictured in the skies from year to year, showing a graphic symbolism in the great world or macrocosm what will eventually take place in man, the little world or microcosm. We are all destined to experience the things that Jesus experienced, including the Immaculate Conception, which is a prerequisite to the life of saints and saviors of varying degrees. By understanding this great cosmic symbol, we shall more easily understand its application to the individual human being.

The sun is "THE LIGHT OF THE WORLD" in a material sense. When In winter time it reaches the extreme southern declination at the solstice on December 23rd, the people in the northern hemisphere, where all the present religions have had their birth, are plunged into the deepest darkness and bereft of the all-sustaining vital power emanating from the sun, which is them partly dead so far as its influence upon men in concerned. It is therefore necessary that a new light shine in the darkness, that a SUN OF GOOD be born to same humanity from the cold and famine which must inevitably result if the sun were to remain in the southern position which he occupies at the winter solstice.

On the night between the 24th and 25th of December, the sun having commenced to slowly rise toward the earth's equator, the zodiacal sign of Virgo, the immaculate celestial Virgin, is on the eastern horizon in all northern latitudes (in the hours immediately preceding midnight). In the science of astrology, it is the sign and degree on the eastern horizon at the time of birth which determine the form or body of the creature then born. Therefore, the Sun of Good is said to have been born of Virgo, the sublime celestial Virgin, who remains as pure after giving birth to her Sun Child as she was before. By analogy the Son of God who comes to save his fellow men must also be born of an immaculate spiritual virgin.

From what has been said it is evident that a great period of preparation precedes the entrance of a Christian Mystic into the present sphere of human life, though he in his physical consciousness is usually entirely unaware of the fact of the great adventure in store for him. In all probability his childhood days and early youth will pass in obscurity, while he lives an inner life of unusual depth, unconsciously preparing himself for the Baptism, which is the first of the nine steps of this method of attainment.

MYSTIC RITE OF BAPTISM

It is noteworthy that nearly all religious systems have prescribed ablutions previous to the performance of religious duties, and the worship performed in the ancient Atlantean Mystery Temple, the Tabernacle in the Wilderness, was no exception, as we have seen from the previous articles on "Symbols of Ancient and Modern Initiation." After having obtained justification by sacrifice on the Brazen Altar, the candidate was compelled to wash in the Laver of Consecration, the Molten Sea, before he was allowed to enter upon the duties of his ministry in the sanctuary proper. And it is in conformity with this rule that we find the Hero of the Gospels going to the river Jordan, where He underwent the mystic rite of Baptism. When He rose, we learn that the Spirit descended upon Him. Therefore, it is obvious that those who follow the Christian Mystic Path of Initiation must also be similarly baptized before they can receive the Spirit, which is to be their true guide through all the trials before them.

But what constitutes Baptism is a question which has called forth arguments of almost unbelievable intensity. Some contend that it is a sprinkling with water, and other insist upon the immersion of the whole body. Some say that it is sufficient to take an infant into church, sprinkle it with water despite its protests, and presto! it becomes a Christian, an heir of heaven; whereas should it unfortunately die before this sacred rite is performed, it must inevitably go to hell.

Others take the more logical position that the desire of an individual for admission into the church is the prime factor necessary to make the rite effective, and therefore wait until adult age before the performance of the ceremony, which requires an immersion of the whole body in water. But whether the rite is performed in infancy or in later life, it seems strange that momentary immersion or sprinkling with water should have the power to save the soul; and when we examine the subsequent life of those who have thus been baptized, even in adult age and with their full consent and desire, we find little or no improvement in the great majority. Therefore, it seems evident that this cannot be the proper rite, because the Spirit has not descended upon them. Consequently, we must look for another explanation of what constitutes a true mystic rite of Baptism.

A story is told of an Ottoman king who declared war on a neighboring nation, fought a number of battles against it with varying success, but was finally conquered and taken captive to the palace of the victor, where he was compelled to work in the most menial capacity as a slave. After many years fortune favored him, and he escaped to a far country, where by hard work he acquired a small estate, married, and had a number of children, who grew up around him. Finally, he found himself upon his deathbed at a very ripe old age, and in the exertion of drawing his last breath he raised himself upon his pillow and looked about him, but there were no sons and daughters there. He was not in the place which he had regarded as home for so many years, but in his own palace which he thought he had left in his youth, and he was as young as when he left it. There he found himself sitting in a chair with a basin of water close to his chin and a servant engaged in washing his hair and beard. He had just immersed his face in the water when the dream of going to war had started, and a lifetime had been lived in dreamland during the few seconds it took until he raised his face.

There are thousands of other instances to show that outside the physical world time is nonexistent and the happenings of millennia are easily inspected in a few moments. It is also well known that when people are under water and in the act of drowning, their whole preceding life is reenacted before their eyes with crystal clarity, even the minutest details which have been forgotten during the passing years standing our sharply. Thus, there must be and is a storehouse of events which may be contacted under certain conditions when the senses are stilled and we are near sleep or death.

To make this last sentence clear it should be understood and borne in mind that man is a composite being, having finer vehicles which interpenetrate the physical body, usually regarded as the whole man. During death and sleep this dense body is unconscious on account of a complete separation between it and the finer vehicles; but this separation is only partial during dream-filled sleep and prior to drowning. This condition enables the spirit to impress events upon the brain with more or less accuracy according to circumstances, particularly those incidents which are connected with itself. In the light of these things we shall understand what really constitutes the rite of Baptism.

According to the Nebular Theory that which is now the earth was at one time a luminous fire-mist, which gradually cooled by contact with the cold of space. This meeting of heat with cold generated moisture, which evaporated and rose from the heated center, until the cold condensed it and it fell again as moisture upon the heated world. The surface of the earth being thus subjected to alternate liquidation and evaporation for ages, it finally crystallized into a shell which perfectly covered the fiery center.

This soft moisture-laden shell naturally generated a mist, which surrounded the planet as an atmosphere, and this was the cradle of everything that has its being upon the earth: man, animal, and plant. The Bible describes this condition in the second chapter of Genesis, where we are told that at the time of the first man a mist went up from the earth, "for it had not yet rained." This condition evidently continued until the Flood, when the moisture finally descended and left the atmosphere clear so that the rainbow was seen for the first time, the darkness was dispelled, and the age of alternation, day and night, summer and winter, commenced.

By a study of the cosmology and the pictorial account of evolution given in the Northern Eddas, treasured among the sages of Scandinavia before the Christian era, we may learn more of this period in the earth's history and the bearing which it has upon our subject. As we teach our children, by means of stories and pictures, truths that they could not intellectually grasp, so the divine leaders of mankind were wont to teach the infant souls in their charge by pictures and allegories, and through these prepare them for a higher and nobler teaching of a later day. The great epic poem which is called "The Lay of the Niebelung," gives us the story of which we are in search, the cosmic origin of the rite of Baptism and why it is necessarily the preliminary step in the spiritual unfoldment of the Christian Mystic.

The cosmogony of the Eddas is similar to that of the Bible is some respects, and in others gives points which bear out the theory of Laplace. We quote from the poetical version of Oehlenschlaeger:

"In the Being's earliest Dawn

All was one dark abyss,

Nor heaven nor earth was known.

Chill noxious fogs and ice,

North from murk Niflheim's hole,

Piled up in mountains lay;

From Muspel's radiant pole,

Southwards fire held the sway.

"Then after ages passed,

Mid in the chaos met

A warm breath, Niflheim's blast,

Cold with prolific heat.

Hence pregnant drops were formed,

Which by the parent air

From Muspel's region warmed,

Produced great Aurgelmer."

Thus, by the action of heat and cold Aurgelmer, or as he is also called, the Giant Ymer, was first formed. This was the pregnant seed ground whence came the spiritual Hierarchies, the spirits of the earth, air, and water, and finally man. At the same time the All-Father created the Cow Audumla, from whose four teats issued four streams of milk, which nourished all beings. These are the four ethers, one of which now sustains mineral, two feed the plant, three the animal, and all four the human kingdom. In the Bible they are the four rivers which went forth out of Eden.

Eventually, as postulated by science, a crust must have been formed by the continued boiling of the water, and from this drying crust a mist must have ascended as taught in the second chapter of Genesis. By degrees the mist must have cooled and condensed, shutting out the light of the sun, so that it would have been impossible for early mankind to perceive the body even had they possessed the physical vision. But under such conditions they had no more need of eyes that a mole which burrows in the ground. They were not blind, however, for were told that "THEY SAW GOD"; and as "spiritual things (and beings) are spiritually perceived," they must have been gifted with spiritual sight. In the spiritual worlds there is a different standard of reality than here, which is the basis of myths.

Under these conditions there could be no clashing of interests, and humanity regarded itself as the children of one great Father while they lived under the water of ancient Atlantis. Egoism did not come into the world until the mist had condensed and they had left the watery atmosphere of Atlantis. When their eyes had been opened so that they could perceive the physical world and the things therein, when each saw himself or herself as separate and apart from all others, the consciousness of "me and mine, thee and thine," took shape in the nascent minds, and a grasping greed replaced the fellow feeling which obtained under the waters of early Atlantis.

From that time to the present stage of egoism has been considered the legitimate attitude, and even in our boasted civilization altruism remains a Utopian dream not to be indulged in by practical people. Had mankind been allowed to travel the path of egoism without let or hindrance, it is difficult to see where it all would have ended. But under the immutable Law of Consequence every cause must produce an adequate effect; the principle of suffering was born from sin for the benevolent purpose of guiding us back to the path of virtue. It takes much suffering and many lives to accomplish this purpose, but finally when we have become men of sorrows and acquainted with grief, when we have cultivated that keen and ready sympathy which feels all the woe of the world, when the Christ has been born within, there comes to the Christian Mystic that ardent aspiration to seek and to save those who are lost and show them the way to everlasting light and peace.

But to show the way, we must know the way; without a true understanding of the CAUSE OF SORROW we cannot teach others to obtain permanent peace. Nor can this understanding of sorrow, sin, and death be obtained from books, lectures, or even the personal teachings of another; at least an impression sufficiently intense to fill the aspirant's whole being cannot be conveyed in that way.

Baptism alone will accomplish the purpose in an adequate manner; therefore, the first step in the life of a Christian Mystic is Baptism. But when we say Baptism, we do not necessarily mean a physical Baptism where the candidate is either sprinkled or immersed and where he makes certain promises to the one who baptizes him.

The Mystic Baptism may take place in a desert as easily on an island, for it is a spiritual process to attain a spiritual purpose. It may take place at any time during the night or day, in summer or winter, for it occurs at the moment when the candidate feels with sufficient intensity the longing to know the cause of sorrow and alleviate it. Then the Spirit is conducted under the waters of Atlantis, where it sees the primal condition of brotherly love and kindness; where it perceives God as the great Father of His children, who are there surrounded by His wonderful love. And by the conscious return to this Ocean of Love, the candidate becomes so thoroughly imbued with the feeling of kinship that the spirit of egoism is banished from him forever. It is because of this saturation with the Universal Spirit that is able later to say: "If a man takes your coat, give him you cloak also; if he asks you to walk one mile with him, go with him two miles."

Feeling himself one and all, the candidate does not even consider the murder of himself as mistreatment, but can say: "Father, forgive them." They are identical with himself, who suffers by their action; he is the aggressor as well as the victim. Such is the true Spiritual Baptism of the Christian Mystic, and any other baptism that does not produce this universal fellow feeling is not worthy of the name.

THE TEMPTATION

We often hear about devout Christians complain of their periods of depression. At times they are almost in the seventh heaven of spiritual exaltation, they all but see the face of Christ and feel as if He were guiding their every step; then without any warning and without any cause that they can discover the clouds gather, the Savior hides His face, and the world grows black for a period. They cannot work, they cannot pray; the world has no attraction, and the gate of heaven seems shut against them, with the result that life appears worthless so long as this spiritual expression lasts.

The reason is, of course, that these people live in their emotions, and under the immutable Law of Alternation the pendulum is bound to swing as far to one side of the neutral point as it has swung to the other. The brighter the light, the deeper the shadow, and the greater the exaltation, the deeper the depression of spirit which follows it. Only those who by cold reason restrain their emotions escape the periods of depression, but they never taste the heavenly bliss of exaltation either. AND IT IS THIS EMOTIONAL OUTPOURING OF HIMSELF WHICH FURNISHED THE CHRISTIAN MYSTIC WITH THE DYNAMIC ENERGY TO PROJECT HIMSELF INTO THE INVISIBLE WORLDS, WHERE HE BECOMES ONE WITH THE SPIRITUAL IDEAL WHICH HAS BECKONED HIM ON AND AWAKENED IN HIS SOUL THE POWER TO RISE TO IT, as the sun built the eye wherewith, we perceive it. The nestling takes many a tumble ere it learns to use its wings with assurance, and the aspirant upon the path of Christian Mysticism may soar to the very throne of God times out of number and then fall to the lowest pit of hell's despair. But some time he will overcome the world, defy the Law of Alternation, and rise by the power of the Spirit to the Father of Spirits, free from the toils of emotion, filled with the peace that passeth understanding.

But that is the end attained only after Golgotha and the Mystic Baptism, the latter of which we discussed in the preceding chapter. Moreover, it is only the beginning of the active career of the Christian Mystic, in which he becomes thoroughly saturated with the tremendous fact of the unity of all life, and imbued with a fellow feeling for all creatures to such an extent that henceforth he can not only enunciate but practice the tenets of the Sermon on the Mount.

Did the spiritual experiences of the Christian Mystic take him no further, it would still be the most wonderful adventure in the world, and the magnitude of the event is beyond words, the consequences only dimly imaginable. Most students of the higher philosophies believe in the brotherhood of man from the mental conviction that we have all emanated from the same source, as rays emanate from the sun.

But there is an abyss of inconceivable depth and width between this cold intellectual conception and the baptismal saturation of the Christian Mystic, who feels it is his heart and in every fiber of his being with such an intensity that it is actually painful to him; it fills him with such a yearning, aching love as that expressed in the words of the Christ: "Jerusalem, Jerusalem, how often would I have gathered thy children together, even as a hen gathereth her chickens under her wings;" a brooding, yearning, and achingly protective love which asks nothing for self-save only the privilege to nurture, to shield, and to cherish. Were even a faint resemblance to such a universal fellow feeling abroad among humanity in this dark day, what a paradise earth would be.

Instead of every man's hand being against his brother to slay with the sword, with rivalry and competition, or to destroy his morals and degrade him by prison stripes or industrial bondage under the whiplash of necessity, we should have neither warriors nor prisoners but a happy contented world, living in peace and harmony, learning the lessons which our Father in Heaven aims to teach us in this material condition. AND ALL THE MISERY IN THE WORLD MAY BE ACCOUNTED FOR BY THE FACT THAT IF WE BELIEVE IN THE BIBLE AT ALL, WE BELIEVE WITH OUR HEAD AND NOT WITH OUR HEART.

When we came up through the waters of Baptism, the Atlantean Flood, into the Rainbow Age of alternating seasons, we became prey to the changing emotions which whirl us hither and yon upon the sea of life. The cold faith restrained by reason entertained by the majority of professing Christians may give them a need of patience and mental valance which bears them up under the trials of life, but when the majority get the LIVING FAITH of the Christian Mystic which laughs at reason because it is HEART-FELT, then the Age of Alternation will be past, the rainbow will fall with the clouds and the air which now composes the atmosphere, and there will be a new heaven of pure ether, where we shall receive the Baptism of Spirit and "THERE SHALL BE PEACE" (Jerusalem).

We are still in the Rainbow Age and subject to its low, so we may realize that as the Baptism of the Christian Mystic occurs at a time of spiritual exaltation, it must necessarily be followed by a reaction. The tremendous magnitude of the revelation overpowers him, he cannot realize it or contain it in his fleshly vehicle, so he flees the haunts of men and betakes himself to the solitude allegorically represented as a desert.

So rapt is he in his sublime discovery that for the time being in his ecstasy he sees the Loom of Life upon which the bodies of all that live are woven, from the least to the greatest-the mouse and the man, the hunter and his prey, the warrior and his victim. But to him they are not separate and apart, for he also beholds the one divine thread of golden life-light "which runs through all and doth all unite."

Nay, more, he hears in each the flaming keynote sounding its aspirations and voicing its hopes and fears, and he perceives this composite color sound as the world anthem of God made flesh. This is at first entirely beyond his comprehension; the tremendous magnitude of the discovery hides it from him, and he cannot conceive what it is that he sees and feels, for there are no words to describe it, and no concept can cover it. But by degrees it dawns upon him that HE IS AT THE VERY FOUNTAIN OF LIFE, beholding, nay, more, FEELING its every pulse beat, and with this comprehension he reaches the climax of his ecstasy.

So rapt has the Christian Mystic been in his beautiful adventure that bodily wants have been completely forgotten till the ecstasy has passed, and it is therefore only natural that the feeling of hunger should be his first conscious want upon his return to the normal state of consciousness; and also naturally comes the voice of temptation: "COMMAND THAT THESE STONES BE MADE BREAD."

Few passages of the sacred Scriptures are darker that the opening verses of the Gospel of St. John: "In the beginning was the word . . . .and without it was not anything made that was made." A slight study of the science of sound soon makes us familiar with the fact that sound is vibration and that different sounds will mold sand or other light materials into figures of varying form. The Christian Mystic may be entirely ignorant of this fact from the scientific point of view, but he has learned at the Fountain of Life to sing the SONG OF BEING, which cradles into existence whatever such a master musician desires. There is one basic key for the indigestible mineral stone, but a modification will turn it to gold wherewith to purchase the means of sustenance, and another keynote peculiar to the vegetable kingdom will turn it into food, a fact known to all advanced occultists who practice incantations legitimately for spiritual purposes but never for material profit.

But the Christian Mystic who has just emerged from his Baptism in the Fountain of Life immediately shrinks in horror at the suggestion of using his newly discovered power for a selfish purpose. It was the very soul quality of unselfishness that led him to the waters of consecration in the Fountain of life, and sooner would he sacrifice all, even life itself, that use this new-found power to spare himself a pang of pain. Did he not see also the Woe of the World? And does he not feel it in his great hearth with such an intensity that the hunger at once disappears and is forgotten? He may, will, and does use this wonderful power freely to feed the thousands that gather to hear him, but never for selfish purposes else he would upset the equilibrium of the world.

The Christian Mystic does not reason this out, however. As often stated, he has not reason, but he has a much safer guide in the interior voice which always speaks to him in moments when a decision must be made. "MAN DOES NOT LIVE BY BREAD ALONE, BUT BY EVERY WORD THAT PROCEEDETH FROM GOD"; another mystery. There is not need to partake of earthly bread for one who has access to the Fountain of Life. The more our thoughts are centered in God, the less we shall care for the so-called pleasures of the table, and by feeding our gross bodies sparingly on selected simple foods we shall obtain an illumination of spirit impossible to one who indulges in an excessive diet of coarse foods which nourish the lower nature.

Some of the saints have used fasting and castigation as a means of soul growth, but that is a mistaken method for reasons given in an article on "Fasting for Soul Growth" published in the December 1915 number of "Rays from the Rose Cross." The Elder Brothers of humanity who understand the Law and live accordingly use food only at intervals measured by years. The word of God is to them a "living bread." So, it becomes also to the Christian Mystic, and the Temptation instead of working his downfall has led him to greater heights.

THE TRANSFIGURATION

We remember that by the mystic processes of the true Spiritual Baptism the aspirant becomes so thoroughly saturated with the Universal Spirit that as a matter of actual fact, feeling, and experience he becomes one with all that lives, moves, and has its being, one with the pulsating divine Life which surges in rhythmic cadence through the least and the greatest alike; and having caught the keynote of the celestial song he is then endued with a power of tremendous magnitude, which he may use either for good or ill. It should be understood and remembered that though gunpowder and dynamite facilitate farming when used for blowing up tree stumps which would otherwise require a great deal of manual labor to extract, they may also be used for destructive purposes as in the great European war. Spiritual powers also may be used for good or ill depending upon the motive and character of the one who wields them.

Therefore, whoever has successfully undergone the rite of Baptism and thereby acquired spiritual power is forthwith tempted that it may be concerned decided whether he will range himself upon the side of good or evil. At this point he becomes either a future "Parsifal," a "Christ," a "Herod," or a "Klingsor" who fights the Knights of the Holy Grail with all the powers and resources of the Black Brotherhood.

There is a tendency in modern materialistic science to repudiate as fable, worthy of attention only among superstitious servant girls and foolish old women, the ideas commonly believed in as late as the Middle Ages, that such spiritual communities as the Knights of the Grail at one time existed, or that there are such beings as the "Black Brothers." Occult societies in the last half century have educated thousands to the fact that the Good Brothers are still in evidence and may be found by those who seek them in the proper way. Now unfortunately the tendency among this class of people is to accept anyone on his unsupported claims as a Master or an adept.

But even among this class there are few who take the existence of the Black Brothers seriously, or realize what an enormous amount of damage they are doing in the world, and how they are aided and abetted by the general tendency of humanity to cater to the lusts of the flesh. As the good forces, which are symbolized as the servants of the Holy Grail, live and grow by unselfish service which enhances the luster of the glowing Grail Cup, so the Powers of Evil, known as the Black Grail and represented in the Bible as the court of Herod, feed on pride and sensuality, voluptuousness and passion, embodied in the figure of Salome, who glories in the murder of John the Baptist and the innocents. It was shown in the legend of the Grail as embodied in Wagner's "Parsifal" that when the Knights were denied the inspiration from the Grail Cup, on which they fed and which spurred them onto deeds of greater love and service, their courage flagged and they became inert. Similarly with the Brothers of the Black Grail. Unless they are provided with words of wickedness they will die from starvation.

Therefore, they are ever active in the world stirring up strife and inciting others to evil. Were not this pernicious activity counteracted in a great measure by the Elder Brothers at their midnight services at which they make themselves magnets for all the evil thoughts in the Western World and then by the alchemy of sublime love transmute them to good, a cataclysm of still greater magnitude that the recent World War would have occurred long ago. As it is, the Genius of Evil has been held within bounds in some measure at least. Were humanity not so ready to range itself on the side of evil, success would have been greater. But it is hoped that the spiritual awakening started by the war will result in turning the scale and give the construction agencies in evolution the upper hand.

It is a wonderful power which is centered in the Christian Mystic at the time of his Baptism by the descent and concentration within him of the Universal Spirit; and when he has refused during the period of temptation to desecrate it for personal profit or power, he must of necessity give it vent in another direction, for he is impelled by an irresistible inner urge which will not allow him to settle down to an inert, inactive life of prayer and meditation.

The power of God is upon him to preach and glad tidings to humanity, to help and heal. We know that a stove which is filled with burning fuel cannot help heating the surrounding atmosphere; neither can the Christian Mystic help radiating the divine compassion which fills his heart to overflowing, nor is he is doubt whom to love or whom to serve or where to find his opportunity. As the stove filled with burning fuel radiates heat to all who are within its sphere of radiation, so the Christian Mystic feels the love of God burning within his heart and is continually radiating it to all with whom he comes in contact.

As the heated stove draws to itself by its genial warmth those who are suffering with physical cold, so the warm love rays of the Christian Mystic are as a magnet to all those whose hearts are chilled by the cruelty of the world, by man's inhumanity to man.

If the stove were empty but endowed with the faculty of speech, it might preach forever the gospel of warmth to those who are physically cold, but even the finest oratory would fail to satisfy its audience. When it has been filled with fuel and radiates warmth, there will be no need of preaching. Men will come to it and be satisfied. Similarly, a sermon on brotherhood by one who has not lived in the "Fountain of Life" will sound hollow. The true Mystic need not preach. His every act, even his silent presence, is more powerful that all the most deeply thought-out discourses of learned doctors of philosophy.

There is a story of St. Francis of Assisi which particularly illustrates this fact, and which we trust may serve to drive it home, for its exceedingly important. It is said that one day St. Francis went to a young brother in the monastery with which he was then connected and said to him: "Brother, let us go down to the village and preach to them." The young brother was naturally overjoyed at the honor and opportunity of accompanying so hold a man as St. Francis, and together the two started toward the village, talking all the while about spiritual things and the life that leads to God.

Engrossed in this conversation they passed through the village, walking along its various streets, now and then stopping to speak a kindly word to one or another of the villagers. After having made a circuit of the village St. Francis was heading toward the road which led to the monastery when of a sudden the young brother reminded him of his intention to preach in the village and asked him if he had forgotten it. To this St. Francis answered: "My son, are you not aware that all the while we have been in this village we have been preaching to the people all around us?

In the first place, our simple dress proclaims the fact that we are devoted to the service of God, and as soon as anyone sees us his thoughts naturally turn heavenward. Be sure that every one of the villagers has been watching us, taking note of our demeanor to see in how far it conforms with our profession. They have listened to our words to find whether they were about spiritual or profane subjects. They have watched our gestures and have noted that the words of sympathy we dispensed came straight from our hearts and went deep into theirs. We have been preaching a far more powerful sermon that if we had gone into the market place, called them around us, and started to harangue them with an exhortation to holiness."

St. Francis was a Christian Mystic in the deepest sense of the word, and being taught from within by the spirit of God he knew well the mysteries of life, as did Jacob Boehme and other holy men who have been similarly taught. They are in a certain sense wiser than the wisest of the intellectual school, but it is not necessary for them to expound great mysteries in order to fulfill their mission and serve as guide posts to others who are also seeking God. The very simplicity of their words and acts carries with it the power of conviction. Naturally, of course, all do not rise to the same heights.

All have not the same powers any more than all the stoves are of the same size and have the same heating capacity. Those who follow the Christian Mystic path, from the least to the greatest, have experienced the powers conveyed by Baptism according to their capacity. They have been tempted to use those powers in an evil direction for personal gain, and having overcome the desire for the world and worldly things they have turned to the path of ministry and service as Christ did; their lives are marked not so much by what they have said as by what they have done.

The true Christian Mystic is easily distinguished. He never uses the six-week days to prepare for a grand oratorical effort to thrill his hearers on Sunday, but spends every day alike in humble endeavor to do the Master's will regardless of outward applause. Thus, unconsciously he works up toward that grand climax which in the history of the noblest of all who have trod this path is spoken of as the "Transfiguration."

The Transfiguration is an alchemical process by which the physical body formed by the chemistry of physiological processes is turned into a living stone such as is mentioned in the Bible. The medieval alchemists who were seeking the Philosopher's Stone were not concerned with transmutation of such dross as material god, but aimed at the greater goal as indicated above.

Moisture gathered in the clouds falls to earth as rain when it has condensed sufficiently, and it is again evaporated into clouds by the heat of the sun. This is the primal cosmic formula. Spirit also condenses itself into matter and becomes mineral. But though it be crystallized into the harness of flint, life still remains, and by the alchemy of nature working through another life stream the dense mineral constituents of the soil are transmuted to a more flexible structure in the plant, which may be used as food for animal and man.

These substances become sentient flesh by the alchemy of assimilation. When we note the changes in the structure of the human body evidenced by comparison of the Bushmen, Chinese, Hindus, Latins, Celts, and Anglo-Saxons, it is plainly apparent that the flesh of man is even now undergoing a refining process which is eradicating the coarser, grosser substances. In time by evolution this process of spiritualization will render our flesh transparent and radiant with the Light that shines within, radiant as the face of Moses, the body of Buddha, and the Christ at the Transfiguration.

At present the effulgence of the indwelling Spirit is effectually darkened by our dense body, but we may draw hop even from the science of chemistry. There is nothing on earth so rare and precious as radium, the luminous extract of the dense black mineral called pitchblende; and there is nothing so rare as that precious extract of the human body, the radiant Christ. At present we are laboring to form the Christ within, but when the inner Christ has grown to full stature, He will shine through the transparent body as the LIGHT OF THE WORLD.

It is an anatomical fact of common knowledge that the spinal cord is divided into three sections, from which the motor, sensory, and sympathetic nerves are controlled. Astrologically these are ruled by the moon, Mars, and Mercury, which are divine Hierarchies that have played a great role in human evolution through the nervous systems indicated.

Among the ancient alchemists these were designated by the three alchemical elements, salt, sulphur, and mercury. Between them and upon them played the spinal Spirit Fire of Neptune. It rose in a serpentine column through the spinal cord to the ventricles of the brain. In the great majority of mankind, the Spirit Fire is still exceedingly weak. But whenever a spiritual awakening occurs in anyone such as that which takes place in a genuine conversion, or better still at the Baptism of the Christian Mystic, the down pouring of the Spirit, which is an actual fact, augments the spinal Spirit Fire to an almost unbelievable extent, and forthwith a process of regeneration begins whereby the gross substances of the threefold body of many are gradually thrown out, rendering the vehicles more permeable and quickly responsive to spiritual impulses. The further the process if carried, the more efficient servants they become in the vineyard of the Master.

The spiritual awakening which starts this process of regeneration in the Christian Mystic who purifies himself by prayer and service, comes also of course to those who are seeking God by way of knowledge and service, but it acts in a different way, which is noted by the spiritual investigator.

In the Christian Mystic the regenerative spinal Spirit Fire is concentrated principally upon the lunar segment of the spinal cord, which governs the sympathetic nerves under the rulership of Jehovah. Therefore, his spiritual growth is accomplished by faith as simple, childlike, and unquestioning as it was in the days of early Atlantis when men were mindless. He therefore draws down the great white Light of Deity reflected through Jehovah, the Holy Spirit, and attains to the whole wisdom of the world without the necessity of laboring for it intellectually. This gradually transmutes his body into THE WHITE PHILOSOPHER'S STONE, THE DIAMOND SOUL.

In those, on the other hand, whose minds are strong and insistent on knowing the reason why and the wherefore of every dictum and dogma, the Spinal Fire of regeneration plays upon the segments of the red Mars and the colorless Mercury, endeavoring to infuse desire with reason, to purify the former of the primal passion that it may become chaste as the rose, and thus transmute the body into the RUBY SOUL, THE RED PHILOSOPHER'S STONE, TRIED BY FIRE, PURIFIED, A CREATIVE BUDDING INDIVIDUALITY.

All who are upon the Path, whether the path of occultism or of mysticism, are weaving the "golden wedding garment" by this work from within and from without. In some the gold is exceedingly pale, and in others it is deeply red. But eventually when the process of Transfiguration has been completed, or rather when it is nearing completion, the extremes will blend, and the transfigured bodies will become balanced in color, for the occultist must learn the lesson of deep devotion, and the Christian Mystic must learn how to acquire knowledge by his own efforts without drawing upon the universal source of all wisdom.

This view gives us a deeper insight into the Transfiguration reported in the Gospels. We should remember distinctly that IT WAS THE VEHICLES OF JESUS WHICH WERE TRANSFIGURED temporarily by the indwelling Christ Spirit. But even while allowing for the enormous potency of the Christ Spirit in effecting the Transfiguration it is evident that Jesus must be a sublime character without a peer. The Transfiguration as seen in the Memory of Nature reveals his body as a dazzling white, thus showing his dependence upon the Father, the Universal Spirit. There is a great diversity in present attainments, but in the kingdom of Christ the differences will gradually disappear, and a uniform color indicating both knowledge and devotion will be acquired by all. This color will correspond to the pink color seen by occultists as the Spiritual Sun, the vehicle of the Father. When this has been accomplished, the Transfiguration of humanity will be complete. We shall then be one with our Father, and His kingdom will have come.

THE LAST SUPPER AND THE FOOT WASHING

We are told in the Gospels which relate the story of the Christian Mystic Initiation, how on the night when Christ had partaken of the Last Supper with His disciples, His ministry being finished at that time, He rose from the table and girded Himself with a towel, then poured water into a basin and commenced to wash His disciples' feet, an act of the most humble service, but prompted by an important occult consideration. Comparatively few realize that when we rise in the scale of evolution, we do so by trampling upon the bodies of our weaker brothers; consciously or unconsciously we crush them and use them as stepping-stones to attain our own ends. This assertion holds good concerning all the kingdoms in nature. When a life wave has been brought down to the nadir of involution and encrusted in mineral form, that is immediately seized upon by another slightly higher life wave, which takes the disintegrating mineral crystal, adapts it to its own ends as crystalloid, and assimilates it as part of a plant form.

If there were no minerals which could thus be seized upon, disintegrated, and transformed, plant life would be an impossibility. Then again, the plant forms are taken by numerous classes of animals, masticated to a pulp, devoured, and made to serve as food for this higher kingdom. If there were no plants, animals would be an impossibility; and the same principle holds good in spiritual evolution for if there were no pupils standing on the lower round of the ladder of knowledge and requiring instruction, there would be no need for a teacher. But here there is one all-important difference. The teacher grows by GIVING to his pupils and serving them. From their shoulders he steps to a higher rung on the ladder of knowledge HE LIFTS HIMSELF BY LIFTING THEM, but nevertheless he owes them a debt of gratitude, which is symbolically acknowledged and liquidated by the foot washing-an act of humble service to those who have served him.

When we realize that nature, which is the expression of God, is continually exerting itself to create and bring forth, we may also understand that whoever kills anything, be it ever so little and seemingly insignificant, is to that extent thwarting God's purpose. This applies particularly to the aspirant to the higher life, and therefore the Christ exhorted His disciples to be wise as serpents but harmless as doves notwithstanding. But no matter how earnest our desire to follow the precept of harmlessness, our constitutional tendencies and necessities force us to kill at every moment of our lives, and it is not only in the great things that we are constantly committing murder.

It was comparatively easy for the seeking soul symbolized by Parsifal to break the bow wherewith he had shot the swan of the Grail knights when it had been explained to him what a wrong, he had committed. From that time Parsifal was committed to the life of harmlessness so far as the great things were concerned. All earnest aspirants follow him readily in that act once it has dawned upon them how subversive of soul growth is the practice of partaking of food which requires the death of an animal.

But even the noblest and most gentle among mankind is poisoning those about him with every breath and being poisoned by them in turn, for all exhale the death-dealing carbon dioxide, and we are therefore a menace to one another. Nor is this a far-fetched idea; it is a very real danger which will become much more manifest in course of time when mankind becomes more sensitive.

In a disabled submarine or under similar conditions where a number of people are together the carbon dioxide exhaled by them quickly makes the atmosphere unable to sustain life. There is a story from the Indian Mutiny of how a number of English prisoners were huddled in a room in which there was only one small opening for air. In a very short time the oxygen was exhausted, and the poor prisoners began to fight one another like beasts in order to obtain a place near that air inlet, and they fought until nearly all had died from the struggle and asphyxiation.

The same principle is illustrated in the ancient Atlantean Mystery Temple, the Tabernacle in the Wilderness, where we find a nauseating stench and a suffocating smoke ascending from the Altar of Burnt Offerings, where the poison-laden bodies of the UNWILLING VICTIMS sacrificed for sin were consumed, and where the light shone but dimly through the enveloping smoke. This we may contrast with the light which emanated clear and bright from the Seven-branched Candlestick fed by the olive oil extracted from the chaste plant, and where the incense symbolized by the WILLING SERVICE of devoted priests rose to heaven as a sweet savor. This we are told in many places, was pleasing to Deity, while the blood of the unwilling victims, the bulls and the goats, was a source of grief and displeasure to God, who delights most in the sacrifice of prayer, which helps the devotee and harms no one.

It has been stated concerning some of the saints that they emitted a sweet odor, and as we have often had occasion to say, this is no mere fanciful story-it is an occult fact. The great majority of mankind inhale during every moment of life the vitalizing oxygen contained in the surrounding atmosphere. At every expiration we exhale a charge of carbon dioxide which is a deadly poison and which would certainly vitiate the air in time if the pure and chaste plant did not inhale this poison, use a part of it to build bodies that last sometimes for many centuries or even millennia as instanced in the redwoods of California, and give us back the rest in the form of pure oxygen which we need for our life.

These carboniferous plant bodies by certain further processes of nature have in the past become mineralized and turned to stone instead of disintegrating. We find them today as coal, THE PERISHABLE PHILOSOPHER'S STONE MADE BY NATURAL MEANS IN NATURE'S LABORATORY. But the Philosopher's Stone may also be made artificially by man from his own body. It should be understood once and for all that the Philosopher's Stone is not made in an exterior chemical laboratory, but that the body is the workshop of the Spirit which contains all the elements necessary to produce this ELIXIR VITAE, and that the Philosopher's Stone is not exterior to the body, but THE ALCHEMIST HIMSELF BECOMES THE PHILOSOPHER'S STONE. The salt, sulphur, and mercury emblematically contained in the three segments of the spinal cord, which control the sympathetic, motor, and sensory nerves and are played upon by the Neptunian spinal Spirit Fire, constitute the essential elements in the alchemical process.

It needs no argument to show that indulgence in sensuality, brutality, and bestiality makes the body coarse. Contrariwise, devotion to Deity, an attitude of perpetual prayer, a feeling of love and compassion for all that lives and moves, loving thoughts sent out to all beings and those inevitably received in return, all invariably have the effect of refining and spiritualizing the nature. We speak of a person of that sort as breathing or radiating love, an expression which much more nearly describes the actual fact than most people imagine, for as a matter of actual observation the percentage of poison contained in the breath of an individual is in exact proportion to the evil in his nature and inner life and the thoughts he thinks.

The Hindu Yogi makes a practice of sealing up the candidate for a certain grade of Initiation in a cave which is not much larger than his body. There he must live for a number of weeks breathing the same air over and over again to demonstrate practically that he has ceased exhaling the death-dealing carbon dioxide and is beginning to build his body therefrom.

The Philosopher's Stone then is not a body of the same nature as the plant, though it is pure and chaste, but it is A CELESTIAL BODY such as that whereof St. Paul speaks in the 5th chapter of Second Corinthians, a body which becomes immortal as a diamond or a ruby stone. It is not hard and inflexible as the mineral; it is A SOFT DIAMOND or ruby, and by every act of the nature described the Christian Mystic is building this body, though he is probably unconscious thereof for a long time. When he has attained to this degree of holiness it is not necessary for him to perform the foot washing so far as concerns the physical pupil who helps him to rise, but he will always have the feeling of gratitude, symbolized by that act, toward those whom he is fortunate enough to attract to himself as disciples and to whom he may give the living bread which nourishes them to immortality.

Students will realize that this is part of the process which eventually culminates in the Transfiguration, but it should also be realized that in the Christian Mystic Initiation there are no set and definite degrees. The candidate looks to the Christ as the author and finisher of his faith, seeking to imitate Him and follow in His steps through every moment of existence. Thus, the various stages which we are considering are reached by processes of soul growth which simultaneously bring him to higher aspects of all these steps that we are now analyzing.

In this respect the Christian Mystic Initiation differs radically from the processes in vogue among the Rosicrucian's, in which an UNDERSTANDING upon the part of the candidate of that which is to take place is considered indispensable. But there comes a time at which the Christian Mystic must and does realize the path before him, and that is what constitutes Gethsemane, which we will consider in the next chapter.

GETHSEMANE THE GARDEN OF GRIEF

And when they had sung a hymn, they went out into the Mount of Olives. "And Jesus saith unto them, All ye shall be offended because of me this night; for it is written, I will smite the Shepherd, and the sheep shall be scattered. But after that I am risen I will go before you into Galilee.

"But Peter said unto him, Although all shall be offended, yet will not I. "And Jesus saith unto him, Verily, I say unto thee that this day, even in this night, before the cock crow twice, thou shalt deny me thrice.

"But he spake the more vehemently, If I should die with thee, I will not deny thee in any wise. Likewise, also said they all. "And they came to a place which was named Gethsemane: and He saith to His disciples, Sit ye here while I shall pray. And He taketh with Him

Peter and James and John, and began to be sore amazed, and to be very heavy; and saith unto them, My soul is exceedingly sorrowful unto death: tarry ye here and watch. And He went forward a little, and fell on the ground, and prayed that if it were possible the hour might pass from him. And He said, Abba, Father, all things are possible unto thee; take away this cup from me: Nevertheless, not what I will, but what thou wilt. And he cometh and findeth them sleeping, and saith unto Peter, Simon, sleepest thou? Couldst not thou watch one hour? Watch ye and pray lest ye enter into temptation. The spirit truly is ready, but the flesh is weak." -MARK, 14:26-38.

In the foregoing Gospel narrative we have one of the saddest and most difficult of the experiences of the Christian Mystic outlined in spiritual form. During all his previous experience he has wandered blindly along, that is to say, blind to the fact that he is on the Path which if consistently followed leads to a definite goal, but being also keenly alert to the slightest sigh of every suffering soul. He has concentrated all his efforts upon alleviating their pain physically, morally, or mentally; he has served them in any and every capacity; he has taught them the gospel of love, "Thou shalt love thy neighbor as thyself"; and he has been A LIVING EXAMPLE to all in its practice.

Therefore, he has drawn to himself a little band of friends whom he loves with the tenderest of affection. Them has he also taught and served unstintingly, even to the foot washing. But during this period of service, he has become so saturated with the sorrows of the world that he is indeed a MAN of SORROWS and acquainted with grief as no one else can be.

This is a very definite experience of the Christian Mystic, and it is the most important factor in furthering his spiritual progress. So long as we are bored when people come to us and tell us their troubles, so long as we run away from them and seek to escape hearing their tales of woe, we are far from the Path. Even when we listen to them and have schooled ourselves not to show that we are bored, when we say with our lips only a few sympathetic words that fall flat on the sufferer's ear, we gain nothing in spiritual growth. It is absolutely essential to the Christian Mystic that he become so attuned to the world's woe that he feels every pang as his own hurt and stores it up within his heart.

When PARSIFAL stood in the temple of the Holy Grail and saw the suffering of Amfortas the stricken Grail King, he was mute with sympathy and compassion for a long time after the procession had passed out of the hall, and consequently could not answer the questions of Gurnemanz, and it was that deep fellow feeling which prompted him to seek for the spear that should heal Amfortas. IT WAS THE PAIN OF AMFORTAS FELT IN THE HEART OF PARSIFAL BY SYMPATHY WHICH HELD HIM FIRMLY BALANCED UPON THE PATH OF VIRTUE WHEN TEMPTATION WAS STRONGEST. It was that deep pain of compassion which urged him through many years to seek the suffering Grail King, and finally when he had found Amfortas, this deep, heartfelt fellow feeling enabled him to pour forth the healing balm.

As it is shown in the soul myth of Parsifal, so it is in the actual life and experience of the Christian Mystic: he must drink deeply of the cup of sorrow, he must drain it to the very dregs so that by the cumulative pain which threatens to burst his heart he may pour himself out unreservedly and unstintedly for the healing and helping of the world. Then Gethsemane, the garden of grief, is a familiar place to him, watered with tears for the sorrows and sufferings of humanity.

Through all his years of self-sacrifice his little band of friends had been the consolation of Jesus. He had already learned to renounce the ties of blood. "Who is my mother and my brother? They that do the will of my Father." Though no true Christian neglects his social obligations or withholds love from his family, the spiritual ties are nevertheless the strongest, and through them comes the crowning grief; through the desertion of his spiritual friends, he learns to drink to the dregs the cup of sorrow. He does not blame them for their desertion but excuses them with the words, "The Spirit is indeed willing, but the flesh is weak," for he knows by his own experience how true this is. But he finds that in the supreme sorrow they cannot comfort him, and therefore he turns to THE ONLY SOURCE OF COMFORT, THE FATHER IN HEAVEN. He has arrived at the point where human endurance seems to have reached its limit, and he prays to be spared a greater ordeal, but with a blind trust in the Father he bows his will and offers all unreservedly.

That is the moment of realization. Having drunk the cup of sorrow to the dregs, being deserted by all, he experiences that temporary awful fear of being utterly alone which is one of the most terrible if not the most terrible experience that can come into the life of a human being. All the world seems dark about. He knows that in spite of all the good he has done or tried to do the powers of darkness are seeking to slay him. He knows that the mob that a few days before had cried "Hosanna" will on the morrow be ready to shout "Crucify! Crucify!" His relatives and now his last few friends have fled, and they were also even ready to deny.

But when we are on the pinnacle of grief, we are nearest to the throne of grace. The agony and grief, the sorrow and the suffering borne within the Christian Mystic's breast are more priceless and precious than the wealth of the Indies, for when he has lost all human companionship and when he has given himself over unreservedly to the Father a transmutation takes place: the grief is turned to compassion, the only power in the world that can fortify a man about to mount the hill of Golgotha and give his life for humanity, not a sacrifice of death but a LIVING SACRIFICE, lifting himself by lifting others.

THE STIGMATA AND THE CRUCIFIXION

As we said in the beginning of this series of articles, the Christian Mystic Initiation differs radically from the Occult Initiation undertaken by those who approach the Path from the intellectual side. But all paths converge at Gethsemane, where the candidate for Initiation is saturated with sorrow which flowers into compassion, a yearning mother love which has only one all-absorbing desire; to pour itself out for the alleviation of the sorrow of the world to save and to succor all that are weak and heavy-laden, to comfort them and give them rest. At that point the eyes of the Christian Mystic are opened to a full realization of the world's woe and his mission as a Savior; and the occultist also finds here the heart of love which alone can give zest and zeal in the quest. By the union of the mind and the heart both are ready for the next step, which involved the development of the STIGMATA, a necessary preparation for the mystic death and resurrection. The Gospel narrative tells the story of the STIGMATA in the following words, the opening scene being in the Garden of Gethsemane: "Judas then having received a band of men and officers from the chief priests and Pharisees came thither with lanterns, torches, and weapons. Jesus therefore knowing all things that should come upon Him went forth and said unto them, Whom seek ye? They answered Him, Jesus of Nazareth.

Jesus said unto them, I am He.....Then the band and the captain and the officers of the Jews took Jesus and bound Him and led Him away to Annas first.....The high priest then asked of His disciples and of His doctrine. Jesus answered him, I spake openly to the world.....Why asketh though me?

Ask them which heard me what I have said unto them; behold they know what I have said. Now Annas had sent Him bound unto Caiaphas the high priest.....Then they led Jesus from Caiaphas unto the hall of judgment..... "Pilate then went out unto them and said, what accusation bring you against this man? They answered and said unto him, If He were not a malefactor we would not have delivered Him unto thee.....Then Pilate entered into the judgment hall again, and called Jesus, and said unto Him, Art though the King of the Jews? Jesus answered him, Sayest thou this thing of thyself or did others tell it to thee of me?.....My kingdom is not of this world: if my kingdom were of this world, then would my servants fight that I should not be delivered to the Jews; but now is my kingdom not from hence.

Pilate therefore said unto him, Art thou a king then? Jesus answered; Thou sayest that I am a king. To this end was I born, and for this cause came into the world that I should bear witness unto the truth. Everyone that is of the truth heareth my voice. Pilate said unto Him, What is truth?.....Then he went out again unto the Jews and saith unto them, I find in Him no fault at all. But we have a custom that I should release unto you one at the Passover; will ye therefore that I release unto you the King of the Jews? Then cried they all again saying, Not this man, but Barabbas. Now Barabbas was a robber. Pilate therefore took Jesus and SCOURGED Him. And the soldiers platted A CROWN OF THORNS and put it on His head, and they put on Him a purple robe and said, Hail, King of the Jews; and they smote him with their hands.

"Pilate therefore went forth again and saith unto them, behold I bring Him forth unto you that ye may know that I find no fault in Him. Then came Jesus forth wearing the crown of thorns and the purple robe. And Pilate saith unto them, Behold the man! When the chief priests therefore, and officers saw Him, they cried out, saying, Crucify Him, Crucify Him. Pilate saith unto them, Take ye Him and crucify Him; for I find no fault in Him.

The Jews answered him, We have a law and by our law He ought to die, because He made Himself the Son of God.....Pilate sought to release Him, but the Jews cried out saying, If thou let this man go, thou art not Caesar's friend; whoever maketh himself a king speaketh against Caesar.....They cried out, Away with Him, away with Him, crucify Him. Pilate saith unto them, Shall I crucify your king? The chief priests answered, we have no king but Caesar. Then delivered he Him therefore unto them to be crucified. And they took Jesus and led Him away.

And He, bearing His cross, went forth into a place called the PLACE OF A SKULL, which is, in the Hebrew, Golgotha. There they CRUCIFIED Him and two others with Him, one on either side and Jesus in the midst. And Pilate wrote a title and put it on the cross. And the writing was, JESUS OF NAZARETH, THE KING OF THE JEWS."

We have here the account of how the STIGMATA or punctures were produced in the Hero of the Gospels, though the location is not quite correctly described, and the process is represented in a narrative form differing widely from the manner in which these things really happen. But we stand here before one of the Mysteries which must remain sealed for the profane, though the underlying mystical facts are as plain as daylight to those who know. The physical body is not by any means the real man. Tangible, solid, and pulsating with life as we find it, it is really the most dead part of the human being, crystallized into a matrix of finer vehicles which are invisible to our ordinary physical sight.

If we place a basin of water in a freezing temperature, the water soon congeals into ice, and when we examine this ice, we find that it is made up of innumerable little crystals having various geometrical forms and lines of demarcation. There are etheric lines of forces which were present in the water before it congealed. As the water was hardened and molded along these lines, so our physical bodies have congealed and solidified along the etheric lines of force of our invisible vital body, which is thus in the ordinary course of life inextricably bound to the physical body, waking or sleeping, until death brings dissolution of the tie.

But as Initiation involves the liberation of the REAL MAN from the body of sin and death that he may soar into the subtler spheres at will and return to the body at his pleasure, it is obvious that before that can be accomplished, before the object of Initiation can be attained, the interlocking grip of the physical body and the etheric vehicle which is so strong and rigid in ordinary humanity, must be dissolved. As they are most closely bound together in the palms of the hands, the arches of the feet, and the head, the occult schools concentrate their efforts upon severing the connection at these points, and produce the STIGMATA invisibly.

The Christian Mystic lacks knowledge of how to perform the act without producing an exterior manifestation. The STIGMATA develop in him spontaneously by constant contemplation of Christ and unceasing efforts to imitate Him in all things. These exterior STIGMATA comprise not only the wounds in the hands and feet and that in the side but also those impressed by the crown of thorns and by the scourging. The most remarkable example of stigmatization is that said to have occurred in 1224 to Francis of Assisi on the mountain of Alverno. Being absorbed in contemplation of the Passion he saw a seraph approaching, blazing with fire and having between its wings the figure of the Crucified. St. Francis became aware that in hands, feet, and side he had received externally the marks of crucifixion. These marks continued during the two years until his death, and are claimed to have been seen by many eyewitnesses, including Pope Alexander the Fourth.

The Dominicans disputed the fact, but at length made the same claim for Catherine of Sienna, whose STIGMATA were explained as having at her own request been made invisible to others. The Franciscans appealed to Sixtus the Fourth who forbade representation of St. Catherine to made with the STIGMATA. Still the fact of the STIGMATA is recorded in the Breviary Office, and Benedict the 13th granted the Dominicans a Feast in commemoration of it. Others, especially women who have the positive vital body, are claimed to have received some or all of the STIGMATA. The last to be canonized by the Catholic Church for this reason was Veronica Giuliana (1831). More recent cases are those of Anna Catherine Emmerich, who became a nun at Agnetenberg;

L'Estatica Maria Von Moerl of Caldero; Louise Lateau, whose STIGMATA were said to bleed every Friday; and Mrs. Girling of the Newport Shaker community.

But whether the STIGMATA are visible or invisible the effect is the same. The spiritual currents generated in the vital body of such a person are so powerful that the body is scourged by them as it were, particularly in the region of the head, where they produce a feeling akin to that of the crown of thorns. Thus, there finally dawns upon the person a full realization that the physical body is a cross which he is bearing, a prison and not the real man. This brings him to the next step in his Initiation, viz., the crucifixion, which is experienced by the development of the other centers in his hands and feet where the vital body is thus being severed from the dense vehicle.

We are told in the Gospel story that Pilate placed a sign reading, "JESUS NAZARENUS REX JUDAEOREM on Jesus' cross, and this is translated in the authorized version to mean, "Jesus of Nazareth the King of the Jews." But the initials INRI placed upon the cross represent the names of the four elements in Hebrew: IAM, water; NOUR, fire; RUACH, spirit or vital air; and IABESHAH, earth. This is the occult key to the mystery of crucifixion, for it symbolizes in the first place the salt, sulphur, mercury, and azoth which were used by the ancient alchemists to make the Philosopher's Stone, the universal solvent, the ELIXIR-VITAE.

The two "I's" (IAM and IABESHAH) represent the saline lunar water: a, in a fluidic state holding salt in solution, and b, the coagulated extract of this water, the "SALT OF THE EARTH"; in other words, the finer fluidic vehicles of man and his dense body. N (NOUR) in Hebrew stands for fire and the combustible elements, chief among which are SULPHUR and PHOSPHORUS so necessary to oxidation, without which warm blood would be an impossibility. The Ego under this condition could not function in the body nor could thought find a material expression. R (RUACH) is the Hebrew equivalent for the spirit, AZOTH, functioning in the MERCURIAL mind. Thus, the four letters INRI placed over the cross of Christ according to the Gospel story represent composite man, the Thinker, at the point in his spiritual development where he is getting ready for liberation from the cross of his dense vehicle.

Proceeding further along the same line of elucidation we may note that INRI is the symbol of the crucified candidate for the following additional reasons: IAM is the Hebrew word signifying water, the fluidic LUNAR, moon element which forms the principal part of the human body (about 87 per cent). This word is also the symbol of the finer fluidic vehicles of desire and emotion. NOUR, the Hebrew word signifying fire, is a symbolic representation of the heat-producing red blood laden with martial Mars iron, fire, and energy, which the occultist sees coursing as a gas through the veins and arteries of the human body infusing it with energy and ambition without which there could be neither material nor spiritual progress. It also represents the sulphur and phosphorus necessary for the material manifestation of thought as already mentioned.

RUACH, the Hebrew word for spirit or vital air, is an excellent symbol of the Ego clothed in the mercurial Mercury mind, which makes MAN and enables him to control and direct his bodily vehicles and activities in a rational manner. IABESHAH is the Hebrew word for earth, representing the solid fleshy part which makes up the CRUCIFORM EARTHY BODY crystallized within the finer vehicles at birth and severed from them in the ordinary course of things at death, or in the extraordinary event that we learn to die the mystic death and ascend to the glories of the higher spheres for a time.

This stage of the Christian Mystic's spiritual development therefore involves a reversal of the creative force from its ordinary downward course where it is wasted in generation to satisfy the passions, to an upward course through the tripartite spinal cord, whose three segments are ruled by the moon, Mars, and Mercury respectively, and where the rays of Neptune then lights THE REGENERATIVE SPINAL SPIRIT FIRE. This mounting upward sets the pituitary body and the pineal gland into vibration, opening up the spiritual sight; and striking the frontal sinus it starts the CROWN OF THORNS throbbing with pain as the bond with the physical body is burned by the sacred Spirit Fire, which wakes this center from its age-long sleep to a throbbing, pulsating life sweeping onward to the other centers in the FIVE-POINTED STIGMATIC STAR.

They are also vitalized, and the whole vehicle becomes aglow with a golden glory. Then with a final wrench the great vortex of the desire body located in the liver is liberated, and the martial energy contained in that vehicle propels upward the SIDEREAL VEHICLE (so-called because the STIGMATA in the head, hands, and feet are located in the same positions relative to one another as the points in a five pointed star), which ascends through THE SKULL (Golgotha), while the CRUCIFIED CHRISTIAN utters his triumphant cry, "Consummatum est" (it has been accomplished), and soars into the subtler spheres to seek Jesus whose life he has imitated with such success and from whom he is thenceforth inseparable. Jesus is his Teacher and his guide to the kingdom of Christ, where all shall be united in one body to learn and to practice the RELIGION OF THE FATHER, to whom the kingdom will eventually revert that He may be All in All.

ARCANA COELESTIA

By EMANUEL SWEDENBORG - 1688 - 1772

*From the Book Arcana Coelestia.

From the mere letter of the Word of the Old Testament no one would ever discern the fact that this part of the Word contains deep secrets of heaven, and that everything within it both in general and in particular bears reference to the Lord, to His heaven, to the church, to religious belief, and to all things connected therewith; for from the letter or sense of the letter all that anyone can see is that-to speak generally-everything therein has reference merely to the external rites and ordinances of the Jewish Church. Yet the truth is that everywhere in that Word there are internal things which never appear at all in the external things except a very few which the Lord revealed and explained to the Apostles; such as that the sacrifices signify the Lord; that the land of Canaan and Jerusalem signify heaven-on which account they are called the Heavenly Canaan and Jerusalem-and that Paradise has a similar signification.

The Christian world however is as yet profoundly unaware of the fact that all things in the Word both in general and in particular, nay, the very smallest particulars down to the most minute iota, signify and enfold within them spiritual and heavenly things, and therefore the Old Testament is but little cared for. Yet that the Word is really of this character might be known from the single consideration that being the Lord's and from the Lord it must of necessity contain within it such things as belong to heaven, to the church, and to religious belief, and that unless it did so it could not be called the Lord's Word, nor could it be said to have any life in it. For whence comes its life except from those things that belong to life, that is to say, except from the fact that everything in it both in general and in particular bears reference to the Lord, who is the very Life itself; so that anything which does not inwardly regard Him is not alive; and it may be truly said that any expression in the Word that does not enfold Him within it, that is, which does not in its own way bear reference to Him, is not Divine.

Without such a Life, the Word as to the letter is dead. The case in this respect is the same as it is with man, who-as is known in the Christian world-is both internal and external. When separated from the internal man, the external man is the body, and is therefore dead; for it is the internal man that is alive and that causes the external man to be so, the internal man being the soul. So is it with the Word, which, in respect to the letter alone, is like the body without the soul.

While the mind cleaves to the literal sense alone, no one can possibly see that such things are contained within it. Thus, in these first chapters of Genesis, nothing is discoverable from the sense of the letter other than that the creation of the world is treated of, and the garden of Eden which is called Paradise, and Adam as the first created man. Who supposes anything else? But it will be sufficiently established in the following pages that these matters contain arcana which have never yet been revealed; and in fact, that the first chapter of Genesis in the internal sense treats in general of the new creation of man, or of his regeneration, and specifically of the Most Ancient Church; and this in such a manner that there is not the least expression which does not represent, signify, and enfold within it these things.

That this is really the case no one can possibly know except from the Lord. It may therefore be stated in advance that of the Lord's Divine mercy it has been granted me now for some years to be constantly and uninterruptedly in company with spirits and angels, hearing them speak and in turn speaking with them. In this way it has been given me to hear and see wonderful things in the other life which have never before come to the knowledge of any man, nor into his idea. I have been instructed in regard to the different kinds of spirits; the state of souls after death; hell, or the lamentable state of the unfaithful; heaven, or the blessed state of the faithful; and especially in regard to the doctrine of faith which is acknowledged in the universal heaven; on which subjects, of the Lord's Divine mercy, more will be said in the following pages. 1. In the beginning God created the heavens and the earth. 2. And the earth was a void and emptiness, and thick darkness was upon the faces of the deep. And the Spirit of God moved upon the faces of the waters. 3. And God said, Let there be light, and there was light. 4. And God saw the light, that it was good; and God distinguished between the light and the darkness. 5. And God called the light day, and the darkness He called night. And the evening and the morning were the first day. 6. And God said, Let there be an expanse in the midst of the waters, and let it distinguish between the waters in the waters. 7. And God made the expanse, and made a distinction between the waters which were under the expanse, and the waters which were above the expanse; and it was so. 8. And God called the expanse heaven. And the evening and the morning were the second day. 9. And God said, Let the waters under the heaven be gathered together in one place, and let the dry [land] appear; and it was so. 10. And God called the dry [land] earth, and the gathering together of the waters called He sees; and God saw that it was good. 11.

And God said, Let the earth bring forth the tender herb, the herb yielding seed, and the fruit tree bearing fruit after its kind, whose seed is in itself, upon the earth; and it was so. 12. And the earth brought forth the tender herb, the herb yielding seed after its kind, and the tree bearing fruit, whose seed was in itself, after its kind; and God saw that it was good. 13. And the evening and the morning were the third day. 14. And God said, Let there be luminaries in the expanse of the heavens, to distinguish between the day and the night; and let them be for signs, and for seasons, and for days, and for years. 15. And let them be for luminaries in the expanse of the heavens, to give light upon the earth; and it was so. 16. And God made two great luminaries, the greater luminary to rule by day, and the lesser luminary to rule by night; and the stars. 17. And God set them in the expanse of the heavens, to give light upon the earth; 18. And to rule in the day, and in the night, and to distinguish between the light and the darkness; and God saw that it was good. 19. And the evening and the morning were the fourth day. 20. And God said, Let the waters cause to creep forth the creeping thing, the living soul; and let fowl fly above the earth upon the faces of the expanse of the heavens. 21. And God created great whales, and every living soul that creepeth, which the waters caused to creep forth after their kinds, and every winged fowl after its kind; and God saw that it was good. 22. And God blessed them, saying, Be fruitful and multiply, and fill the waters in the seas, and the fowl shall be multiplied in the earth. 23. And the evening and the morning were the fifth day. 24. And God said, Let the earth bring forth the living soul after its kind; the beast, and the thing moving itself, and the wild animal of the earth, after its kind; and it was so. 25. And God made the wild animal of the earth after its kind, and the beast after its kind, and everything that creepeth on the ground after its kind;

and God saw that it was good. 26. And God said, Let us make man in our image, after our likeness; and let them have dominion over the fish of the sea, and over the fowl of the heavens, and over the beast, and over all the earth, and over every creeping thing that creepeth upon the earth. 27. And God created man in His own image, in the image of God created He him; male and female created He them. 28. And God blessed them, and God said unto them, Be fruitful, and multiply, and replenish the earth, and subdue it; and have dominion over the fish of the sea, and over the fowl of the heavens, and over every living thing that creepeth upon the earth. 29. And God said, Behold, I give you every herb bearing seed which is upon the faces of all the earth, and every tree in which is fruit; the tree yielding seed, to you it shall be for food. 30. And to every wild animal of the earth, and to every fowl of the heavens, and to everything that creepeth upon the earth wherein is a living soul, every green herb for food; and it was so. 31. And God saw everything that He had made, and behold it was very good. And the evening and the morning were the sixth day.

THE CONTENTS

The six days, or periods, which are so many successive states of the regeneration of man, are in general as follows. The first state is that which precedes, including both the state from infancy, and that immediately before regeneration. This is called a "void" "emptiness" and "thick darkness." And the first motion, which is the Lord's mercy, is "the Spirit of God moving upon the faces of the waters."

The second state is when a distinction is made between those things which are of the Lord, and those which are proper to man. The things which are of the Lord are called in the word "remains" and here are especially knowledges of faith, which have been learned from infancy, and which are stored up, and are not manifested until the man comes into this state. At the present day this state seldom exists without temptation, misfortune, or sorrow, by which the things of the body and the world, that is, such as are proper to man, are brought into quiescence, and as it were die. Thus, the things which belong to the external man are separated from those which belong to the internal man. In the internal man are the remains, stored up by the Lord unto this time, and for this use.

The third state is that of repentance, in which the man, from his internal man, speaks piously and devoutly, and brings forth goods, like works of charity, but which nevertheless are inanimate, because he thinks they are from himself. These goods are called the "tender grass" and also the "herb yielding seed" and afterwards the "tree bearing fruit."

The fourth state is when the man becomes affected with love, and illuminated by faith. He indeed previously discoursed piously, and brought forth goods, but he did so in consequence of the temptation and straightness' under which he labored, and not from faith and charity; wherefore faith and charity are now enkindled in his internal man, and are called two "luminaries."

The fifth state is when the man discourses from faith, and thereby confirms himself in truth and good: the things then produced by him are animate, and are called the "fish of the sea" and the "birds of the heavens."

The sixth state is when, from faith, and thence from love, he speaks what is true, and does what is good: the things which he then brings forth are called the "living soul" and the "beast." And as he then begins to act at once and together from both faith and love, he becomes a spiritual man, who is called an "image." His spiritual life is delighted and sustained by such things as belong to the knowledges of faith, and to works of charity, which are called his "food;" and his natural life is delighted and sustained by those which belong to the body and the senses; whence a combat arises, until love gains the dominion, and he becomes a celestial man.

Those who are being regenerated do not all arrive at this state. The greatest part, at this day, attain only the first state; some only the second; others the third, fourth, or fifth; few the sixth; and scarcely anyone the seventh.

THE INTERNAL SENSE

In the following work, by the name Lord is meant the Savior of the world, Jesus Christ, and Him only; and He is called "the Lord" without the addition of other names. Throughout the universal heaven He it is who is acknowledged and adored as Lord, because He has all sovereign power in the heavens and on earth. He also commanded His disciples so to call Him, saying, "Ye call Me Lord, and ye say well, for I am" (John 13:13). And after His resurrection His disciples called Him "the Lord."

In the universal heaven they know no other Father than the Lord, because He and the Father are one, as He Himself has said: I am the way, the truth, and the life. Philip saith, Show us the Father; Jesus saith to him, Am I so long time with you, and hast thou not known Me, Philip? He that hath seen Me hath seen the Father; how sayest thou then, Show us the Father? believest thou not that I am in the Father, and the Father in Me? believe Me that I am in the Father and the Father in Me (John 14:6, 8-11).

Verse 1. In the beginning God created the heavens [coelum] and the earth. The most ancient time is called "the beginning." By the prophets it is in various places called the "days of old" [antiquitatis] and also the "days of eternity." The "beginning" also involves the first period when man is being regenerated, for he is then born anew, and receives life. Regeneration itself is therefore called a "new creation" of man. The expressions to "create" to "form" to "make" in almost all parts of the prophetic writings signify to regenerate, yet with a difference in the signification. As in Isaiah: Everyone that is called by My name, I have created him for My glory, I have formed him, yea, I have made him (Isa. 43:7). And therefore the Lord is called the "Redeemer" the "Former from the womb" the "Maker" and also the "Creator;" as in the same Prophet: I am Jehovah your Holy One, the Creator of Israel, your King (Isa. 43:15). In David: The people that is created shall praise Jah (Ps. 102:18). Again: Thou sendest forth Thy spirit, they are created, and Thou renewest the faces of the ground (Ps. 104:30). That "heaven" signifies the internal man; and "earth" the external man before regeneration, may be seen from what follows.

Verse 2. And the earth was a void and emptiness, and darkness was upon the faces of the deep [abyssi]; and the Spirit of God was brooding upon the faces of the waters. Before his regeneration, man is called the "earth void and empty" and also the "ground" wherein nothing of good and truth has been sown; "void" denotes where there is nothing of good, and "empty" where there is nothing of truth. Hence comes "thick darkness" that is, stupidity, and an ignorance of all things belonging to faith in the Lord, and consequently of all things belonging to spiritual and heavenly life. Such a man is thus described by the Lord through Jeremiah: My people is stupid, they have not known Me; they are foolish sons, and are not intelligent; they are wise to do evil, but to do good they have no knowledge. I beheld the earth, and lo a void and emptiness, and the heavens, and they had no light (Jer. 4:22-23).

The "faces of the deep" are the cupidities of the unregenerate man, and the falsities thence originating, of which he wholly consists, and in which he is totally immersed. In this state, having no light, he is like a "deep" or something obscure and confused. Such persons are also called "deeps" and "depths of the sea" in many parts of the Word, which are "dried up" or "wasted" before man is regenerated. As in Isaiah: Awake as in the ancient days, in the generations of old. Art not thou it that drieth up the sea, the waters of the great deep, that maketh the depths of the sea a way for the ransomed to pass over? Therefore, the redeemed of Jehovah shall return (Isa. 51:9-11). Such a man also, when seen from heaven, appears like a black mass, destitute of vitality. The same expressions likewise in general involve the vastation of man, frequently spoken of by the Prophets, which precedes regeneration; for before man can know what is true, and be affected with what is good, there must be a removal of such things as hinder and resist their admission; thus, the old man must need die, before the new man can be conceived.

By the "Spirit of God" is meant the Lord's mercy, which is said to "move" or "brood" as a hen broods over her eggs. The things over which it moves are such as the Lord has hidden and treasured up in man, which in the Word throughout are called remains or a remnant, consisting of the knowledges of the true and of the good, which never come into light or day, until external things are vastated (T*he action or process of emptying or purifying someone or something, typically violently or drastically*). These knowledges are here called "the faces of the waters."

Verse 3. And God said, Let there be light, and there was light. The first state is when the man begins to know that the good and the true are something higher. Men who are altogether external do not even know what good and truth are; for they fancy all things to be good that belong to the love of self and the love of the world; and all things to be true that favor these loves; not being aware that such goods are evils, and such truths falsities. But when man is conceived anew, he then begins for the first time to know that his goods are not goods, and also, as he comes more into the light, that the Lord is, and that He is good and truth itself.

That men ought to know that the Lord is, He Himself teaches in John: Except ye believe that I am, ye shall die in your sins (John 8:24). Also, that the Lord is good itself, or life, and truth itself, or light, and consequently that there is neither good nor truth except from the Lord, is thus declared: In the beginning was the Word, and the Word was with God, and God was the Word. All things were made by Him, and without Him was not anything made that was made. In Him was life, and the life was the light of men. And the light shineth in darkness. He was the true light, which lighteth every man that cometh into the world (John 1:1, 3-4, 9).

Verses 4, 5. And God saw the light, that it was good, and God distinguished between the light and the darkness. And God called the light day, and the dark He called night. Light is called "good" because it is from the Lord, who is good itself, The "darkness" means all those things which, before man is conceived and born anew, have appeared like light, because evil has appeared like good, and the false like the true; yet they are darkness, consisting merely of the things proper to man himself, which still remain. Whatsoever is of the Lord is compared to "day" because it is of the light; and whatsoever is man's own is compared to "night" because it is of darkness. These comparisons frequently occur in the Word.

Verse 5. And the evening and the morning were the first day. What is meant by "evening" and what by "morning" can now be discerned. "Evening" means every preceding state, because it is a state of shade, or of falsity and of no faith; "morning" is every subsequent state, being one of light, or of truth and of the knowledges of faith, "Evening" in a general sense, signifies all things that are of man's own; but "morning" whatever is of the Lord, as is said through David: The spirit of Jehovah spake in me, and His word was on my tongue; the God of Israel said, the Rock of Israel spake to me.

He is as the light of the morning, when the sun ariseth, even a morning without clouds, when from brightness, from rain, the tender herb springeth out of the earth (2 Sam. 23:2-4). As it is "evening" when there is no faith, and "morning" when there is faith, therefore the coming of the Lord into the world is called "morning;"

and the time when He comes, because then there is no faith, is called "evening" as in Daniel: The Holy One said unto me, Even unto evening when it becomes morning, two thousand and three hundred (Dan. 8:14, 26). In like manner "morning" is used in the Word to denote every coming of the Lord, consequently it is an expression of new creation.

Nothing is more common in the Word than for "day" to be used to denote time itself. As in Isaiah: The day of Jehovah is at hand. Behold, the day of Jehovah cometh. I will shake the heavens, and the earth shall be shaken out of her place: in the day of the wrath of Mine anger. Her time is near to come, and her days shall not be prolonged (Isa. 13:6, 9, 13, 22). And in the same Prophet: Her antiquity is of ancient days. And it shall come to pass in that day that Tyre shall be forgotten seventy years, according to the days of one king (Isa. 23:7, 15). As "day" is used to denote time, it is also used to denote the state of that time, as in Jeremiah: Woe unto us, for the day is gone down, for the shadows of the evening are stretched out (Jer. 6:4). And again: If ye shall make vain My covenant of the day, and My covenant of the night, so that there be not day and night in their season (Jer. 23:20, also 25). And again: Renew our days, as of old (Lam. 5:21).

Verse 6. And God said, Let there be an expanse in the midst of the waters, and let it distinguish between the waters in the waters. After the spirit of God, or the Lord's mercy, has brought forth into day the knowledges of the true and of the good, and has given the first light, that the Lord is, that He is good itself, and truth itself, and that there is no good and truth but from Him, He then makes a distinction between the internal man and the external, consequently between the knowledges [cognitiones] that are in the internal man, and the memory-knowledges [scientifica] that belong to the external man. 24-1 The internal man is called an "expanse;" the knowledges [cognitiones] which are in the internal man are called "the waters above the expanse;" and the memory-knowledges of the external man are called "the waters beneath the expanse." Man, before he is being regenerated, does not even know that any internal man exists, much less is he acquainted with its nature and quality. He supposes the internal and the external man to be not distinct from each other. For, being immersed in bodily and worldly things, he has also immersed in them the things that belong to his internal man, and has made of things that are distinct a confused and obscure unit.

Therefore it is first said, "Let there be an expanse in the midst of the waters" and then, "Let it distinguish between the waters in the waters;" but not, Let it distinguish between the waters which are "under" the expanse and the waters which are "above" the expanse, as is afterwards said in the next verses: And God made the expanse, and made a distinction between the waters which were under the expanse, and the waters which were above the expanse, and it was so. And God called the expanse heaven (Gen. 1:7-8). The next thing therefore that man observes in the course of regeneration is that he begins to know that there is an internal man, or that the things which are in the internal man are goods and truths, which are of the Lord alone. Now as the external man, when being regenerated, is of such a nature that he still supposes the goods that he does to be done of himself, and the truths that he speaks to be spoken of himself, and whereas, being such, he is led by them of the Lord, as by things of his own, to do what is good and to speak what is true, therefore mention is first made of a distinction of the waters under the expanse, and afterwards of those above the expanse. It is also an arcanum of heaven, that man, by things of his own, as well by the fallacies of the senses as by cupidities, is led and bent by the Lord to things that are true and good, and thus that every movement and moment of regeneration, both in general and in particular, proceeds from evening to morning, thus from the external man to the internal, or from "earth" to "heaven." Therefore, the expanse, or internal man, is now called "heaven."

To "spread out the earth and stretch out the heavens" is a common form of speaking with the Prophets, when treating of the regeneration of man. As in Isaiah: Thus, saith Jehovah thy Redeemer, and He that formed thee from the womb; I am Jehovah that maketh all things, that stretcheth forth the heavens alone, that spreadeth abroad the earth by Myself (Isa. 44:24). And again, where the advent of the Lord is openly spoken of: A bruised reed shall He not break, and the smoking flax shall He not quench; He shall bring forth judgment unto truth (Isa. 42:3); that is, He does not break fallacies, nor quench cupidities, but bends them to what is true and good; and therefore it follows, Jehovah God createth the heavens, and stretcheth them out; He spreadeth out the earth, and the productions thereof; He giveth breath unto the people upon it, and spirit to them that walk therein (Isa. 42:5). Not to mention other passages to the same purport.

Verse 8. And the evening and the morning were the second day. The meaning of "evening" of "morning" and of "day" was shown above at verse 5.

Verse 9. And God said, Let the waters under the heaven be gathered together to one place, and let the dry [land] appear; and it was so. When it is known that there is both an internal and an external man, and that truths and goods flow in from, or through, the internal man to the external, from the Lord, although it does not so appear, then those truths and goods, or the knowledges of the true and the good in the regenerating man, are stored up in his memory, and are classed among its knowledges [scientifica]; for whatsoever is insinuated into the memory of the external man, whether it be natural, or spiritual, or celestial, abides there as memory-knowledge [scientificum], and is brought forth thence by the Lord. These knowledges are the "waters gathered together into one place" and are called "seas" but the external man himself is called the "dry [land]" and presently "earth" as in what follows.

Verse 10. And God called the dry [land] earth, and the gathering together of the waters called He seas; and God saw that it was good. It is a very common thing in the Word for "waters" to signify knowledges [cognitiones et scientifica], and consequently for "seas" to signify a collection of knowledges. As in Isaiah: The earth shall be full of the knowledge [scientia] of Jehovah, as the waters cover the sea (Isa. 11:9). And in the same Prophet, where a lack of knowledges [cognitionum et scientificorum] is treated of: The waters shall fail from the sea, and the river shall be dried up and become utterly dry, and the streams shall recede (Isa. 19:5-6).

In Haggai, speaking of a new church: I will shake the heavens and the earth, and the sea and the dry [land]; and I will shake all nations; and the desire of all nations shall come; and I will fill this house with glory (Hag. 2:6-7). And concerning man in the process of regeneration, in Zechariah: There shall be one day, it is known to Jehovah; not day, nor night; but it shall come to pass that at evening time it shall be light; and it shall be in that day that living waters shall go out from Jerusalem, part of them toward the eastern sea, and part of them toward the hinder sea (Zech. 14:7-8). David also, describing a vastated man who is to be regenerated and who will worship the Lord: Jehovah despiseth not His prisoners; let the heavens and the earth praise Him, the seas and everything that creepeth therein (Ps. 69:33-34). That the "earth" signifies a recipient, appears from Zechariah: Jehovah stretcheth forth the heavens, and layeth the foundation of the earth, and formeth the spirit of man in the midst of him (Zech. 12:1).

Verses 11, 12. And God said, Let the earth bring forth the tender herb, the herb yielding seed, and the fruit tree bearing fruit after its kind, whose seed is in itself, upon the earth; and it was so. And the earth brought forth the tender herb, the herb yielding seed after its kind, and the tree bearing fruit, whose seed was in itself, after its kind; and God saw that it was good. When the "earth" or man, has been thus prepared to receive celestial seeds from the Lord, and to produce something of what is good and true, then the Lord first causes some tender thing to spring forth, which is called the "tender herb;" then something more useful, which again bears seed in itself, and is called the "herb yielding seed;" and at length something good which becomes fruitful, and is called the "tree bearing fruit, whose seed is in itself" each according to its own kind.

The man who is being regenerated is at first of such a quality that he supposes the good which he does, and the truth which he speaks, to be from himself, when in reality all good and all truth are from the Lord, so that whosoever supposes them to be from himself has not as yet the life of true faith, which nevertheless he may afterwards receive; for he cannot as yet believe that they are from the Lord, because he is only in a state of preparation for the reception of the life of faith. This state is here represented by things inanimate, and the succeeding one of the life of faith, by animate things. The Lord is He who sows, the "seed" is His Word, and the "earth" is man, as He himself has deigned to declare (Matt. 13:19-24, 37-39; Mark 4:14-21; Luke 8:11-16). To the same purport He gives this description: So is the kingdom of God, as a man when he casteth seed into the earth, and sleepeth and riseth night and day, and the seed groweth and riseth up, he knoweth not how; for the earth bringeth forth fruit of herself, first the blade, then the ear, after that the full corn in the ear (Mark 4:26-28). By the "kingdom of God" in the universal sense, is meant the universal heaven; in a sense less universal, the true church of the Lord; and in a particular sense, everyone who is of true faith, or who is regenerate by a life of faith. Wherefore such a person is also called "heaven" because heaven is in him; and likewise, the "kingdom of God" because the kingdom of God is in him as the Lord Himself teaches in Luke: Being demanded of the Pharisees when the kingdom of God should come, He answered them, and said, The kingdom of God cometh not with observation; neither shall they say, Lo here! or, Lo there! for behold, the kingdom of God is within you (Luke 17:20-21). This is the third successive stage of the regeneration of man, being his state of repentance, and in like manner proceeding from shade to light, or from evening to morning; wherefore it is said (verse 13), "and the evening and the morning were the third day."

Verses 14-17. And God said, Let there be luminaries in the expanse of the heavens, to distinguish between the day and the night; and let them be for signs, and for seasons, and for days, and for years; and let them be for luminaries in the expanse of the heavens, to give light upon the earth; and it was so. And God made two great luminaries, the greater luminary to rule by day, and the lesser luminary to rule by night; and the stars. And God set them in the expanse of the heavens, to give light upon the earth. What is meant by "great luminaries" cannot be clearly understood unless it is first known what is the essence of faith, and also what is its progress with those who are being created anew.

The very essence and life of faith is the Lord alone, for he who does not believe in the Lord cannot have life, as He himself has declared in John: He that believeth on the Son hath eternal life, but he that believeth not on the Son shall not see life, but the wrath of God shall abide upon him (John 3:36). The progression of faith with those who are being created anew is as follows. At first, they have no life, for it is only in the good and the true that there is life, and none in the evil and the false; afterwards they receive life from the Lord by faith, first by faith of the memory, which is a faith of mere knowledge [fides scientifica]; next by faith in the understanding, which is an intellectual faith; lastly by faith in the heart, which is the faith of love, or saving faith. The first two kinds of faith are represented from verse 3 to verse 13, by things inanimate, but faith vivified by love is represented from verse 20 to verse 25, by animate things. For this reason, love, and faith thence derived, are now here first treated of, and are called "luminaries;" love being "the greater luminary which rules by day;" faith derived from love "the lesser luminary which rules by night;" and as these two luminaries ought to make a one, it is said of them, in the singular number, "Let there be luminaries" [sit luminaria], and not in the plural [sint luminaria]. Love and faith in the internal man are like heat and light in the external corporeal man, for which reason the former are represented by the latter. It is on this account that luminaries are said to be "set in the expanse of heaven" or in the internal man; a great luminary in its will, and a lesser one in its understanding; but they appear in the will and the understanding only as does the light of the sun in its recipient objects. It is the Lord's mercy alone that affects the will with love, and the understanding with truth or faith.

That the "great luminaries" signify love and faith, and are also called "sun, moon, and stars" is evident from the Prophets, as in Ezekiel: When I shall extinguish thee, I will cover the heavens and make the stars thereof black; I will cover the sun with a cloud, and the moon shall not give her light; all the luminaries of the light of heaven will I make black over thee, and I will set darkness upon thy land (32:7, 8). In this passage Pharaoh and the Egyptians are treated of, by whom are meant, in the Word, the principle of mere sense and of mere knowledge [sensuale et scientificum]; and here, that by things of sense and of mere knowledge [sensualia et scientifica], love and faith had been extinguished. So in Isaiah: The day of Jehovah cometh to set the land in desolation, for the stars of heaven and the constellations thereof shall not give their light the sun is darkened in his going forth, and the moon shall not cause her light to shine (13:9, 10).

Again, in Joel: The day of Jehovah cometh, a day of darkness and of thick darkness; the earth trembleth before Him, the heavens are in commotion; the sun and the moon are blackened, and the stars withdraw their brightness (2:1, 2, 10). Again, in Isaiah, speaking of the advent of the Lord and the enlightening of the Gentiles, consequently of a new church, and in particular of all who are in darkness, and receive light, and are being regenerated: Arise, shine, for thy light is come behold darkness covers the earth, and thick darkness the peoples, and Jehovah shall arise upon thee, and the Gentiles shall come to thy light, and kings to the brightness of thy rising, Jehovah shall be to thee a light of eternity, thy sun shall no more go down, neither shall thy moon withdraw itself, for Jehovah shall be to thee a light of eternity (60:1-3, 20). So in David: Jehovah in intelligence maketh the heavens, He stretcheth out the earth above the waters He maketh great luminaries the sun to rule by day, the moon and stars to rule by night (Ps. 136:5-9). And again: Glorify ye Jehovah, sun and moon glorify Him, all ye stars of light glorify Him, ye heavens of heavens, and ye waters that are above the heavens (Ps. 148:3, 4). In all thee passages, "luminaries" signify love and faith.

It was because "luminaries" represented and signified love and faith toward the Lord that it was ordained in the Jewish Church that a perpetual luminary should be kept burning from evening till morning, for every ordinance in that church was representative of the Lord. Of this luminary it is written: Command the sons of Israel that they take oil for the luminary, to cause the lamp to ascend continually: in the tabernacle of the congregation without the veil, which is before the testimony, shall Aaron and his sons order it from evening even until morning, before Jehovah (Exod. 27:20, 21). That these things signify love and faith, which the Lord kindles and causes to give light in the internal man, and through the internal man in the external, will of the Lord's Divine mercy be shown in its proper place.

Love and faith are first called "great luminaries" and afterwards love is called a "greater luminary" and faith a "lesser luminary;" and it is said of love that it shall "rule by day" and of faith that it shall "rule by night." As these are arcana which are hidden, especially in this end of days, it is permitted of the Lord's Divine mercy to explain them. The reason why these arcana are more especially concealed in this end of days is that now is the consummation of the age, when there is scarcely any love, and consequently scarcely any faith, as the Lord Himself foretold in the Evangelists in these words: The sun shall be darkened, and the moon shall not give her light, and the stars shall fall from heaven, and the powers of the heavens shall be shaken (Matt. 24:29). By the "sun" is here meant love, which is darkened; by the "moon" faith, which does not give light; and by the "stars" the knowledges of faith, which fall from heaven, and which are the "virtues and powers of the heavens." The Most Ancient Church acknowledged no other faith than love itself. The celestial angels also do not know what faith is except that which is of love.

The universal heaven is a heaven of love, for there is no other life in the heavens than the life of love. From this is derived all heavenly happiness, which is so great that nothing of it admits of description, nor can ever be conceived by any human idea. Those who are under the influence of love, love the Lord from the heart, but yet know, declare, and perceive, that all love, and consequently all life-which is of love alone-and thus all happiness, come solely from the Lord, and that they have not the least of love, of life, or of happiness, from themselves. That it is the Lord from whom all love comes, was also represented by the great luminary or "sun" at His transfiguration, for it is written: His face did shine as the sun, and his raiment was white as the light (Matt. 17:2). Inmost things are signified by the face, and the things that proceed from them, by the raiment. Thus, the Lord's Divine was signified by the "sun" or love; and His Human by the "light" or wisdom proceeding from love.

It is in everyone's power very well to know that no life is possible without some love, and that no joy is possible except that which flows from love. Such however as is the love, such is the life, and such the joy: if you were to remove loves, or what is the same thing, desires-for these are of love-thought would instantly cease, and you would become like a dead person, as has been shown me to the life. The loves of self and of the world have in them some resemblance to life and to joy, but as they are altogether contrary to true love, which consists in a man's loving the Lord above all things, and his neighbor as himself, it must be evident that they are not loves, but hatreds, for in proportion as anyone loves himself and the world, in the same proportion he hates his neighbor, and thereby the Lord. Wherefore true love is love to the Lord, and true life is the life of love from Him, and true joy is the joy of that life. There can be but one true love, and therefore but one true life, whence flow true joys and true felicities, such as are those of the angels in the heavens.

Love and faith admit of no separation, because they constitute one and the same thing; and therefore, when mention is first made of "luminaries" they are regarded as one, and it is said, "Let there be [sit] luminaries in the expanse of the heavens." Concerning this circumstance, it is permitted me to relate the following wonderful particulars. The celestial angels, by virtue of the celestial love in which they are from the Lord, are from that love in all the knowledges of faith, and are in such a life and light of intelligence that scarcely anything of it can be described. But, on the other hand, spirits who are in the knowledge of the doctrinals of faith, without love, are in such a coldness of life and obscurity of light that they cannot even approach the first threshold of the court of the heavens, but flee back again. Some of them, while not living according to His precepts, say that they have believed in the Lord, and it was of such that the Lord said in Matthew: Not everyone that saith unto Me, Lord, Lord, shall enter into the kingdom of the heavens, but he that doeth My will: many will say to Me in that day, Lord, Lord, have we not prophesied through Thy name (Matt. 7:21, 22, to the end). Hence it is evident that those who are in love are also in faith, and thereby in heavenly life, but not those who say they are in faith, and are not in the life of love.

The life of faith without love is like the light of the sun without heat, as in the time of winter, when nothing grows, but all things are torpid and dead; whereas faith proceeding from love is like the light of the sun in the time of spring, when all things grow and flourish in consequence of the sun's fructifying heat. It is precisely similar in regard to spiritual and heavenly things, which are usually represented in the Word by such as exist in the world and on the face of the earth. No faith; and faith without love, are also compared by the Lord to "winter" where He foretells the consummation of the age, in Mark: Pray ye that your flight be not in the winter, for those shall be days of affliction (Mark 13:18-19). "Flight" means the last time, and also that of every man when he dies. "Winter" is a life destitute of love; the "day of affliction" is its miserable state in the other life.

Man has two faculties: will and understanding. When the understanding is governed by the will they together constitute one mind, and thus one life, for then what the man wills and does he also thinks and intends. But when the understanding is at variance with the will (as with those who say they have faith, and yet live in contradiction to faith), then the one mind is divided into two, one of which desires to exalt itself into heaven, while the other tends toward hell; and since the will is the doer in every act, the whole man would plunge headlong into hell if it were not that the Lord has mercy on him.

They who have separated faith from love do not even know what faith is. When thinking of faith, some imagine it to be mere thought, some that it is thought directed toward the Lord, few that it is the doctrine of faith. But faith is not only a knowledge and acknowledgment of all things that the doctrine of faith comprises, but especially is it an obedience to all things that the doctrine of faith teaches. The primary point that it teaches, and that which men should obey, is love to the Lord, and love toward the neighbor, for if a man is not in this, he is not in faith. This the Lord teaches so plainly as to leave no doubt concerning it, in Mark: The foremost of all the commandments is, Hear, O Israel, the Lord our God is one Lord; therefore thou shalt love the Lord thy God with all thy heart, and with all thy soul, and with all thy mind, and with all thy strength: this is the foremost commandment; and the second is like, namely this, Thou shalt love thy neighbor as thyself; there is none other commandment greater than these (Mark 12:29-31). In Matthew, the Lord calls the former of these the "first and great commandment" and says that "on these commandments hang all the law and the Prophets" (Matt. 22:37-41). The "law and the Prophets" are the universal doctrine of faith, and the whole Word.

It is said that the luminaries shall be "for signs, and for seasons, and for days, and for years." In these words are contained more arcana than can at present be unfolded, although in the literal sense nothing of the kind appears. Suffice it here to observe that there are alternations of things spiritual and celestial, both in general and in particular, which are compared to the changes of days and of years. The changes of days are from morning to midday, thence to evening, and through night to morning; and the changes of years are similar, being from spring to summer, thence to autumn, and through winter to spring. Hence come the alternations of heat and light, and also of the productions of the earth.

To these changes are compared the alternations of things spiritual and celestial. Life without such alternations and varieties would be uniform, consequently no life at all; nor would good and truth be discerned or distinguished, much less perceived. These alternations are in the Prophets called "ordinances" [statuta](*Statute*), as in Jeremiah: Said Jehovah, who giveth the sun for a light by day, and the ordinances of the moon and of the stars for a light by night, . . these statutes shall not recede from before me (Jer. 31:35-36). And in the same Prophet: Said Jehovah, If My covenant of day and night stand not, and if I have not appointed the ordinances of heaven and earth (Jer. 33:25). But concerning these things, of the Lord's Divine mercy, at Genesis 8:22.

Verse 15. And to rule in the day, and in the night, and to distinguish between the light and the darkness; and God saw that it was good. By the "day" is meant good, by the "night" evil; and therefore goods are called works of the day, but evils works of the night; by the "light" is meant truth, and by the "darkness" falsity, as the Lord says: Men loved darkness rather than light. He that doeth truth cometh to the light (John 3:19, 21). Verse 19. And the evening and the morning were the fourth day.

Verse 20. And God said, Let the waters cause to creep forth the creeping thing, the living soul; and let fowl fly above the earth upon the faces of the expanse of the heavens. After the great luminaries have been kindled and placed in the internal man, and the external receives light from them, then the man first begins to live. Heretofore he can scarcely be said to have lived, inasmuch as the good which he did he supposed that he did of himself, and the truth which he spoke that he spoke of himself; and since man of himself is dead, and there is in him nothing but what is evil and false, therefore whatsoever he produces from himself is not alive, insomuch that he cannot, from himself, do good that in itself is good. That man cannot even think what is good, nor will what is good, consequently cannot do what is good, except from the Lord, must be plain to everyone from the doctrine of faith, for the Lord says in Matthew: He that soweth the good seed is the Son of man (Matt. 13:37). Nor can any good come except from the real Fountain of good, which is One only, as He says in another place: None is good save One, God (Luke 18:19). Nevertheless, when the Lord is resuscitating man, that is, regenerating him, to life, He permits him at first to suppose that he does what is good and speaks what is true from himself, for at that time he is incapable of conceiving otherwise, nor can he in any other way be led to believe, and afterwards to perceive, that all good and truth are from the Lord alone.

While man is thinking in such a way his truths and goods are compared to the "tender grass" and also to the "herb yielding seed" and lastly to the "tree bearing fruit" all of which are inanimate; but now that he is vivified by love and faith, and believes that the Lord works all the good that he does and all the truth that he speaks, he is compared first to the "creeping things of the water" and to the "fowls which fly above the earth" and also to "beasts" which are all animate things, and are called "living souls."

By the "creeping things which the waters bring forth" are signified the memory-knowledges [scientifica] which belong to the external man; by "birds" in general, rational and intellectual things, of which the latter belong to the internal man. That the "creeping things of the waters" or "ishes" signify memory-knowledges, is plain from Isaiah: I came and there was no man; at My rebuke I dry up the sea, I make the rivers a wilderness; their fish shall stink because there is no water and shall die for thirst; I clothe the heavens with blackness (Isa. 50:2-3). But it is still plainer from Ezekiel, where the Lord describes the new temple, or a new church in general, and the man of the church, or a regenerate person; for everyone who is regenerate is a temple of the Lord: The Lord Jehovah said unto me, These waters that shall issue to the boundary toward the east, and shall come toward the sea, being led into the sea, and the waters shall be healed; and it shall come to pass that every living soul that shall creep forth, whithersoever the water of the rivers shall come, shall live, and there shall be exceeding much fish, because those waters shall come thither, and they shall heal, and everything shall live whither the river cometh; and it shall come to pass that fishers shall stand upon it from En-gedi to En-eglaim, with the spreading of nets shall they be; their fish shall be according to its kind, as the fish of the great sea, exceeding many (Ezek. 47:8-10). "Fishers from En-gedi unto En-eglaim" with the "spreading of nets" signify those who shall instruct the natural man in the truths of faith. That "birds" signify things rational and intellectual, is evident from the Prophets; as in Isaiah: Calling a bird from the east, the man of My counsel from a distant land (Isa. 46:11). And in Jeremiah: I beheld and lo there was no man, and all the birds of the heavens were fled (Jer. 4:25). In Ezekiel: I will plant a shoot of a lofty cedar, and it shall lift up a branch, and shall bear fruit, and be a magnificent cedar; and under it shall dwell every fowl of every wing, in the shadow of the branches thereof shall they dwell (Ezek. 17:22-23). And in Hosea, speaking of a new church, or of a regenerate man: And in that day will I make a covenant for them with the wild beast of the field, and with the fowls of heaven, and with the moving thing of the ground (Hos. 2:18). That "wild beast" does not signify wild beast, nor "bird" bird, must be evident to everyone, for the Lord is said to "make a new covenant" with them.

Whatever is proper to man has no life in itself, and whenever it is made manifest to the sight it appears hard, like a bony and black substance; but whatever is from the Lord has life, containing within it that which is spiritual and celestial, which when presented to view appears human and living. It may seem incredible but is nevertheless most true, that every single expression, every single idea, and every least of thought in an angelic spirit, is alive, containing in its minutest particulars an affection that proceeds from the Lord, who is life itself. And therefore, whatsoever things are from the Lord, have life in them, because they contain faith toward Him, and are here signified by the "living soul:" they have also a species of body, here signified by "what moves itself" or "creeps." These truths, however, are as yet deep secrets to man, and are now mentioned only because the "living soul" and the "thing moving itself" are treated of.

Verse 21. And God created great whales, and every living soul that creepeth, which the waters made to creep forth, after their kinds, and every winged fowl after its kind; and God saw that it was good. "Fishes" as before said, signify memory-knowledges, now animated by faith from the Lord, and thus alive. "Whales" signify their general principles, in subordination to which, and from which, are the particulars; for there is nothing in the universe that is not under some general principle, as a means that it may exist and subsist.

"Whales" or "great fishes" are sometimes mentioned by the Prophets, and they there signify the generals of memory-knowledges. Pharaoh the king of Egypt (by whom is represented human wisdom or intelligence, that is, knowledge [scientia] in general), is called a "great whale." As in Ezekiel: Behold, I am against thee, Pharaoh king of Egypt, the great whale that lieth in the midst of his rivers, that hath said, My river is mine own, and I have made myself (Ezek. 29:3). And in another place: Take up a lamentation for Pharaoh king of Egypt, and say unto him, Thou art as a whale in the seas, and hast gone forth in thy rivers, and hast troubled the waters with thy feet (Ezek. 32:2), by which words are signified those who desire to enter into the mysteries of faith by means of memory-knowledges, and thus from themselves.

In Isaiah: In that day Jehovah, with His hard and great and strong sword, shall visit upon leviathan the longish [oblongum] serpent, even leviathan the crooked serpent, and He shall slay the whales that are in the sea (Isa. 27:1). By "slaying the whales that are in the sea" is signified that such persons are ignorant of even the general principles of truth. So in Jeremiah: Nebuchadnezzar the king of Babylon hath devoured me, he hath troubled me, he hath made me an empty vessel, he hath swallowed me as a whale, he hath filled his belly with my delicacies, he hath cast me out (Jer. 51:34),denoting that he had swallowed the knowledges of faith, here called "delicacies" as the whale did Jonah; a "whale" denoting those who possess the general principles of the knowledges of faith as mere memory-knowledges, and act in this manner.

Verse 22. And God blessed them, saying, Be fruitful, and multiply, and fill the waters in the seas, and the fowl shall be multiplied in the earth. Everything that has in itself life from the Lord fructifies and multiplies itself immensely; not so much while the man lives in the body, but to an amazing degree in the other life. To "be fruitful" in the Word, is predicated of the things that are of love, and to "multiply" of the things that are of faith; the "fruit" which is of love contains "seed" by which it so greatly multiplies itself. The Lord's "blessing" also in the Word signifies fructification and multiplication, because they proceed from it. Verse 23. And the evening and the morning were the fifth day.

Verses 24 - 25. And God said, Let the earth bring forth the living soul after its kind, the beast, and the moving thing, and the wild animal of the earth after its kind; and it was so. And God made the wild animal of the earth after its kind, and the beast after its kind, and everything that creepeth on the ground after its kind; and God saw that it was good. Man, like the earth, can produce nothing of good unless the knowledges of faith are first sown in him, whereby he may know what is to be believed and done. It is the office of the understanding to hear the Word, and of the will to do it.

To hear the Word and not to do it, is like saying that we believe when we do not live according to our belief; in which case we separate hearing and doing, and thus have a divided mind, and become of those whom the Lord calls "foolish" in the following passage: Whosoever heareth My words, and doeth them, I will liken unto a wise man who built his house upon a rock: but everyone that heareth My words, and doeth them not, I liken to a foolish man, who built his house upon the sand (Matt. 7:24, 26).The things that belong to the understanding are signified-as before shown-by the "creeping things which the waters bring forth" and also by the "fowl upon the earth" and "upon the faces of the expanse;" but those which are of the will are signified here by the "living soul which the earth produces" and by the "beast" and "creeping thing" and also by the "wild animal of that earth."

Those who lived in the most ancient times thus signified the things relating to the understanding and to the will; and therefore, in the Prophets, and constantly in the Word of the Old Testament, the like things are represented by different kinds of animals. Beasts are of two kinds; the evil, so called because they are hurtful; and the good, which are harmless. Evils in man are signified by evil beasts, as by bears, wolves, dogs; and the things which are good and gentle, by beasts of a like nature, as by heifers, sheep, and lambs. The "beasts" here referred to are good and gentle ones, and thus signify affections, because it here treats of those who are being regenerated. The lower things in man, which have more connection with the body, are called "wild animals of that earth" and are cupidity's and pleasures.

That "beasts" signify man's affections-evil affections with the evil, and good affections with the good-is evident from numerous passages in the Word, as in Ezekiel: Behold, I am for you, and I will look back to you, that ye may be tilled and sown, and I will multiply upon you man and beast, and they shall be multiplied and bring forth fruit; and I will cause you to dwell as in your ancient times (Ezek. 36:9, 11, treating of regeneration). In Joel: Be not afraid ye beasts of My field, for the dwelling places of the wilderness are become grassy (Joel 2:22). In David also: So foolish was I, I was as a beast before Thee (Ps. 73:22). In Jeremiah, treating of regeneration: Behold the days come, saith Jehovah, that I will sow the house of Israel and the house of Judah with the seed of man, and with the seed of beast, and I will watch over them to build and to plant (Jer. 31:27-28). "Wild animals" have a similar signification, as in Hosea: In that day will I make a covenant for them with the wild animal of the field, and with the fowl of the heavens, and with the creeping thing of the earth (Hos. 2:18). In Job: Thou shalt not be afraid of the wild animals of the earth, for thy covenant is with the stones of the field, and the wild animals of the field shall be at peace with thee (Job 5:22-23). In Ezekiel: I will make with you a covenant of peace, and will cause the evil wild animal to cease out of the land, that they may dwell confidently in the wilderness (Ezek. 34:25). In Isaiah: The wild animals of the field shall honor me, because I have given waters in the wilderness (Isa. 43:20). In Ezekiel: All the fowls of the heavens made their nests in his boughs, and under his branches did all the wild animals of the field bring forth their young, and under his shadow dwelt all great nations (Ezek. 31:6).

This is said of the Assyrian, by whom is signified the spiritual man, and who is compared to the garden of Eden. In David: Glorify ye Him, all His angels, glorify Jehovah from the earth, ye whales, fruit trees, wild animal, and every beast, creeping thing, and flying fowl (Ps. 148:2, 7, 9-10). Here mention is made of the same things-as "whales" the "fruit tree" "wild animal" the "beast" "creeping thing" and "fowl" which, unless they had signified living principles in man, could never have been called upon to glorify Jehovah. The Prophets carefully distinguish between "beasts" and "wild animals of the earth" and "beasts" and "wild animals of the field." Nevertheless, goods in man are called "beasts" just as those who are nearest the Lord in heaven are called "animals" both in Ezekiel and in John: All the angels stood round about the throne, and the elders, and the four animals, 46-1 and fell before the throne on their faces, and worshiped the Lamb (Rev. 7:11; 19:4). Those also who have the gospel preached to them are called "creatures" because they are to be created anew: Go ye into all the world, and preach the gospel to every creature (Mark 16:15).

That these words contain arcana relating to regeneration, is evident also from its being said in the foregoing verse that the earth should bring forth the living soul, the beast, and the wild animal of the earth whereas in the following verse the order is changed, and it said that God made the wild animal of the earth and likewise the beast; for at first, and afterwards until he becomes celestial, man brings forth as of himself; and thus regeneration begins from the external man, and proceeds to the internal; therefore here there is another order, and external things are mentioned first.

Hence then it appears that man is in the fifth state of regeneration when he speaks from a principle of faith, which belongs to the understanding, and thereby confirms himself in the true and in the good. The things then brought forth by him are animate, and are called the "fishes of the sea and the fowl of the heavens." He is in the sixth state, when from faith, which is of the understanding, and from love thence derived, which is of the will, he speaks truths, and does goods; what he then brings forth being called the "living soul" and the "beast." And as he then begins to act from love, as well as from faith, he becomes a spiritual man, who is called an "image of God" which is the subject now treated of.

Verse 26. And God said, Let us make man in our image, after our likeness; and let them have dominion over the fish of the sea, and over the fowl of the heavens, and over the beast, and over all the earth, and over every creeping thing that creepeth upon the earth. In the Most Ancient Church, with the members of which the Lord conversed face to face, the Lord appeared as a Man; concerning which much might be related, but the time has not yet arrived. On this account they called no one "man" but the Lord Himself, and the things which were of Him; neither did they call themselves "men" but only those things in themselves-as all the good of love and all the truth of faith-which they perceived they had from the Lord. These they said were "of man" because they were of the Lord. Hence in the Prophets, by "man" and the "Son of man" in the supreme sense, is meant the Lord; and in the internal sense, wisdom and intelligence; thus, everyone who is regenerate.

As in Jeremiah: I beheld the earth, and lo, it was void and emptiness, and the heavens, and they had no light. I beheld and lo there was no man, and all the birds of the heavens were fled (Jer. 4:23, 25). In Isaiah, where, in the internal sense, by "man", is meant a regenerate person, and in the supreme sense, the Lord himself, as the One Man: Thus, saith Jehovah the Holy One of Israel, and his Former, I have made the earth, and created man upon it; I, even My hands have stretched out the heavens, and all their army have I commanded (Isa. 45:11-12). The Lord therefore appeared to the prophets as a man, as in Ezekiel: Above the expanse, as the appearance of a sapphire stone, the likeness of a throne, and upon the likeness of the throne was the likeness as the appearance of a man above upon it (Ezek. 1:26). And when seen by Daniel He was called the "Son of man" that is, the man, which is the same thing: I saw, and behold, one like the Son of man came with the clouds of heaven, and came to the Ancient of days, and they brought Him near before Him; and there was given Him dominion, and glory, and a kingdom, that all people, and nations, and languages should serve Him. His dominion is an everlasting dominion, which shall not pass away, and His kingdom that which shall not be destroyed (Dan. 7:13-14). The Lord also frequently calls Himself the "Son of man" that is, the man, and, as in Daniel, foretells His coming in glory: Then shall they see the Son of man coming in the clouds of heaven with power and great glory (Matt. 24:30). The "clouds of heaven" are the literal sense of the Word; "power and great glory" are the internal sense of the Word, which in all things both in general and in particular has reference solely to the Lord and His kingdom; and it is from this that the internal sense derives its power and glory.

The Most Ancient Church understood by the "image of the Lord" more than can be expressed. Man is altogether ignorant that he is governed of the Lord through angels and spirits, and that with everyone there are at least two spirits, and two angels. By spirits man has communication with the world of spirits, and by angels with heaven. Without communication by means of spirits with the world of spirits, and by means of angels with heaven, and thus through heaven with the Lord, man could not live at all; his life entirely depends on this conjunction, so that if the spirits and angels were to withdraw, he would instantly perish. While man is unregenerate he is governed quite otherwise than when regenerated.

While unregenerate there are evil spirits with him, who so domineer over him that the angels, though present, are scarcely able to do anything more than merely guide him so that he may not plunge into the lowest evil, and bend him to some good-in fact bend him to good by means of his own cupidities, and to truth by means of the fallacies of the senses. He then has communication with the world of spirits through the spirits who are with him, but not so much with heaven, because evil spirits rule, and the angels only avert their rule. But when the man is regenerate, the angels rule, and inspire him with all goods and truths, and with fear and horror of evils and falsities. The angels indeed lead, but only as ministers, for it is the Lord alone who governs man through angels and spirits. And as this is done through the ministry of angels, it is here first said, in the plural number, "Let us make man in our image;" and yet because the Lord alone governs and disposes, it is said in the following verse, in the singular number, "God created him in His own image." This the Lord also plainly declares in Isaiah: Thus, saith Jehovah thy Redeemer, and He that formed thee from the womb, I Jehovah make all things, stretching forth the heavens alone, spreading abroad the earth by Myself (Isa. 44:24). The angels moreover themselves confess that there is no power in them, but that they act from the Lord alone.

THE ROSICRUCIAN'S OR KNIGHTS OF THE ROSY CROSS

(From "The Dreamer," London, 1754.)

From hence, my noble friend conducted me to the college of the Rosicrucian's, or the Knights of the Rosy Cross. This order of Knighthood is very ancient, and was greatly respected, while they strictly observed the statutes of their founder. For they are enjoined to be meek and humble, to be charitable and hospitable. And therefore, the primitive Rosicrucian's employed their whole revenues in entertaining the pilgrim and the stranger, and in feeding the poor and hungry. While they practiced these virtues, of which they make profession, when they are elected into the college; while they were temperate, vigilant and laborious, they preserved their independency, and enjoyed with honor as great immunities, as the present Knights of Malta. But, as they haven ow entirely departed from all the rules of their institution, and are become proud and luxurious, covetous and ambitious, they are likewise the most corrupt and servile crew in all the land of the Papyropolites. Some years have passed since they renounced the independency of their order, both for themselves and their successors, by a formal act, and agreed to obey implicitly all the commands, which from time to time they should receive from the Intendants of the Mill. But they have lately consented to a decree, by which they are become odious to the whole nation. For they have not only obliged themselves to lay aside the cross, which has hitherto been constantly worn on their habits, but to practice the same ceremonies, with regard to this sacred badge of their order, which are used by the Dutch merchants and sailors, who are admitted into the empire of Japan. So that, whenever a Rosicrucian is mentioned, this proverbial saying is applied to him, *In Tartara, jufferis ibit*, not only for his servility, but to signify his dealings with the people of those regions, from whence he imports the waters of Lethe. But while the Rosicrucian's are the most abject flatterers of men in power, they treat their inferiors, especially their younger brothers, of which there is a numerous tribe, with the greatest insolence and contempt, and suffer the latter, in violation of the most sacred injunctions of their common parent, to languish in poverty, and want even the common necessaries of life.

The Knights of the Rosy Cross, says my friendly conductor, are those *adepts* who were formerly supposed to possess the philosopher's stone, or the secret of compounding a medicine, which, according to their report, would make the person, who swallowed it, immortal. By this artifice they raised in their several districts large contributions, especially among the old maids and widows, who of all beings are the most-fond of life. I know a Rosy Cross, who, by the iniquity of the times and the aid of a peculiar cant, from the quality of a grave-digger, hath been elected into this honorable brotherhood, and hath since acquired one of the most lucrative commandries belonging to the order. His whole business is diligently to attend a large body of these ancient females, whom he dignifies with the title of. his disciples, and never fails to extract a purse of gold from them once a day. And at the same time, that he pretends to make them immortal, he makes their wills, and takes particular care, that his own name shall be found in the first class of the legatees. The face of this Rosicrucian is a composed counterfeit; and it would puzzle all of the optics of physiognomy, or even the most penetrating genius, to define his real character, and investigate the disposition of his mind. I took some pains, since I arrived in this country, to inform myself of his most secret actions, and by that means I discovered his most exquisite hypocrisy.

But, tho' it sufficiently appeared, that this grand Elixir had not half so much virtue, as Ward's pill, yet the Rosicrucian's, in those ages of ignorance and superstition, were able to maintain their reputation by ascribing the ill success of the medicine to the inaptitude or incredulity of the patient. Even, in our more enlightened age, the Rosicrucian Elixir has been in some kind of credit, and was not quite exploded, till Gulliver published his travels. His history of the Struldbrugs must convince every person of common sense, that nothing can be more absurd and ridiculous, than a desire of never dying, and that, if the grand Elixir could make a man immortal, it would make him the most miserable creature in the universe. However, the Rosicrucian's, after this medicine was out of vogue, preserved their character of adepts by introducing another of singular virtue, and which never fails to answer the purpose, for which it is administered. I mean the water of oblivion, which, as I have said before, cannot be imported without their direction and assistance: and they may now appeal to common experience for the efficacy of this medicine, since it has been so successfully tried on the Band of Four Hundred, and consequently has proved of such notable service to a trading nation. It has indeed sometimes happened; that a young Knight, who has been troubled with a hypochondriac melancholy, owing to an ill habit of body, or to a disappointment, when one of his brethren hath been preferred to a rich commandry before him, in order to eradicate the seeds of his distemper, hath overdosed himself with the water of *Lethe*. The consequence of this has been fatal: For he has not only forgot all that he ever knew, or had learned; but has been rendered utterly incapable of knowing, or learning more, or of improving his mind in any manner, by his commerce with men or books, for the future. These Knights are styled in the ancient registers of the college, *Homines plumbei*, and they are distinguished now by the same appellation. I know that one of the poets of this country ascribes the *Plumbeitie* of the Rosicrucian's to the want of genius, or a defect in their education, and imputes their admission into so honorable an order to corruption, or a want of discernment in the electors. But I will not enter into a discussion of this point, or, whether the men of little learning, or the men of much craft (into which division the Rosy Crosses at present naturally fall), are to have the preference in the judgment of their superiors.

It will be proper to inform you, before I leave them, that the Rosicrucian's are not Knights of chivalry. They are neither trained to arms, nor acquainted with those maxims of honor and gallantry, which form a modern hero. In case of a foreign or domestic war, they rather chose by their harangues to inspire their neighbors with courage, than give any proofs of it themselves. On these occasions, *Fungar vice cotis* **[Be as a whetstone for others to be sharpened upon]** etc., is their constant motto; and in this practice they have sometimes succeeded beyond all expectation. However, there are some of them who have been so bold as to gird their loins with the sword: and their present great master is as full of martial ardor, as he is of piety and devotion; and is ever prepared, in time of danger, both to pray and to fight for his friends and his country. I will likewise add, that I may not seem to speak with prejudice, or draw the character of these Knights altogether in profile, that I have known as excellent men of this order, as are to be found in the whole human species; and I doubt whether the chevaliers B-- and D--, lately deceased, have left their equals behind them.

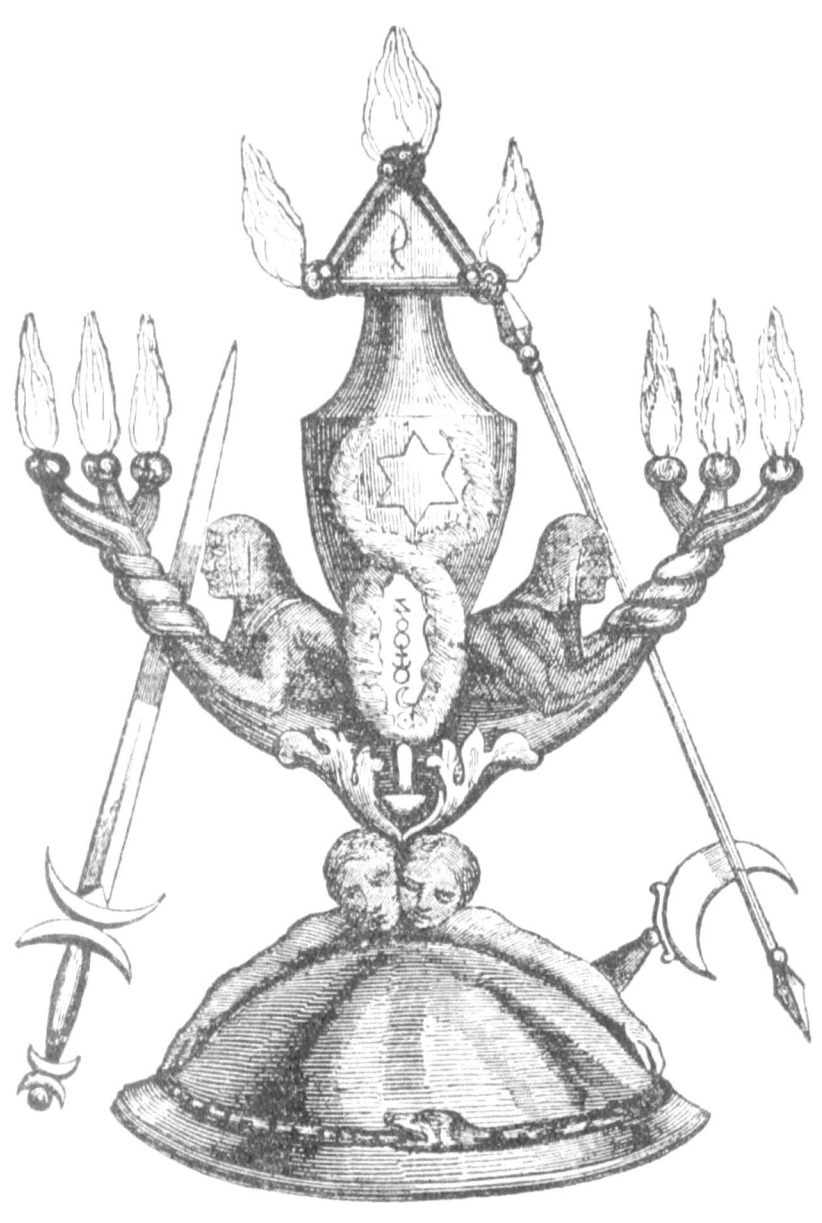

THE PHILOSOPHER'S STONE

(Translated from an old German Rosicrucian Manual script of F.H.)

By FRANZ HARTMANN 1838 - 1912

Some years ago, after having long and earnestly prayed to Good, the unmanifested, incomprehensible cause of all things, I was attracted to Him, and by the power of his Holy Spirit through whom all wisdom descends upon us, and who has been sent to us through Christ, from the Father, he illuminated my inner sight so that I was able to recognize the *Centrum in Trigono Centri*, **[The center is in the triangle of the center.]** which is the only and veritable substance for the preparation of The Philosopher's Stone. But although I know this substance, and had it actually in my possession for over five years, nevertheless I did not know how to obtain from it the Blood of lite Red Lion, and the Gluten of the White Engle, neither did I know the processes by which these substances could be mixed, bottled, and sealed up, or bow they were to be treated by the secret fire, a process which requires a great deal of knowledge, prudence, and cautiousness.

I had studied to a great extent the writings, parables; and allegories of various writers, and I had used great efforts to understand their enigmas, many of which were evidently the inventions of their own fancy; but I found at last that all of their prescribed methods for the preparation of The Philosopher's Stone were nothing but fables. All their *purifications, sublimations, distillations, rectifications, and coagulations*, together with their stoves and retorts, crucibles, pots, sand and water baths, etc., were entirely useless and worthless for my purpose, and I began to realize the wisdom of Theophrastus Paracelsus, who said in regard to that stone, that it is a great mistake to seek for it in material and external things, and that the people who do so are very foolish, because instead of following Nature, they follow their own brains, which do not know what Nature requires. Nature in her nobility does not require any artificial methods to produce what she desires. She produces everything out of her own substance, and in that substance, we must seek for her. He who deserves her will find her hidden there. But not every one is able to read the book of Nature, and this is a truth which I found out by my own experience;

for although the true substance for the preparation of The Philosopher's Stone was in my own possession for over five years, nevertheless it was only in the sixth year that I received the key to the mystery by a secret revelation from God.

To open the secrets of Nature a key is required. This key was in the possession of the ancient patriarchs, prophets, and Adepts, but they always kept it hidden away, so that none but the worthy should come into its possession; for if the foolish or evil-disposed were to know the mysteries of Nature, a great deal of evil would be the result.

In the following description I have revealed as much of these mysteries as I am permitted to reveal, and I have been strongly forbidden to speak more explicitly and plainly. Those who read these pages merely with their external understanding will obtain very little valuable information; but to those who read them by the light of the true faith, shining from the ever-burning fires upon the altars erected in the sanctuary of their own hearts, the meaning will be plain. They will obtain sweet fruits, and become and remain forever true brothers of the Golden and Rosy Cross, and members of our inseparable fraternity.

But to those who desire to know my name, and who might charge me with being too much reserved if I do not reveal it, I will describe it as follows, so that they will have no cause to complain: The number of my name is MDCXII, and in this number the whole of my name is fully inscribed into the book of Nature by eleven dead and seven living ones. Moreover, the fifth letter is the fifth part of the eighth, and the fifteenth the fifth part of the twelfth. Let this be sufficient for your purpose.

"Learn to know all, but keep thyself unknown." - IRENÆUS.

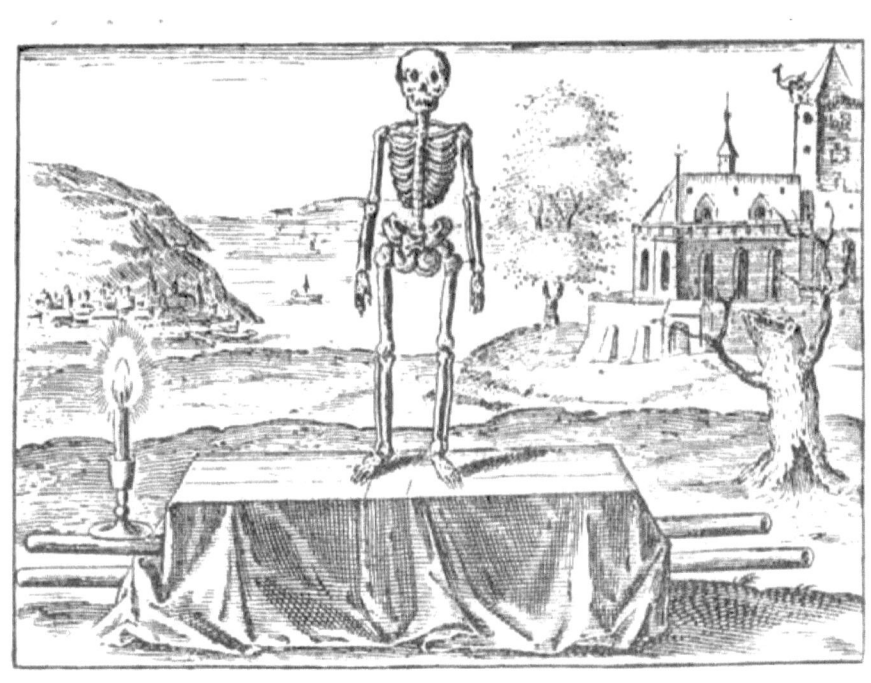

A ROSICRUCIAN ALLEGORY

By JOHN HEYDON - 1629 - 1667

There is a mountain situated in the midst of the earth or center of the world, which is both small and great. It is soft also above measure, hard and strong. It is far off and near at hand; but, by the Providence of God, it is invisible. In it, are hidden most ample treasures, which the world is not able to value. This mountain, by the envy of the devil, is compassed about with very cruel beasts and ravenous birds, which make the way thither both difficult and dangerous; and, therefore, hitherto, because the time is not yet come, the way thither could not be sought after by all, but only by the worthy man's self-labor and investigation. To this mountain you shall go in a certain night, when it comes most long and dark, and see that you prepare yourself by prayer. Insist upon the way that leads to the mountain, but ask not of any man where it lies; only follow your guide, who will offer himself to you, and will meet you in the way.

The guide will bring you to the mountain at midnight, when all things are silent and dark. It is necessary that you arm yourself with a resolute, heroic courage, lest you fear those things that will happen, and fall back. You need no sward or other bodily weapon, only call upon your God, sincerely and heartily seeking him.

When you have discovered the mountain, the first miracle that will appear is this a most vehement and very great wind will shake the whole mountain and shatter the rocks to pieces. You will be encountered by lions, dragons and other terrible wild beasts; but fear not any of these things. Be resolute and take heed that you return not, for your guide that brought you thither will not suffer any evil to befall you. As to the treasure, it is not yet discovered, but it is very near. After this wind will come an earthquake, which will overthrow those things which the wind had left. Be sure you fall not off. The earthquake being past, there will follow a fire that will consume the earthly rubbish and discover the treasure, but as yet you cannot see it. After all these things, and near daybreak, there shall be a great calm, and you shall see the daystar arise, and the darkness will disappear. You will conceive a great treasure; the chiefest thing and the most perfect is a certain exalted tincture, with which the world, if it served God and were worthy of such gifts, might be tinged and turned into the most pure gold.

THE PHILOSOPHER'S STONE

By Gen. N. B. BUFORD - 1807 - 1883

(This lecture on "The Philosopher's Stone" was delivered before the Chicago Philosophical Society by its president, General N. B. Buford.)

The most precious jewel ever coveted by man is the Philosopher's Stone. It has been diligently sought for in all ages. The science of Alchemy was cultivated earnestly during the Middle Ages by two classes of men. By one class the Philosopher's Stone was used to denigrate the agent by which the baser metals could be turned into gold. By another, and a wiser class, it was used synonymously with the "Pearl of Great Price!" The gold sought for was the Truth. This latter class of thinkers has existed from the earliest periods of which we possess written records, and its peculiar style, using symbols, as more expressive than words, is found abundantly in the Old and New Testaments. Both classes exercised a great influence over all Europe from the seventh to the seventeenth century. The student may discover the evidences that Dante, Shakespeare, and Cervantes were thoroughly acquainted with the science. Many of the "dark sayings" of these geniuses can only be understood by interpreting them in harmony with the mystical writers. The sonnets of Shakespeare, which have puzzled the learned ever since they were written; and his purely imaginative dramas, "Midsummer Night's Dream" and "The Tempest," are made clear in the light of nature, truth and reason, when thus interpreted. The same may be said of the allegory of "Marcella," in the early chapters of Don Quixote.

What I know of this science is mainly derived from the conversations and writings of General Ethan Allen Hitchcock, of whom I shall give you a brief account. He was the son of Judge Samuel Hitchcock, of Vermont, and the grandson of the celebrated Ethan Allen, whom you all remember, at the beginning of the War of the Revolution, demanded the surrender of Fort Ticonderoga, "In the name of the Great Jehovah and the Continental Congress!" General Hitchcock was born in 1798, graduated at West Point in 1817, served with his regiment in the Southern States, where, before he was twenty-one, he became noted for his metaphysical ideas and knowledge of the Platonic philosophy. He became commandant of the cadets at West Point, in 1831. Next, he served with distinction in the Florida and Mexican wars. After the latter, he traveled for two years in Europe, a student, and returned, singularly fitted to communicate the mystical ideas of the Hermetic philosophers, of whose writings he had become the possessor of more than one thousand volumes and pamphlets. He then became the General commanding our troops in California, where he continued from 1851 to 1854, during which time he frustrated attempts designed to separate our newly acquired territory on the Pacific slope from the Union. In consequence of this patriotic conduct, he was soon involved in an unpleasantness with the Secretary of War, Jefferson Davis, which led to his resignation in 1855. After this event he made his home in St. Louis, devoting himself solely to the acquisition of knowledge, and the writing and publishing his philosophical speculations. I pass over these now, soon to return to them, in order to state, that when the signs of the rebellion began to take form, after the election of Mr. Lincoln, he wielded the ablest pen in the West, publishing his articles in the St. Louis Republican, persuading the State of Missouri and the other border States to stand by the flag. In accordance with his noble principles, he was one of the first of the retired officers to volunteer his services to the Union. I shall not detail the facts that led to their tardy acceptance by the government; but, on the tenth of February, 1862, he was commissioned a Major-General, and assigned to duty at the War department, where he rendered valuable. services. He soon acquired the entire confidence of Mr. Stanton, the sagacious Secretary of War, and a higher place, the love of Mr. Lincoln.

General Hitchcock's first publication on what he used to call The Problem of Life was "Remarks on Alchemy," published in 1857, showing that the Philosopher's Stone was a symbol. It is to this work that I desire to draw your especial attention tonight; but, before I enter upon it, I think proper to notice his other writings, which, if properly studied, may prove the best introduction of the study of the ONE TRUTH, to which he devoted his age as well as his youth.

His second book, published in 1858, was entitled "Swedenborg, a Hermetic Philosopher," in which he proves that that remarkable man, who quoted no works of other authors, was a master of all the writings of the Alchemists; and that his method, as far as he had any, was built out of Spinoza. Next followed, in 1860, two volumes, "Christ the Spirit," being an attempt to state the primitive view of Christianity. To properly notice this great work would take up my whole evening. He interprets the Gospels so as to present their divine truths as the Spirit of Christ, which dwells in all men who are the true sons of God. The spirit of virtue, the spirit of conscience, the spirit of the soul communing with the Infinite, and obedient to His will. He makes clear to his readers, that among the Jews at the advent of Christ there was a secret society called the Essenes, whose ethical principles and religious observances were essentially the same as those taught in the New Testament - love of God, love of virtue, love of man. This sect is often spoken of in the Gospels, there called "the brethren." He makes it appear probable that the Gospels were the secret books of this society, and he is sustained in his interpretation of them by the writings of the learned Philo the Jew, of Alexandria, who was born twenty years before Jesus, and lived to an extreme age; and by Origen, one of the most learned of the Christian Fathers. I shall recommend this book to all my hearers by quoting the words of an eminent clergyman, who says of it:

"A sweeter moral atmosphere we never breathed than pervades every paragraph of these two volumes. There is no harshness, there is no intolerance, there is no dogmatism, no assumption of superior wisdom. Its charity is perfect, for there is no air of charitableness about it; it is the good will of an honest, believing and gentle mind. We can scarcely think of a theologian who might not with profit sit at the feet of this brave soldier and listen as he talks of religion."

Next, in 1863, he published "*The Red Book of Appin*," a fairy story. It, with other fairy stories, are interpreted. In it one may learn how to interpret the deepest mystics, and the most imaginative poets.

In 1865, he published "Remarks on the Sonnets of Shakespeare," which has proven a key for the understanding of that most Wonderful work, the puzzle of the scholars and commentators for nearly three centuries, now made as clear as they are beautiful and wise. The same year he published the poem of Spenser, "Collin

Clouts Come Home Againe," explained, to which he happily applied the insight and the learning exhibited in the previous volumes.

And last, in 1866, he published "Notes on the Vita Nuova" of Dante. He proves these three works were written in the Hermetic vein, and by understanding that science we at once see that Beatrice was not a mere woman, but to Dante a celestial vision - Heavenly Wisdom personified.

Now to my work. Our author has proved that MAN was the subject of Alchemy, and that the object of the ART was the perfection, or at least, the improvement of man. The salvation of man, his transformation from evil to good, or his passage from a state of nature to a state of grace, was symbolized under the figure of the transmutation of metals. The Alchemists all symbolized under words, gold, silver, lead; salt, sulphur, mercury; sol, luna, wine, etc. The various opinions of the writers on the questions of God, nature, and man, all developed from lint central point, which is MAN, the image of God. Now if these symbolic works had found no echo in the human heart, they would have perished; but the fact is, they have been preserved through all past ages, awakening as much interest now in the minds of those who study them as when first published, which proves they have struck a vein of imperishable truth.

The Alchemists were the reformers in the dark ages, when the spirit of religion was buried· under forms and ceremonies; when superstition was taught for truth, and the hierarchy was armed with civil power and used it to suppress all intellectual freedom. In that midnight of moral and intellectual darkness, it was a light from Heaven; but the truth was treated of in their books as the elixir of life, the universal medicine, the philosopher's stone, only understood by the initiated. The writings of these peculiar thinkers, these spiritually minded free men, were necessarily written in symbols, to secure them from the persecutions of the hierarchy of the inquisition, many of the writers were monks. The truth, when it finds a lodgment in the human heart, is predominant. The "still small voice" was their secret. They were the genuinely religious men of their time. Their writings prove that they were students of Plato and Aristotle; also, of mathematics and astronomy. It was they who were preparing the world for the discoveries in chemistry, in medicine, and the laws of the natural world which have been steadily increasing up to this time.

It was his superiority in knowledge that caused Roger Bacon to be called a magician, and Galileo to be compelled by the church to deny the fact that he had discovered that the earth moved.

The effulgence of this light of truth and science in spreading over Europe necessarily produced the great reformation, of which Martin Luther was the leader. He was acquainted with Alchemy, and translated one of the Hermetic books, "Theologia Germanica," in corroboration of his teachings; and the writings of a holy monk, Thomas a Kempis, who was one of them, from that time became equally popular with both Protestants and Catholics, which continues to be a fact at this day. I shall now quote some of these alchemical writers, and first, Sandivogius, who lived and wrote in 1650. "There is abundance of knowledge, yet but little truth known. I know of but two ways that are ordained for getting wisdom, namely: the Book of God and the book of Nature; and these also, but as they are read with reason. Many look upon the former as a thing below them; upon the latter, as a ground of atheism, and therefore neglect both. It is my judgment, that as to search the scriptures is most necessary; so without reason it is impossible to understand them. Faith without reason is but implicity. If I cannot understand by reason how a thing is, yet I will see that a thing is so, before I will believe it to be so. I will ground my believing upon reason; I will improve my reason by philosophy.

"When God made man after his own image, how was that? Was it not by making him a rational creature? Men, therefore, that lay aside reason, in the regarding of sacred mysteries, do but un-man themselves, and become involved in labyrinths of errors. Hence, their religion is degenerated into irritational notions. And further on: "The Most High Creator was willing to manifest all natural things unto man; wherefore, He showed to us that celestial things themselves were naturally made, by which His absolute and incomprehensible power and wisdom might be so much the more freely acknowledged; of all which things the Alchemists in the light of nature, as in a looking glass, have a clear sight. For which cause they esteemed this art, not out of covetousness for gold or silver, but for knowledge's sake, not only of all natural things, but also the power of the Creator; but they were willing to speak of the things only sparingly and figuratively, lest the Divine mysteries by which nature is illustrated should be discovered by the unworthy; which thou (reader), if thou knowest how to know thyself, and art not of a stiff neck, mayest easily comprehend, created as thou art in the likeness of the great world, yea, after the image of God."

The Arabians, at the highest of their power, when they had conquered Alexandria, all the North of Africa, and Spain, were for a time the most advanced philosophers and physicians of the civilized world. I next quote one of them, Alipilli:

"The highest wisdom consists in this, for man to know himself, because in him God has placed His eternal word, by which all things were made and upheld, to be his light and life, by which he is capable of knowing all things both in time and eternity. Therefore, let the high inquirers and reachers into the deep mysteries of nature, learn first to know what they have in themselves, before they seek into foreign matters without them; and by the divine power within them, let them first heal themselves, and transmute their own souls; then they may go on prosperously, and seek with good success the mysteries and wonders of God in all natural things.

"I admonish thee that desirest to dive into the inmost parts of nature, if that which thou seekest thou findest not within thee, thou wilt never find it without thee. The universal orb of the world contains not so great mysteries and excellencies as a little man, formed by God in his own image. And he who desires the primacy among the students of nature, will nowhere find a greater or better field of study than himself. So, with a loud voice I proclaim: O, man, know thyself! In thee is hid the treasure of treasures!"

In as clear a manner, George Ripley declares the subject of the stone, in the following lines:

"For as of one mass was made all things

Right, so must it in our practice be,

All our secrets of one image must spring:

In philosopher's books, therefore, who wishes may see,

Our stone is called the less world, one and three."

That is, the stone is man, of one nature, of body, soul, and spirit.

In the "Alchemists' Enchiridon," published in 1672, man is indicated as the stone, as follows:

"Now will I manifest to thee the nature of the stone of the philosophers, appareled with a triple garment, even this stone of riches and charity, the stone of relief from languishment; in which is contained every secret, being a divine mystery and gift of God, than which there is nothing in this world more sublime. "Therefore, diligently observe: it is appareled with a triple garment, that is to say, with a body, soul, and spirit."

Thus, again, it appears man is the central object in all alchemical books; yet not man as he is an individual, but as he is a Nature, containing or manifesting the great world, or as he is the Image of God.

I will next quote Geber, another Arabian, whose strange mode of expression gave rise to our word "gibberish."

"The artist should be intent on the true end only, because our art is reserved in the divine will of God, and is given to, or withheld from, whom He will." He speaks of the stone as a "medicine rejoicing and preserving the body in youth." This in alchemical language is immortality, and how can it be better preserve than as perpetual youth?

Here is one of the prescriptions for obtaining perpetual youth:

"Take a pound of persistence, and wash it with the water of your eyes; then let lie by your heart; then take of the best faith, hope, and charity, you can get a like quantity, and mix all together; use this confection every day. Then take both your hands full of good works and keep them close in a clear conscience, and use as occasion requires."

Had Ponce de Leon understood this recipe, he might have been saved his trials and journeys in Florida in pursuit of the fountain of perpetual youth.

No Alchemist supports his views by appeals to authority. He would have every doctrine tested by "the possibility of nature." He acknowledges no master but One. He would have all things brought to the standard of truth; but truth must be submitted to God, who is All in All - the One Master.

The Alchemists in Christian countries received the doctrines of Jesus as true in themselves, or in the nature of things; but they were not accepted as true simply on the ground that Jesus announced them, with them the "wisdom of the doctrine established the truth of Christianity, not the miracles. The wisdom of the doctrine is the truth of it, and this is the authority of God."

I now come to the announcement that the conscience is the starting point in pursuit of the philosopher's stone. A consideration of more importance that all others is that conscience cannot be said to err; in other words, the conscience cannot sin. It sits in judgment upon every man, approving the good and condemning the bad, but in itself it is incorruptible. When we say a man has a bad conscience, we do not properly speak of the conscience, but of the man, whom a good conscience condemns! The error is not in the conscience, but in the judgment employed in applying means for the accomplishment of ends. The conscience has reference to ends, and not to means. A man is approved or condemned according to the end he aims at. If the end is approved by the wise, a mistake in the means, however lamented, commands pity and not condemnation.

The highest of all religious duties is that of obedience to God. It is right for the creature to obey the Creator. An obedience rendered on any other ground than right would not be free; and if produced by hope of reward or fear of punishment is destitute of virtue. A sense of duty made cheerful by love is the true ground of that perfect obedience to God which it is the object of all pure religion to secure. Fear never made, or can make, a man religious.

The key to a true life is nothing else but a true life itself; and this is the root of all philosophy which aims at the elevation of man, and in fine it is the root itself, or rather it is root, body, and branches. In vain, then, do men go out of themselves for that which can only be found within themselves.

By symbolism the Alchemists escape the difficulty of treating the subject in ordinary language; for the meaning of the terms employed must be taught by the nature of things; they must be tested by "the possibility of nature." They tell us, whoever departs from nature is lost, and must commence his work anew. Whoever is without the bounds of nature is in error.

When the Alchemists speak of a long life all one of the gifts of the stone, they mean immortality; when they attribute to the stone the virtues of a universe medicine, the cure of all diseases; they mean to deny the positive nature of evil, and thus deny its perpetuity; when they tell us that the stone is "the cut throat of covetousness and of all evil desires," they mean that all evil affections disappear in the light of truth, as darkness yields to the presence of light.

Hermetic philosophy is not a doctrine; it is properly a practice. It is the practice of truth, justice, and goodness. Now the law of conscience being the law of God in the soul of man, obedience to it becomes of the first importance to all men. Very few, in these days, recognize the conscience as the oracle of God, the Immanuel, and guide to his presence. The power of man is defined by the knowledge of God - his acceptance of it, and his submission to it. A right view of this will explain the power and weakness of man, the power being measured by reason, the weakness by passion. Such lessons as these eminently fit the Hermetic philosopher for the instruction of young men. Passion unseats reason. They repeatedly cry out: "O Man, Know Thyself."

All the Hermetic writers quote the Egyptian Hermes, not the later Greek one, as of men, the highest source of thought and knowledge, or the Logos embodied, and hence called him Trismegistus. The Neoplatonists also attributed to him the same superiority. The Hermetic creed is embraced in what is - called the Smaragdine (or Emerald) Table. It is attributed to Hermes; but its real history, like that of the church creed itself, is entirely unknown. I shall proceed to compare them. It is admitted both by the churchmen and philosophers that the principal points are in harmony in the two creeds on the vital points of both of them. The Hermetic creed on the Smaragdine Table reads thus:

I. This is true and far distant from a lie: whatsoever is below is like that which is above; and that which is above is like that which is below, by this is acquired and perfected the miracle of one thing. There is a positive affirmation of something as true; and God is truth; in the above and below we recognize the heaven and earth of the creed: for these are declared to be the work of God, who cannot make anything contrary to his own nature. Now, the clear parallel to the first article of the church creed is as follows:

(1) I believe in God the Father Almighty, maker of heaven and earth. The second article of the Hermetic creed is:

II. Also, as all things were made from one, by the help of one; so all things are made from one thing by conjunction. By this (one) we recognize the Logos, word, in the Gospel of John. This word, in the creed, is the person. The second article of the church creed reads:

(2) And in Jesus Christ, his only son, our Lord. The third article of the Hermetic creed reads:

III. The father thereof is the sun, and the mother is the moon; the wind carries it in its belly, and the nurse thereof is the earth.

Here the sun and the moon must be taken as symbols of the invisible father and the visible mother of all things, commonly called nature. The allusion to wind and to the earth is a declaration that living things must have air and body, life being the subject of both creeds.

The third article of the church creed expresses this, thus:

(3) Who was conceived by the Holy Ghost, (and) born of the Virgin Mary. The fourth article of the Hermetic creed reads:

IV. This the mother or fountain of all perfection; and its power is perfect and entire, if it be changed into earth.

This article will recall to your minds the fact that John, the beloved disciple, was perfected at the foot of the cross by the reception of the mother, which in the Hermetic creed is called the mother, or fountain of all perfection. The earth is here used as a symbol of what the Hermetic philosophers call the fixation of the matter of the philosopher's stone, which is their mode of teaching the necessity of practice; no doctrine being considered as established until introduced into life and made actual by practice. The fifth article of the Hermetic creed reads thus:

V. Separate the earth from the fire, and the subtle and thin from the gross and thick; but prudently, with long suffering, gentleness, and patience, and. with wisdom and judgment.

This means the preparation of their art: the purification of the matter of the stone; in one word, the purification of man; the separation of the earth from the fire, the pure from the impure, which can only be done by wisdom and patience; there being nothing more difficult in our lives than to bring about a reformation of a man confirmed in e vii habits.

The sixth article of the Hermetic creed still refers to the one.

VI. It ascends from earth up to heaven, and descends again from the heavens to the earth, and receives the powers and efficacy of the superiors and inferiors. The parallel of this is found in the articles of the church creed from the fourth to the eighth. They all refer to the one, who is the subject of both creeds.

(4) (He, the one) suffered under Pontius' Pilate, was crucified, dead, and buried;

(5) He descended into hell;

(6) The third day he arose from the dead;

(7) He ascended into heaven, and sitteth on the right hand of God the Father Almighty; From whence he shall come to judge the quick and the dead.

In the church creed, the one is said to pass from earth to heaven, and from thence descend again to earth with wonderful powers, which now follows in the seventh and eighth articles of the Hermetic creed.

VII. In this work, you acquire to yourself the wealth and glory of the whole world; drive therefore from you all cloudiness, or obscurity, and darkness, and blindness. The wealth and glory signify truth and wisdom, which the spirit may acquire in the successful experiences of life. The parallel of the eighth church article above recited, is found in the article of the Hermetic creed.

VIII. For the work, increasing or going on in strength, adds strength to strength, forestalling and over-topping all other fortitudes and powers, and is able to subjugate and conquer all things, whether they be thin and subtle, or thick and solid bodies Here the power of the one over the quick and the dead, the power over all things in the church creed, is parallelled by the thin and subtle (the living), and the thick and solid (the dead) in the Hermetic creed.

The two creeds are evidently couched in mystical language, and they refer to the same mystery, represented as history in the visible church, but spiritually discerned, by the followers of the esoteric view. The remaining articles of the church creed are instructions in points of faith.

(9) I believe in the Holy Ghost,

(10) The Holy Catholic Church; the communion of saints;

(11) The forgiveness of sins;

(12) The resurrection of the body; and the life everlasting. Amen.

The Hermetic creed concludes as follows:

IX. In this manner was the world made; and hence are wonderful conjunctions or joining's together of matter and parts there, and the marvelous, when in this way it was done, by which these wonders are effected.

X. And for this cause I am called Hermes Trismegistus; for that I have the knowledge and understanding of the philosophy of the three principles of the universe. My doctrine or discourse, which I have here delivered concerning the solar work, is complete and perfect.

This is the whole of the creed of the Hermetic philosophers who saw in it the doctrine of what they call the great work of making the philosopher's stone. The three principles of the universe is another expression for the trinity, which they all believed in, though they entered into no controversies about persons, substances or things.

That Swedenborg was one of the most remarkable men of modern times is believed by all the scholars who have studied his writings. He was a proficient in al the sciences, an engineer of genius, and was noble in the highest attributes of man. When about fifty years old his thoughts were exclusively turned to religion. He calls his new state the opening of his internal sight; as if a supernatural influence had been exerted upon him, which we attributed to the Lord. General Hitchcock has proved that he was thoroughly acquainted with the principles of the Hermetic writers, and also with Spinoza. The principle upon which the heavenly arcana was written is usually called that of correspondence. He thus states it:

"There is not anything in the mind to which something of the body does not correspond; and this which corresponds may be called the embodying of that." In the Smaragdine Table, thus read, this principle was thus announced:

"That which is above is as that which is beneath, and that which is beneath is as that which is above, to work the miracles. of one thing."

The "above" and "beneath" are the spiritual and natural worlds of Swedenborg; and the "one thing" is the Lord; the life of the two worlds. In the language of Swedenborg, the Lord is the end, the spiritual world the cause, and the natural world is the effect; yet the effect contains the cause, and both express the life, call them salt, sulphur, and mercury, and we shall express the same in alchemical language. The natural world, the visible is a world of effect, and symbolizes or "corresponds," to the spiritual world, and would be nothing without it, as the spiritual, in its turn, would be nothing without the life, the "one thing" in all. This doctrine has been thus expressed:

"Heaven above, heaven beneath, stars above, stars beneath. All that is above is also beneath. Understand this and be happy."

The principle of correspondence is also found in Plato: "His intelligible word, or world of ideas, contains the types or patterns of all natural things in the universe; our houses, our ships, our furniture, and our implements."

The Alchemists were of the opinion that true religion cannot be taught. It may be preached about, talked about, and written about; but there always remains something in the depths of a religious soul which cannot be expressed in language. Hence the line:

"Expressive silence muse his praise," is the best utterance of a true religious feeling. The final step, the entrance into "light," is not taken by any force of mere human will. This is one of the reasons for the use in all past ages of symbolic writing.

We may now see how the Hermetic philosophers handled the subject of man's free will. To obtain the idea of God's omnipotence in the usual sense, and of the eternity and immutability of His decrees, as extending to all things, and at the same time, the notion of man's free agency, as if he possessed an actual power of his own, is impossible. Whoever holds these two opinions must necessarily carry about a conflict within himself. One or both sets of ideas should be purified, in order to produce harmony. If the philosopher's stone could solve this question, it might be worth seeking if for nothing else. Let us hear the Hermetic writers:

"Let the power of God be called sulphur, and the power of man, mercury; then find a salt that shall be their unity. This is the problem. The philosopher may find that the controversy lies between two of the elements or principles of man, and must last until the third principle is recognized, which, though last discovered, is the first in order, and stands above, as it were, the other two, and through it decides, though it takes no part in the controversy. This third principle, when awakened in man, his God given intuition, he no longer 'opines' about things, but 'knows.' The Alchemist call this knowledge 'The gift of God.' God must be the author and finisher of our faith, if we have a true faith!"

Perhaps you may discover an analogy in what I shall next quote.

"Two of the principles of the Alchemists are called extremes, but an invisible one includes the two inseparably, as one idea with two images. When the idea is realized, its illustrations become multitudinous. Let us examine this one: Wronging and being wronged are the two extremes, caused by excess and deficiency; then comes justice by equality in the middle. Justice is the regulating principle of the universe, operating silently and invisibly, but as surely, as it is absolutely beyond the control of man. The link between the human and Divine, matter and spirit, has never been revealed. Is not this the philosopher's stone?"

It is impossible in a single hour to more than indicate the symbolism used by the Hermetic philosophers. I shall indicate a few of them: salt, sulphur, and mercury are the words commonly used for body, soul and spirit, but not invariably. The way indicates the conscience. A circle indicates nature now returning into itself. We use the word nature for the true mother; the gives us a clue to walk by, to guide use if we lose the clue, we fall into difficulties; her laws are everlasting commandments. The hand is used as the symbol of power; a fearful beast for a bad passion; a tree for a firm principle, rooted in the ground with its branches ascending to heaven. The black state of the matter is the one that can only be made white, by repentance.

Six boys and a little girl, the seven champions of Christendom, Prudence, Temperance, Fortitude, Justice, Faith, Hope, and Charity. The plain ring indicates Humility. His horse, his pride. He turns his horse, indicates he reflects. The sun, the all-seeing eye, the moon, are used as emblems of the reason, the conscience, and the affections. The flail, that which separates the wheat from the straw, truth from error. The sea, life.

Gold, truth. I have copied in a note-book more than two hundred of these symbols and their interpretations.

I shall next quote Eckhart, one of the German mystics, born 1250, became a monk, and died in 1329. He did not use Hermetic language, and so was condemned by the hierarchy, but escaped punishment by dying.

He affirmed: "All religious truth lay within the sphere of human reason. The universe is that which truly exists. The soul is immaterial. The faculties of the soul are the external senses, and the lower and higher faculties. The lower faculties are the empirical understanding, the heart (organ of passions) and the appetitive faculty. The higher faculties are memory, reason, and will. The soul is not subject to the conditions of time and space The soul is something intermediate between God and created things. The highest activity of the soul is that of cognition. There are three species of cognition: sensible, rational, and super-rational; only the last reaches the whole truth. Whatever can be expressed by words is comprehended by the lower faculties, but the higher ones are not satisfied with so little; they constantly press further on, till they reach the source from whence the soul originally flowed forth. Knowledge is the foundation of all essence, the ground of love, the determining power of the will. Love is the principle of all virtues; love strives after the good.

The lowest faculties of the soul must be subordinated to the highest, and the highest to God. At the judgment day, it is not God who pronounces judgment, but man, who passes judgment on himself!"

I have quoted enough to show that the mystical elements in Eckhart were his conception of the highest activity of the reason as an immediate intellectual intuition; his demand that the individual self should be given up, and his doctrine of complete union with God as the supreme end of man. It was from reading General Hitchcock's books, commencing fifteen years ago, that my mind became fixed in the study of philosophy. I discovered the difference between thinking, essences, and opinions. The doctrine of an unchangeable order of Providence is as old as philosophy. The art of prophesying is divination concerning the future from things that are present and past. For neither is the original of anything with out a cause, nor the foreknowledge of any thing without a reason. It this is, that *preceded*; again, if this *is*, that *shall be*. The knowledge of the consequence is a rational thing; but sense gives the anticipation to reason.

The union of sense and reason in the soul is said to be a mystical marriage. On the one side nature is seen as a blind force; on the other a life perfectly free. That there is a com· bination of these views resulting in a beautiful harmony, is the assertion of the Hermetic philosophers, while they have told us that their view is an incommunicable secret through the senses. This, in religion, I take to be a species of inspiration which has been felt in all ages. It is the common ground of true poetry, true philosophy, and true religion. The philosopher alone may attempt to explain this unity, but he is not satisfied with what he says. He told of it as the immutable; upon which, those who hear infer a fatality, that he does not mean at all. But after exhausting words and endeavoring to enunciate the unspeakable, the pious soul calls it God, and forbids all attempts to represent it by images.

In one word, the spirit is free, but finds its freedom only in recognizing itself in God, and then can submit to nothing else. Nothing in the universe can be proved but by the assumption of something unchangeable, not requiring proof; but this is God, conceived in His immutability. It is because God does not change, and anything remains true from one instant to another.

In conclusion, I must be allowed to say that it is with unaffected diffidence I have discoursed here tonight. I felt sure I could not do it justice. I even feared I might not make no impression at all. But it was through this class of studies that I found my may into the portico of the thinkers, and I have continued to find the way pleasant.

Careful study of these writings has enabled me to interpret a fairy story; next to discover, as I believe, Shakespeare's meaning in handling the problem of life. "He made nature his love, and she made him her child." Next to interpret Goethe's hidden treasures in "Wilhelm Meister," which is written in the Hermetic vein from beginning to end. Perhaps my best lesson was to learn "To try all things by the possibility of nature," and was thus led on to the study of Descartes, Leibnitz, Spinoza, thus back to Plato, and thus the fountains of Greek thought; thence forward to Kant and Hegel.

Have I found the philosopher's stone? Have I found the pearl of great price? No. To those who'd find it the transmutation will be real. It will turn the wicked to righteousness. The God spoken of by the searchers for the stone, is Truth, pure and simple. "Reason is the eye of the soul," for, as the eye cannot see without light, so neither can reason know without instruction. "It is the gift of God."

THE ROSICRUCIAN'S

By ALEX. WILDER, M. D. - 1823 - 1909

The first attention of the great world was called to the Rosicrucian's in 1610 by the appearance of an anonymous little book entitled *The Discovery of the Brotherhood of the Honorable order of the Rosy Cross*, dedicated to the scholars of Europe. It stated that Christian Rosenkreutz had come from the East where he had acquired a thorough knowledge of arcane learning. He died in 1484, and it appears that he had enjoined his disciples not to make his doctrines public till the expiration of one hundred and twenty years. I notice a slight variance in this from the statement of Lord Bulwer Lytton: "The Arabians of Damus in 1378 taught to a wandering German the secrets which founded the institution of the Rosicrucian's." Nikolai, the author of "Temple Herren," assigns the authorship of "The Discovery," etc., to Johann Valentine Andrea, a Lutheran Mystic divine of Wurtemburg. The Emperor of Germany at the time was Rudolf II, the greatest patron of magical and mystic studies ever recorded in history. The book created a prodigious excitement. It contained the descriptions of a select body of eight men, who abode in a secret crypt styled "The Temple of the Holy Ghost," where they prosecuted the study of occult lore. Search was made for it with great eagerness. Charlatans everywhere in Germany pretended to belong to the Mysterious Brotherhood and reaped golden harvests from the credulity of the ignorant. Occult medical treatment possesses a wonderful fascination in our own day, and the pretense of extraordinary learning gives ample occasion for superstitious arrogance and unprincipled stupidity.

The clergy assailed the little volume and invoked on the head of its author the fires of heaven, declaring that he ought to be broken on the wheel for his impiety. Such were the atrocious remedies of the Middle Ages for dissent and protest. The crusades against the Manichean Provengals, the sanguinary wars against the Saracens, themselves but Christian sectaries, the wholesale proscriptions and executions of the *soldiers of Mithras* after mock trials for witchcraft, the burning of Temple Knights, the massacres of the Waldenses in cold blood by the soldiers of the infamous dukes of

Savoy - a crime which cost them the inheritance of the British throne -are so many arguments for keeping knowledge secret. Our own country is not exempt. When Bishop Ives turned Roman Catholic and Henry Kiddie announced himself a Spiritualist, their former associates impugned their soundness of mind. We have madhouses, public and private, in which persons may be incarcerated for months and years upon a process differing little in form and operation from the *lettres de cachet*, by virtue of which Frenchmen were immured without trial or even crime, in the Bastile during the reign of Pompadour.

The *Doketae* of the early Christian centuries had the maxim: "Learn to know all, but keep thyself unknown." The writer of the little story of Rosenkreutz and his Mystic Order, obeyed that rule. The Brotherhood who are known as Rosicrucian's have kept themselves so thoroughly secret, that although the philosopher Descartes advertised all over Germany for information concerning them, he utterly failed.

The Rosy Cross, or red rose impaled upon a cross, had been the badge of the Templars. Despite their suppression in 1307, this Order continued as late as the reign of Francis I., who burned four of them. That king had also caused the Albigenses to be extirpated from Provence with extraordinary ferocity. Like all the Gnostics and Ophites they had secret doctrines, symbols and tokens for mutual recognition. The symbols of the Rosicrucian's were generally like those of these societies. They interwove in their system religion and philosophy, the latter comprising alchemy and astrology, and made use of the peculiar dictum of the alchemists and other mystics to express their ideas. To this fact much of the obscurity is due, which many will find in the treatise of Hargrave Jennings.

Mr. Jennings's book relates to a topic which has more than once created the liveliest interest in Europe. The learned have searched carefully for the *Temple Herren*; the half-learned have denied its existence. The modern school of disciples of the Sankhya and Epikcuros, who have bowed God out of the universe, have but jeers for all such matters. With them the day for sober argument has passed, if indeed, it ever dawned.

One blemish is on Mr. Jennings's work, a fault too frequently common. The sentences are often painfully interwrought, so as to nullify their meaning. Some may say that this is done for purposes of concealment of the arcane idea. It is a bad explanation, and the author has himself set it aside by the remark that the Rosicrucian's "were really men appearing like real men, carrying, in very deed, through the world, *eternally-forbidden secrets*, safe, however, in the fact that they were sure never to be believed." We are tempted therefore to hold him to the rule, that the obscurely uttered is the obscurely thought. We give him the benefit however of his own plea, similar to that, perhaps, of Herodotus:

"We have drawn to ourselves a certain portion of reticence, up to which margin we may freely comment; though we absolutely refuse to overpass it with too distinct explanations, or to enlarge further on the strange persuasions of the Rosicrucian's."

There is no fault to be found with this; but we suggest that conscientious readers will thank a man who states accurately what they agree with, and will be almost equally grateful to the one who states clearly what they most distrust from. "What they want is either truth or error; not a muddle between them."

Lord Lytton's two romances, "Zanoni" and "The Strange Story," give much interesting information respecting the Mysterious Brotherhood, and will repay the curious for their careful study. There have been many Glyndons, occasionally a Zanoni, possibly a Mejnour; is there anywhere a Louis Grayle living out of whom the immortal entity has perished?

The author of "The Discovery," etc., was familiar with the writings of Paracelsus and Van Helmont. He has made liberal use of their ideas and expressions. Indeed, the following distinguished persons, all of them proficient in kabbalistic and theosophy learning, are included as Rosicrucian adepts, namely Raymond Lully (died, 1315); John Reuchlin, the instructor of Martin Luther; Giovanni Picus Mirandola (died, 1494); Cornelius Agrippa (died, 1535); John Baptist Van Helmont (died, 1644); Henry More (died, 1687); and Robert Flood (died, 1637); from whose works Mr. Jennings has largely compiled his treatise. In the little book ascribed to Andrea, the declaration appears that the Rosicrucian's contemplated no political movement hostile to the ruling powers. Their aim was to diminish human suffering, diffuse education, advance learning, science, and enlightenment; and in short to substitute love and benevolence for the antagonisms of self-interest and unworthy ambition.

Nevertheless, the readers of "Zanoni" will observe a vigorous protest against the doctrine of equality among mankind. "Level all conditions today, and you only smooth away all obstacles to tyranny tomorrow. A nation that aspires to quality is unfit for freedom. Diffuse all the knowledge the earth contains equally over all mankind today, and some men will be the wiser tomorrow. The wiser the few in one generation, the wiser will be the multitude in the next. These men, to commence their era of improvement and equality are jealous even of the Creator. They would deny an intelligence – a God!"

The Rosicrucian doctrine, it need not be added, is essentially theistic. Its adepts were often members of Christian communions. They mingled in the pursuits of everyday life, passed for men of business, served others kindly but in an undemonstrative· manner, with no apparent motive except a kind disposition, yet lived in a world apart, and were taken for anything except what they really were.

There was a peculiar method of expression in their writings which renders it somewhat difficult to comprehend whether they were discoursing about physical sciences, or in symbols. They certainly professed to know the art of transmutation, or making gold, and the compounding of the elixir of life by which to prolong existence for an indefinite period. And more, also, they claimed the control of nature and the invisible forces and spirits – that God was their master and all else obligated to their service. How far this was figurative speech, as the late General Hitchcock interpreted it, we may conjecture; but plainly Lord Lytton and Mr. Jennings regard it as more or less literal.

In the writings of Count de Gabalis we find the address of the Grand Master to neophytes, which shows what was actually claimed. The following is a copy:

"You are now to learn how to command all nature. God alone will be your master; philosophers alone will be your equals. The supernal intelligences will be ambitious to obey your desire; the evil demons will not dare approach where you are. Your voice will make them tremble in the depths of the abyss. The invisible hosts of the four elements will deem themselves happy to minister to you.

"Have you learned what it is to be a man?

"Are you not weary of serving as a slave – you who were born for dominion?"

Despite any seeming charlatanry which this may seem to exhibit, a defined philosophy permeates every doctrine. Man possesses a threefold mode of existence. The animal or physical life is rudimentary, and characterized by impressions, appetites and necessary activities. Next is the psychic, from which proceed purpose and self-consciousness. Beyond and above these is the spiritual *esse*, or real thing. "We believe in God," says Jacobi, "not by reason of the Nature which conceals him, but by reason of the supernatural in others, which alone reveals him and proves him to exist."

Can metals be transmuted? It is reported that Raymond Lully produced gold for the use of Edward I of England. Thomas Vaughan (Eugenius Philalethes), "tells us of himself that going to a goldsmith to sell twelve hundred marks' worth of gold, the man told him at first sight that it never came out of the mines, but was the production of art, as it was not of the standard of any known kingdom." General Hitchcock thinks this figurative of celestial gold, which cannot be made current among men, because "the natural man discerneth not the things of the spirit, because they are foolishness to him and can only be spiritually discerned." Yet I do not see why a knowledge of atoms and a law of combinations and forces, would not enable a person to refine ore substance and procure its change into another form.

The Elixir of Life. Is not the immortality which spiritual life denotes, the true elixir vita:, and the regeneration of man from a sensual to a spiritual life, the true transformation of base metal into gold? Did Paracelsus mean more than this? Did the brethren of the Holy Cross? Did any of the Alchemists or Hermetists?

Some have supposed the legend of the Wandering Jew, whom death overlooked, to have been derived from some conception of the Rosicrucian's. "All that we profess to do is this, said Mejnour to Glyndon," to find out the secrets of the human frame, to know why the parts ossify and the blood stagnates, and to apply continual preventives to the effects of time. This is not magic! it is the art of medicine rightly understood."

Artephius is said to have invented a kabbalistic magnet which attracted the aura or "mysterious spirit of human efflorescence and prosperous bodily growth out of young men," so that he could apply it to himself. The story of King David and Abishag is directly in point. Physicians have observed the enhancing of some persons' vital forces by sleeping or only social intimacy with those more vigorous than themselves; and public speakers know well how they are weakened or strengthened by persons in their audience. It is more than likely that oriental harems are often supplied with women for the express purpose of recruiting exhausted vital energy by this form of vampirism.

Robert Boyle, however, mentions a medicated preparation which was given to an old woman of seventy, and restored so many phenomena of maidenhood as to alarm her and compel its discontinuance. The story is also told of a Signor Gualdi, who appeared in Venice in the seventeenth century, who exhibited to a visitor a picture of himself by Titian, then two hundred years dead. Thomas Vaughan, "who certainly was a Rosicrucian adept, if there ever was one, led a wandering life and fell often into great perplexities and dangers from the mere suspicion that he possessed extraordinary secrets. He was born about the year 1612, and it was believed by those of his fraternity" as late as 1740, that he was still living. "Nay," says the writer quoted, "it is further asserted, that this very individual is the president of the Illuminated in Europe, and that he sits as such in all their annual meetings."

Nevertheless, "there may have been men who have possessed these gifts, that is, the power of making gold and of perpetuating their lives," who despised a wealth that they could not enjoy, and declined a perpetuated life which could only add to their weariness. There is the languishment for the ever. lost original home in this tearful mortal state."

Why the Rosicrucian's are a Secret Order. "We of the secret knowledge," says Robert Fludd, "do wrap ourselves in mystery, to avoid the objurgation and importunity or violence of those who conceive that we cannot be philosophers unless we put our knowledge to some ordinary worldly use. There is scarcely one who thinks about us who does not believe that our society has no existence; because, as he truly declares, he has never met any of us. And he concludes that there is no such brotherhood, because, in his vanity, we do not seek him to be our fellow."

Poverty and Chastity. "Maidhood and virginity is a phenomenon independent of creation, and bears through the worlds, visible and invisible, the world's immortal, the impress and seal upon its forehead, of God's Rest, not of his Activity. Hence, its sacredness in all religions and under all beliefs." In plainer speech, Activity is masculine, and Rest, as its contrast, is abstinence from production. Nature means "bringing forth."

The Rosicrucian's held that God was to be known supernaturally, above the action and operation of nature. Indeed, in the world of nature, he is veiled, hidden away, and it is impossible to know him. Hence, the Illuminated brothers regarded the celibate state as infinitely more consonant with the inventions of Providence. "It is not generally known," says Mr. Jennings, "that the true Rosicrucian's bound themselves to obligations of comparative poverty and absolute chastity in the world, with certain dispensations and remissions. that fully answered their purpose; for they were not necessarily solitary people; on the contrary they were frequently gregarious, and mixed freely with all classes, though privately admitting no law but their own."

Old Mejnour, in his cloister, calm and passionless, living on through the ages, and Zanoni, still young with all his weight of years since Chaldea was a country, yet capable of love and its sacrifices, and ready to lay off existence for another's sake, are pretty fair illustrations.

Fire Worship. The early men believed that they lived after dying. Observing that warmth characterized the living they venerated fire as denoting the Great Ancestral Spirit – the Father in heaven. It was not the God, but only his symbol. The gods appeared in fire, not because they were constituted of it, but because it was most like them. Every religion, Hamitic, Semitic, Aryan – was a fire religion. The central fire burned on the altar in the secret crypt of every sanctuary, alike for Mazda, Agui, Yava, Moloch, and Apollo.

The Assyrian Magi carried the moving flame before the marching hosts, and their Bedouin kinsmen in advance of the caravan – "a pillar of cloud by day and a column of fire by night." All over Asia, Africa, Europe, and America are the fire symbols. The menhir or dolmen, the monolith, the baitulos, the obelisk, pyramid, triangle, church spire, each denotes the flame, and typifies the God who appears in fire. The serpent with his head darting thither, and thither, and running along the ground without organs of locomotion, was received as the living model of the flame. It typifies also the intestinal structure of the body, which is really its essential portion. So, too, the umbilicus is in its way a serpent. From the navel of Vishnu proceeded the lotos and Brahma came forth. Our umbilical connection is never really severed. As the remotest twig is connected with the trunk of the tree and draws sap from it, so we all in an analogous manner, derive vital influxes from all who precede us, by that great maternal chain which extends for each of us back into the indefinite past. All this, too, the fire symbolizes.

The torch, the candle, the bonfire, have the same arcane meaning and are so used whether by Pagans, Moslems, Jews, or Christians.

The Unseen Spirits and Potencies. The horseshoe placed over a door, the pentacle or "wizard's foot," have been a theme of merriment for some, and regarded as a superstition by others. Paracelsus taught of elementary and elemental spirits. Bulwer Lytton describes them "some of surpassing wisdom, some of horrible malignity, some hostile as fiends to men, others as gentle as messengers between earth and heaven."

"It is awing thought," says our author, "but spirits and supernatural embodiments -unperceived by our limited, vulgar senses- may make their daily walk among us, invisible in the ways of the world. It may indeed be that they are sometimes suddenly happened upon, or, as it were, surprised. The world, although so silent, may be noisy with ghostly feet. The unseen ministers may every day pass in and out among our ways, and we all the time think we have the world to ourselves. It is, as it were, to this inside, unsuspected world, that these recognitive, deprecatory signs of horseshoes and of charms are addressed; that the harming presences, unprovoked may pass harmless; that the zealous watch of the Unseen over us may be assuaged in the acknowledgment; that the unrecognized presences amidst us, if met with an unconsciousness for which man cannot be accountable, may not be offended with carelessness in regard of them for which he may be punishable."

This World and The Next. The Rosicrucian's held that all things visible and invisible were produced by the contention of light and darkness. They, therefore, contained a deposit of light which it may take ages to evolve. All minerals have in this spark of light the rudimentary possibility of plants and growing organisms; all plants have rudimentary sensitives which might (in the ages) enable them to perfect and transmute into locomotive new creatures, lesser or higher in their greater or nobler or meaner in their functions; thus all may pass off by sideroads into more distinguished highways of completer advance – allowing their original spark of light to expand and thrill with higher and. more vivid force, and to urge forward with more abounding, informed purpose.

The Rosicrucian's claimed not to be circumscribed by the limits of the present world, but to be able to pass into the next, to work in it and to come back safe out of it, bring them trophies with them – gold, and the elixir of life. Man was to have lived as the angels, of an impregnable, impassable vitality; taking his respiration, not by short snatches, as it were, but as out of the great cup of the centuries. He was to be the spectator of nature – not nature his spectator. The real objects of the adepts were in truth to remain no longer slaves to those things supposed to by necessities, but to remove back to Heaven's original intentions, to indicate the purpose of God, and tread degradation under foot.

It will be seen that the Rosicrucian do-es not discard the scriptures. He only looks into their interior, away from their apparent sense which is illusory and often untruthful. The man is ignorant who deems the mystic an unbeliever.

The Mystic Sleep. The author of the work "The Rosicrucian's" is far from being clear in his utterances respecting sleep and its revelations. The mode of expression which he employs is not attractive to me. It is not so difficult to understand, but it has a disagreeable verbosity which wearies, and finally creates a feeling of dissatisfaction.

Here is Bulwer Lytton: "Man's first initiation is in TRANCE. In dreams commences all human knowledge; in dreams hovers over measureless space the first faint bridge between spirit and spirit - the world and the worlds beyond."

Mr. Jennings says: "Our highest knowledge – the most refined 'sum up' of the thinnest sighted metaphysics, is peremptorily forced back upon us when we sway beyond the practice of 'second causes.' All is guess over that brink. All is cloud where the pathway ends. Man falls asleep helpless when the great veil is dropped over him to isolate his understanding. All is possible in 'sleep' because dreams are in life. God is in sleep. And God, who is in sleep, although he is a reality away from us, is a delusion when sought to be demonstrated to us. And sleep – which is men's thoughts, or the dreams are – is the stumbling block over which the whole comprehensible theory of man parts into nothing, and falls into obscurity; as in which dream he is himself alone, perhaps mad. "Man is not a maker. Man gets nothing that is outside of him. He only obtains that which is already in him. He is in this world. But he is not of another world. His helplessness, unsupported, is perfectly ridiculous. He only lives - forgetting himself. He 'falls asleep' blindly 'into the morrow!'"

There have been secret fraternities as far back as the history of mankind. All the ancient priesthoods in every country had mysteries and a secret society among themselves. Ancient science was kept carefully hidden. It may have been necessary; some, like swine, tread all learning under foot; others, like dogs, tear the teacher. Besides, knowledge is power; and they who possess it are the kings of men. It is too fashionable to decry the clergy as our lords and tyrants; they are not even freemen in a proper sense. In Protestant Christendom there is no real priest-caste; and among the Romanists, I suspect the lower clergymen are outside the pale.

There were philosophical societies, arcane like the Gnostics, and Eclectic Platonists, for many centuries. The Pagans, who after Theodosius, adhered to their worship, hid their secrets, their initiation, and their mystic jargon. I conjecture the magic and witchcraft of the Middle Ages to have been the Mithraic Institute which had been disseminated through the Roman empire.

I suppose that the Rosicrucian's have existed; I doubt whether there are any now. All of whom I knew that pretended to be such were charlatans. None of our present secret societies antedate that Order; certainly, they do not come up at its sublime ideal. There may be something of the kind in the East, but the Moslems have pretty effectually annihilated the most of them. The communes of later date can hardly be considered as heirs or successors of the old brotherhoods. If any test was required to show this it would be found in their love of display, their meretricious exhibitions, and their assiduous endeavors to become notorious.

CRYPTIC QUATERNIONS

A. D. A. M. "Anatole, Dysis, Arctos, Mesembrion" (The initials of the four stars, representing the four quarters of the earth, forming the name Adam, says Bede).

A. G. L. A. "Atah Gihor Lolam Adonai" (Thou art mighty forever, O LORD). On the Shield of David.

E. L. O. M. "Eagle, Lion, Ox, Man" (the initial of the Cherubim, also the ancient division of the Zodiac.)

H R D M. "Heredem," or Heredom, perhaps from the Greek, "the holy house." Royal Order of Scotland: 1° Heredom. 2° Rosy Cross. Tradition has it that the Order originated in the Island of I-Colm-Kill.

I. A. A. T. "Ignis. Aer, Aqua, Terra" (Fire, Air, Water, Earth. On the rings of German Rose Croix Masons.

I. N. R. I. "Iesus Nazarenus Rex Iudreorum" (Jesus of Nazareth the King of the Jews). On the Cross.

I. N. R. L. "Igne Natura Renavator Integra" (By fire nature is perfectly renewed). A Rosicrucian explanation.

I. H. S. V. "In Hoc Signo Vinces" (In this sign we conquer).

I H V H. (The Tetragrammaton.) "Jehovah."

I. N. R. I. "Iammim Nour Rouah, Iabescheh" (Used in a Philosophical Lodge to represent Fire, Salt, Sulphur, (and) Mercury).

M. C. B. I. "Mi Camocha, Baalim, Jehovah" (Who is like unto thee among the gods, O JEHOVAH). Maccabees.

M. H. S. U. Maher-Shalal-Hash-Baz, "He hasteneth to the spoils."

M. M. T. P. "Mene, Mene, Tekel, Peres" (Numbered, numbered, weighed, divided).

S. P. Q. R. "Senatus Populusque Romanus" (The Senate and Roman People).

CHRISTIAN ROSENKREUZ AND THE ROSICRUCIAN'S

By W. WYNN WESTCOTT, M. D. - 1848 - 1925

The Rosicrucian's of medieval Germany form a group of mystic philosophers, assembling, studying and teaching in private the esoteric doctrines of religion, philosophy and occult science, which their founder, Christian Rosenkreuz, had learned from the Arabian sages, who were in their turn the inheritors of the culture of Alexandria. This great city of Egypt, a chief emporium of commerce and a center of intellectual learning, flourished, before the rise· of the Imperial power of Rome, falling at length before the martial prowess of the Romans, who, having conquered took great pains to destroy the arts and sciences or the Egypt they had overrun and subdued; for they seem to have had a wholesome fear of those magical arts, which as tradition had informed them, flourished in the Nile valley; which same tradition is also familiar to English people through our acquaintance with the book of Genesis, whose reputed author was taught in Egypt all the arts and sciences he possessed, even as the Bible itself tells us, although the orthodox are apt to slur over this assertion of the Old Testament narrative.

Our present world has taken almost no notice of the Rosicrucian philosophy, nor until the last thirty-five years of any mysticism, and when it does condescend to stoop from its utilitarian and money-making occupations, it is only to condemn all such studies, root and branch, as waste of time and loss of energy. The very name of "Christian Rosenkreuz," the founder of Rosicrucianism, would meet with hardly any sign of recognition in the best social and literary circles of this country; and yet the mere publication in 1614 of a little pamphlet in Germany, narrating the mode of foundation and the aim of the Rosicrucian Order, made such a stir throughout Europe, that even today there are extant six hundred tracts for and against the reality and the bona fides of the doctrines of the Order; which tracts were written and printed in Germany and France alone, within a hundred years of the issue of the original *Fama*

Fraternitatis, or narrative of the establishment of the Society of Christian Rosenkreuz.

In estimating the relative importance of so voluminous a literature, we must remember that the era 1600-1700 was far different than the age in which we live. The printing press, although available to the few and rich, was still a rarity, and the daily newspaper had not been thought of. Certainly, no book that has been, printed within the last fifty years has created one tithe of the flutter, in the world of the learned, that was caused by this thirty-three page Latin pamphlet, published in German in the year 1614.

The Reformation, we must remember, had just become an accomplished fact; it was a sweeping change that bad affected a vast tract of semi-civilized country, and perhaps some explanation of the outcry against the Rosy Cross was a form of protest against another possible attempt at the conversion of men, like the Reformation of Catholicism which had preceded it, and had, while making great improvements, greatly unsettled men's minds, and had shaken European religious and social life to its foundations. The narrative, then, of Christian Rosenkreuz created a veritable intellectual panic among the learned, and it was a ferment which did not complete its work for several generations. That its effect was on the whole a good one, need not be doubted by us, for whatever may be the merits or the demerits of Rosicrucianism as a system of philosophy or ethics, its promulgation certainly tended to widen men's intellectual conceptions, to show that the prevailing standards and forms of religion were not the only possible forms of high spiritual thought and aspiration, and that even the time-expired formulae of Egyptian culture were susceptible of a later development not wholly unsuitable, and not unworthy the attention of a later age. Why indeed should it not have been so, seeing that for 1600 years in Europe the nations had reposed in a state of apathy without culture, had made almost no progress, and bad been hide bound by the fetters of a religious establishment which boasted itself on its exclusiveness, its control of all that God gave or man could receive, and formulated and practiced the dogma that there was no revelation but one – the Bible – and that the Bible was unsuitable to the people, whose sole duty was to support a priesthood, from whose personal attention and propitiation alone was any good to be obtained.

So long as vast nations were taught that neither mind, nor intellect, nor man's spiritual soul required any further culture, nor any further enlightenment than could be obtained from listening to the only infallible book in a language not understood of the people; it is easy to perceive why Germany in 1600 was behind Alexandria of the year 1, alike in culture, in science and in art.

Reform of any sort, new presentments of truth of any kind, always stink in the nostrils of men who have a vested interest in maintaining things as they are; and history has repeatedly shown that even beneficed ministers will stoop to misrepresentation and falsehood in order to sustain their own interests and God given rights, in their mind's consonant with the right divine of Kings – another now exploded superstition. Small wonder then that the *Fama Fralernitatis Crucis* raised up a storm of passion, and that its followers were assailed by every form of abuse and every vile epithet that the Billingsgate of clerical intolerance of that day could supply. For the clergy, be it remembered, with the pupils of the clergy, were alone able to read and write, and it was but one man in a thousand who, having received education from orthodox sources, dared to express an opinion of his own. Of such a sort were the few defenders of Rosenkreuz, and their pamphlets are mostly anonymous, to avoid open persecution, while the writers who wrote in condemnation signed their names in full with many ecclesiastic titles. None of the minor clergy, whatever they thought or felt in private, dared publish any defense of a teacher or school which conflicted with the dominant faith; a few exalted clerics, Priors and Abbots, did, as I shall no doubt be reminded, both profess and practice Hermetic science and alchemy; but then an Abbot – as he of Spanheim, I mean the notable Trithemius; or a Prior like Valentine; or a Bishop, like he of Ratisbon, Albertus Magnus, were living in safety among a crowd of retainers, and the Holy Father's arm was a long way off, and he did not unnecessarily degrade a priest of high rank unless for contumacy to some personal order – while on the other hand each one of ten thousand common parish priests could easily be cajoled into a visit to a neighboring monastery and there be retained until released by a merciful Karma.

It seems to me that there is a parallelism, and I hope to be able to show to you that there is an analogy, and some points of resemblance between the appearance of Christian Rosenkreuz in

Germany, and the coming of your own H. P. B. as a teacher bearing witness to the light within her, and being inspired by knowledge gained in the East by travel and initiation there; the difference being that in the former case the few thousand learned of all Europe were alone approached by a printed manifesto while in our time the whole nation is approached by personal teaching, supplemented by the use of the press. Let us see shortly what is known historically of this Rose Cross Order, whose manifesto excited so great an interest.

The book *Fama Frateruitatis* narrates that about the years 1375-1450, there flourished a very learned man, who, having spent many years in travel through the East – Asia Minor, Chaldea, Arabia and Fez – came again to Europe, and after a residence among the Moors in Spain, returned to his native state in Germany, fulfilled with the Hermetic Sciences and capable in magical arts, with knowledge he had acquired by many initiations in Eastern lands. He adopted a covered mystic name, as medieval teachers mostly did; the name he took was "Christian Rosenkreuz," or Christian Rose Cross, or more shortly C.R., with a Signum or seal of a Rose on a cross formed of six squares; such a cross which as if closed up would form a cube. He settled in a certain retired place and drew around him a select circle of friends and pupils who were ultimately, after training, received by him into the grades of mystic initiation which he had himself collected.

After some years of tuition and elementary practice these initiates set to work and built, or caused to be built for themselves, a Temple or Lodge House, or Home: they called it "*Domus Santti Spiritus*," the House of the Divine Spirit. Here they settled and this was their abode, study, and laboratory, from this they went forth in turn in deeds of mercy and of healing, and of teaching, and of observation. From this first circle there were formed other circles in succession, the elders teaching the juniors, and so was the secret knowledge both preserved and extended. C. R. lived to a very advanced age – 106 years – and dying at last was buried, as had been arranged by him and the members of the inner circle, in a special vault within their Domus, or secret dwelling place. Some form of embalming was used, and the vault was decorated with grand and beautiful emblems, designs and implements. The Magus was enclosed in a specially prepared tomb, and was laid to rest with his own special consecrated insignia. The vault was closed, and upon the door was fixed a brazen plate, upon which was engraved an inscription of a prophetic explanation of his own, that in 120 years after his death his tomb should be reopened and his doctrines, in a modified form, once more made public, and not only to a few, but to the learned in general; this plate was then covered up and the presence of the vault quite masked.

The members of C. R.'s inner circle appear to have died off each in his turn, until at last there remained no one who could tell the secret of where the great Instructor lay, and where was the secret chamber of which all had heard, and which all were forbidden to seek. The brothers were content to refrain from seeking; trusting in a promise that a time should come when, in the natural course of events, C. R. should rise again, or at least in the spirit, that is, his doctrines and fame should be published. The 120 years passed away, and the Order still flourished; faithful initiates still studied, watched and waited, until the fateful hour was struck on the clock of time, and in 1584 the secret was discovered. I will read from the original work, in its earliest English translation by "Eugenius Philalethes," that is, Thomas Vaughan, printed in London, 1652:

"The year following after N. N. had performed his school right, and was minded now to travel, being for that purpose sufficiently provided with Fortunatus' purse he thought (being a good Architect) to alter something of this building, and to make it more fit; in such renewing he lighted upon the Memorial Table, which was cast of brass, and containeth all the brethren, with some few other things; this he would transfer in another more fitting vault, for where or when Fra R.C. died, or in what country he was buried, was by our predecessor, concealed and unknown to us. In this Tablet stuck a great nail somewhat strong, so that when he was with force drawn out, he took with him an indifferent big stone out of the thin wall, or plaster of the hidden door, and so unlooked for, uncovered the door, wherefore we did with joy and longing throw down the rest of the wall, and cleared the door, upon which that was written in great letters, '*Post CXX Annos Patebo*' with the year of the Lord under it; therefore we gave God thanks, and let it rest that same night because first we would overlook our Rotam.

"In the morning following we opened the door and there appeared to our sight a vault of seven sides and corners, every side five feet broad and the height of eight feet. Although the Sun never shined in this Vault, nevertheless it was enlightened by another sun, which had learned this from the Sun, and was situated in the upper part of the center of the ceiling; in the midst, instead of a tomb stone, was a round altar covered over with a plate of brass, and thereon this engraven: *A. C. R. C. Hoc universi compendium unius mihi sepulchrum fici*: "Round about the circle or brim stood:

Jesus mihi omnia.

"In the middle were four figures, enclosed in circles, whose circumscription was:

1. *Nequaquam vacuum*, No void exists.

2. *Legis fugum*, The yoke of the law.

3. *Libertas Evangelii*, The liberty of the doctrine.

4. *Dei gloria intacta*, The unsullied glory divine.

"This is all clear and bright, as also the seventh side and the two Heptagoni, so we kneeled together down, and gave thanks to the sole wise, sole mighty, and sole eternal God, who hath taught us more than all men's wit could have found out, praised be His Holy Name. The vault was parted in three parts: the upper part or ceiling, the wall or side, the ground or floor.

"Of the upper part you shall understand no more of it, at this time, but that it was divided to the seven sides in the triangle, which was in the bright center; but what therein is contained, you shall (God willing), (that are desirous of our society) behold the same with your own eyes, but every side or wall is parted into ten squares, every one with their several figures and sentences, as they are truly showed and set forth concentratum here in our book. Now as yet we had not seen the dead body of our careful and wise, father; we therefore removed the altar aside, there we lifted up a strong plate of brass, and found a fair and worthy body, whole and unconsumed, as the same is here lively counterfeited with all the ornaments and attires; in his hand he held a parchment book, called **T**; the which, next unto the Bible, is our greatest treasure, which ought to be delivered to the censure of the world, At the end of this book standeth this eulogium, which then follows in Latin – it may be shortly translated thus –

'A seed sown in the breast Ihesus.'

"'Christian Rose Cross sprung from a noble and famous German family. The man of his age for the most subtle imaginations and divine revelations, and one of unwearied labor in the search for heaven's mysteries and those also of humanity; he was scarcely admitted to a more than Regal or Imperial Gaza (or treasure house) during his journeys in Arabia and Africa; he instituted and became the custodian for posterity of these arts; he formed the *Minutum Mumdum*, which related the past, present and future. He lived more than a century, and passed away, not of disease, but at the call of God; away from the embrace and last kiss of his brethren, and so returned to divinity.

"He was a beloved father, a very dear brother, a most faithful teacher, and the most enduring friend. He lies concealed here for 120 years.

"Underneath this inscription there were five signatures of members of the First Circle, and three of the Second Circle."

Back to Mr. Westcott:

I am not of those who scoff at all that seems at first sight improbable, and to me this does not seem a very impressive narrative. Many of you as Theosophists must see nothing wildly improbable about it; and it may seem to you within the range of things possible; but I admit that the truth of the narrative is not proven. No person as an entire outsider has ever seen this embalmed body, or this vault, or this *Domas Sandi Spiritus*, which was built about 1460, and opened about 1584; or at any rate no notable man has asserted in print that he has seen it. But would such an outsider be at all likely to see it? – at least not without first martyring the Fraters of the Order.

Be just to Rosicrucianism and its origin, and history; ask yourselves what absolute proof you have of the fact of many other historical events; proof I mean independent of the evidence of those who had already convinced themselves and of those who have a personal object to serve in establishing the truth of any alleged occurrence – such as the death of Jesus by crucifixion, the Trojan War, or of the striking incident in the conversion of Saul of Tarsus, or of the former existence of the Pharos of Alexandria.

And, on the other hand, of what value is negative evidence in such a discussion. The fact that the works of Josephus have no mention of Jesus which is not a forgery, is no proof that a gentle, wise and revered spiritual divine teacher did not preach in the time of the Emperor Tiberius, in Jerusalem; nor is the fact that neither

Lord Bacon, nor Frederick the Great, nor Pope Pio Nono, nor Spinoza, nor Huxley has ever asserted that he has seen the Vault of Christian Rosenkreuz, any reason for denying its existence in 1484 or 1600, or at any time since then.

I would undertake to obtain in a week, in any large town in England, a thousand signatures to a document attesting that no living Theosophist had ever been seen by them, or to a document testifying that no evidence existed which went to show that the Theosophists had a Sanctum in which rested the ashes of their late revered teacher, in a room suffused with the peace which now at length dwells over the memory of the character, at once so enthusiastic and so contemplative – and of her personality, at once aggressive and so endearing.

Thousands of persons of culture, and hundreds of occultists and pseudo-occultists, could be found willing to testify that they were not in possession of any evidence that successors of "Rosy Cross the Adept" still exist in England; or that any such a vault exists here or anywhere else in Europe. Yet that need not upset my belief, or your belief, if you hold it, that Adept Rosicrucian's do still exist; nor will it upset the fact that I have met a person in this very Blavatsky Lodge (who was known to most of the elders in Theosophy among you) who assured me of the truth of these assertions, and who claimed to have seen such a vault. Not that I am weak enough, or so ignorant of human nature as to suppose that any statement of mine would make you believe, nor do I want you to believe this. Seeing is believing, and if you cannot see, you are not to be blamed, BY ME, for not believing; but take my former case as to the Theosophical Headquarters, of this assertion there are many of you here present who, having seen, could testify to its truth, and so, I suppose, do believe, and so the gist of my argument may come to such of you. So much then for the History of the Order of C. R., first issued in 1610, and printed again and distributed in considerable numbers in 1614. A great outcry arose at once, and it is to be observed that the Fama, issued alone in 1610, was, when issued in 1614, in a revised form, bound up with a second tract, the *Confessio Fraternitatis*. This is important, because the two works vary exceedingly as to the matter and manner.

The first, Fama, treats of the 1450-80 period of Europe, when Roman Catholicism was unchallenged only by Mahommedanism, and a few remaining descendants of the pagan philosophers, and by Hermetic pupils; while second, the Confessio, issued in 1614, and no doubt then written – but it is anonymous – appeared after the throes of the Reformation, and it is tinctured deeply with the notions of Luther, and with Protestant crudities; and so differs widely from the purely Hermetico philosophic or Gnostic-Christian form of the earlier work.

I have no objection to urge against the notion which has been formulated by Edward Macbean, among others, that the Fama was written by a true follower of Christian Rosenkreuz's original Order, and that the latter was written by John Valentine Andrea, a well-known German theologian and mystic who flourished at that time. He may have been a low grade initiate of the Rosicrucian Order and have been ordered to publish this *Confessio* to temper the storm which had been set up by the first tract. This effect, however, did not follow, and the polemic fury of the literati continued in full force for many, many years.

Many modern critics have accepted this suggestion that this Andrea wrote the *Confessio*: but they err from want of study, who say that both are from the same hand; as well say that Jeremiah wrote the Book of Esther, so much also do they differ in style, and in that case too, one is apologetic, and the other is historic or fable – at least a narrative.

So much for the history of the founding of the Order, now what is stated of the tenets? We must presume that an Order founded on a basis of philosophy gathered in Arabia and Africa was not simply a Christian one. The claim also to magical power negatives the idea that the doctrines were orthodox; and, yet we find a profession of Christianity running through the volume. We must remember that C. R. began life as a pupil in a cloister, and was the associate in early life of monks; we must bear in mind that out of Europe, in the East, Christianity was Gnostic, and that the Gnostics and Neo-Platonists, although to a Roman Catholic or Protestant decidedly heretical, were yet inspired by Christian ideals – although they could not realize the accepted admixture of the God and Man in Christ, yet, insisted on the Christ teaching of the Man Jesus.

Similarly, so we today, having mostly entered upon the Eastern Theosophy from a Christian education, still are largely tinctured with our basic theology and still use Christian language and types and symbols in our new ideals of the higher principles of man and humanity. For example, read the Theosophic works of Brothers Kingsland and Brodie Innes. For this reason, it seems to me, that this hook, explanatory of an Eastern occultism, yet using frequently Christian terms; must be read as though the Christian allusions were to a Gnostic and not to a Catholic Christ spirit and man Jesus; for Jesus to the Hermetist is the shortened form of Yehoshua, which title is formed of the letters of the Kabalistic Yod, Hek, Van, Heh, having interposed the letter Shin, the emblem of the spark of the Divine overshadowing each human soul. This Yod Heh Yan Heh, the Incommunicable Name, being the origin of the common God name Jehovah, but to the Kabalist was not the jealous God of the Jewish nation, but a glyph of the divine creative forces which emanate from the highest God ideal, yet manifested and certainly not individualized.

As to the tenets of the Order next. The Fama begins with a tribute to the mercy and goodness if the Wise and Merciful God, by which a more perfect knowledge of two subjects is obtained –Jesus Christ and Nature, not these two – as of equal importance. God is thanked for the raising of some men who are able to bring Arts to perfection; and then finally that man might understand his own nobleness and worth, and why he is called Microcosmos – that is, I take it, man's unlimited range of improvement and that he is a mirrored reflection of the Macrocosm, the Divine Universe of Manifestation.

Men are chided for adhering to short-sighted doctrines, as of Aristotle and Galen, when the greater Truth lies before them; of those teachers it is added, that had they been offered the knowledge of the Rosicrucian initiation they would have accepted it with much joy. It is then explained that C. R., on his return from his travels, offered to the learned the elements of his Eastern lore; he showed them the errors of their church and how the whole *Philosophia Moralis* might be amended. But it is added – "these things were to them a laughing matter, for being a new thing up to them that feared that great Name should be lessened, if they should now begin to acknowledge their many years' errors, to which they had grown accustomed, and wherewith they had gained them enough."

That was the secret, the secret of the failure of C. R. to become a public teacher, and such the reason why the idea occurred to him of founding a new Order which should work for a General

Reformation in silence and secrecy, and undisturbed by the scoffs of the world either too ignorant or too self-seeking to be taught. Some pages further on the general agreement of the members is given:

1. That no public profession of any superior knowledge should be made; but that members should when able endeavor to cure the sick, and that gratis.

2. That they should not make themselves conspicuous by any special garment or insignia, to the world.

3. That they should yearly meet in assembly and mutually instruct each other in the knowledge gained since they last met.

4. That every member should select a worthy person to succeed him as pupil.

5. That the letters C.R. should be their mark, seal and character, ever keeping them in mind of their Founder, and of Christ the spirit, and of the Rose of Silence.

6. To keep the Society secret at least One Hundred Years.

This point was certainly well kept; but after that time many members did write themselves, no doubt by permission, as a Frater R.C.

Other references to their ideas and habits, and their unusual powers abound in the Fama. For instance, it is said, although they could not live longer than the time appointed by God, yet were they free from disease and pain. That Frater J. O. was very expert in the Kabala, the mystic philosophy of the Chaldee and Hebrew initiates. That their burial places should all be kept secret, they claimed the secret of the art of embalming. They claimed the knowledge of the secret of the Ever-burning Lamp, which is so often referred to in the medieval occult authors. The power of foresight, as shown by the inscription on the Vault door. In the Vault were found, *inter alia*, "wonderful artificial songs"; these we may take to be what the Eastern adepts call Mantrams, that is, portions of language in a certain rhythm for recitations in magical ceremonies. They condemned gold-making for profit and luxury as being accursed, calling transmutation but a Paragon or side work.

And lastly we read in the Fama:

"Our philosophy is not a new invention, but as Adam after his fall received it, and as Moses and Solomon used it, also she ought not to be much doubted of or contradicted by other opinions or meanings; but seeing that Truth is always peaceful and brief and always like herself and especially accorded by with Jesus *in omni parte* and all members. And as he is the true Image of the Father, so is she his image. It shall not be said that this is true only of philosophy, but true according to Theology. And wherein Plato, Aristotle, Pythagoras and others did hit the mark, and wherein Enoch, Moses and Soloman did excel, but especially in what that wonderful book the Bible agreeth. All that same concurreth and makes a sphere or globe whose total parts are equidistant from the center."

There follows the *Confessio Fraternitati's*, written to the learned of Europe, and which is said to contain thirty-seven reasons of the purpose and intention of the Society. Curiously enough, that tract does not contain any series of thirty-seven reasons, or thirty-seven paragraphs, but is a very discursive relation of the doctrines of the Fraters. As a whole its tenets differ from those of the Fama, and are plainly tinctured with post-reformation ideas, indeed we find the Pope called Antichrist. So, it seems safe to decide that this tract is rather by John Valentine Andrea, the Protestant Theologian, than by men deeply inspired by the mysticism and magic of a man raised to Adeptship by Oriental Sages.

Time will not permit of any review of the Confessio, nor of any glance at the lives and works of those philosophers who have since styled themselves Fraters of the R.D., so I hasten to conclude with a short summary, and with the analogies between the origin of the R.C. and the Theosophical Society. As a critic, then, of the Rosicrucian's, viewed from the standpoint of the *Fama Fraternitatis* – their own manifesto to the world, it seems that the Order was essentially a brotherhood of philosophers living in a Christian country, and professing a normal Christianity of Gnostic type, yet essentially a band of students of Oriental lore and Eastern magical arts, professing and practicing Kabalistic divination and the knowledge of the ultra-natural planes of being.

As such they had to encounter the rampant hostility of the orthodoxy of their time, and hence needed to shroud themselves under an impenetrable veil of seclusion; they only appeared in public singly, and without any mark of their character; and lastly, when abroad they devoted themselves first to charity and healing, and then to the acquisition of more knowledge and experiment.

I am now to point out certain resemblances, possibly entirely superficial, which seem to me to exist between the narrative of Christian Rosenkreuz and the origin of the Theosophic propaganda.

Let no error be made by you as to what is here said: The Rosicrucian establishment, admitting of no demonstration, may be, if it seems good to you, regarded as a myth. Theosophy is to us a great fact. But as for myself I studied Western mysticism twenty years before I became a pupil of this school, and I esteem it highly, and so it is for me no slight to Theosophy to compare it to the work of Christian Rosenkreuz. I admit that the present work of the Theosophical Society is exalted in its aim, and is becoming universal in its distribution, and so far, excels the role of the ideal Rosicrucian, whose zeal was much more turned to personal development; as such, however, I am prepared to contend for the value of Hermetic initiation; but that is not before you at this time.

My attention is the more admissible because H. P. B. ever declared that the school of learned men who instructed HER to promulgate their doctrines, has been in continuous existence for ages; and that they have at several times, notably in the closing twenty-five years of each century, authorized and guided some effort at the spread of true occult philosophy. Until the contrary is proved, it is admissible to argue that the legend of Christian Rosenkreuz narrates a minor display of this principle and practice; that the attempt was a failure was no proof of its unworthiness, for H. P. B. repeatedly said that her own promulgation of faith might easily subside into failure and into insignificance, unless some great-hearted souls and enthusiastic pupils were strong enough to carry it over such a period of natural decadence.

I have to ask to be allowed to say a few words of explanation.

I have not come here at this time because I am a Theosophist; but on the contrary, I have been asked to speak on the Rosicrucian's, because I have the pleasure to hold a high office in the Rosicrucian Society of England, so might reasonably be supposed to have studied the history of that Order. But to avoid misconception, I wish to say that the Society of Rosicrucian's in Anglia is a Masonic Body – it is composed of Freemasons who have associated themselves together to study the old Rosicrucian books in the light of history, and to trace the connection between Rosicrucianism and the origins of Freemasonry, a connection which has been alleged to exist by many historians belonging to the outer world.

The members of this Order, as such, make no claim to be in possession of the secret wisdom of the pupils of Christian Rosenkreuz, and I am very desirous that no one should leave with the impression that I speak as anything more than a critic of history, or with the notion that I have any part or lot in a personal claim to magic arts.

I ask this favor of you all as referring to this lecture in conversation, because even if I were a member of the old Society, and had any powers beyond those you possess, I should not make public a claim to the possession of them; because I hold it at all times absurd for any one to lay claim to the possession of any abnormal powers which he is not willing to demonstrate, or is not able to show to the public, or at least to all who ask; so that seeing they might believe, and believing understand.

May we not then observe a parallel between the promulgations of the doctrines of Christian Rosenkreuz and the establishment of the Theosophical Society and H. P. B.'s inner group of students. In each case the instruction in Mystic Philosophy came from the East; in the former case from Asia Minor, Arabia, Africa, and notably Fez; in the latter from India, Thibet and Egypt.

In each case the inspiration and actual founding of the Order is really due to one alone; in the former case by a man, in the latter by a woman.

In each case the Order appears to have been founded in the closing quarter of a century.

In each case the Initiator laid some part of his or her store of learning before the world, and in each case the learning was a "laughing matter unto them," and the teacher was the butt for scorn and ridicule. In each case the teaching is based upon a foundation of Ethics and a high standard of morality, and the suggestion is made that such a course of life may lead to abnormal or magical powers. In each case, the teacher, disgusted with a vain-glorious and hypocritical world, fell back upon the formation of a select band of pupils bound together by a solemn contract, and stimulated by enthusiasm.

In each case, an early step was the foundation of a home and special dwelling set apart for work, study and contemplation. In each case the founder passes away and is regarded by sorrowing pupils as dearest friend, most learned teacher, and beloved chief.

In one case we find the expenditure of loving care and skill in preserving the remains of the Master; and in the other we find an Urn of Ashes preserved by loving hands and placed in respectful privacy in her own chamber; and lastly, as Christian Rosenkreuz left the prophetic, and perhaps allegorical assertion, to be found by his successors of the third generation, that he, or his name and doctrine, should reappear; even so did H. P. B., as I understand, affirm that she would return, in another form indeed, but still the same Ego, and individual, in a stage still farther on in the path to full Adeptship.

You will all, as Theosophists struggling to the light, hope that even as we read that the pupils of Rosy Cross, one hundred and twenty years after his death, showed the vitality of their Order, so may this Lodge founded by your great inspirer, Helena Petrovna Blavatsky, continue to flourish and extend until time shall be no more with you.

THE HERMETIC PHILOSOPHERS

By HARGRAVE JENNINGS - 1817 - 1890

There was among the sages a writer, Artephius, whose productions are very famous among the Hermetic Philosophers, – insomuch that the noble Olaus Borrichius, an excellent writer and a most candid critic, recommends these books to the attentive perusal of those who would acquire knowledge of this sublime philosophy. He is said to have invented a cabalistic magnet which possessed the extraordinary property of secretly attracting the aura, or mysterious spirit of human efflorescence, out of young men and these benign and healthful springs of life he gathered up, and applied by his art to himself, by inspiration, transudation, or otherwise, – so that he concentrated in his own body, waning in age, the accumulated rejuvenescence of many young people; the individual owners of which new, fresh life suffered in proportion to the extent in which he preyed vitally upon them, and some of them were exhausted by this enchanter, and died. This was because their fresh young vitality had been unconsciously drawn out of them in his baneful, devouring society, which was unsuspected because it was delightful. Now, this seems absurd; but it is not so absurd as we suppose.

Sacred history affords some authority to this kind of opinion. We are all acquainted with the history of King David, to whom, when he grew old and stricken in years, Abishag, the Shunamite, was brought-a damsel described as "very fair;" and we are told that she "lay in his bosom," and that thereby he "gat heat" which means vital heat, – but that the king "knew her not." This latter clause in I Kings i. 4, all the larger critics, including those who speak in the commentaries of Munster, Grotius, Vossius, and others, interpret in the same way. The seraglios of the Mohammedans have more of this less lustful meaning, probably, than is commonly supposed. The ancient physicians appear to have been thoroughly acquainted with the advantages of the companionship, without indulgence, of the young to the old in the renewal of their vital powers.

The elixir of life was also prepared by other and less criminal means than those singular ones hinted above. It was produced out of the secret chemical laboratories of Nature by some adepts. The famous chemist, Robert Boyle, mentions a preparation in his works, of which Dr. Le Fevre gave him an account in the presence of a famous physician and of another learned man. An intimate friend of the physician, as Hoyle relates, had given, out of curiosity, a small quantity of this medicated wine to an old female domestic; and this, being agreeable to the taste, had been partaken of for ten or twelve days by the woman, who was near seventy years of age, but whom the doctor did not inform what the liquor was nor what he was expecting that it might effect. A great change did occur with this old woman; for she acquired much greater activity, a sort of bloom came to her countenance, her face was becoming much more agreeable; and beyond this, as a still more decided step backward to her youthful period, certain *purgationes* came upon her again with sufficiently severe indications to frighten her very much; so that the doctor, greatly surprised at his success, was compelled to forego his further experiments, and to suppress all mention of this miraculous new cordial, for fear of alarming people with novelties, - in regard to which they are very tenacious, having prejudices.

But with respect to centenarians, some persons have been mentioned as having survived for hundreds of years, moving as occasion demanded from country to country; when the time arrived that in the natural course of things they should die, merely changing their names, and reappearing in another place as new persons, – they having long survived all who knew them, and thus being safe from the risk of discovery. The Rosicrucian's almost jealously guarded these secrets, speaking in enigmas and parables for the most part; and they adopted as their motto the advice of one of their number, one of the Gnostic of the early Christian period: "Learn to know all, but keep thyself unknown." Further, it is not generally known that the true Rosicrucian's bound themselves to obligations of poverty and chastity in the world, with certain dispensations and remissions that fully answered their purpose; for they were not necessarily solitary people; on the contrary, they were frequently gregarious, and mixed freely with all classes.

Their notions of poverty, or comparative poverty, were different from those that usually prevail. They felt that neither monarchs, nor the wealth of monarchs, could aggrandize those who already esteemed themselves the superiors of all children of men; and therefore, though. declining riches, they were voluntary in the renunciation of them. They held to chastity, because, entertaining some peculiar notions about the real position in creation of the female sex, the Enlightened or Illuminated Brothers held the monastic or celibate state to be greatly that more consonant with the intentions of Providence, since in every thing possible to man's frail nature they sought to trample on the pollutions of this his state in flesh. They trusted the great lines of Nature, not in the whole, but in part, as they believed Nature was in certain sense a betrayer, and that she was not wholly the benevolent power to endow, as accorded with the prevailing motion. We wish not to discuss more amply than this the extremely refined and abstruse protested views of these fantastic religionist, who ignored Nature. We have drawn to ourselves a certain frontier of reticence, up to which we may freely comment; and the limit is quite extended enough for the present popular purpose, – though we absolutely refuse to overpass it with too distinct explanation, or to enlarge further on the strange persuasions of the Rosicrucian's.

There is related, upon excellent authority, to have happened an extraordinary incident at Venice, that made a very great stir among the talkers in that ancient place, and which we will here supply at length, as due to so mysterious and amusing an episode. Every one who has visited Venice in these days, and still more those of old-fashioned time who have put their experience of it on record, are aware that freedom and ease among persons who make a good appearance prevail there to an extent that, in this reserved and diffident country, is difficult to realize. This doubt of respectability until conviction disarms has a certain constrained and unamiable effect on our English manners, though it occasionally secures us from imposition, at the expense perhaps of our accessibility. A stranger who arrived in Venice one summer, towards the end of the seventeenth century, and who took up his residence in one of the best sections of the town, by the considerable figure which he made, and through his own manners, which were polished, composed, and elegant, was admitted into the best company, - this though he came with no introductions, nor did any body exactly know who or what he was. His figure was exceedingly well proportioned, his face oval and long, his forehead ample and pale, and the intellectual faculties were surprisingly brought out, and in distinguished prominence. His hair was long, dark, and flowing; his smile inexpressibly fascinating, yet sad; and the deep light of his eyes seemed laden, to the attention sometimes of those noting him, with the sentiments and the experience of the historic periods. But this conversation, when he chose to converse, and his attainments and knowledge, were marvelous; though he seemed always striving to keep himself back, and to avoid saying too much, yet not with an ostentatious reticence. He went by the name of Signor Gualdi, and was looked upon as a plain private gentleman, of moderate independent estate. He was an interesting character, in short.

This gentleman remained at Venice for some months; and was known by the name of the "Sober Signor" among the common people, on account of the regularity of his life, the composed simplicity of his manners, and the quietness of his costume; for he always wore dark clothes, and these of a plain, unpretending style. Three things were remarked of him during his stay at Venice. The first was, that he had a small collection of fine pictures, which he readily showed to every body that desired it; the next, that he was perfectly versed in all arts and sciences, and spoke always with such minute particularity as astonished-nay, silenced -all who heard him, because he seemed to have been present at the things which he related, making the most unexpected corrections in small facts sometimes. And it was, in the third place, observed that he never wrote or received any letter, never desired any credit, but always paid for every thing in ready money, and made no use of bankers, bills of exchange, or letters of credit. However, he always seemed to have enough, and he lived respectably, though with no attempt at splendor or show.

Signor Gualdi met, shortly after his arrival at Venice, one day, at the coffee-house which he was in the habit of frequenting, a Venetian nobleman of sociable manners, who was very fond of art; and this pair used to engage in sundry discussions; and they had many conversations concerning the various objects and pursuits which were interesting to both of them. Acquaintance ripened into friendly esteem; and the nobleman invited Signor Gualdi to his private house, whereat -for he was a widower-Signor Gualdi first met the nobleman's daughter, a very beautiful young maiden of eighteen, of much intelligence, and of great accomplishments. The nobleman's daughter was just introduced at her father's house from a convent, or *peusion*, where she had been educated by the nuns. This young lady, in short, from constantly being in his society, and listening to his narratives, gradually fell in love with the mysterious stranger, much for the reasons of Desdemona; though Signor Gualdi was no swarthy Moor, but only a well-educated gentleman -a thinker rather than a doer. At times indeed, his countenance seemed to grow splendid in expression; and he boasted certainly wonderous discourse; and a strange and weird fascination would grow up about him, as it were when, he became more than usually pleased and animated. Altogether, when you were set thinking about him, he seemed a puzzling person, and of rare gifts; though when mixing with the crowd you would scarcely distinguish him from the crowd; nor would you observe him, unless there was something akin to him in you excited by his talk.

And now for a few remarks on the imputed character of these Rosicrucian's. And in regard to them, however their existence is disbelieved, the matters of fact we meet with, sprinkled- but very sparingly -in the history of these hermetic people, are so astonishing, and at the same time are preferred with such confidence, that if we disbelieve, – which it is impossible to avoid, and that from the preposterous nature of their pretensions, – we cannot escape the conviction that, if there is not foundation for it, their impudence is most audacious. They speak of all mankind as infinitely beneath them; their pride is beyond idea, although they are most humble in exterior. They glory in poverty, and declare that it is the state ordered for them; and this though they boast universal riches. They decline all human affections, or submit to them as advisable escapes only-appearances of loving obligations, which are assumed for convenient acceptance, or for passing in a world which is composed of them, or of their supposal. They mingle most gracefully in the society of women, with hearts wholly incapable of softness in this direction; and they criticize them in their own minds as altogether another order of beings from men. They are most simple and deferential in their exterior; and yet the self value that fills their hearts ceases it self-glorying expansion only with the boundless skies. Up to a certain point they are the sincerest people in the world; but rock is soft to their impenetrability afterward. In comparison to the hermetic adepts, monarch are poor, and their greatest accumulations are contemptible. By the side of the sages, the most learned are mere dolts and blockheads They make no movement toward fame, because they abnegate and disdain it. If they become famous, it is in spite of themselves; they seek no honors, because there can be no gratification in honors to such people. Their greatest wish is to steal unnoticed through the world, and to amuse themselves with the world because they are in it, and because they find it about them. Thus, toward mankind they are negative; toward everything else, positive, self contained, self-illuminated, self – every thing; but always prepared to do good, wherever possible or safe.

To this immeasurable exaltation, what standard of measure, or what appreciation, can you apply? Ordinary estimates fail in the idea of it. Either the state of these occult philosophers is the height of sublimity, or it is the height of absurdity. Not being competent to understand them or their claims, the world insists that these are futile. The result entirely depends upon there being fact or fancy in the ideas of the hermetic philosophers. The puzzling part of the investigation is, that the treatises of these profound writers abound in the most acute discourse upon difficult subjects, and certain splendid passages upon all subjects, – upon the nature of metals, upon medical science, upon the unsupposed properties of simples, upon theological and ontological speculations, and upon science and objects of thought generally -upon all these matters they enlarge to the reader splendidly.

THE ANCIENT ROSICRUCIAN'S

The Rosicrucian Society instituted in the fourteenth century was an extraordinary Brotherhood, exciting curiosity and commanding attention and scrutiny. The members delved in abstruse studies: many became anchorites, and were engrossed in mystic philosophy and theosophy. This strange Fraternity, asserted by some authorities to have been instituted by Roger Bacon near the close of the thirteenth century, filled the world with renown as to their incomprehensible doctrines and presumed abilities. They claimed to be the exponents of the true Cabala, as embracing theosophy as well as the science of numbers. They ate said to delve in strange things and deep Mysteries; to be enwrapped in the Occult Sciences, sometime vulgarly termed the "Black Art"; and in the secrets of Magic and Sorcery, which are looked upon by the critical eyes of the world as tending to the supernatural, and a class of studies to be avoided.

These Mystics, for whom great philanthropy is claimed, and not without reason, are heard of as early as the commencement of the fourteenth century in the person of Raymond Lully, the renowned scholiast and metaphysical chemist, who proved to be an adept in the doctrines taught at the German Seat of Hermetic Learning in 1302, and who died in 1315. Fidelity and Secrecy were the first care of the Brotherhood. They claimed a kinship to the ancient philosophies of Egypt, the Chaldeans, the Magi of Persia, and even the Gymnosophists of India. They were unobtrusive and retiring in the extreme. They were learned in the principles and sciences of Chemistry, Hermeticism, Magnetism, Astrology, Astronomy, and Theosophy, by which they obtained great powers through their discoveries, and aimed at the universal solvent – the Philosopher's Stone-thereby striving to acquire the power of transmuting baser metals into silver and gold, and of indefinitely prolonging human life. As a Fraternity they were distinct from the Cabalist, Illuminati, and Carbonari, and in this relation, they have been largely and unpleasantly misrepresented. Ignorance and prejudice on the part of the learned as to the real purposes of the Rosicrucian's and as to the beneficence of that Fraternity has wrought them great injustice. Science is infinitely indebted to this Order. The renowned reviver of Oriental literature, John Reuchlin, who died in 1522; the famous philosopher and classic scholar, John Picus di Mirandola, who died in 1484; the celebrated divine and distinguished philosopher, Cornelius Henry Agrippa, who died in 1535; the remarkable chemist and physician, John Baptist Von Helmont, who died in 1644; and the famous physician and philosopher, Robert Fludd, who died in 1637, all attest the power and unquestioned prominence of the famous Brotherhood. It is not the part of wisdom to disdain the Astrological and Hermetic Association of Elias Ashmole, author of the "Way to Bliss." All Europe was permeated by this secret organization, and the renown of the Brotherhood was pre-eminent about the year 1615. Wessel's "Fama Fraternitatis," the curious work "Secretioris Philosophiæ Consideratis," and "Cum Consideratis Fraternitatis," by P. A. Gabella, with Fludd's "Apologia," the "Chemische Hochzeit of Christian Rosenkreuz," by Valentine Andrae; and the endless volumes, such as the "Fama Ramissa," establish the high rank in which the Brotherhood was held. It's curious, unique, and attractive Rosaic doctrines interested the masses of scholars of the sixteenth and seventeenth centuries. With the Rosicrucian's worldly grandeur faded before intellectual elevation. They were simple in their attire, and passed individually through the world unnoticed and unremarked, save by deeds of benevolence and humanity.

The Modern Rosicrucian's

The Modern Society of Rosicrucian's was given its present definite form by Robert Wentworth Little, of England, but a few years ago; it is founded upon, the remains or the embers of an old German association which has come under his observation during some of his researches. Brother Little Anglicized it, giving it more perfect system, and placing it in that condition in which it was received in the United States. The purpose of Robert Wentworth Little was to create a literary organization, having in view a base for the collection and deposit of Archeological and Historical subjects pertaining to Freemasonry, Secret Societies in general, and interesting provincial matter; to inspire a greater disposition to obtain historical truth and to displace error; to bring to light much in relation to a certain class of scientists and scholars, and the results of their life-labors, that were gradually dying away in the memories of men. To accomplish this end, he called about him some of his most prominent English and Scottish Masonic friends inclined to literary pursuits, and they awarded their approval and hearty co-operation. The Rosicrucian Societies for England and for Scotland were immediately established; and in 1876 the Order was planted in the Dominion of Canada by authority of Prince Rhodokanakis, of Greece, in which latter country it had been introduced from England. It was introduced and organized in the United States in 1879. The Society also exists in Ireland, in Tunis, in China, in India, and New Zealand.

EARLY ROSICRUCIAN'S

By Frater WILLIAM CARPENTER - 1797 - 1874

I hope I shall not be thought to be trespassing upon the ground which our very learned and indefatigable Frater Hughan is occupying in the pages of The Rosicrucian, in calling attention to one or two earlier publications anent our fraternity, than any he or Brother Charles P. Cooper have noticed, though. I can hardly think that they have not met with them in their varied and extensive researches.

The *Fama Fraternitatis*, which Frater Hughan is reproducing in our pages, is dated 1659, and Brother Cooper, as he states, mentions a work of three years earlier date. Mr. Vaughan, in his *Hours with the Mystics*, however, gives us the substance of a little book which appeared in 1610 and excited a great sensation throughout Germany. It was entitled, The Discovery of lite Brotherhood of the *Honourable Order of the Rosy Cross*, and it was dedicated to all the scholars and magnates of Europe. "It commenced," says Mr. Vaughan, "with an imaginary dialogue between the Seven Sages of Greece and other worthies of antiquity, on the best method of accomplishing a general reform in those evil times. The suggestion of Seneca is adopted, as most feasible; namely, a secret confederacy of wise philanthropists, who shall labor everywhere in unison for this desirable end The book then announces the actual existence of such an association. One Christian Rosenkrentz, whose travels in the East had enriched him with the highest treasures of occult lore, is said to have communicated his wisdom, under a vow of secrecy, to eight disciples, for whom he erected a mysterious dwelling place, called The Temple of the Holy Ghost. It is stated further, that this long-hidden residence had been at last discovered, and within it the body of Rosenkrentz, untouched by corruption, though, since his death, 120 years had passed away. The surviving disciples cooperate in their project of reform, to advertise their names. They themselves indicate neither names nor place of rendezvous. They describe themselves as true protestants. They expressly assert that they contemplate no political movement in hostility to the reigning powers. Their sole aim is the diminution of the fearful sum of human suffering, the spread of education, the advancement of learning, science, universal enlightenment and love. Traditions and manuscripts in their possession have given them, they say, the power of gold-making, with other potent secrets; but by their wealth they set little store. They have arcana, in comparison with which the secret of the alchemist is a trifle. But all is subordinate, with, them, to their one high purpose of benefiting their fellows both in body and soul. This famous book gave rise to keen discussion: some regarding the association of Rosicrucian's, which it professed to describe, as a fabulous, and others as a real society. The author of the production, who was discovered to be Valentine Andrea, at length published a treatise explaining that the work which had given rise to so much angry discussion was wholly fictitious. But this did not prevent many from continuing to believe in the existence of the Rosicrucian brotherhood, and professing to be acquainted with its secrets."

The date of this work, as I have stated, is 1610, and Eliphas Levi states, in his *Histaire de la Magie*, that in the Spring of 1623 the following strange proclamation was found posted in the streets of Paris:

"We, Deputies of the Rose Cross Brothers, sojourn, visible and invisible, in this town, by the grace of the Most High, towards Whom the heart of the wise turn; we teach, without any exterior means, the spoken languages of the countries we inhabit, and we draw men, like ourselves, from terrors and from death. If any one desire to see us from curiosity only, he will never communicate with us; but if his will carries of the Institute call on the learned and devout, who desire to since the thought joined to the real will of the reader is sufficient to make unknown to him, and him to us." Public attention was much excited by this mysterious proclamation, and if any one was heard to ask, "Who are the Brothers of the Rose Cross?" some unknown person took the questioner aside, and gravely said, "Predestined to the reform which must soon be accomplished throughout the universe, the Rose-Cross are the depositaries of the supreme wisdom, and the peaceable possessors of all the gifts of nature, which they can dispense at their will. Wherever they may be, they know everything that happens, in the rest of the world, better than if they were present; they are subject neither to hunger nor to thirst, and they fear neither old age nor sickness. They can command the most powerful spirits and genii. God has covered them with a cloud, to conceal them from their enemies, and though you had eyes more piercing than those of the eagle, you could not see them, but when they will. They hold their general assembly in the pyramids of Egypt; but those pyramids are to them like the rock whence issued the stream of Moses; they are with them in the desert, and will be until their entrance into the land of promise."

The authority for this story I do not know. It is curious, and the merest tyro in occult learning will at once perceive its allegorical character. But what of its early date?

THE ORIGIN OF SOCIETIES

From time immemorial, in all ages of the world, and in all the phases of the world's history, men have always tried, by forming themselves into groups or societies, to command a certain position which would be to them the base of some future empire or state, and which eventually gave rise to most of the famous empires of antiquity. After these empires we find colonies dispatched to different parts of the world, and they carrying with them the germs of a civilization that they had been brought up in, eventually succeeded in scattering far and wide those seeds of human knowledge and human wisdom which, after a lapse of ages, sprung up so beautifully on the different barbaric shores where they were sown, and produced nations so prominent in the world's history, that ofttimes we are compelled to turn to tradition and mythic lore, and by trying to thread our way through this serious labyrinth of unexplored learning attempt at all hazards to form a something out of nothing. The first man we find at the head of the great society formed by man was Nimrod, a mighty hunter, and after the confusion of tongues, or as some have more properly asserted, after the confusion that arose as to what purpose the stupendous fabric they were then erecting was to be put, they then divided themselves into different bands or societies, and each band or society electing a leader, scattered themselves far and wide over the earth. From these arose chiefs or heads of tribes, Patriarchs or fathers, Governors and Kings, or chief Magistrates of the commonwealth, and eventually we find in many instances these succeeded by Emperors. For many ages they seemed to have remained in a sort of quiescent state, until that restlessness, for which man is so very much noted, began to be apparent; for it seems that, having ascended so far in the scale of human pride and ambition, they commenced to descend on the other side and to form noted societies, many of which have become famous in the world's history. In the foremost ranks we may mention that society which existed in Egypt, and to which the pyramids of today owe their architectural fame. Next in order comes that celebrated society of Greece, of which all the entreaties of the Greeks could not suffice for Epaminondas to become a member; and then, in the order of succession, we find the Knights Templar, from whom it is thought the present Masonic body owes its origin, although we think that we may safely assert that with a little patience, we may trace its existence to ages long before the rise of Christianity; in fine, we may almost hazard to ray that the Knights Templar took their insignia from the body Masonic, and by no wild conjecture we declare it to be, if not the same, yet almost to be the same, and if not existing alone, yet co-existent with that society in Egypt, which laid down the plans in the priestly halls of Thebes for the erection of the pyramids.

THE RED BOOK OF APPIN

BY Gen. E. A. HITCHCOCK - 1798 - 1870

Once upon a time there lived a man at Appin, Argyleshire, and he took to his house an orphan boy. When the boy was grown up, he was sent to Herd, and upon a day of days, and him herding, there came a fine gentleman where he was, who asked him to become his servant, and (promised) that he would give him plenty to eat and drink, clothes, and great wages. The boy told him that he would like very much to get a good suit of clothes, but that he would not engage till he would see his Master; but the fine gentleman would have him engaged without delay: this the boy would not do upon any terms, till he would see his Master. 'Well,' said the gentleman, 'in the meantime, write your name in this Book.' Saying this, he put his hand into his outer pocket, and pulling out a large RED BOOK, he told the boy to write his name in the Book. This the boy would not do; neither would he tell his name, till he would acquaint his Master first. 'Now,' said the gentleman, 'since you will neither engage nor tell me your name till you see your present Master, be sure to meet me about sunset to· morrow, at a certain place.' The boy promised that he would be sure to meet him at the place about sunsetting. When the boy came home, he told his Master what the gentleman said to him. 'Poor boy,' says he, 'a fine master he would make; lucky for you that you neither engaged nor wrote your name in his Book: but since you promised to meet him, you must go; but as you value your life do as I tell you.' His master gave him a sword, and at the same time told him to be sure and be at the place mentioned a while before sunset, and to draw a circle round himself with the point of his sword in the name of the Trinity. 'When you do this, draw a cross in the center of the circle; upon which you will stand yourself; and don't move out of that position till the rising of the sun next morning.' He also told him that the gentleman would wish him to come out of the circle to put his name in the Book; but that upon no account was he to leave the circle. 'But ask the Book till you would write your name yourself, and when once you get hold of the Book keep it; he cannot touch a hair of your head, if you keep inside of the circle.'

"So, the boy was at the place long before the gentleman made his appearance; but sure enough he came after sunset; he tried all his arts to get the boy outside of the circle, to sign his name in the Red Book; but the boy would not move one foot out of the place where he stood; but at the long last he handed the Book to the boy, so as to write his name therein. The Book was no sooner inside the circle, – than it fell out of the gentleman's hand inside the circle; the boy cautiously stretches out his hand for the Book, and as soon as he got hold of it, he put it into his oxter. When the fine gentleman saw that he did not mean to give him back the Book, he got furious; and at last he transformed himself into a great many likenesses, blowing fire and brimstone out of his mouth and nostrils; at times he would appear as a horse; other times as a huge cat, and a fearful beast; he was going round the circle the length of the night: when day was beginning to break he let out one fearful screech; he put himself into the likeness of a large raven, and he was soon out of the boy's sight. The boy still remained where he was till he saw the sun in the morning, which no sooner he observed than he took to his soles home as fast as he could. He gave the Book to his Master; and this is how the far-famed RED BOOK was got."

OLD MANUSCRIPT FOUND AT ALEXANDRIA

THE PREFACE TO THE TRANSLATION

A member of the Abyssinian Mercantile Company discovered in Alexandria an ancient house formerly occupied by Grecian friars, in whose to oblivion-abandoned library was found an old pergament. A French literate, accidentally present, at once commenced deciphering it, but a missionary in the ardor of fanatical orthodoxy tried by all means to destroy the antique document. But the efforts of the Jesuit missionary do not seem to have been successful, as a copy of the Latin original was written, which copy found its way into Germany. It has been proved from the archeological discoveries made on the spot, that the house where the pergament was found, was owned and occupied by the Order of Essenes. Further, that the document found was the only remains of literature from the once well-filled library of this scientific and religious Order of brotherhood. The French literate who first conceived the importance and historical worth of the manuscript, tried hard to enrich the French Academy with the original, but owing to the intrigues of the Jesuits mission in Egypt, bent on destroying a document so detrimental to their doctrines, he was not successful, although it was preserved principally through the interference of influential Abyssinian merchants, and Pythagorical societies, from whom the copy above spoken of came into the modern institution of Freemasons, and a society in Germany now possesses the, without doubt, only copy in existence.

As regards the discovered antique document, it consisted of a letter which the so called "Terapeut" (the elder), the highest esteemed member of the-brotherhood, had written to his brethren in Alexandria, in the name of the brotherhood in Jerusalem. This letter was written by him only a few years after the death of Jesus, giving a full description of the life, doctrine and death of Jesus, who the letter proves to have belonged to and had been a member of their brotherhood. Rumors of his miracles and finally of his martyrdom had also reached Alexandria, and as the brethren there had a conviction that he was their brother preached their doctrines, used their sign of recognition and lived in accordance with their rules, they manifested a desire to be informed on the subject, as to the real truth of the matter. To obtain this information, their leader, or "Terapeut," had written a letter to his colleague in Jerusalem, who in reply wrote the Jetter from which we obtain a clear and truthful account of this important and interesting subject. It is a fact, that never has been doubted by those familiar with ancient history, that the Essenes always spoke and wrote the strictest truth, and this added to their moral and scientific lives, puts an end to any doubt as to the correctness and genuineness of the information given in this ancient discovered letter.

Although not at first organized among the Jews, this Order existed already in the days of the "Maccabai," and with them it assumed more of a national outward form, at the same time maintaining most of the ancient Pythagorical doctrines. Most of the members were agriculturalist and gardeners, and assembled together to promote virtue and wisdom among themselves; furthermore, they devoted themselves, especially in the higher degrees, to the art of healing, induced thereto through their studies of nature and art, and were well acquainted with the effects of most then known plants and minerals for recruiting the human system. This knowledge they made useful by healing and comforting the sick. They were true communists, and all put their gains in the common treasury. Before sunrise they never spoke to each other of earthly matters, but met in prayer at the break of day. Having taken their morning meal and put on a peculiar kind of working clothes, they proceeded to their place of work. At noon they again came together, and having washed their hands and feet, and dressed themselves in clean white robes, they ate their dinner together. According to their moral standing and ability, they were divided into four classes or degrees. In the first degree were especially adopted children (the Essenes hardly ever married), but in case an adult wished to be admitted into their Order, it was necessary to go through a very severe moral trial for the term of three years. It was strictly prohibited for a ·ember of higher degree to divulge any of the secrets of his degree to any of the lower rank.

The punishment for such a trespass was expulsion from the brotherhood. Nothing but a strictly moral life, wisdom, godliness, and excellency in science entitled to the higher degrees. In their domestic life they exercised hospitality and benevolence, kept the rules of the Order strictly, and never took any interest or part whatever in politics and revolutions. Thus, they showed a thoroughly peaceable disposition. Their greeting and sign of recognition was "Peace be with you." At their meals they broke the bread and passed the cup, and worshipped "Jehovah," but never made no sacrifice in the temple, but performed their ceremonies in their homes They knew no higher virtue than to suffer and die for their belief; accordingly, death did not terrify them, as much more, as they believed the spirit a prisoner in the body, to be released through death, then to be returned to the celestial glory. Deceit and profanity were considered grave sins, as well as quarreling and vengeance, and looked upon with abhorrence.

This Order, of which the present Freemasonry is the modern issue, was at the time of Jesus widely diffused through Palestine and Egypt, and had their colonies scattered all over the country. They always kept up a congenial fraternal feeling in their meetings, and gave each other information about the affairs of the brotherhood. They counted among their members men of all professions and stations in society, and although comprising a great many learned men and rich persons (who sometimes found it in their interest to keep this secret), they never did exclude the poor or other persons in moderate circumstances.

Thus, we have all reasons to credit this letter, dictated by the love of truth, and written by a man who had been an eyewitness to most of the important transactions in the life and death of Jesus, who as a member of their Order, was embraced by them by all the fraternal devotion of the Order.

The article on an "Old Manuscript Found at Alexandria," is the preface of a small volume, published in Chicago thirty-five years ago, and has been out of print for several years. The first edition was entitled:

"Important Concealed Information, Obtained from an Old Manuscript Found in Alexandria, which shows that Jesus, in a Trance was taken down from the Cross, brought to Life again, and in reality died six months after, within a Secret Religious Society, called Essen Brethren, of which he was a member."

The preface was written by the translator. The text of the translation comprises 64 pages, and the translator's closing remarks 16 pages. The second part of the volume contains an essay on "The Order of Essenes Among the Jewish People," of 32 pages. The frontispiece to the volume is a portrait of Jesus, with the statement that this picture fs the oldest known, and found on a tomb in the, Catacombs.

THE ROSICRUCIAN'S IN THE UNITED STATES

BY S. C. GOULD, VIII° - 1840 -1909

The earliest known reference to the Rosicrucian's in literature is dated at Cassel, 1614. Then there appeared an anonymously printed book entitled *"Fama Fraternitatis Benedicti Ordinis Rosæ Crucis,"* or translated, *"The History of the Fraternity of the Meritorious Order of the Rosy Cross,"* addressed to the learned in general and to the governors of Europe. There is evidence that this work was circulated in manuscript in 1610.

Soon afterwards, perhaps in the same year, but certainly in 1616, the "Fama Fraternitatis" was reprinted, and with it still another tractate entitled "Confessio Fraternitatis," being a statement of the doctrines of the Society, without the history. The doctrines and objects in this second tract are more fully explained. In the first there are reference to the Reformed Church; while in the second the current of thought is plainly Lutheran. The chief work of the Reformation took place between 1610-1660; that is, between the dates of the closing and opening of the vault, 1484-1604. (*Post centum vinginti annos patebo.*) It has been generally conceded by nearly all writers of Rosicrucian history that the author of "Fama Fraternitatis," was Johann Valentine Andreas, who claimed or assumed that the founder of the Rosicrucian was one Christian Rosenkreuz, on which name there has been much speculation as to the personage, whether real or pseudonymous. The real authorship of the second tractate has been held somewhat in doubt, although Andreas became its publisher. He was Abbot of Adleburg, a theologian, a mystic and reformer. These books created an immense stir in the public mind and among mystics. Many other tracts soon followed, both for and against the existence of such a Society.

Many editions and several translations of these books soon followed. The first English translation was by Thomas Vaughan (*"Eugenius Philalethes"*), in 1652; and this translation has been reprinted several times in England and America. From 1610 to 1700, there were published to the world a large number of books in support of the real history of the Rosicrucian's, and some that discredited their doctrines and even their existence.

We have already published several quite lengthy essays on the origin, history, objects and purposes of this arcane society by those who are authorities, Drs. Franz Hartmann, Kenneth R. H. Mackenzie, W. Wynn Westcott, Alex. Wilder; also, by Charles Mackay, Albert Mackey, Hargraves Jennings. John Yarker, and others, which articles should be read by all who desire to become familiar with the Society from 1402 to 1866.

SOCIETAS ROSICRUCIANA IN ANGLIA

The Society in Anglia was founded in England by Robert Wentworth Little, an eminent Freemason. He became the first Supreme Magus and Master General of the College in 1867, and continued as such till 1818 when he died on April 12, at the age of 39 years. Frater Little left a sealed letter appointing as his successor as Supreme Magus Dr. William Robert Woodman who accepted the office on April 5 and continued until 1891 when he died December 20, leaving a sealed letter, with his nephew addressed to the Society, appointing as his successor as Supreme Magus Dr. William Wynn Westcott who on February 25, 1902, the next regular quarterly session, was officially proclaimed as such. He is the present Supreme Magus of the Society in Anglia. The Metropolitan College in London dates from 1867. Supreme Magus Little soon founded other Colleges by warrants and otherwise in England, Scotia, Canada and other countries.

Several of the Colleges in England and Scotia have printed a portion of their transactions, and the papers read, and furnished them to their members, and exchanged them with other Colleges. The Metropolitan College of London have preserved all records, or nearly so, and thus precludes their loss by fire or otherwise. The Rosicrucian, a quarterly journal, published in London, 1868-1879, contains a resume of its proceedings for that time, when that publication ceased. From 1885 to 1907 inclusive, the College has privately printed its transactions, and papers read as supplements, in annual volumes. A list of these essays, with the names of the authors, and dates when read, have already been published in The Rosicrucian Brotherhood (Vol. I, No. r, and Vol. II, No. 2), 23 volumes thus far having been printed; and some of the papers have been reprinted from the annual volumes for the use of their authors. The Rosicrucian archives of the editor of this journal contain these Trans. actions and papers.

THE ROSICRUCIAN SOCIETY IN THE UNITED STATES

The fame of the Rosicrucian Society in England led a number of eminent Freemasons in the United States to an effort in 1877, to introduce it here. Accordingly, these brothers in July, 1878, received from York College admission to the Society in England. They petitioned the High Council of England for Warrant to constitute a Society in the United States, but owing to some delay or misunderstanding the petition lapsed. These Fraters then petitioned for a Warrant from the Rosicrucian Society in Scotia (chartered by the English Society) which was duly received, and in December, 1879, Philadelphia College was established, for Pennsylvania, under the special rule of Frater Charles E. Meyer; and in April, 1880, the New York College, for New York State, under Frater Albert G. Goodall; being charted by the High Council of Scotia, for the purpose of forming a High Council for the United States. These two Colleges met April 19, 1880, and formed and established a High Council for the United States, which was officially recognized in June, 1880, by the Supreme Magus of Anglia. Applications for two more State Colleges having been made the same were granted one for Boston College, for Massachusetts, on May 9, 1880; and for Baltimore College, for Maryland, on May 10, 1880. These four Colleges, through their representatives, met in Boston, Mass., September 21, 1880, and with their inherent powers formed and adopted a Constitution and consecrated the four Colleges, Boston under Frater Alfred F. Chapman, and Baltimore under Frater Thomas J. Shryock. The Council also chartered Burlington College for Vermont under Geo. O. Tyler; and "reproclaimed said creation, formation, and constitution of such Society and Order under the distinctive title, *Societats Rosicruciana* in the United Slates of America, holding the Sovereign power of governing itself and regulating all the grades of the Society of the Rosicrucian's within the boundary of the United States; of determining and perpetuating the Ritual and Philosophy of the Society, in substantial accordance with that under which it was warranted."

The officers of the High Council, Societatis Rosicruciana, in the United States of America, were as follows:

Supreme Magus- Charles E. Meyer, Philadelphia, Pa.
Senior Substitute Magus- Albert G. Goodall, New York.
Junior Substitute Magus- Alfred F. Chapman, Boston, Mass.
Treasurer General- Thomas J. Shryock, Baltimore, Md.
Secretary General- Charles T. McClenachan, New York.

The complement of the officers for the High Council was:

6, Primus Ancient; 7, Secundus Ancient; 8, Tertius Ancient;
9, Quartus Ancient; 10, Quintus Ancient; 11, Sextus Ancient;
12, Septus Ancient; 13, Precentor; 14, Conductor of Novices;
15, Torch Bearer; 16, Herald; 7, Guardian of the Caverns;
18, Medalist.

The adopted Constitution of September 18, 1880, affirmed September 21, 1880, was printed and promulgated to the four Colleges and these at once commenced active work. Members were selected from Master Masons in good standing. Only one College in each State or Territory without the consent of one or all already existing there. Each College had 17 officers: Chief Adept; Celebrant; Suffragan; Treasurer; Secretary; Primus, Secundus, Tertius, and Quartus Ancients; Conductor of Novices; Organist; First and Second Heralds; Guardian of the Caverns; Medalist; and Acolyte.

Each College, in conformity with the history and traditions of the Society and ancient usage, is limited to 72 members, who shall be "Active Members." Every Frater, on admission shall select for himself a brief Latin motto to be registered with the Secretary, which motto is to be appended to his signature in communications relating to the society; no two Fraters can select the same motto.

There are Nine Grades (or degrees) in this Rosicrucian system divided into three orders of four, three, and two Grades:

The First Order– 1º, Zelator; IIº Theoricus; IIIº Practicus; IVº Philosophus.

The Second Order– Vº Adeptus Junior; VIº Adeptus Seinor; VIIº Adeptus Exemptus.

The Third Order– VIIIº Magister Templi, (an official grade); IXº Chief Adept, which is held by an official appointment and constitutes a Provincial Magus.

One of the leading purposes of this Society is to explore into the Archeological, historical and traditional subjects of Ancient and Aboriginal Societies, pertaining to Rosicrucianism, Freemasonry, Druidism, and other Secret Cults and Orders; to read papers on these and allied subjects; to print and distribute the same for the enlightenment of the Brotherhoods. These American Colleges for several years did important work along these lines of research and investigation. We are not cognizant of what and how many such papers were read before the New York and Baltimore Colleges as none have come under our notice, and suppose none of them ever got into print. However, in the middle '80's they became inactive and are now dormant. The Philadelphia College flourished for a few years, and some excellent and elaborate papers were read, and printed. We have one of these in our collection, by Frater John Sartain, which has passed into its second edition, but is without a date:

"The Four Elements." A Paper read before the Philadelphia College, Societas Rosicruciana, U. S. A. "Out of chaos and darkness into light." By Frater John Sartain. Second edition. Frontispiece is a portrait of the author.

This copy contains a facsimile copy of Frater Sartain's certificate of elevation to the third or highest Order of the Society, on the 22d day of July, 1887, and that he was enrolled in the *Liber Aureas* on the 30th day of July, 1887, as a member and Ron. VIIIº Degree. Signed Wm. Robt. Woodman, Supreme Magus, and Wm. Wynn

Westcott, Secretary General. The Philadelphia College appears to have become inactive in the late '80's and is now dormant.

The Boston College warranted May 9, 1880, and chartered June 5, 1880, grew slowly the first years. The writer of this article was the eighteenth Frater enrolled in chronological order and thus completed the first quarter of its limited membership. He also attended nearly all stated meetings, and some specials, from his admission, during its activity. He privately printed the quarterly leaflet membership register, with their selected mottoes, and admission dates, presenting these to the Fraters at the banquets for reference and record. Banquets were held at the quarterly sessions and quite elaborate ones at the annual and some special convocations.

The literary features were usually produced at the quarterly meetings, after the business and conferring of grades. Papers on subjects within the scope of the Society were read and discussed; some of these were read at the banquets, between the courses served, these feasts lasting from seven to twelve, P.M. Room 16, for obvious reasons, was The Adytum, at "Young's."

We have thus far very briefly sketched the succession of the Rosicrucian Society in its official or more organized outward form in 1866, when it was formulated upon relics, documents, and cryptic history, down to 1879, when it was introduced into the United States as an exoteric body.

A Society had been organized in Canada September 19, 1876 by a Warrant from Prince Rhodocanakis, Supreme Magus of the Kingdom of Greece.

In 1870, Hargraves Jennings published his work in London, "The Rosicrucian's. Their Rites and Mysteries." A volume 356 pages, although quite sporadic, and perhaps ubiquitous, as to contents, soon found its way to America, and the incognito of the Brotherhood were soon familiar with the gist of it. In less than ten years, a second edition of this work was published by J. W. Bouton, in New York, the same year that the College in Philadelphia was established, "Who are the Rosicrucian's, and what are their teachings?" has been propounded to us hundreds of times within the past fifty odd years. It was in the early '50's when we were a youth that we became much interested in the cult of several arcane Societies, – Druidism, Rosicrucianism, and Freemasonry.

"The Rosicrucian's lived among men, yet were apart from them; they could not be found, because they had no organization or society; they are humble and quiet in exterior, and yet judge the world somewhat beneath them in exterior show; they are quite indifferent as to putting their knowledge to a commercial use; they do not seek for fame, and care not for distinction or honors; they are generally quite sociable."

It was not necessary, therefore, to be identified with a Lodge, Society, or Order, to be a Rosicrucian. There have been many such in even this country; there many are such today, but the world does not know them, neither are they members of organized societies, but we know some of them. Suffice it to say we became one in the '50's, the theosophical sum of which year is 16, but no matter here how, and identified ourself with the English Order, February 10, 1885, in Boston, so as to be in touch with other congenial spirits, and other avenues of fraternal strength.

HERMETIC BROTHERHOOD TEMPLE TALKS

By SOLARIUS

Planes of Consciousness

1. Consciousness is not a thing, but a condition; a mode of the Divine Action. Consciousness says of itself: "Before creation was, I am." Consciousness is the imminence of the Almighty in creation. Just as all power and energy in creation is an expression of His omnipotence; so all consciousness in creation is an expression of His omnipresence. It is scientifically true that, "not a sparrow falleth to the ground without the Father."

2. Consciousness may be compared to the great central light of the universe for without it all manifestation would be as darkness. The parable of creation says that up to a certain period "darkness was on the face of the deep." The divine consciousness was involved (rolled up,—clothed,—hidden) in matter and, consciousness was involved for expression, creation could not become self-conscious, until a certain condition of evolvement, unfoldment or development of potentiality should be attained. Waiting the evolution of a proper vehicle it is said that— "the Light shineth in darkness and the darkness comprehendeth it not."

3. Creation is the vehicle for the expression of the light of the Divine consciousness in order that it may be able to "enlighten every man that cometh into the world," and creation was instituted that out of it and through it there might be perfected individualized spiritual entities that would be fitted to dwell with God in eternal companionship.

4. As creation is the vehicle for the general diffusion of the light of consciousness so is the physical body the particular vehicle for its diffusion to the individual soul and, in its turn the soul is the vehicle for the individualization of the Divine Spirit which, when perfected becomes that apex and crown of creation— "Son of Man and Son of God."

5. The consciousness that is involved in the mineral element and which gives to it a separate and distinct character of its own and which prompts it to respond invariably to certain chemical and other affinities is evidently on a lower plane than that consciousness which dwells in the plant and prompts it to respond to what we call the laws of vegetable life. On a still higher plane of development is the consciousness that dwells in free moving life organism and which prompts them to go forth and seek that form of substance that they deem best for the prolongation of their existence. So, the consciousness of the fish that dwells in the water, the bird that dwells in the air and the animal that roams the surface of the earth; each dwells in its own specific plane of consciousness.

6. The mineral, the plant, the fish, the bird and the animal, each one is, or may be, entirely righteous in its station of life. Its measure of rightness is the same as is measured to all creatures. The plant, the fish, the beast and the man are all measured with the same measuring rod. If the organism is in harmony with the divine mode of action on its plane of consciousness, it lives and makes progress, if not its existence is hampered and finally terminates. This is the divine mode of action that science calls "the survival of the fittest." The organism becomes perfect in his kind and advances in consciousness in proportion as it conforms to the harmonic law or it degenerates and deteriorates as it recedes from it. "There is one law and He that worketh is One."

7. The element and the plant are not self-conscious except possibly in some dim and indefinable degree. Action on their plane of consciousness is more or less automatic and action and re-action on this plane has its seat and origin in the eternal and exact nature and power of universal consciousness itself.

8. Above the plant in the scale of development comes free moving, independent living organisms and on this plane comes self-recognition. Here the light that shineth in darkness begins to be apprehended, self-knowledge begins, and from this plane, looking upward, the comprehension of that light is based upon the capacity of the organism, its measure being indicated by the centralization and complexity of the physical organization.

Here life recognizes itself and says: "I am." It also recognizes itself in relation to its environment and says, "I will become."

The Divine Consciousness involved in matter is the underlying cause and energy of that orderly system of progressive development that we call by the name of "evolution." This truth is concealed in the mystic saying, viz: "Spirit clothes itself to come down and strips itself to go up."

9. Above the domain of Automatic Consciousness there are four grand divisions or great planes of conscious corresponding to the four-fold nature of man, viz: Physical Self-consciousness; Mental Self-consciousness; Moral Self-consciousness; Spiritual Self-consciousness.

In conformity to the known laws of progressive development, it is evident that all organisms in the line of evolution must "emerge," or grow out of, the lower grand division before they can become capable of sustained existence in the grand division next above. This capacity is acquired by perfecting and improving the physical vehicle to such a degree that it has the ability to enter into relation with and to respond to the varied requirements of an environment of higher conscious potentiality.

The organism must not only be a condition of rightness with the plane on which it dwells, its native environment, but it must develop extra and surplus energy or power sufficient to carry it into the higher plane and begin its comprehension of the fact that something exists, in consciousness, that has more power, more freedom and possesses a more desirable outlet for its energies. This new knowledge gives the organism the necessary incentive, the stimulus to strive for a higher attainment.

Here, as elsewhere, the mode is the same. The organism that would rise to a higher plane of existence must first overcome, it must strive to enter into the "straight gate," it must become master of the things of the lower heritage before it is entitled to become a dweller in the plane above. The Father is always saying: "To him that overcometh I will give the inheritance."

Spiritual evolution finds its counterpart and correspondence in physical evolution. Study the lower and you have the key to the mysteries of the higher. Law on one plane does not conflict with law on any other plane, for what we call "law" is the Divine Mode of Action.

"There is one law and He that worketh is One." The unfolding and perception of consciousness is the unfolding and perception of the existence of the Spirit of the Almighty, omnipresent in the manifest universe.

The soul is always pure spirit but it is of the substance aspect of the divine manifestation, whereas what we designate as spirit is of the energizing aspect of the divine manifestation.

God is One, but divinity in action is, to us, inconceivable unless we predicate something to be acted upon; hence the appearance of duality.

Further: Action not only requires something to be acted upon, but it requires a result or a consequence of the action itself; hence the divine in manifestation has not only the appearance of duality but also the appearance of trinity.

In reality, all is one, but as our finite minds can only grasp a limited portion of the problems of infinity, in order to satisfy our mental craving for an explanation we reduce it to finite terms and speak of these factors as appearances.

We speak of the One as having the aspect of Father Mother and in assigning a place to soul we refer it to the motherhood aspect, while in speaking of Spirit we place it in the Fatherhood aspect; consequently, in the evolution and manifestation of the divine man the soul has, mystically, the position of Mary, mother of Christ. This is one of the most beautiful topics in the whole range of Mystic Philosophy and it will be taken up and treated more in detail later on.

10. Consciousness as applied to the organic Kingdom has its beginning in what is popularly called "the divine spark" that is said to dwell in every form of life. Each separate cell is a center of consciousness, a cell soul so to speak and the polarization or focusing of all the cells to a central point is what makes the aggregate consciousness of the organism. This is the reason why centralization and complexity of physical organization is the measure of the degree of the consciousness of the organization.

Further: Inasmuch as the cell consciousness is developed in degree and character adapted to the requirements or functions of different organs, i.e. the consciousness of muscle cells, the lung cells, the blood making cells, etc., etc., each class being developed and specialized on different lines and to a high degree of special efficiency, it follows that the "Congress" formed by the polarization of all their "cell souls" to a central assemblage, the harmonious union of all these "divine sparks" will produce an individual consciousness which will be far more capable, comprehensive and powerful than would be indicated by the sum of their separate capacities for, by the union of all these potentialities in one, an additional power or intensity of localization is acquired that raises the aggregate to a higher plane of efficiency that in effect transcends them all.

11. One individual is more potent than another simply for the reason that his vehicle of expression (physical body) has greater specialization and complexity developed to a higher degree of efficiency and all massed in a central organ of greater and finer capacity. This organ is called the brain. For example, a person born blind is limited in consciousness; light exists for all but he cannot cognize it because his organic limitations prohibit him from relating himself to it.

12. The individualization of consciousness is cumulative. Life on each plane of consciousness develops the power to apprehend the life of the plane next above. States of consciousness depend upon our perception. If we could develop a new sense we would come into a comparatively new world of sensation, and until we do begin to develop such a necessary sense we cannot relate ourselves to anything higher than the plane on which we dwell. This is the reason that "the natural man knoweth not the things of the spirit." In order to acquire knowledge of spiritual things we must enter into a "life of relation" with a spiritual environment. This is the reason why "faith" is spoken of by the Master as being necessary as a beginning in spiritual life and faith has its root in inherent consciousness and is therefore a very reasonable thing to exercise.

13. Until we become masters and dwellers on the upper plane, we must of necessity lead a seemingly dual life, for we cannot become dwellers on the higher plane until we have become understandingly acquainted with it. In the meantime, the process of overcoming and gaining the mastery over the lower condition is constantly going forward. The criticism so freely voiced regarding the shortcomings of struggling Christians is very unjust and has its seat in gross ignorance. The child must creep before it can walk and the attempt at walking brings many a fall, yet in time the child overcomes and demonstrates his mastery, in the interval it is unjust and ungenerous to multiply discouragements.

Until we know more ourselves, and understand the "things of God" better and more correctly, our greatest present need is less arrogance and more charity, and we should remember that the individual that has mastered the physical environment and the vehicle of his expression in it, has no more need of earth contact; he has acquired the "Wedding Garment" and it is fit and proper that he take his place in the upper room. Doctor Jekyll and Mr. Hyde in a more or less modified form are factors of progress, always have been and always will be until creation shall have accomplished its perfect work.

14. Consciousness is the gateway through which God makes himself known to all those who have made themselves capable of knowing Him, and educated and spiritualized manhood always had been and always will be His vehicle of manifestation. It is literally and scientifically true that such are, in fact, "the Temples of the Holy Spirit." Professor Le Conte, of blessed memory, says: "The objects of nature are objectified, eternalized, materialized, states of divine consciousness." "God is immanent—resident in nature. Nature is the house of many mansions in which He forever dwells. The forces of nature are different forms of His energy, acting directly in all times and places." "The laws of nature are the modes of operation of the divine energy. Invailable because He is perfect. No other view is any longer tenable."

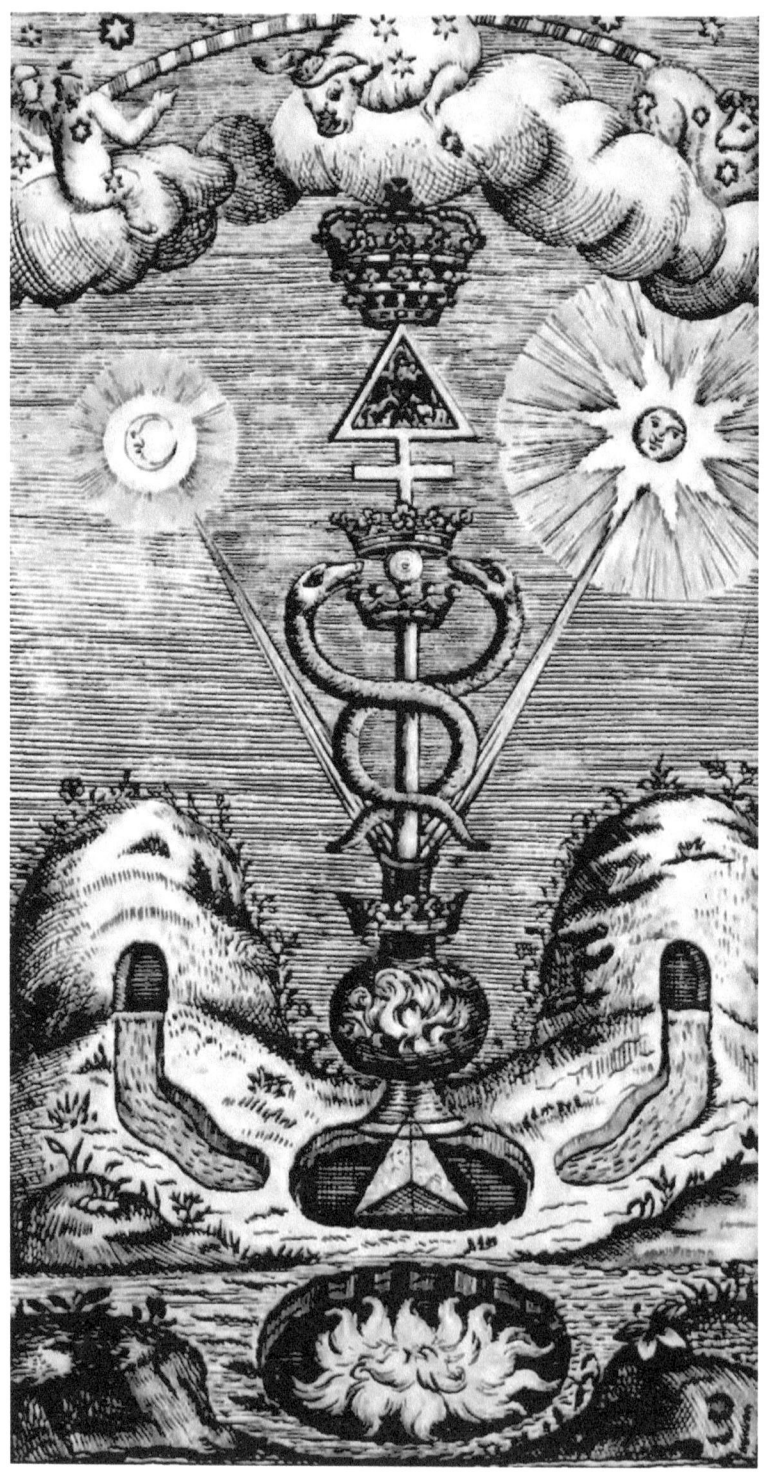

THE ROSIE CRUCIAN PRAYER TO GOD

JESUS Mim OMNIA.

"Oh Thou everywhere and good of All, whatsoever I do, remember, I beseech thee, that I am but Dust, but as a Vapor sprung from Earth, which even thy smallest Breath can scatter; Thou hast given me a soul, and Laws to govern it; let that Eternal Rule, which thou didst first appoint to sway Man, order me; make me careful to point at thy Glory in all my ways; and where I cannot rightly know Thee, that not only my understanding, but my ignorance may honor thee. Thou art All that can be perfect; Thy Revelation hath made me happy; be not angry, Divine One, God the most high Creator, if it please thee, suffer these revealed Secrets, thy Gifts alone, not for my praise, but to thy Glory, to manifest themselves. I beseech thee most gracious God, they may not fall into the hand of ignorant envious persons that cloud these truths to thy disgrace, saying, they are not lawful to be published, because what God reveals, is to be kept secret. But Rosie Crucian Philosophers lay up this Secret into the bosom of God, which I have presumed to manifest clearly and plainly. I beseech the Trinity, it may be printed as I have written it, that the truth may no more be darkened with ambiguous language. Good God, besides thee nothing is. Oh, stream thyself into my Soul, and flow it with thy Grace, thy Illumination, and thy Revelation. Make me to depend on Thee; Thou delightest that Man should account Thee as his King and not hide what Honey of Knowledge he hath revealed. I cast myself as an honorer of Thee at thy feet. establish my confidence in Thee, for thou art the fountain of all bounty, and canst not but be merciful, nor canst thou deceive the humbled Soul that trusts Thee: And because I cannot be defended by Thee, unless I live after thy Laws, keep me, my Soul's Sovereign, in the obedience of thy Will, and that I wound not my Conscience with vice, and hiding thy Gifts and Graces bestowed upon me; for this I know will destroy me within, and make thy Illuminating Spirit leave me: I am afraid I have already infinitely swerved from the Revelations of that Divine Guide, which thou hast commanded to direct me to the Truth; and for this I am a sad Prostrate and Penitent at the foot of thy Throne; I appeal only to the abundance of thy Remissions. my God, my God, I know it is a mystery beyond the vast Soul's apprehension, and therefore deep enough for man to rest in safety in. Thou Being of all Beings, cause me to work myself to Thee, and into the receiving arms of thy paternal Mercies throw myself. For outward things I thank Thee, and such as I have, I give unto others, in the name of the Trinity, freely and faithfully, without hiding anything of what was revealed to me, and experienced to be no Diabolical Delusion or Dream, but the Adjectamenta of thy richer Graces; the Mines and deprivation are both in thy hands. In what thou hast given me I am content. Good God ray thyself into my Soul, give me but a heart to please Thee, I beg no more than thou hast given, and that to continue me, uncontemnedly and unpittiedly honest. Save me from the Devil, Lusts and Men: and for those fond dotages of Mortality, which would weigh down my Soul to Lowness and Debauchment, let it be my glory (planting myself in a Noble height above them) to condemn them. Take me from myself, and fill me but with thee. Sum up thy blessings in those two, that I may be rightly good and wise; And these for thy eternal Truths' sake grant and make grateful."

The Holy Guide, 1652.

FINIS

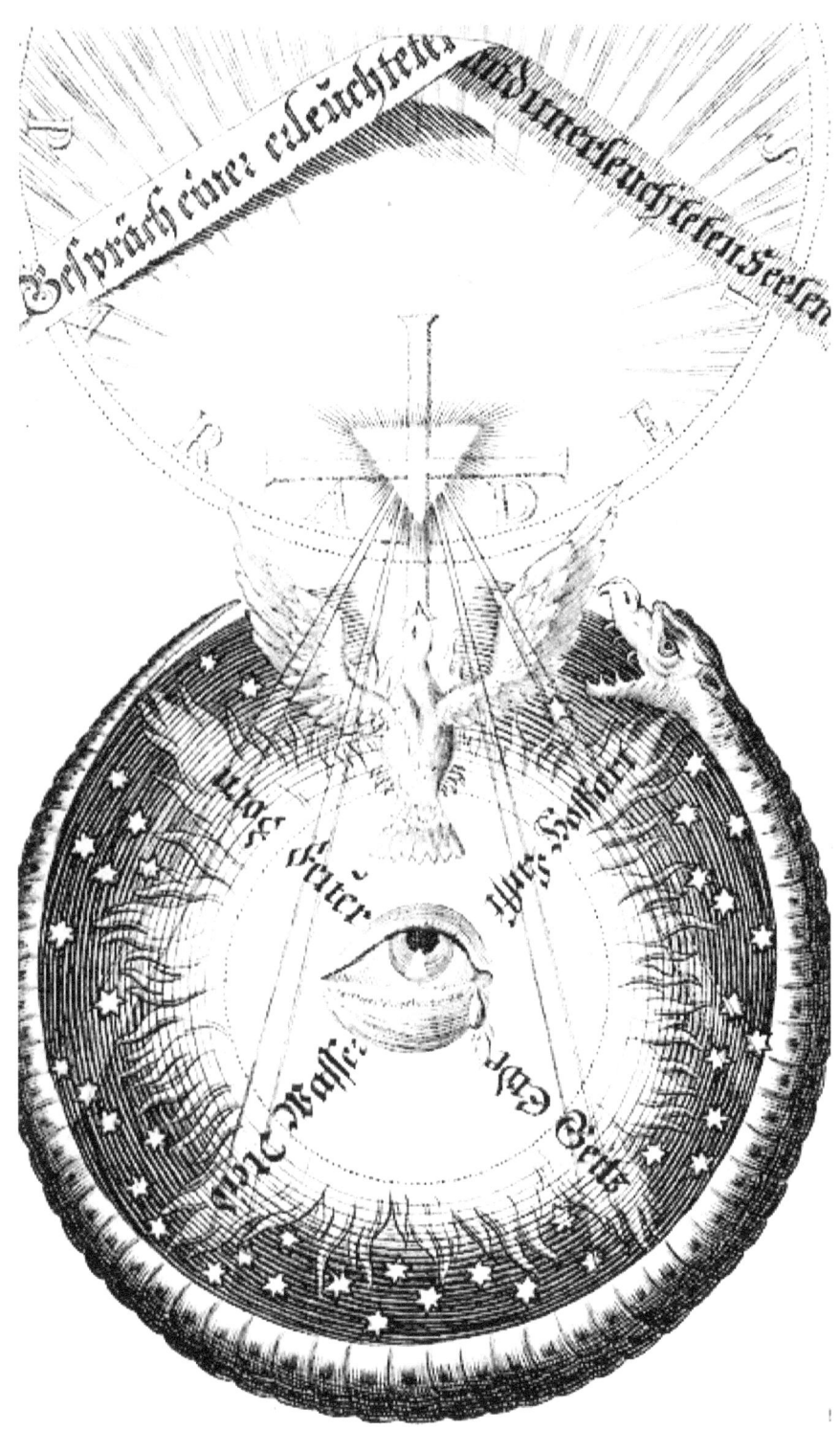

Original Authors' Portraits

WYNN WESTCOTT

MAURICE MAGRE

DR. T. J. BETIERO

MAGUS INCOGNITO AKA
(William Walker Atkinson)

JNANA MARGA AKA
(Robert Adams)

MANLY P. HALL   RUDOLF STEINER

R.S. CLYMER   MAX HEINDEL

CHARLES FILLMORE

A. E. WAITE

EMANUEL SWEDENBORG

JOHN HAYDEN

Gen. JOHN BUFORD   FRANZ HARTMANN

ALEXANDER WILDER   Gen. ETHAN A. HITCHCOCK

WILLIAM W. ATKINSON

References

For further life enrichment and knowledge.

Soul.org

Other Books by the Managing Editor

Manly P. Hall All-Seeing Eye Series:
Book First, Second, and Third
Manly P. Hall Seeker of More Intelligent Life Series:
Book I-IV
Hiram E. Buttler Exoteric Christianity
Arthur Waite Forgotten Essays, Book I & II
The Initiates Speak
George Oliver Masonic Writings
Walter L. Wilmshurst Forgotten Essays
Joseph Fort Newton Forgotten Essays
H. Stanley Redgrove Forgotten Essays
Freemasons – South Dakota Territory, Book A – K
Freemasons – South Dakota Territory, Book L – Z

> For latest books, please visit:
> Parallel47North.com/collections/esoteric-books
> Contact: Info@Parallel47North.com

About Managing Editor

Darrell Jordan is an acolyte of the August Fraternity, former Noble Grand-IOOF and Freemason.

He is also a member of the Theosophical and Philalethes Societies.

Darrell Jordan

www.ingramcontent.com/pod-product-compliance
Lightning Source LLC
Chambersburg PA
CBHW020311010526
44107CB00001B/70